Rebels & Devils

naive voluntarism
equality in mediocrity
desperate hunger for an enemy
artificial hate

William S. Burroughs
The Foremost Literary Figure of Our Time,
author of *Naked Lunch* and many other works

REBELS & DEVILS
The Psychology of Liberation

Edited by Christopher S. Hyatt, Ph.D.

Introduced by S. Jason Black
Foreword by Nicholas Tharcher

With Contributions By

William S. Burroughs • Timothy Leary, Ph.D.
Robert Anton Wilson • Aleister Crowley
Israel Regardie • Austin Osman Spare
Jack Parsons • Genesis P-Orridge
Peter J. Carroll • Osho Rajneesh
Phil Hine • Lon Milo DuQuette
James Wasserman

and

Jay Bremyer • David Jay Brown
Harry Crosby • Shari Dee Crowley
Edwin Drummond • Jim Goldiner
Douglas Grant • Eric Gullichsen
J.E. Hardee • Diana Rose Hartmann
Steven Heller • Richard Kaczynski
Dave Lee • Peter J. Lima
Joseph C. Lisiewski • C.G. Lopez
Adam Matza • Adrian Romany Omelas
Ian Read • Rodolfo Scarfalloto
Germaine W. Shames • Floyd Smith
Daniel Suders • Robert F. Williams, Jr.
Jack S. Willis • Templum Nigri Solis
Ad Veritatem IX°

NEW FALCON PUBLICATIONS
TEMPE, ARIZONA, U.S.A.

International Standard Book Number: 1-56184-153-6
Library of Congress Catalog Card Number: 94-69288

First Edition 1996
Second Revised Edition 2000

This book is an extensive revision of the title
Undoing Yourself, Too by Christopher S. Hyatt, Ph.D.
originally published by Falcon Press, 1988

Cover Art by Denise Cuttita
Based on a design by C. S. Hyatt, Ph.D.
and originally executed by S. Jason Black
Book Concept by C. S. Hyatt, Ph.D.

The paper used in this publication meets the minimum requirements of the American National Standard for Permanence of Paper for Printed Library Materials Z39.48-1984

Address all inquiries to:
NEW FALCON PUBLICATIONS
1739 East Broadway Road #1-277
Tempe, AZ 85282 U.S.A.
(or)
320 East Charleston Blvd. • #204-286
Las Vegas, NV 89104 U.S.A.

website: http://www.newfalcon.com
email: info@newfalcon.com

Dedicated to
William S. Burroughs,
Timothy Leary, Ph.D.,
Robert F. Williams, Jr.
&
Stephani Williams

"He divines remedies against injuries;
he knows how to turn serious accidents
to his own advantage;
whatever does not kill him
makes him stronger."

Friedrich Nietzsche
Ecce Homo

ACKNOWLEDGMENTS

Our deepest appreciation goes out to the mage of the era, William S. Burroughs for his contributions to this book and for his life's work;

To Robert F. Williams, Jr., Stephani Williams and Douglas Grant for their assistance in coordinating *The World of Chaos* section;

To the members of the IOT Pact who contributed to this project;

To Hymenaeus Beta X° for his permission to use the Crowley material and for his valuable assistance with the Austin Osman Spare and Jack Parsons selections;

To S. Jason Black for his incomparable art work including the drawings on pages 38, 60, 116, 182, and 252 and the *VoodooMan* comic (from a concept by Christopher S. Hyatt, Ph.D.);

To Robert F. Williams, Jr. and Stephani Williams for the photographs of William S. Burroughs on pages 2, 46, 51, and 430 and for the photograph of Ian Read on page 204;

To Genesis P-Orridge for the pictures on pages 380, 400, and 407;

To Chris Morgan for the Golden Dawn symbol on page 170;

To Chic C. Wedge for the photographs of Christopher S. Hyatt, Ph.D. on pages 8, 106, 318 and 378.

To Anderson Slade for the graphics on pages 52 and 65;

To Douglas Grant for the graphic art on page 180;

To Michael Moynihan/Blood Axis, Box 3527, Portland OR 97208 U.S.A. for the photographs on pages 196 and 203;

To Floyd Smith for the graphic on page 274;

To Edwin Drummond for the photographs on pages 408 and 429;

To Richard Wardell for the photographs of Marjatta DeAnnA on pages 12, 130, 254, 260, 264 and 310;

To Nicholas Tharcher for book design and typesetting;

To Nancy Wasserman for her ruthless editing;

To all of the authors, artists, photographers and models who made this work possible;

and

To Rebels & Devils Everywhere!

Christopher S. Hyatt, Ph.D.

TABLE OF CONTENTS

Part II — The World Of Chaos

Part III — VoodooMan

Part IV -- Struggles

Part V — Reprogramming The Self

Part VI — The Beginning

FLESH WARRIORS

The Making Of A Rebel And A Devil?

by Christopher S. Hyatt, Ph.D.

If you look into the eye of the Buddha
be prepared to find everything and nothing—
—all at Once.

When he put the gun to my head at 16 I left home. I walked dark city streets littered with flashing lights and well filled hustler bars.

Everywhere I went I found the same thing. Fragile leather coats, sheep-lined suede, ripped tweed, family restaurants stacked with white gravy-stained coffee cups.

Humans moving around, each propelled by something unknowable to them, each going in a direction unique to that person's experience, yet each perversely similar.

When the sun passed an invisible line it was business as usual. Beautiful straight-nyloned women forgetting that some man, somewhere, was making millions constructing their coffins. Men in suits checking their zippers.

Once, a Rebbe asked his congregation why they had so little time to pray and follow Torah. They responded they were too busy making a living. He laughed, and said, "the graveyard is close enough, don't be in such a hurry to find a new one—slow down, it will catch up with you soon enough."

At 16 I didn't realize that I lived within the rushes of my mind, as if it had a reality beyond its own cutting room. There was a big sign on my forehead. "Owners permission required to enter."

My mother was a cripple. She got away with murder. She manipulated the entire world with the sight of her pretzeled hands. At five she dressed me in a pure white suit. I was handsome and proud and so was she. I thought I was a sailor, a captain of a great ship.

I was strong-willed, like her in so many ways. Her struggles were my struggles. I grew to hate her. She courted me, hoping that somehow I could fix her shattered life. Excited, I began to build a new world for us. My erector set and my trains filled with imagination and determination to straighten her feet and repair her bloated knees. I was strung out between hope and fear. I ran around the house chasing my dog with her used syringes. She removed the needles so I couldn't hurt myself.

I had a dream. I was sitting on a green bench in a lush park. She passed and sat next to me. She was beautiful. I asked her to marry me. I woke up. The dream terrified me. I still remember my erection.

Although she hated my father, their door closed on me every night. During the day I was her helpless Knight, at night her dejected suitor. My aunt suggested that I come and live with her, but my mother refused. Until her dying day she never forgave my aunt for asking.

I started my car and picked up Big Mike. The plan was simple. He had staked out an apartment, the guy would be at work. He would climb up the fire escape, and I would drive the getaway car. I was thrilled. When we reached the apartment I parked—the engine running at fast idle.

The car and I were shaking to different beats. I couldn't stop trembling. I felt that I was wearing out. I greased myself with a stiff swig. I saw Big Mike open the window and climb through. With one leg hanging out the window I was reassured by his smile. This was the first time I did anything like this. He and Huby had robbed a few stores at gun point. For him this was easy. For me it was living hell. This was the beginning of learning how to tolerate eternity. This ability would come in handy latter. The car door opened and Big Mike slid in. In his hand was a warm, worn bag overflowing with wrinkled clothes. I started to ask him what we got. He yelled, go man go. Safe, we began splitting up the loot. Each of us kept a piece of clothes. What was left was a broken watch and a few dollars in change. We bought some beer and Lucky Strikes, found an abandoned house and got drunk. It was night and we had other plans. About 8 or 9 of us were going to visit Claire. She was ugly but she would fuck anyone. Big Mike and I arrived late, five or six guys had already fucked her. Big Mike hopped in the car. A minute or so later he returned. "Next," was the cry. I pretended I was too drunk. I threw up.

I climbed through my bedroom window. No one heard me. I hid in the closet, shivering.

I sneaked into the bathroom, soaked the stolen shirt with cold water and washed. I hid the shirt under my bed. I wanted to masturbate, regretting that I didn't fuck Claire with the rest of them. I couldn't. I got up early clutching the shirt to my chest and threw it into someone else's garbage pail. I felt safe. I was in control. My father wouldn't be home for another hour or so. I heard my mother call me. I went into her room. She lay in bed, two pillows propping up her head. She was always ugly in that position. I saw her twisted toes protruding from the blanket. Her big toe crossing over the next one like someone hoping for luck. I gently covered them. She reached for me with her flaccid claws. I could feel them on my back. I tried to hide my disgust, but she was too smart. She asked me to help her up so she could go to the bathroom. I flashed a smile wondering if I left a mess from the night before.

I got ready for school. My hangover would soon be eased from a hidden stash of Silver Satin. My grandmother had bought me a few bottles the day before. I could always get her to buy booze when my nerve failed. The cops had been hot looking for the guys who were buying booze and selling it to the good kids for a hefty profit. I would need all the nerve I could muster that day. It was my turn to buy that night.

I picked up Big Mike and a few other guys and drove. Everyone laughed at me for throwing up the night before just when it was my turn. Driving through the high school gate my tension rose. Everyday was hell. I wondered what would happen today. Big Mike knew he would be kicked out soon. All the teachers had it in for him.

We were a sight, stumbling out of the car, dressed in leather and heavy boots. Our hair was nicely greased. Big Mike had a curl sticking out over his forehead which jumped up and down as we strutted into the Principal's office for our lecture on tardiness. Big Mike laughed, while the Dean of Punishment wailed on. Big Mike saluted with a, yes sir, and we found our next class. All the hall monitors hung their heads as we walked by, all but one, who asked us where we were going. Big Mike smiled. "After school, punk." We kept walking. The school monitor chased us, Big Mike turned and punched him in the gut. He bent over and Big Mike kicked him. But for his muffled groan there was dead silence.

I slid down in my chair my feet pushing hard on the chair in front of me. The student didn't dare complain. He knew I ran with a bad crowd. My head low and tilted to the side I snuck a peek at my teacher's legs, desperately trying to see up her dress. She was gorgeous. I was in love with her. My excitement ceased when I saw her belly. I hated her husband. She was lecturing on angles. I had finished algebra with a C or a D, but I couldn't get the squares or the triangles. I looked at her legs again, my eyes jumping over her belly to her tits then her face and hair. All I wanted, was to touch her hair, for now. I would even settle for her soft lovely arm. But it wasn't in the cards. Today, I wonder if she is still alive—she was a good ten years older than me.

The last bell rang and we all met at the car. Big Mike was already in the back seat sipping some bourbon. He was laughing. That meant he had a plan. He saw one of the teachers escorting a student to his car. She was one of the class beauties and the teacher was one of Mike's tormented victims. Big Mike knew how to aggravate the teachers. He was an expert in humiliation. It was rumored that Big Mike's I.Q. was over 150.

The teacher was Jewish, one of the few in the Christian ghetto. He taught English. He once humiliated me for not being able to memorize and recite a poem. I hated him. Big Mike's plan was to call his wife and tell her that her husband and a woman were involved in a car accident. He also called the girl's parents. He left everything else to fate. The next day we observed the results. Big Mike's trick was the talk of the school. There was no place for the teacher and the girl to hide. I took pride in the small part I played. Big Mike used my coins to make the phone call. I never found out if they were innocent or really getting it on. I prefer to believe they were getting it on. To this day I don't know how Big Mike found the phone numbers. Probably, it was something simple, like looking in the phone book. I have no doubt that Big Mike had been waiting for fate to catch up to his victim for some time, and it did.

At 9:30 pm we pulled up to the liquor store. It was the one I used a few months before to score a case of Scotch. The owner knew I was under-age, but an additional ten bucks and a false I.D. was enough to get the job done. This time I felt weird, there were two young girls waiting on the counter. Big Mike got behind the wheel and I walked into the store. I ordered a quart of beer and a case of mixed booze. I took out the money and laid it down. One girl picked it up, put it in the register and handed me my change. I picked up the box and walked out. As my body cleared the door, I saw red lights and heard sirens. Cops flooded in from all corners. Big Mike and the other guys jumped out of the car and started running. I dropped my package and ran. I stopped—a gun pointed in my face. He grabbed my arm and handcuffed me to himself. The other cops were chasing Big Mike and the guys. The cop took me to an unmarked squad car, uncuffed himself, and cuffed me to the steering wheel. He slammed the door shut and joined the chase. I was trapped. I automatically tugged at the steering wheel. I sat back in total panic and waited. Every minute or so my hand twitched at the wheel. Maybe I should try harder, I thought. I almost convinced myself that I could get away if I wanted to. I couldn't bear the sense of futility. It was beyond my control. They arrested both the girls for selling liquor to a minor; later I found out that they were also minors. No one else was caught. Big Mike and the guys got away.

This liquor store had been under surveillance for weeks. That night was the sting and I was the flesh. They grilled me. I kept my mouth shut. I told them to call my father. He was a cop and maybe for once in his life he would do something with his authority that would help me. The girls said I had I.D., but for some reason that evening I didn't carry it.

When we hit the station I was searched again. They found my real I.D. and called my father. In the meantime I was pushed into a cell. The cops laughed, trying to get me to tell them who was with me. I remained loyal to the code, just like any West Pointer. I was as good as they were. The code was everything. If I broke it I was done. Besides, I needed self-respect and status. My arrest and silence gave me that. Unknown to me, my father and the officer-in-charge decided to leave me in jail until the morning. They were teaching me a lesson. What the lesson was I can only speculate. The next morning my father arrived and handed the officer-in-charge some money; they let me go on the proviso that I testify against the owner of the store. I nodded. The code didn't include him.

Six weeks later my father and I were in court with hundreds of other people waiting for a preliminary hearing. My case was called within a few minutes. The Judge asked me my name and age and did I buy the liquor and did I use a false I.D. I responded, head hanging, saying that I did buy the liquor and that I didn't have or use a false I.D.

People were moving in all directions, people handcuffed to guards, people whispering, the Judge talking to someone, and I kept my head hanging and waiting. I thought, another lesson in eternity. Finally, I looked up at his voice—case dismissed. He added the usual condition that he didn't want to see me again.

My father dragged me firmly to the car and I listened to him drone. He was concerned that what I did could have cost him his job. I knew that was a lie; he was appointed to a life sentence as a petty bureaucrat, and couldn't lose his job unless he got caught. I had learned very early that not getting caught was just about the solution to every problem. If you were caught then those who hadn't yet been caught had to make an example of you, unless of course you knew the right people.

When we reached home a wave of nausea came over me. I would now have to face the greatest judge of all—my crippled mother. I would have to listen, again and again, how I was making her sicker. If I were really unlucky I would have to listen to her tell me how her health was ruined by my birth. Worse yet, the old man would have to listen too.

A Year Passed

The policeman stopped me at 0100 or so and asked me who I was and where I was going. His ruddy nose sniffing for booze and drugs. His hangover yearned for the right connection and I smelled right.

Shivering, I handed him a piece of paper. He swayed incoherently as he studied it.

On it were scribbles, seals and numbers, a collage of old meals, maybe he thought it a napkin, maybe he was attracted to the food. Before I could say anything, his bad breath pronounced my name.

At once he knew who I was, and all at once I knew too.

We were from two different corners of hell. Hunting season had just begun. As his bullseye glowed I reached for the detective special in my back pocket.

Instead of shooting him I smiled and was instantly Enlightened. I repeated to myself, fear, fear, fear. Think fear, remember hope. I repeated it three more times. He mumbled on, sniffing for my fumes, unconsciously caressing the document between his fat little fingers.

A piece of dried food fell from my shirt to the ground and I smiled, knowing I had ruined something precious for him. The two devils knew the game was about to end. The winner would be the one who could contort his face the best.

A Zen Master himself, belching one simple word, he answered a number of perplexing questions. "Loitering." Yes, I said in an excited voice to myself, I was loitering. His nose twitched reaching for the drink I had swallowed minutes earlier.

For the first time in my life I knew everything.

I even knew what God had felt when Adam created Him.

This was a rare experience, I thought, a pink seventeen year old rat knowing so much.

I knew who I was and what I was doing.

As his mouth prepared to open, the scars on his face forming a smile, my exhilaration grew— anticipating more—

He asked, "Where are you going?" I pointed to an all night coffee shop. I now knew what God couldn't know—the spoken word alone didn't create the world, creation also required a pointing finger. I stared at his blue trigger-finger. How many men died from his bad diet, flat sex life, and unpaid bills? He was sentenced to his ghetto for 25 years. I only had to do four. I stopped thinking about the present knowing his last thought before he died would be more interesting. I began to imagine what it would be. I looked straight into his eyes searching his veins for a clue.

Finally, finally, maybe I thought, he would ask me one more question. He said, breaking wind, "Why are you out so late?"

I didn't know and my world fell apart.

From knowing everything to knowing nothing—I couldn't take it—one tear fell—striking my cheek. He yelled, "Go home." I nodded, thanking him, not telling him that I had no home to go to. I thought of shooting him and ridding humanity of two disturbing influences.

I felt sorry for myself. Having tasted the truth, I couldn't turn back. Something in me had changed and I was scared. I knew that everyone was like Christ building a coffin from the leftover parts of their cross. I cried. I laughed.

When the sun came up I found myself on the beach lying in the sand. My head pounded, the residue of cheap wine rushing through me.

I looked at my clothes. They were bloody, dirty and wrinkled. Did I kill him, after all? No.

My morning erection lost, I remembered where the blood came from. The terror ended my headache. The blood was from a friend who had had a fight with a marine over a piece of pizza. Carrot pushed the knife. I always thought that was a funny name for a guy who could knife a Nun. There was nothing sweet about him.

Still, I didn't know whose blood it was. I stopped caring about names. I just wanted it off me. I was lucky it happened after the incident with the cop. God and Satan had other plans for me.

My mind ran wild with the possibilities of what could have happened if it had occurred before the cop stopped me. I imagined the hard time—crushing my hope of getting out of this red, white and blue ghetto—I had seen blood before—blood was cheap.

But the Gods were kind, it didn't come down that way. I calmed down, and my headache dialed in. A brain tumor, I thought.

Reaching into my pocket I found a comb and a crushed "bennie." I laughed, another decision to make, but this one was easy. Bennie had a name, the comb didn't.

It was getting warm, there was a slight breeze. I could hear sails slapping in the distance. I took off my shirt, wrapped it around my bloated belly and walked toward a newly built concrete head. I wondered how much piss had collected around the drain system from the night before? Beach heads in Venice in those days were always a surprise. Drunks, addicts and servicemen had their own form of art.

I felt tense and sick. Within a few moments the tension was gone. Bennie was a good friend—snow-white, bitter and fast.

My stomach and bladder emptied, my mind and emotions shifted to idle. I smiled. I thought of Tennyson's *Ulysses,* the only thing left in my skull from my high school ghetto. I got caught selling booze on campus. The Deans put their skulls together and decided it would be best if I "resigned." My parents were angry, but I didn't care, I simply worked, wandered and had fun—and then jetted to boot camp hell.

I liked Ulysses. He copped his own form of madness and death. This was my plan. He also gave me the horrifying impression that nothing in life would ever be enough. Man's deepest soul could never be satisfied.

I splashed some water on my face and combed my hair. It was Sunday and quiet. The smell wasn't too bad. I was in charge again. I had 13

hours left before returning to my uniform. I had lost my uniform somewhere. I began to worry. I said, "fuck it." Bennie was now at full speed. I
shifted into fifth.

I hitchhiked to Hollywood. I found my comrades eating and chattering
at the coffee shop. People ran to and fro. Life was happening again. We
could pretend that we had a real plan. We believed strongly in our plan.
Someone passed a pint of whiskey around under the table. One pass and
it was gone. Death was frightened by too much hope.

We began to plan out the day. The goal—to score. Each had our own
idea of what that word meant. It could mean sex, money, booze, a fight,
drugs, a free lunch, a party, a ride in a stolen car, beating up a queer.
Usually it meant boredom.

We pretended that we knew how and where to score. We were
confident that we wouldn't have to spend the rest of the day on the street
until the bus came to take us back.

As usual, things just seemed to happen. An event, a person, or just time
would change everything. This time we spent the day on the sand with
some beach girls and cheap booze. Next time, who knows, a fight, jail, or
sore feet. Hollywood cared little for the weekend flesh warriors who
marched the streets looking for a special fix knowing all the time
anything would do.

Three years passed and I had directed myself into marriage and fatherhood. I no longer thought of Ulysses. I was surprised how I reacted to
family life. I was scared. I gained twenty pounds. It was nice having easy
sex.

No one had told me of the horrors born from lust. I wondered why they
had forgotten to tell me. I felt that I was getting more stupid as I was
getting older. This, as I was to find out later, was a result of higher
education. Decisions were harder to make. Every three units was a letter
on my death certificate.

With all the experience I had had, with all the lectures I was subjected
to, no one told me that I might be scared of marriage and fatherhood. I
waited, patiently, for guidance.

No answers came, just hate. I yearned for the beach and my fingers
scratched through my pockets looking for Bennie.

I was living with two strangers, one called my wife and the other my
son. My wife had a family and they were my in-laws. It all seemed
strange to me. Who were these people? I took a big swig of Vodka.
"Let's see," I said, "repeat what you just said. She is my wife, he is my
son and those 'grins' sitting in a straight line are my in-laws. That has to
be the answer." I took another swig of Vodka, and a quick hit off a joint.

Another answer came, they were all strangers, stuck together by labels. No one seemed to know anyone, yet each of us had a label and with each label came duties—roles—responsibilities. We were related by labels. I laughed and hated it all. I began to have fantasies about sailing around the world. I wondered if I could move fast enough not to be caught by the speed of my own thoughts. No, that would require a jet.

Everyone appeared content and seemed to know what to do next, except me. I felt strange, artificial and trapped. I thought of Ulysses. I bought a book of collected poems. The first one I turned to was *The Second Coming* by W. B. Yeats. I liked the poem.

Though I didn't know what to do next, somehow I did things. Maybe this is the way things are done. Some of my acts were applauded, others were scorned, but most of them went unnoticed. I thought life was crazy like a string with a definite beginning and end, painted over with sine waves.

I longed to be at sea.

One day I bought a kitten. The woman called wife didn't like it. I'll call her, the woman, She Who Must Be Obeyed. One day the kitten landed on the head of my son and scratched him. She took the kitten to the vet and had its claws removed. I never saw the kitten again. She Who Must Be Obeyed told me that it had died during the operation. I felt hurt and angry. She was disappointed in me for feeling that way. Somehow, I was demonstrating my inconsideration again.

We had a terrible fight and I got in my car and stormed off. At 0300 or so the police stopped me and asked me the same questions I was asked years before. I felt frightened, yet I started to feel good again. I showed them a different piece of paper and gave them some new answers. They seemed satisfied and I was happy. For the first time in a long time I knew what I was doing and who I was.

I went home and beat her up. "Whose child is it really?" "Mine or that Doctor you were sleeping with even the day before we got married?"

We moved and shortly divorced. I didn't know how it all happened. The lawyers were yelling, she was crying, her family was swearing, and I was laughing. I thought of Yeats and began to smile. After all it was all falling apart.

Finally, I was handed a few pieces of clean paper with seals and scribbles. I stared at them and didn't know what to do. My lawyer asked me what was wrong. I told him that I didn't understand. He replied that the papers said that I was a free man. It was almost all over. She Who Must Be Obeyed was no longer my wife. She was a stranger. But did I still have a son? He was not a stranger. The blood tests were inconclusive. They both disappeared.

My lawyer told me to keep the papers in a safe place. I started a file. I found other papers which I put in the file. The file got too big so I started another one.

I remembered the rest of my lawyer's conversation as I fiddled with these files. "Who knows" he said, "someday you might need these papers, particularly if you want to get married again. You should be grateful, you got off easy this time." Little did I know that he was right. As time passed I finally concluded that I was a serial monogamist and those papers did come in handy in speeding up my addiction.

After leaving the courthouse I felt relieved and strange. Questions kept haunting me. "Who owned me? Who did I belong too? What happened? Where am I? Why did this happen?"

I knew that this episode, or for that matter anything else in my life, was not *my* intention. In fact my life was not my intention. I did not desire it, no matter what the Hindus have pawned off on the Americans. I did not create it. Yet, there I was.

Everyone else seemed to know what do. Everyone else seemed to know where they were going. I did have a mother and a father and a family. But who were these people? Where did they come from? I must be some sort of malcontent, a misfit, Yeah that's it. I'm a misfit. My father did call me that, when he pointed the detective special at my brain. That's it, I'm a misfit. I lit a joint, kicked down hard and drove off.

With every thump of the motorcycle I kept asking, "Who planned this? This planet is crazy. It's time to get off. It's time for a new species. What? Am I mad?" These mantras were driving me nuts.

Finally the answer came, it was the Sea that planned it all out. Her again! I thought I was nuts, or the pot was bad. How could the sea plan anything? It had to be God, or Satan, or Yeats. Yes, it was Yeats. I was just following Yeats' plan. If it was Yeats, he had to be nuts too. I laughed, down shifted, braked and pulled in behind a new glowing smile.

Thirty-six years or so have passed and I am sitting at a Macintosh writing this.

I still don't know how I got here and where I am going. I don't feel bad about this. It is no longer necessary to know what is going to happen next.

One day I will disappear in the same way I appeared. I do not know when, just like before. It will just happen. One day, I will be gone. Until then I will just keeping doing and being done to.

If you look into the eye of the Buddha
be prepared to find everything and nothing—
—all at Once.

FOREWORD

by Nicholas Tharcher

"When he put the gun to my head at 16 I left home."
— Christopher S. Hyatt, Ph.D.

If you've read this far, you already know that this is a remarkable book. It brings together some of the most talented, controversial and rebellious people on the planet today. Many are world-famous, some are lesser-known, but every contributor, in every article, in every aspect of their lives has but one focus: to bring freedom to their world.

In all of human history the essence of the independent mind has been the need to think and act according to standards from *within,* not *without*: to follow one's own path, not that of the crowd. Inevitably, it follows that anyone with an independent mind must become, as the dictionary says, 'one who resists or opposes an authority or established convention': a *rebel.* Usually rebellion is done so quietly that no one notices. But, when others recognize the rebel's disobedience, we have a *Rebel* with a capital *R.* If *enough* people come to agree with, and follow, the Rebel, we now have a *Devil.* (On the other hand, if enough follow the Devil, we may now have a Leader, a Hero, a Martyr, an Innovator or any number of other *good* things.)

Rebels and Devils create. Sometimes the creations are labeled 'beautiful' and 'good' by others—whether the creations are inventions that make 'our' lives longer and easier, art 'we' admire, or leadership that produces ends 'we' approve of. More often these creations are seen as 'bad' and 'dangerous'—inventions that take away 'our' jobs, art 'we' find offensive or dangerous, or leadership that results in mass murder 'we' disapprove of.

'Society' hates the price of its own progress. Its 'representatives' claim to want the benefits of the (approved of) products of the 'innovator' without the risk of the (unapproved of) products of the 'criminal'. Almost every society has mechanisms to harness and take advantage of certain kinds of rebels: shamans, inventors, priests, teachers, soldiers. Some societies have been more clever than others in the effort to contain the Rebel: physically active people are 'encouraged' to become soldiers, police officers or professional athletes (i.e., entertainers); mystically inclined people become shamans or priests; artistically creative people are 'patronized.' The Rebel is thus made to feel dependent on the social structure; dependency breeds fear, and fear is control.

Some societies, however, have recognized that trying to harness the person of independent mind is inherently dangerous and, rather than risk change and inevitable destruction, have accepted total stagnation. Among these have been the medieval periods of Europe and Japan, and the grey futures portrayed in such novels as Ayn Rand's *Anthem* and George Orwell's *1984*.

Within this collection you will find many forms and styles of expression, which, we feel, befits a volume extolling the virtues of the Rebel. There is prose, poetry, fiction, non-fiction, words, photographs, drawings, a complete comic book, and more.

Part I — Prescription for Rebellion, contains a wide variety of pieces which describe the nature of rebellion. The title is taken from the work of the psychologist, Robert Lindner, Ph.D. of whom Christopher Hyatt has much to say in his lead article. (You have already met the remarkable Dr. Hyatt in the *Prologue* of this book.)

We are especially delighted to welcome William S. Burroughs to these pages. Few writers of the modern era have contributed as much to the cause of freedom as he. *Paradise Mislaid,* one of his last works before his death in 1997, is exquisite Burroughs: masterfully written, lyrical, poignant and angry. No one can read it and escape understanding the nature of rebellion from the perspective of both the Rebel and entrenched society. No one can read it and not be faced with some hard and uncomfortable questions about his own life.

Next, Jim Wasserman gives us a lesson in practical civics, asking whether government officials can ever be our 'friends.' After reading this article you may not be surprised to learn that the man who presided over the deaths in Waco, Texas and Ruby Ridge, Idaho is the same 'liberal' 'Democrat' president who said only a short time later that no one has the *right* to say bad things about the police and that anyone who dislikes the government cannot 'love' his 'country.' If you recall phrases such as 'My country right or wrong,' and 'Love it or leave it' from the 1960s, you may also understand that there are *no differences* among politicians whether they are labeled liberal, conservative, Democrat, Republican, Communist, Nazi, or anything else. *No* differences. They all want *exactly the same thing*: the power to dictate your life at the point of a gun.

Next, a remarkable poem by the late Episcopal Priest, Daniel Suders, presents a 14-step program for people who are sick of Alcoholics

Anonymous; then comes a poem by Aleister Crowley, who is generally considered the father of modern Western magickal traditions and who was Rebel enough to be tossed out of several countries and Devil enough to be called 'the wickedest man alive.' (Since he loved to play to an audience, he often signed his name 'The Beast 666.') Following this is a brief description of aspects of Crowley's philosophy; then another essay on Crowley's philosophy by the late Jack Parsons, rocket scientist and a founder of Jet Propulsion Laboratory.

Austin Osman Spare may have affected the development of the Western magickal traditions as deeply as Crowley—though perhaps more quietly. His diatribe, *Anathema of Zos,* however, is anything but quiet. Harry Crosby's poem, *Assassin,* may be somewhat less vindictive, but is certainly no less lyrical.

Another piece by Dr. Hyatt asks the fundamental—but rarely asked—question of ethics: 'Who owns you?' If more people would honestly confront this question—and stand by their answer—most 'issues' of politics (and, indeed, of all human relationships) would dissolve into the insignificant and fetid swamp in which they belong.

Next is a poem by Jim Goldiner—one of three in this volume—that may inspire you to reread (or read!) Kafka's *The Trial.* Appropriately, the enlightened master and master outcast Osho (Bhagwan Shree) Rajneesh next discusses the difference between two frequently confused ideas: rebellion and revolution. 'I don't preach revolution. I am utterly against revolution. ...my word for the future, and for those who are intelligent enough in the present, is *rebellion.*' If you have ever felt that rebellion and revolution were the same—or even related—you may think again as you read this selection.

Next, Diana Rose Hartmann presents an incisive essay on the Rebel and Devil from a feminist perspective. (As you read this piece you will be reminded that 'feminist' does not have to signify a pseudo-victimized, tight-lipped, life-hating bitch—as some would have it.)

Then comes an interview with one of the greatest Western magicians of all time, Dr. Israel Regardie. It's hard to believe that Regardie has been gone from us so long. Even in his seventies he had a youthful spirit, full of jokes and pranks. Many who have read his scholarly works on Western mysticism will be quite surprised—perhaps even shocked—to see this side of him.

Part I closes with Richard Kaczynski's observations of Aleister Crowley's love-hate relationship with several 'taboo' subjects including sex, drugs, and death. Appropriately, we then open another 'taboo' world in *Part II — The World of Chaos.*

This section consists of contributions by many of the foremost representatives of a relatively modern branch of Western mysticism: Chaos

Magick. Of course, most people are more than a little leery of *any* sort of occultism, calling it satanic, demonic, 'black,' and so forth. But even among Western occultists, the Chaos practitioner is often considered a Rebel. See for yourself what the cutting edge of occultism looks like.

Part III consists of a single selection—the 'comic book' *VoodooMan* conceived and executed by Christopher Hyatt and S. Jason Black.

Part IV — Struggles, shows us the sometimes painful, sometimes comical side of the operating Rebel. Here you will see the day-to-day price the Rebel has always faced in the struggle to live, to create and to be free.

This section opens with the Adam Matza's poem, "Prelude to a One-Night Stand" which begins: 'I need a body-sized condom to protect me from your malaise.' (Maybe you've been there, too; I know I have.)

Then comes the fiction (?) of Germaine Shames (who wonders what it would be like to make love with a terrorist), and the historical perspective of Lon Milo DuQuette (as he reminds us that Christianity has *always* been more than willing to use murder to eliminate independent thought).

Next, the first of two contributions by Reichian therapist Dr. Jack Willis, deals with 'The Black Art of Psychotherapy.' Many people who wish to pursue some form of therapy have wondered what 'flavor' would be best for them. Dr. Willis can help you. He can also help you assess the competence of your therapist, and the effectiveness of your therapy. At the same time, he is sure to piss off any number of therapists as he dares to compare their work to that of black magicians. (Most therapists, of course, would not appreciate the connection—except, perhaps, a very few such as the brilliant psychiatrist Thomas Szasz, the author of such books as *The Myth of Mental Illness* and *The Manufacture of Madness: A Comparative Study of the Inquisition and the Mental Health Movement.*)

Jay Bremyer's beautiful and lyrical prose (or is it poetry?) revists the religious and secular hysteria at the turn of the Christian millennium, and impels us to consider, once again: Is there intellligent life on Earth?

True, the Struggle for freedom can be extremely painful. But Floyd Smith's poetry reminds us that the Struggle can also have great rewards.

Finally, as 'Saint Francis Visits Satan,' Rudy Scarfalloto reminds us that personal integrity is an essential part of the Struggle. Indeed, without it, freedom is impossible.

Part V — Reprogramming the Self, provides practical suggestions to those who would be free. Robert Anton Wilson, one of the most insightful, witty and prolific writers of our time, starts this section with a primer on the mechanisms of the brain and how to use them to your benefit. The body of his work covers science, mysticism, science fiction, history, social philosophy, literature, sex—and almost everything else.

Next, the eminent psychologist Dr. Timothy Leary and cyber-expert Eric Gullichsen combine their expertise to provide a number of practical alternatives to involuntary death. This article is especially significant, for, as we went to press with the first edition of this book, Dr. Leary had announced that he was in the terminal stages of cancer. He said: 'When I found out I was terminally ill—and I know this can be misinterpreted—I was thrilled... How you die is the most important thing you ever do. It's the exit, the final scene of the glorious epic of your life.'[1]

Next, physicist Joseph Lisiewski, Ph.D. explores the mysteries of language in our rather curious, and generally futile, attempts to 'become someone.' Following this is a second poem by Jim Goldiner.

James Wasserman returns with another 'civics lesson.' This time he addresses the question: How do individuals ultimately control the rapacious nature inherent to politicians? No form of government can do it. No laws can do it. No elections can do it. Only the power of a well-armed citizenry can give us a 'fighting chance' to become, and remain, free. As former U.S. Vice-President Hubert Humphrey said: 'One of the chief guarantees of freedom *under any government,* no matter how popular and respected, is the right of the citizen to keep and bear arms. [It] is one more safeguard against a tyranny which now appears remote in America, but which historically *has proved to be always possible.'* [Emphasis added] Most politicians will do *anything* to disarm honest citizens; after all, a helpless population is *so* much easier to bully, intimidate and control.

The second contribution by Dr. Jack Willis deals with a subject almost everyone believes they know something about: morality. After reading *The Virtue of Personal Liberation,* however, you may begin to question some of your beliefs, especially about children and child-rearing. (Of course, you should question *all* of your beliefs. The odds are you have never developed, derived or verified much of anything in your head. Almost everything rattling around your brain was put there by someone else, who got it from someone else, who got it from someone else, etc. *ad nauseum.)* Is the notion of morality important to the Rebel? Judge for yourself.

The next two contributions introduce a remarkable place in Phoenix, Arizona. The Mountain Temple Center has been made available to a wide variety of 'esoteric' groups (wiccans, Golden Dawners, goths, mystics, voodooists, and sometimes even the sweetness-and-light crowd) for seminars, classes, rituals and more. The first article discusses the

---

[1] Dr. Leary died on May 31, 1996. A longtime supporter of space exploration and colonization, some of his ashes were launched into space in 1997.

background and nature of The Mountain. The second... Well, come to The Mountain and see for yourself. Things can get rather weird at times.

Politicians seem to have an inexhaustible variety of methods to accrue more power to themselves. During the last century or so, one of the most effective techniques has been the ongoing 'war on (some) people who use (some) drugs.' Prisons throughout the world (and especially in the U.S.) are filled to overflowing with non-violent people whose only 'crime' has been the misfortune to get caught with certain chemicals in their possession. David Brown revisits some of the origins of this war, reminding us—once again—what politicians do for a living.

There are many ways for the rebel to develop the skills to resist and fight oppression. Certainly one of the best is the use of martial arts training. C.G. Lopez and J.E. Hardee, both experts themselves, consider the martial artist: 'skilled in two battles, within and without, is an excellent example of a rebel in our midst.'

Then, Ericksonian-style hypnotherapist Dr. Steven Heller tackles the issue of trance: how we—and those around us—are hypnotized by language. We close this section with another poem by Jim Goldiner.

In *Part VI — The Beginning,* we welcome Genesis P-Orridge, musician and magickian *extraordinaire.* His unique style, his observations, proverbs, poetry and prose defy description. If you find his style more than a bit unusual, stay with it: you will find the journey worth the trip.

Finally, poet, climber and political activist Edwin Drummond, whose exploits include climbing the Statue of Liberty in New York, Nelson's Column in London and the Embarcadero Building in San Francisco to promote peace and freedom (and which has put him in the hands of the police more than once), turns his boundless energy to his ongoing project to free Geronimo Pratt from prison.[1]

But first, we turn to S. Jason Black as he glorifies the Marquis de Sade...

---

[1] In 1997, after 27 years in prison, Pratt's murder conviction was overturned.

INTRODUCTION

How The Marquis de Sade Saved My Life

by S. Jason Black

Author of the Falcon titles:
Tantra Without Tears
Pacts With The Devil
Urban Voodoo

"The thinking man who scorns the prejudices of simpletons necessarily becomes the enemy of simpletons. He must expect as much, and laugh at the inevitable."

— Donatien Alphonse Francoise, Marquis de Sade

This book, and what I consider its "sister" books, have a rather odd history—at least for me and for those others that I have talked to regarding their first encounters with the subject matter within. The original title of an earlier, and much different version of this book was *Undoing Yourself, Too*, which—in form and content—was intended as a sequel to the now classic and forever-selling *Undoing Yourself With Energized Meditation and Other Devices* by Christopher S. Hyatt, Ph.D. The third volume in this triumvirate is *Cosmic Trigger I: Final Secret of the Illuminati* by Robert Anton Wilson. (All are published by New Falcon Publications.)

Like magic lamps found in junk shops or grimoires in the basement of a recently deceased grandmother, they always seem to come as a surprise and have a disturbing and often permanently life-changing effect. For my part, I was led into the morass of the Illuminati, or the Nine Unknown Men, or the Great White Brotherhood or whomever by a slightly more circuitous route. I grew up in the midwest, just outside of Kansas City, Missouri, and while culturally Kansas City wasn't bad at all—in fact, the best metropolitan area in the state (St. Louis is a sinkhole)—it was difficult for me to find items that weren't available at any large B. Dalton's.

It was, in fact, in just such a place that I made the discovery that was to have possibly the largest impact on my world view of any before or since.

I was wandering bored and hypnotized from rack to rack hoping to god for something decent to read when an extremely thick, plain book caught my eye. Unlike its garish neighbors, the cover was decorated only with elegant script, dominated by a name: *Marquis de Sade*. For me he was only a name with a sinister reputation. I had never even set eyes on a book by Aleister Crowley or any of the other rascal gurus like Gurdjieff (as if I could have understood *him* at seventeen!) It was *Philosophy in the Bedroom and Other Writings* published by Grove Press.

Neither mom nor my teachers would approve if I was caught with it. Of course, I bought it instantly.

Please understand that I was not buying a piece of pornography to sneak home and wank off to. Those who expect that of de Sade will, I suppose, get a little of it. On the contrary, I was, at that age, inexplicably mesmerized by the late eighteenth century, so the world of the pre-revolutionary aristocrat was a place that needed no explaining to me. I expected a happy romp (rather diabolical *ala* Dashwood) through the bordellos of Paris, with a lot more nifty detail than I was used to. What I got was a shock.

From the point of view of any "normal" philosophical and social standards that I had ever been exposed to, I might as well have purchased a book by Lucifer for, like Lucifer, de Sade mucked things up and horrified his generation by telling the plain, simple truth about human behavior. Coming from the scion of one of the oldest noble houses in France (going back to the Crusades) this was like one of the popes leaving for posterity a journal of just how many choir boys he *had* sodomized on the altar of St. Peter's.

Preceding Nietzsche by a century and, I must suppose, completely ignorant of left-handed Tantra, he preached a philosophy and a system of self-development not only at odds with "civilization", but which took it into consideration only when it was a useful tool for what he termed his "unique beings", his supermen. I make references to such things as Tantra here in trying to make the unfamiliar reader understand what this man was about, but never forget that he *was* a radical atheist. He was partially raised by a lecherous old uncle who was also a high church official. He attended parties where the rulers of the nation participated in activities which, if I described them in detail, I would probably not be believed, but hey, let *me* give some examples anyway:

The Prince DeConde, head of the family second only in power to the Bourbons themselves had, it seemed, a rather strange little fetish. While having *sex* with his current woman or boy, he would make sure that the bed he was using was near a window. Within range of this window he would also make sure that a common laborer was working on a nearby roof, whether it needed it or not. As he was approaching orgasm, he would reach for a nearby pistol, shoot the workman off of the roof and come like a racehorse.

There are many similar scenes in de Sade's novels most of which are simply assumed to be de Sade's world of fantasy—and some are. But many, like the above, are true, true, true. Those of you familiar with the theories of how fetishes come to be, whether for spiked heels or women with red hair, may be asking yourselves a question that I have been asking ever since learning of the above-mentioned quirk of the lord DeConde: Just what in *HELL* happened to this man to cause him to pop his cookies while shooting a roofer?

But let us go on to something else they probably didn't tell you in history class. King Louis XV of France, as you may know, was the last of his rank to die of natural causes. He became King at the age of five. Among the other wonderful things that his Illustrious predecessor, the Sun King, told him on his death bed was the identity of the Man in the Iron Mask. Oh yes! There really was one. Louis XV passed this tidbit to the unfortunate Louis XVI who carried the secret to his grave. (I don't know about you, but that kind of thing drives me crazy. But I digress.)

Those who have read *Pacts With The Devil: A Chronicle of Sex, Blasphemy and Liberation* (New Falcon Publications, 1993), that I co-authored with Dr. Hyatt, may remember my description of Phillippe, Duc D'Orleans, who became, on the death of the Sun king, Regent of France and guardian to little Louis. This gentleman was a committed devil-worshipper, a political murderer, and would fuck anything that moved. Especially his daughter. Raised in this richly textured environment (for which, I confess, I envy him) Louis became one of the most remarkably compartmentalized personalities in European history. He was, or gave the appearance of being, religiously devout and yet was also a manip-ulative cynic who played two separate secret-police organizations off against each other. Those familiar with modern law enforcement may find that this has become a tradition of sorts. For example, local drug enforcement would rather eat razor blades than cooperate with the federal government's DEA.

At any rate, Louis became quite a connoisseur of nearly everything. At one point during his early adolescence he panicked his guardians because of an intense fondness for stable boys, but this turned out to be a teenage homosexual phase that passed, and the kingdom got its queen and its heirs, for all the good it did them.

While his taste for boys seems to have passed, his taste for youth did not, and the most famous of his mistresses, the Countess DuBarry, desiring to keep his emotional loyalty if not his physical fidelity, either proposed or encouraged the project that became known as "Deer Park."

Deer Park was the nickname of a portion of the grounds of Versailles upon which was built what may have been the most lavish private bordello since the time of the Caesars. If, on an outing, Louis would spot a young lady who, to be polite, struck his fancy, he would enquire of her parents or guardians, pay them a handsome fee, and ensconce them at the park.

Did I mention that the average age of these "young ladies" was around nine?

Earlier I mentioned the King's apparent piety. Whenever he would, uh, desire the society of one of these children (whoops! I mean women), they would both disrobe and before the "act" would retire behind a screen and pray to Little Lord Jesus for forgiveness for the fun about to be had.

The conflicts in the western personality, as personified by Louis (and documented by Freud), should now be clear. It should also be clear that, in America at least, they are still with us. The point of my little detour into eighteenth century French politics will become obvious when we see what it did to the life of our hero the Marquis, who, whatever else he was, was not a hypocrite.

In the year 1768, Easter Sunday to be precise, de Sade had ventured out in search of some amusement, and found it in the form of a certain Rose Keller, an unemployed widow who was reduced to begging alms. The Marquis and Mrs. Keller had a brief conversation and she agreed to accompany him in his carriage to his rented cottage at Arceuil. At this point the story becomes a little confused due to conflicting testimony, but the facts are broadly these: She was taken into a room hung with whips of various sizes and furnished with a cot or bed. She was either instructed or forced to strip and was then asked to do a rather unusual thing.

The Marquis produced a large ivory crucifix, placed it upon the floor and told her to shit on it.

She refused.

He insisted.

Finally, he convinced (or compelled) her to take an enema and poop on Jesus. This aroused his excellency beyond all bounds and he placed her face-down on the cot and whipped her three ways to Tuesday until he climaxed. From all the accounts I have read, there was no genital sex at all.

He then poured a little candle wax on her back for good measure, paid her the promised fee, and let her go. Those familiar with what is now known as S&M will be aware that this theatrical piece is milder by far than it sounds. According to the police reports, the woman was not injured in any significant way—they saw far worse in the bordellos all the time. Why did Rose Keller go to the police? Probably because she tried to blackmail the Marquis and failed.

His excellency had gotten himself in rather a lot of trouble though. This was not the first time he had caused a public scandal and the police kept a close watch on his activities. He gave sworn (and rather sarcastic) testimony in court regarding the event, and was let off with what was more or less a brief house arrest.

Until the King heard about it.

I have already mentioned Louis' interesting combination of pedophilia and piety, and when he read the report on the de Sade escapade (he always read the sex crime files) he went ballistic. By order of the King, the Marquis was apprehended and thrown into prison.

And what do you think the charge was?

Rape? Nope.

Acts against "nature"? Nope.

The charge, my friends, was blasphemy.

Picking up a poor woman off the streets and doing weird things to her (possibly) against her will was no particular problem. But doing number two on the image of Jesus was another matter altogether, and when de Sade realized what the charges were he began to sweat for his life. Louis XV was, after all, the last of the absolute monarchs and could have had the Marquis killed without bothering with an explanation.

It has been said that prison made a writer of de Sade. Recent material released by the current generation of the Sade family shows this was not the case. He had always had the desire to be a published author and there are manuscripts that prove it. This incarceration began to transform a highly intelligent eighteenth century libertine into the greatest philosopher of individual rebellion (the subject of this book), and debunker of social establishments in western history, bar none.

This was the beginning of the end of his life as a wild-living young aristocrat. He was to spend, off and on, a total of twenty-seven years of his life in incarceration and died at the insane asylum at Charenton in 1814. (They didn't particularly think that he was insane, they just didn't know what else to do with him.) We may never know the mature form of his philosophy or his social observations as fully two-thirds of his finished books were either confiscated by Napoleon's spymaster Fouche, or destroyed by his son after his death.

Why was this man so dangerous? Despite his sexual foibles, most of the tales of his activities are either pure myth or taken from one of his novels and related as fact. He did not get his rocks off, like the Prince DeConde, by shooting roofers, but his published principles made him more dangerous than a thousand murderous perverts, and they were basically these (and while far more radical, I suggest the reader compare them to Timothy Leary's rules for self-programming, which helped land him in prison as well.)

1. There is no God. Anything that exists that could remotely be called "God" is that philosophical concept called Nature.

2. All things that exist, including especially every impulse, however bizarre, violent or anti-social, is natural and has its place in nature.

3. Every man, woman or child has the right and obligation to develop his personality, proclivities and the extent of his power *whatever they may be* to the fullest extent of their ability.

4. The above self-development is the only genuine "purpose" in human life, and is not related to rationality or any false notions of progress, which are delusions to manipulate the slave classes.

5. The world is, and always has been, ruled by a natural elite which he referred to as "Unique Beings" or supermen, who hide their existence and activities from the world at large both for survival and to preserve power.

6. All religions, laws and governments exist (knowingly or unknowingly) to preserve the system for the benefit of the elite and to keep the inferiors deluded and productive.

7. Finally, the fully realized "Unique Being" may use his power absolutely as he sees fit for, or against, anyone or anything with recourse to no authority except himself or a greater "Unique Being."

8. The principle activity of nature, like some eternally frustrated artist, is destruction.

Even after the French Revolution, and the supposed liberalization of the French world view, his writings caused great horror. They also, it seems, sold very well.

For those who have read a little de Sade, some modern proof that these "Unique Beings" are far from fantasy has come in the form of a recent biography of J. Edgar Hoover, the long-time head of the FBI, who mercilessly persecuted homosexuals and blackmailed congressmen and presidents, while spending his evenings in silk dresses and sucking off teenage boys. Such men are not unique to this age or any other.

I was raised in a rather liberal background (I do not mean this in the political sense, but the sense that I could read and see more or less what I liked) but still this material came as almost a religious experience. At this time Falcon Press had not yet been founded and so many radical books of philosophy and occult practice simply were not available. Not where I lived at any rate.

When I realized what de Sade was actually saying, not only about the nature of society, but of a man's responsibility for his own self-development, and when I compared the writing to what I saw in the "real" world, I came to three conclusions which I have had no reason to alter. I will illustrate two of these with quotes from authors I discovered some years later:

Do What Thou Wilt Shall Be The Whole of The Law — Aleister Crowley
No communication is possible except between equals.

— Robert Anton Wilson

And the third, which, as far as I know, is my own:

All creativity, with no exception, stems from a criminal relationship vis a vis *society.*

Regarding the last postulate, of course, one must realize that only the failures remain criminals. For the successes, like Mohammed or Paul of Tarsus, history is rearranged for the sake of politeness.

For me the principle connecting theme to the essays in this book is the breaking of social trance so that the individual can make a valiant attempt at becoming "enlightened" or a "Magus" or an "Illuminati". The shape these articles take are to be rude in many ways. First, and most obviously, politically. But there is also talk of "magick" and "psychic phenomena" and other things considered impolite to speak of. I said that de Sade, an eighteenth century atheist, led me to the Illuminati and I will finish this long preamble by explaining how:

I have had what are popularly referred to as "psychic experiences" since I was very small. What may be my earliest memory is of one that occurred (according to my mother) when I was just under three years of age. By the time I had encountered de Sade I was aware of the existence of such things as magic and witchcraft outside the area of fiction. I had also made a study of both clinical and self-hypnosis, and, as a lark, once had myself regressed in hopes of finding past lives. The past life experience was a blowout, but my first encounter with deliberately induced trance was a revelation. I fully understand why both the medical profession and some occultists are terrified by trance. Any culture that masters the techniques of trance will put many doctors and priest/gurus out of work.

I had been lucky enough to find three books, that, had I not been exposed to the intellectual freedom of the Marquis, I would have been afraid to buy (magic is *dangerous* you know): *The Eye in the Triangle: An Interpretation of Aleister Crowley* by Israel Regardie (now published by New Falcon) the aforementioned *Cosmic Trigger: Final Secret of the Illuminati* by Robert Anton Wilson (also now published by New Falcon) and Aleister Crowley's *Magick in Theory and Practice* in the Dover Books edition.

I was alone in the house for about ten days. My mother, who was involved in state politics, was at the capital and I took advantage of the situation. I culled a makeshift ceremony from the little material I had (despite its title, Crowley's book is hardly a full-fledged how-to book) and attempted to call up my "Holy Guardian Angel." I have no idea if I did this, but something certainly happened.

I cleared out the dining room of all furniture, and laid down a circle of masking tape, performed an amateurish banishing, and began. The only things that I remember for sure from the ritual is that I read Crowley's version of the "Bornless Ritual" and some other stuff from *The Eye in the Triangle.* I remember scaring the shit out of myself. The whole thing may have lasted half an hour. I banished, put the dining room furniture back, went to watch TV and waited for the cold sweats to pass.

Mom returned the following day.

That night I went to sleep and awakened instantly, with absolutely no sense of drowsiness and with the total conviction that I had had a long and important conversation with *something* that had told me things that I had to do for my well-being and survival.

I pulled on my bathrobe, walked out into the living room, and announced that, with no financial resources to speak of, I was moving to California.

I did so around the time that Falcon Press was being founded. Among the other significant things that happened in the next two years was my association with a Crowley group that at the time practiced serious magic (a rare animal in the occult world). I worked for a while at Peace Press, the then-publisher of Dr. Timothy Leary, whose work graces these pages and is now published by Falcon. Sometime later I met and began to do work for Dr. Christopher Hyatt, whose reputation as a dangerous *persona non grata* is slowly coming to rival de Sade's. So you see, the opening of a single intellectual door by a maverick French noble has pushed me into a world that the *pashu* around us don't even suspect exists.

May at least one of the works that you find herein do for you what the Divine Marquis did for me so many years ago.

S. Jason Black is a professional writer, illustrator and fine artist and a life-long student and practitioner of Magic and Tantra. He has worked as a professional psychic, much sought after for his accuracy.

PART I

Prescription For Rebellion

"PRESCRIPTION FOR REBELLION" — REVISITED

by Christopher S. Hyatt, Ph.D.

Author (or co-author) of the Falcon titles:
Undoing Yourself With Energized Meditation and Other Devices
The Enochian World of Aleister Crowley: Enochian Sex Magic
Sex Magick, Tantra & Tarot: The Way of the Secret Lover
The Tree of Lies: Become Who You Are
Secrets of Western Tantra
Pacts With The Devil
Urban Voodoo
and others

"Mental health is the ability to deny reality and repress feelings within the boundaries and parameters established by one's peer group(s)."
— Christopher S. Hyatt, Ph.D.

Way back in 1952 Robert Lindner, Ph.D., a noted clinical psychologist with a strong psychoanalytical background, boldly asserted that rebellion was instinctive and was the *quintessence* of the creative personality. However, for Lindner, creativity comes from separating oneself from the collective and the will of the masses. The primary purpose of society says Lindner was, "To bend the will of the individual to the will of the majority, to become as others are by accepting the illusions of the mass..." As such, Lindner viewed psychological symptoms as protests against the surrender of individuality.

He further ventured to say that the instinct to rebel was as important as the sex instinct for the survival of the species, for without rebellion from the "cult of adjustment" and domestication, nothing new arises.

In clinical terms this meant that rebellion was normal and healthy and should be properly channeled—not seen as a problem for society, requiring either imprisonment or "treatment."

This radical idea didn't sit well with the conservative and social-worker mentalities of that decade, nor does it sit any better today. In fact, it may even be worse.

Adjustment to culture and domestication is now practiced by a greater number of middle class and "mid-zonal" professions. This simple fact may have some explanatory value when we consider the "outrageous" acts of rebellion exhibited by youths and adults whose rage seems to have no other place to go except toward self-destruction and "random" acts of violence aimed at others.

Dr. Lindner, a man of many heretical ideas, predicted that psychology and its associated disciplines would, in time, become handmaidens of the State and Big Business. This meant that psychology would lose its value for those who needed it the most.

He believed that both the public and the State would begin to believe that psychology had more to offer than it did. He meant this in the context of forced and coerced adjustment to the values of mediocrity, fate and destiny as preached by educators, clinicians and the clergy.

Anyone who takes the time to investigate modern psychotherapy and counseling would have to agree with Lindner's predication. Contrary to the modern clinical practice of psychology, Lindner saw psychology this way: "...the various psychotherapies have as their job the recovery of individuals and groups for evolution so that those whose lives would otherwise be wasted can also contribute toward the same end: the coming glorious breakthrough into ... What?"

What a revolutionary re-definition of psychotherapy! Without a doubt any licensed psychotherapist practicing such a psychotherapy in the U.S. today—one which would assist the species in the evolution to a "glorious breakthrough into ... What?"—would be promptly arrested and stripped of his license. This is no exaggeration. Only a few years ago the Attorney General of one State emphasized that any therapist who focused on the practice of experiential therapy (where the therapist shares his or her own struggles with a patient) would be suspected of incompetent practices.

Dr. Lindner's assertions are, of course, unscientific (as if clinical psychology were a science, instead of a legally invented "crutch").

Lindner's definition is heresy and stands squarely against the sleepy-dreamy welfare of the masses who practice their perversions in the privacy of their own "home," while at the same time glaring into the eyes of their neighbors desperately searching for the devil—someone to blame for their dissatisfactions. Dr. Lindner was keenly aware that hypocrisy was the only politically correct stance to take.

Not satisfied with these heresies, Dr. Lindner became bolder, bordering, some would say, on the ridiculous and insane when he suggested that for humanity to reach its true potential, it had to overcome what Lindner termed the "triad of limitations," namely, the effects of *gravity, ignorance and mortality.* What he meant by these are "loosening…the fetters of gravity," removing the bounds set by "…the biologically given equipment of human beings," and making "…longevity, if not immortality…more than a promise." Yes, Dr. Lindner, back in 1952 would have to be considered wacky when you consider the work and plight of Dr. Timothy Leary.

Dr. Lindner wrote his prescription before the "21st century" pioneer whiz kid Dr. Timothy Leary wrote his formula for the future (*S*pace *M*igration, *I*ncreased *I*ntelligence and *L*ife *E*xtension—SMI²LE) in *Exo-Psychology* sometime between 1975–76 while enduring the effects of his forced exile and imprisonment for rebellion. His ground-breaking book is now revised as *Info-Psychology* (1994) and published by New Falcon Publications. It is required reading for rebels and devils everywhere.

Although Leary's work is considered as borderline "crazy" by most academics and the general populace, many "youngsters," including myself, consider his ideas refreshing and hopeful. Unfortunately, Dr. Leary is frequently remembered only for his use of drugs and sometimes even held responsible for "our" present day drug "problem." As such, the corpus of his work, as well as his innovative solutions for today's problems, goes unnoticed. For example, I recently did an unofficial, non-scientific survey of some fourteen college professors and sixty students. Fewer than half the students had ever heard of Leary and 80% of the college professors didn't think very much of him. Some even turned their head at the mention of his name. One clinician called him a "burnt out drug fiend."

Unlike Leary, Lindner was somewhat more respectable in the '50s but he was not satisfied to simply assert his ideas of overcoming the triad of limitations, *gravity, ignorance and death.* (I used the phrase "somewhat more respectable" in opening this paragraph because Dr. Lindner was vehemently opposed to the then popular procedure of pre-frontal lobotomies and electro-convulsive therapies. He referred to this as "knife-happy fingers" and "push-button psychiatry.")

He was bold enough to provide us with a new morality to go along with his theory. Providing new moralities such as Reich's "Love, Work and Knowledge Are The Well-Springs Of Life. Therefore They Should Also Govern It," is alone sufficient to be charged with cultural and religious heresy.

Wilhelm Reich (see Robert Anton Wilson's, *Wilhelm Reich In Hell*, 1995, New Falcon Publications) was not as lucky as Lindner. Reich's books were burned and he died in prison. Lindner simply died young, remembered from time to time for the phrase (not the book) *Rebel*

Without A Cause, Grune and Stratton, 1944. I quote Lindner's morality:
"Anything—thought or deed—which enables man to pierce the three-sided cage described as the triad of limitations, is intrinsically good:
anything which prevents him from so doing is intrinsically bad." Not a
bad ethic coming from a psychologist. It is more than interesting that
Lindner, a Neo-Freudian and expert penologist, viewed normal existence
as a cage and normal human behavior as bordering on the pathological.
Worse, he suggests that restriction and moral inhibition as practiced then
(*and today as well*) are inherently evil, and, if such practices are left un-
checked, might end the future development and freedom of mankind. For
those who might fall into the trap which has possessed many followers of
Reich and Aleister Crowley, Lindner's morality is not a license to do as
one's "whims"—of course, neither was Crowley's nor Reich's. For a
crucial discussion on the issues of freedom and license I suggest Jack
Parson's book *Freedom Is A Two-Edged Sword*, New Falcon (1989).

Unfortunately, Lindner's new morality, not surprisingly, has not found
a large and active following. If Dr. Lindner were alive today he might be
even more deeply saddened by the current moral philosophy of
conformity, altruism and group-think: anything that doesn't support
mediocrity in social life is frowned upon; anyone who stands up for
responsible disobedience is heretical and subject to ostracism or
imprisonment. Dr. Lindner would be still more horrified to find
psychology participating with government and the religious right in the
fight against man's progress over gravity, ignorance and death.

My more-than-passing interest with Lindner was stimulated not by his
popular books, but instead by a book lent to me many years ago by the
Rascal Guru Israel Regardie. The title of this long-overlooked book was
Prescription For Rebellion, Rinehart & Co. Inc. (1952).

In 1991, while reviewing Dr. Regardie's papers, I was pleasantly
surprised to find correspondence between Lindner and Regardie. Their
correspondence was more than professional. It was warm and friendly
and Regardie felt secure enough with Lindner to seek his advice on a
personal issue. Lindner also felt close enough to Regardie to voice his
complaint that his most important ideas went unnoticed. Regardie, of
course, sympathized and attempted to reassure Lindner, as he had done
with many others, that revolutionary ideas such as his often take many
decades before acceptance and application. They discussed the works of
Reich and others who would subsequently find themselves in the hands
of the Inquisition of the '50s.

Sadly, Regardie's timing lacked a sense of history for, as we know,
heretical ideas including those asserted by the rebel Jesus take much
longer than decades to find a receptive vessel.

Regardie, like Lindner, knew that the so-called "higher adjustment" promised by psychotherapy was a lie and, worse, they both knew that Freud (who had been accused of creating this lie) was not the real culprit. Both men, like other rebels and devils, knew that society's "cure" meant surrendering mind and body. Thus, the remedy for mankind's "disease" was acquiescing to collective illusions. Happiness became a modern "pact with the devil." However, this pact required that the individual exchange his oneness—his rebellion, his symptoms—for a promised peace—and I do not mean the blissful peace, promised by the so-called escapist "religion" of Buddhism—but a peace of passivity as promised by the Christian ethic that, according to many modern thinkers, Christianity can't deliver. Regardie, Reich and Nietzsche went so far as to say that Christianity delivered a living death. Nietzsche went further and said it was the religion of the weak and pathetic.

An Alternative To The "Pact With The Devil"

Below are some characteristics of constructive rebellion.

Remember *your* priorities. Do not become distracted from *your* primary goals. As various instincts and desires compete for the center stage of consciousness, it is necessary to remember and reinforce *your* priorities by energy regulation. This is often difficult to do since our true will and desires have been contaminated or replaced by the will and desires of others. However, by proper energy regulation your desires can be rediscovered and channeled productively without unnecessary conflict. I say "unnecessary conflict" because *real* conflict exists and no one is immune from it. Before I discuss other characteristics of constructive rebellion I will discuss proper energy regulation.

Energy Regulation

There are four types of energy direction and two primary cycles.

First, there is *energized enthusiasm* which in turn is usually balanced by *deep relaxation*—the second type of energy. This cycle is the fundamental healthy, creative, rebellious ebb and flow of life. Third, there is *deep tension* and, fourth, *agitated tiredness*. These last two are the primary signs that the fundamental ebb and flow of life is disturbed.

For example: One person has a cup of coffee. The caffeine stimulates him and he feels energized and enthusiastic. The caffeine runs its course and he feels tired and can easily relax. Another person drinks a cup of coffee and feels energized but there is a background of subtle agitation. He feels a sense of free-floating tension which leads to agitated tiredness and manifests as a desire to have a drink. For some people, the alcohol does not relax, but instead energizes *without* loss of the background sense of agitation. But soon the person requires more alcohol and the agitated quality begins to predominate over the energized enthusiasm. Soon the person begins to feel exhausted and drinks to reduce the feelings of agitated tiredness. He hopes to relax but since he is on a disturbed cycle, deep relaxation is next to impossible unless the cycle is broken. This is usually painful, which is nothing more than a signal that the healthy flow of life has been disturbed. Keep in mind that the pain of the disturbed cycle is something that people dislike but the difficulty in breaking the cycle completely and switching over to the healthy cycle is even more disturbing. (Notice the interesting interactive effects of pain.)

Most normal people and many rebels live this way. This is where the power of remembering becomes essential. If you feel agitated and tense remember to exercise or back off—focus on your priorities. Most can't perform this task. They fall into a slump or seek some quick fix which has relieved their pain in the past. Remember, getting off the second cycle and slowly switching to the first can be very unpleasant. This example is in no way limited in its implications to the use of chemicals. More often than not it is applicable to a person's entire lifestyle.

One case comes to mind. A very good looking, friendly young man is fundamentally insecure. This means he is easily agitated. Agitation is painful and he desires to reduce it. He is in a business meeting and makes promises to his associates which are next to impossible to keep. Momentarily his agitation lessens, but as he drives home he begins to worry. When he reaches home he greets his wife and within an hour has sex. Then for no apparent reason he criticizes her. They fight and quickly make up. He has a drink or two and begins to feel tired. He can't rest as a flood of insecurities overtake him. He tries sex again and then blames her for his inability to find sexual release. He takes a pill and goes to sleep.

Waking up he feels agitated tension which he interprets as enthusiasm or the "get-going" feeling. He has two cups of coffee. However, he feels guilt (tension-insecurity) about his behavior toward his wife and then makes her a promise that is difficult to complete. He leaves for work, making up excuses or planning something unethical which might help him fulfill his promises to his associates.

When he reaches work he has come up with a compromise solution. He will lie to someone else and get them to do something that will help him fulfill part of his promise to his other associates. (This is the robbing-Peter-to-pay-Paul game.)

As the day wears on, he wears out. Remembering his promise to his wife, he takes her out to an expensive dinner which he charges on his credit card. He can't afford this, particularly when his job is in jeopardy and he is in debt. He continues with this process for years until he burns himself out. During his burn-out phase he may get fired, divorced, attempt suicide or file bankruptcy. In his mind he sees himself as a first-class manipulator—a rebel against an unjust world. From time to time he gains a sense of pride from his juggling act but, as he ages, fewer and fewer people are taken in by his charm. Finally, he has to change or "go under." Usually he goes down and rebuilds his act on a smaller scale.

Keeping these two cycles in mind we return to our factors of potent rebellion.

The next quality is *focus*. Whatever priorities one has chosen, focus, determination and persistence are essential. To focus means to attend to what you are doing. If you are daydreaming attend to that, but don't daydream when riding your motorcycle. Determination and persistence don't mean agitated tension but the ability to continually focus on your primary goals, particularly on what you can do now to accomplish them.

The fourth and final factor is *practice*. Whatever you are trying to accomplish, practice, practice, practice. Do not feel you are an expert simply because something comes easily. Until you can do something with the assurance of a sleepwalker, you are not an expert. The act of practice is what makes neurotics neurotics and rebels rebels. This is why it is difficult to change bad habits as well as good ones. People get into "habit ruts," some good, but most bad. You can tell if a habit is working by how you feel. Most of the time you should feel on the continuum of energized enthusiasm or deep relaxation. If you are on the other cycle you might have to change your entire life to get off the merry-go-round.

To repeat the four factors:
- —Remembering
- —Energy regulation
- —Focus
- —Practice

The key principle is that a good life in general, and successful rebellion in particular, are the result of oscillating on the energized enthusiasm and deep relaxation continuum. All other things in life have a higher probability of success if you are on the right energy cycle.

Remember, the ultimate goal of rebellion is to break out of the cage you, and society, have "put" you in.

Christopher S. Hyatt, Ph.D. holds degrees in psychology, education and criminal justice. He is a former experimental psychologist, a former clinical psychotherapist and the first person to receive the Professional Certificate in Creative Writing from The University of Arizona. He has written a wide variety of books on psychology, self-transformation, sex magic and Western magical traditions.

William S. Burroughs
author of *Cities of the Red Night,*
The Place of Dead Roads and *The Western Lands*

PARADISE MISLAID

by William S. Burroughs

Paradise is a still picture. Paradise cannot change. The forbidden fruit is Time. And here are Adam and Eve ...

She is eating sardines out of a can with a shoe-horn. She points at Adam with the horn:

"We're going to have to talk about our *relationship* and stuff."

God groans: "What have I done?"

Adam says, real stupid: "Huh?"

She adds, "Adam, we need to *emote!*"

Adam wears a dirty old t-shirt, the dirt so old it's gray. He stands in front of a cheap motel where they live in innocent bliss, surrounded by the Paradise Amusement Park. She hands him the *Big Apple*. He bites into it, and the apple turns into a candied apple. Carousel music. Shots from the shooting gallery. The Ferris wheel turns.

And here is an old clown, with a rusty scythe. A smell about him, sweet and evil and rotten. Not dangerous to a healthy adult, but Adam isn't healthy anymore. He is apple-rotten to the core.

Eve says: "Get out of here, and get me some money, too."

God echoes: "Get out of my Paradise. Get out and hustle, from here to eternity."

So they want me to do an endorsement for Peppy Jeans? What do they expect, a strip-tease? — at my age, in my condition?

"No," they assure me; "nothing that will offend the canons of good taste."

And then they write me as saying: "I was young once, with snakes dancing in my teeth."

Now, wait a minute. What you think I am, some snake-eating geek? And how did snakes get into this, anyhoo? and stuff ... (oh, uh, yes I remember). A man has to draw the line *somewhere.*

Snakes in my teeth, indeedy;
I am not that fucking needy.

"So how is this? — 'When I draw on my Peppy Jeans, I get a peppy feeling.'"

This will be a special-effects striptease, in which the jeans dance offa my ass and I chase them around the stage??

Now in evolution, the most basic thing is to find a *niche* — a niche that only you and yours can occupy — and hold that niche, from here to eternity. It's the old Army game. If you lose that niche, you lose everything you can hold dear. And the worst thing that can happen to any species is *loss of habitat:* loss of the place in which it lives and breathes.

So how you find a niche? Look at yourself, and look around yourself. Here is a recent example: there was no niche for narcs until the Harrison Narcotics Act of 1914 slipped through — like Prohibition, when folks had other things on their mind. Before the Harrison Act, opium, cocaine, morphine could be bought across the counter in any American drugstore, from sea to shining sea. The law created a niche, and it was soon full to overflowing — taking over narcotics research at Lexington, lest any wise-ass find a cure; telling doctors what they can and can't prescribe for their patients — and it keeps screaming for MORE MORE MORE: more personnel, more money.

Now how does one destroy such a cancerous factor? By destroying its habitat: the whole vast network of addicts, buys, stings, confiscations, stool pigeons, in which this creature lives and breathes.

Only thing gets Homo Sap up off his ass is a foot up it. If we don't stop this Reefer Madness, it will eat all our niches out from under us.

Time to streamline the medical profession. Future croakers will specialize in one operation, and know that inside out.

Diagnosis has become a separate specialty. They are known as "D's" and they tend to be of an elitist persuasion:

"Very few people are good at anything. You should see the diagnoses and test schedules passed along by the hospitals. They have an insatiable appetite for tests. The more unnecessary the better, since they necessitate more tests."

The D walks in and sniffs: "Yellow fever. He stinks of raw meat."

"But that's impossible … he hasn't been …"

"What is his trade?"

"Uh, marine insurance."

"He goes on ships?"

"Uh, yes."

"So do mosquitoes."

"Supportive treatment. Prognosis unfavorable. Next case."

A psychiatric case returned for medical review:

"Disorientation … uh, drooling … Here are my tests so far."

"Liver?"

"Enlarged. Possible somatic symptoms. Subject's grandmother died of liver failure."

"The old bag drink?"

"I doubt it. She was a one of those temperance ladies."

"Did you slur out 'drooling'?"

"Uh yes, it didn't seem important ..."

"Wilson's disease ... probably inherited. Treatment clearly indicated."

"Tests, doctor?"

"Look, when I do a D, I do a D — see? She's a classic Wilson. Does she have to slobber it all over you?"

The doctor snarls, and simpers, and sidles out of the room like a disgruntled crab, clutching his tests to his heart, hoping the D will be proven wrong. He isn't. In three months the Wilson is a normal healthy slut.

Next case. The D inhales deeply:

"What a lovely smell of new-mown hay ... Typhoid. Get on it, in the name of Mary."

He turns to the patient: "Ate any good oysters lately?"

"The best. Portuguese oysters. They is known to be the best, like Portuguese Jews."

"Where?"

"Joe's Seafood, at 49th and Third."

"Pass that address along to the Board of Health."

Next case: excruciating headache, chills and fever.

"That's enough. Malaria."

"Malaria in New York City? Didn't you say all cases are addicts?"

"Yes. It thrives in syringes."

"Nothing is true. Everything is permitted."

Last words of Hassan i Sabbah, the Old Man of the Mountain, Master of the Assassins. Interpreted by the ignorant as an invitation to unbridled license. On the contrary, realization involves exacting spiritual training. Everything is permitted *because* nothing is true. Everything is illusion.

"Do what you want is the whole of the law." Aleister Crowley's panacea. How many *know* what they want?

Everyman's ME is the dullest part about him. Who wants to hear about feelings of inadequacy? He'll be telling you about his bowel movements next, if you don't stop him. Just remember that in a case like this, deadly force is admissible. It's him or you.

W. Somerset Maugham thought that he had made the Devil's Bargain. If so, he was taken for a fool. The Devil's Bargain is always a fool's bargain, and especially for a writer. Since the Devil only deals in *quantitative* merchandise. He can make you a rich writer. He can make you famous. But he can't make you a great writer, or even a good writer.

He always tries money first:

"Well, not much to spend it on — eh, Gramps? Well now, how does a young body grab you?"

"Like a pea under a shell: 'Step right up. Hell under the shell.'"

To be young, you have to be *there* in Time. You have to *be* young, with the awkwardness, uncertainty and folly of youth. You have to be eighteen in Time. And you are not eighteen. You are seventy-eight:

"Old fool sold his soul for a strap-on."

"Well, how about an *honorable* bargain? You could be a great research scientist and benefit mankind."

"There are no honorable bargains involving the exchange of qualitative merchandise, like souls and talent, for quantitative merchandise, like money and Time. So fuck off, Satan, and don't take me for dumber than I look."

Every man has the choice, at some moment in his life, to be God.

God put in this clause, and added: "Only a fool would take the job, when he learns that 'all-knowing' is all-*feeling*. A few hours in a cancer ward will usually cure a wise-ass."

God's Bargain and Satan's Bargain are both fool's bargains.

William S. Burroughs
Lawrence, Kansas
September 17, 1994

William S. Burroughs, born February 5, 1914, is the world-renowned author of *Naked Lunch, Queer, Interzones, Junky, The Soft Machine,* and *My Education: A Book of Dreams,* among many other works. He is a member of the American Academy and Institute for Arts and Letters and a *Commandeur de l'Ordre des Arts et des Lettres* of France. He is considered by many to be the foremost literary figure of our time. He died on August 2, 1997.

William S. Burroughs
author of *Queer, Interzones* and *Junky*
among many other works

Liber Anu vel DCXXXV
The Book of Hope
by
Anderson Slade

THE PRICE OF FREEDOM

by James Wasserman

Editor of the Falcon title:
AHA!

Thrill with lissome lust of the light,
O man! My man!
Come careering out of the night
Of Pan! Io Pan!

I have come to realize, at age 46, that Liberty has been the entire basis of my life quest. I have used every technique I could find to maximize my Liberty—meditation, ritual magick, sex, drugs, sobriety, philosophy, personal economics, career orientation. I now believe that an understanding of political liberty is an essential part of my search for spiritual liberty.

Historically the gods of a conquered people become the devils of their conqueror's pantheon. Today's rebels and devils include those of us who still worship yesterday's gods of Individual Liberty and Inherent Individual Rights. Our would-be conquerors are the New World Order addicts, whose cradle-to-grave security and obedience models are inimical to individual Freedom. These power-junkies parade themselves endlessly upon the media stage, camouflaging their daily control-fix under the banner of Compassion, Global Interdependence, and Resource Management. Their addiction has caused them to both advocate and labor toward an abandonment of the Liberty unique to American society.

I too once embraced socialism as part of my learning process—until it became clear that a world bureaucracy run by social planners and civil-servants was one three-dimensional reality I truly had to fear. I now spurn the advance of the Age of the Expert, and the cultural madness in which the machine (designed by the international corporate mind-killers) becomes God. Thus, although I am a business owner, father, husband, law-abiding, tax-paying, U.S. citizen, my political views are those of a modern social pariah.

My spiritual path is identified with the teachings of Aleister Crowley and *The Book of the Law*. A logical corollary of this statement is that I believe in Divine Inspiration. I also believe that *The Book of the Law* was neither the first nor the last time divine inspiration penetrated human consciousness. Further, I believe the American Constitution and its Bill of Rights to be a divinely inspired model of a potential Thelemic society—as later articulated by Crowley in *Liber OZ* (a short tract, written in 1925, that expressed the political philosophy of *The Book of the Law* in words of one syllable). What makes the ideas of both *Liber OZ* and the Bill of Rights so radical is their guarantee of nearly unlimited personal liberty and individual right.

Implicit in seeking to maximize individual liberty is a recognition of the divinity inherent within each human being. Quoting *The Book of the Law*, "Every man and every woman is a star" and "...thou hast no right but to do thy will." These statements posit both a will to do, and an attainable celestial nature at the root of the self. The reigning political goal of a society built on these principles must be the encouragement of maximum individual liberty for the most unfettered growth of the divine inner potential. Simple enough—*if* you believe in the divine inner potential.

Respect for human nature is an absolute prerequisite to a vision of human freedom.

The U.S. Bill of Rights represents the first time in history that individual sovereignty was regarded as *primary*, and government sovereignty as *secondary*. The Declaration of Independence spells out America's founders' understanding of the *origin* of rights in no uncertain terms, "We hold these Truths to be self-evident, that all Men are...endowed by their Creator with certain inalienable Rights..." The inviolate supremacy of the *inalienable* rights acknowledged in the Bill of Rights is protected *from* the State. The "rights" acknowledged by the UN and other New World Order scams are *conditional* upon the will of the State. They are *contingent* rights, "given" or "dispensed" *by* the State. It is impossible to emphasize strongly enough the difference between these two points of view.

The U.S. Constitution purposely sets up an *inefficient* government. This is no accident. Thomas Jefferson spoke of an America government "shackled by the chains of the Constitution." Imagine our New World Order addicts willingly cutting themselves off from their domination-fix.

In the Age of the Expert, the vision of an *inherently successful* humanity is considered a nineteenth century myth that today's "experts" have deemed inoperative. Social planners are heralded as the new deities who will bring order out of the chaos of an *inherently unsuccessful* human-ity's unbridled and destructive passions—and channel these instincts into constructive byways. How they accomplish this modern miracle, of course, may require the use of force. In simpler times, this would be called "Tyranny." Today, "Social Planning for an Orderly and Productive Society Under the Watchful Eye of the Corporate Oligarchy" might be a more long-winded, if politically correct means to describe the same thing. The ultimate end of this philosophy was conclusively forecast by George Orwell in *1984* and Aldous Huxley in *Brave New World.*

The hooded black figures with automatic weapons these days are no longer terrorists—they are government agents. To confirm this, let us invoke the shade of David Koresh and the eighty-some Branch Davidians who perished in the flames with him as the world watched TV. On February 28, 1993, one hundred federal police, armed with automatic weapons and badges showed up on private property, guns a' blazin'. Soon came hundreds more, with hundreds more guns and badges, adding tanks, Bradley Fighting Vehicles, loudspeakers, stadium lights, electronic surveillance equipment, and a mini-army of professional cult busters and "expert deprogrammers." Next came hundreds of pages of newspaper and magazine articles, and hundreds of hours of TV and radio broadcasts, continuing the assault with their "objective" reporting—a barrage of character assassination and unsubstantiated rumor—painting this sect and its young leader as modern incarnations of the anti-Christ. Fifty-one days of torment and slander finally result in the greatest conflagration of modern "law-enforcement." In 45 minutes, the "fortress" of this "heavily armed cult" burns to the ground like the pathetic tinderbox it was all along.

Our globally compassionate political leaders strut and fret their hour upon the stage, each one so willing to "take responsibility" you had to wonder when their jail terms would begin. Meanwhile, ACLU, Amnesty International, and other Establishment conscience-mongers are so silent you could hear a dead child's whimper. Editorial pages poke a few jabs at the BATF just to prove their independence, but the BATF isn't really as popular as the FBI anyway. The bottom line is, nobody cares. Koresh and the Davidians were weird, and had it coming.

Just ever so gradually, the house of cards begins to fall apart. Infor-mation surfaces to contradict the government/media disinformation, and many questions arise. Among a host of issues are the following:

1. The heavily armed cult appears to have owned about 200 rifles, or two per adult resident. Statewide in Texas, average gun ownership runs about four per adult.

2. Irrefutable evidence is provided that the loss of the element of surprise was known to ATF raid leaders before the raid. They shamelessly lied about this for months after the raid.

3. Three of the four dead ATF agents had been Clinton's bodyguards during the 1992 campaign. Unedited video feeds of the raid suggest these three may have been assassinated by another ATF agent, who tossed a grenade, then fired two unaimed machine gun bursts into the room they had just entered.

4. Neither Clinton nor Reno dare acknowledge that their much publicized desire to save the children was the primary cause of the children's death. The FBI turns out not to have been so sure of child abuse after all.

5. Highly respected attorneys who visited Mt. Carmel publicly accuse ATF of firing from helicopters through the ceiling of the women and children's living quarters. They swear the physical evidence supported Koresh's claims that agents fired first.

6. A sane assessment of tanks smashing into wooden walls—behind which were bales of hay, kerosene lamps, diesel generators and propane tanks—casts doubt on claims by an FBI sniper to have observed black-clad masked Davidians setting fires. The sniper's statement is also known to contradict observations by newsmen during the first half hour of the live broadcast of the fire, before the disinformation squad could assemble.

7. A couple of government investigative experts are courageous enough to speak up and pin the tail on Reno, *et al.*

8. And finally a kangaroo court in February, 1994 exposes the extent of the government vendetta against the Branch Davidians. The judge overthrows the jury's innocent verdict with such arrogance that the jury foreman cries on the steps of the courthouse. And thereby undoubtedly sets the precedent for a successful appeal.

9. Multi-million dollar lawsuits against the U.S. government are filed both here and abroad.

10. And finally A&E Network offers a fairly unbiased hour-long report after nearly two years of an almost total media disinformation campaign.

A family in Idaho, the Weavers, gunned down by Federal agents in August, 1992 are also getting some acknowledgment, despite the earlier media blitz against their "white-supremacist," "armed extremist" profile. U.S. Marshals first shoot and kill the family's dog, and then shoot Weaver's 14-year-old son in the back, killing him. Next, 300 feds surround the Weaver cabin. An FBI agent blasts a .30 caliber hole in Mrs. Weaver's head, killing her as she cradles her ten-month-old baby in her arms. After 11 days, a severely wounded Weaver surrenders. He is later acquitted by a jury of his peers. In Weaver's case, he faces a human being for a judge, unlike his Davidian soul-mates. A secret Justice (*sic*) Department report leaked in December, 1994 acknowledges that Mrs. Weaver's Constitutional rights were violated by the FBI's "rules of engagement" for that operation. (Strangely enough, these unconstitutional "rules" were written by one of the same public servants who incinerated the Branch Davidians eight months later.) While all the money or legal precedents in the world can't bring back a son or a wife, Randy Weaver is suing the government and will undoubtedly win. It's a good feeling to know that our government can rely on its taxpayers to cover its financial liabilities when it has been adjudged to have acted improperly.

We Americans are facing a daily information assault designed to persuade us to sacrifice our Liberty in the name of Collective Security. In late 1992, for the first time in history, more people were employed by various levels of local, state, and federal government than were employed by private industry. Those employed by government have only one purpose—to monitor us. We now have more people paid to monitor us, than we have people producing the money to pay our monitors.

The tyrants encroaching in our lives are dangerous because of their insatiable need for more control. In *Naked Lunch,* William S. Burroughs brilliantly describes the exponential grasping of addiction as the "Algebra of Need." Our political addict-experts have pounced into our very beds with their sexual speech codes, and will soon demand we make them responsible for licensing us to produce our children. Later they will insist on determining those children's schooling, profession, and place of residence (all in the name of global ecology, crime-prevention, human rights, etc., *ad nauseam*).

An enforced subservience of the individual to the "common good" is the current meaning of the word "Liberalism." In order to grasp the doublethink involved, read Jack Parson's collection of essays in *Freedom is a Two-Edged Sword,* published by New Falcon Publications. Written in the early 1950's, for Parsons, *Liberalism* meant what we would call today "Individualism," "Constitutionalism," even "Conservatism"(!) In any brainwashing procedure, one of the first patterns that must be broken down is the meaning of words. "Loyalty," "patriotism," "honor," must be gradually turned into their opposites to allow the naturally morally-directed psyche to maintain allegiance to its guiding principles, while acting in a conditioned manner—Orwell's classic FREEDOM IS SLAVERY.

Like any sane and decent person, I am concerned with war and political strife. My experience as a human being however teaches me that evolution and peace cannot be coerced, even in the name of the "greater good." And I become suspicious of people who want to coerce me. For example, even before the "fall" of the Soviet Union and the "liberation" of South Africa, the United States boasted the largest percentage of its citizens in prison in the entire world. And now, the U.S. House and Senate, with cheer-leading from the White House, are attempting to outdo each other to prove how "tough on crime" they can really be. Build More Prisons. Makes sense. After all, since in 1990, 50% of new inmates in New York were imprisoned for the sale or possession of drugs, we need more prisons to make room for criminals as well as pot smokers.

However, I can't find a section of the Constitution or Bill of Rights that allows the Government to imprison people who are not committing crimes against others. In fact, the First Amendment guarantees free-expression; the Fourth Amendment guarantees privacy; and the Ninth and Tenth Amendments tell the Government exactly where it must stop. (Incidentally, there are bills in both the House and Senate to repeal the Second Amendment. And Comrade Clinton is still attempting to ram through legislation and rally public support to abrogate the Fourth Amendment, through warrantless searches in public housing.) If a person commits a crime while under the influence of drugs, he should certainly be imprisoned. If a person commits a crime with a gun, that person should also be severely punished. But the operative phrase is "If a *person* commits a crime"—not "drugs" or "guns."

In the final months of the Kennedy Administration, a 15 member Special Study Group was commissioned to evaluate the ramifications of a world at peace. The group met for two and a half years, after which they submitted their unanimous secret report to the Johnson Administration. One member anonymously leaked the report, which was published as *Report from Iron Mountain on the Possibility and Desirability of Peace,* with Introductory Material by Leonard C. Lewin, Dial Press, 1967.

Discussing the need to find a substitute, in a peaceful society, for the military function of providing an outlet for aggressive young people, as well as employment opportunities for the poor and under-educated, the report states, "Another possible surrogate for the control of potential enemies of society is the reintroduction, in some form consistent with modern technology and political processes, of slavery. Up to now, this has been suggested only in fiction, notably in the works of Wells, Huxley, Orwell, and others engaged in the imaginative anticipation of the sociology of the future. But the fantasies projected in *Brave New World* and *1984* have seemed less and less implausible over the years since their publication. The traditional association of slavery with ancient pre-industrial cultures should not blind us to its adaptability to advanced forms of social organization, nor should its equally traditional incompatibility with Western moral and economic values. It is entirely possible that the development of a sophisticated form of slavery may be an absolute prerequisite for social control for a world at peace."

The sinister perpetrators of the world government hypnotic hoax are powerful people in government, finance, and the media, whose self-importance allows them to feel they are better qualified to run our lives than we are. The really scary part is that we have given them the power to do so. Why? Because they *valued* it *more* than we did. We have been guilty of dereliction of duty. The price of freedom is eternal vigilance. And we have been asleep at the wheel. That personal, individual evasion of moral responsibility is the key to the slavery we are substituting daily for the American Constitutional Freedom that is the birthright of each member of this nation. Living with, and protecting, that terrible Freedom is the unique responsibility of everyone who dare call himself Initiate.

True compassion and true idealism demand that American society honor and defend its unique philosophical underpinnings. We can share this model with the entire world by example, functioning as a beacon of light and hope that all may see. The pathetic, guilt-ridden, hand-wringing and cringing proposed by the New World Order crowd are merely sophisticated psychological tactics to induce subservience. Today, self-aware, independent thinkers can "Just Say No!" to this Globaloney bullshit.

James Wasserman has been studying and practicing the Magical system of Aleister Crowley for over twenty years. He is also a noted author and a strong proponent of freedom and human rights.

THE FOURTEEN STEPS

by Daniel Suders

When all the world is on a program
And the storm of self-indulgence
Is on the horizon

I would like to go to the Bermuda Triangle

And sift through the sands of Amelia Ehrhardt

And take the twelve step program one step further than reality which we all know as $E = mc^2$ and make a pie of thankless guts called fish which blow your hair and illusions up like bonnets of azure musk hens who need to be herded in thousands before you can even begin to understand the program of steps and step by step you will begin to feel better about smiling happy people who invade your home via the television talking about how they climbed the ladder to oblivion and need to make a public spectacle of themselves in order to convince the world that they exist because at the top of rung number twelve awaits the fool.

Indicates the inescapable advance of man in his evolution.

It represents man advancing along the road of evolution with indifference and without stopping, bearing the load of his good or bad actions, stimulated by the tinkling of his thoughts, low anxieties of the moment, low instincts, until he reaches a serene state.

Step One

We must acknowledge a higher fool and admit we are powerless to bear our load or, for that matter, the load of all the great big bullshitters that would like us to cow-tow to their corporate ideas of who we should be.

Repeat three times daily: "I am my higher power!"

Step Two

To understand why we got where we are we need to consult a bus schedule of emotions called hubbards. They will help us know the values that have been implanted in our scarves and free us to cast them to the wind as if shaking out a table cloth full of crumbs. This will give us empty minds and allow us to fill them with our own misconceptions and (fill in your own name) _____'s thoughts about the cosmic results of being born.

Climb a tree and give thanks to your higher power.

Step Three:

Get a rubber stamp with your signature. It will help you seal the deal and imprint your identity on anyone foolish enough to let you do it. You see that we have learned from many years of experience that we imprint who we are on everybody we encounter. So it is best to be "up front" about what we do. It is a well-known fact that we do not see those we meet— we only see little faces of ourselves in their eyes and evaluate ourselves by the way we perceive ourselves in their perceptions of us.

Stamp them til they turn blue.

Step Four:

Many people have made us blue. Kill them by writing their obituary and then burning it. All the people in the world do not care for you so you might as well admit it and move into your own circle of self. This is done by ignoring anything to do with organized religion. The Archbishop of Canterbury and the Pope in his house in Rome and the Dali Lama will try to purge your brains to refuse this most important step. But if you persevere you can wall off your brain to their onslaughts and remain pure beyond what people are trying to do to you.

Suck cock until you can't think.

Step Five:

You have now reached NIRVANA, and you have no need for anything in your head. Do the sighing exercise and long for release from your bondage to bondage. Even this desire will leave you because your jaws are now tired. Too tired to think about the hubbards implanted in you since you were born to well-meaning parents who had similar bondage to bondage. Let the wind storms of the canyons carve you deeply and a low sodium diet clear your soul.

Eat as many french fries as you can hold.

Step Six:

This is the colossal jump into the fire of faith in yourself. It is the time when you fear no fear. To turn back into old ways is enticing but you know you must pull out and move forward. The road is getting straighter... The path more clear. For fog no longer shrouds the way and the dawn is upon you. Write letters to your most beloved folks and let them know they no longer have any power over your emotions and if they try to control you any longer that you will kill them in a rage so uncontrollable that they will have to shoot you up with Thorazine for about ten years.

Go to a Hallmark store and read all the cards.

Step Seven:

The way of the tree grows straight. As you surround yourself with blue energy your program takes a new shape. All the memories you ever had turn into feathers and float away just like the stuffing from the pillow at your first pajama party. And now your bed is made. Float in your own arms and be thankful you have them. (Be thankful you have feet while you are at it otherwise you couldn't walk down the fucking street).

Release yourself to the clouds and float on a see of tranquillity.

Step Eight:

Buy the "Big Book". I spent a lot of time and energy writing the damn thing and I need the residuals to pay the light bill. You know you could do something else for somebody else some time you bozo. You don't have to be so self-centered that you can't do something to make another guy's life a little better. I have dedicated my life to you so you might as well fork over the $14.95 for the Big Picture and learn more about your miserable self-awareness trip O.K.

Get a life you fool!

Step Nine:

I've got this .45 automatic and I'm going to come over to your house and blast the shit out of your cat and your mother-in-law and your goddamn television set. That will surely put a crimp in your fucking serenity. So, lock your door and pray to your fucking higher power that I don't know your address. Better still move out of the country and herd hens in some stinking third-world country where the women don't shave their arm pits and smell like last year's Thanksgiving dinner. And give me a break... I think you are the most ugly motherfucker on the face of the earth.

Eat a hoard of hornets.

Step Ten:

Serenity is as serenity does. So why do you live in my typewriter you bitch? You want my help in doing *your* program. Well. What about mine. You know, if I want a drink I'll have one. And if I want twelve: that's even better. So get off my dress and find some other lesbian to bother. Isn't it enough that I tried to help you? (Even though you are a worthless piece of shit.) I get up every morning to a pile of dishes in the sink, a pile of dirty clothes on the floor and several drunken drug addicts lying around on my sofa listening to fucking Patsy Cline. Don't you think I have it rough? *My serenity is down the toilet.* Twelve steps! I can't even move twelve inches until I've had a drink in the morning.

Go to the liquor store for some more vodka.

Step Eleven:

I've had it with you namby pampy wimps! Slurring your way through *my* life. You wander around like senile walruses looking for beached any-thing. Who told you you could find any answers whatsoever in a book? Your hubbards are yours. Why take mine? The only thing I've got is ammunition to blow your tits to kingdom come. And, by god, I'll do it!

Look out!

Step Twelve:

You have now come very close to the highest good you can achieve. Rejoice and spend time with those souls that have come close to you in your journey. You could not have done this on your own. But the inner strength you have found will enable you to move further than you ever imagined. You will see stars more clearly and unicorns will nestle in your rose bushes. The storms of life will pass unnoticed through the trees of your life... They will bend with the winds of change but stand straight as ever after they have passed. You have discovered roots as deep as the center of the world. They hold you firm but you are not attached to them. They bring you nourishment but you are not hungry. You envy no other human being for you are yours and yours alone. You don't crave any-thing...not even re-runs of Mr. Ed. And in the peace that flows around you, you are completely satisfied and at one. Thank you... Thank you... Thank you...

Turn on the gas for about an hour and light a match.

© 1995 Lion Serpent Publishing *Liber Anu vel DCXXXV The Book of Hope*

THE THIRTEENTH STEP

News Item: Little Rock, Ark. —Thirty two years later, Virginia Kelley still remembers the scene "as clear as day." Her husband was a good man, she recalls, but sometimes bourbon changed him.

The *Los Angeles Times*

Well, the *Los Angeles Times* has something to say about drinking. It is sandwiched between the sports page and the coupons and the big fat bellies of swill readers who believe everything they read because it is the newspaper.

It is the sandpaper that scrapes the rectum of the universe and sings nigaboo songs on the jukeboxes of eternity.

Now, let's get down to this lady—

She says

"Bourbon" changed her hubby

> He was good
> Sometimes
> But "clear as day"
> Bourbon changed him
> And he committed the awful crime
> Of violating step number thirteen

HE HIT HER

Now we all know from our studies that sacred teaching teaches us that the hitting is forbidden (unless changed by bourbon).

> Wagon wheels keep on turning
> Wagon wheels keep on burnin'
> We'll just keep goin' on

THE OLD WEST

Jed

Pecos is just around the corner... But I guess I'll just have to have me another bourbon.

Burt

But the west needs to be won...to be won!

Collette

(She is swooning against the piano)

It is bourbon...bourbon...bourbon. You fools will never win the west. (She is slurring.) You will fill your bellies with that devil's brew and you won't even be able to find your assholes, much less the west!

The Mummy
Leave them alone you bitch! (he begins to unravel.) I like bourbon myself. And if I want bourbon I will have it! (To the bartender) Give me a bourbon!

(The bartender gives him a bourbon and the mummy grabs Collette and presses his dusty rags against her bosom... She is repulsed but also amused as Pope John Paul the Second walks into the room and orders...)

The Pope
Give me a bourbon you poop!

When you read the times from cover to cover you discover the most wonderful things.

Item: Four skulls were found walking in the park scaring poodles

Item: Lesbians are really baskets of strange melons

Item: When you clean your space you have many new and strange things to come

Item: Into

Item: Bourbon changed him

Item: I got you babe

Sonny Bono drank bourbon once and it took him to Cher

George Bush drank bourbon once and it took him to Washington

Phyliss Diller washed her hair in bourbon and the world knows the truth

You Know The Truth And It Is Contained In The Book Of

1. "I didn't like the people so I sent them this stuff."
2. And the people didn't know any difference so they drank of this stuff.
3. And they became sick. But the rulers of the people were wise and decreed that they never drink of the stuff again and they were not changed in their ways but spoke of Patsy Cline and moonlight and noodles.
4. But the wise ones came to their senses one morning and threw out the stuff and the people were not changed any longer or, for that matter, any shorter.
5. There was one, however, that had learned the secret of the stuff and his name was Wanda.
6. Wanda had been born of baboons and star dust.

7. "Do you know my world?" he was fond of asking.
8. "Because I do and it will fit into Gregorian chant!"

Hints:

> When washing the floor with bourbon avoid the fumes
> because they can make you into a

Zombie

Item:

Zombies like to drink
They no like to think
Or they will turn pink
And pull your fucking head off at the roots

Vampire

In nineteen hundred and ninety two
A hungry vampire made a pass at you
He rubbed on your knee
Went to take a pee
And then flew out of the chimney: Hoo!

Werewolf

A monster went to a bargain mart
To get a small bottle of bourbon
He ate three pigs and a crust of bread

Guns 'n Roses

Lombardo Rapacini was out of bourbon. It had been a difficult day to say the least. Or at least to say it was difficult. Or difficult bourbon was out of season as he looked at the empty bottle and wondered how he would get through the night without a shot of difficult bourbon. But bourbon was as bourbon does so he went down to the convenience store in his building where he met seven large ethnic people who wanted to kill the shit out of him.

Seven Large Ethnic People

"To baby whoo you be go?
We is seven and you be one
You got two dollars
And we got none
The government has conspired
Against us and our dependents
And our children just sit and watch
Godzilla movies all day waiting for
A hot lunch

While Tokyo burns
So we all's goin' to kill your
Brown butt and we are goin'
To drink your bourbon"

It is reported that she watched as her husband of thirty four years shoved a broom stick up the most private part of her seven year old lhasa apso, Mimi.

"It was the bourbon... The bourbon..." She sobbed as they carried the sorry pooch to the dustbin.

Ooooooo the times they are a changing
For the worse
And no matter how much crack we smoke
Or how much bourbon we toke
Or the joke we joke
The shit still clings to our cloak

Debbie went to the mailbox to find a very special prize. Ed McMahon was looking out of a little window in an envelope. He was smiling at Debbie. He looked happy...happy...happy. Little Debbie gently took the envelope from Mr. Mailbox and ran to the house. Unfortunately, she ran over Mr. Rake who gave her a nasty crack on the head. Ed McMahon was still smiling so Debbie didn't really mind the large embolism swelling over her left temple.

"Traa-laa-traa-laa," sang Debbie, as she sat at the comfortable kitchen table and inhaled one more bourbon. She was only nine years old but wise beyond her age. She knew Jim Beam was a fine product and she knew Jack Daniels was even better. A wise grandmother had taught her that "Old Gutter-Snipe" from "Lucky's" was about as good.

Anyway, good old Ed was telling her that she had just won seven million dollars from his smiling glassine face behind the envelope. "What a lot of bourbon that will buy,", thought Debbie. "I could even buy a gallon and get real twisted and murder Mrs. Tweezer's camel."

It was at about this time that the United States Senate commissioned a new national anthem.

So Debbie took the seven million dollars she had just won from the smiling face behind the glassine envelope and bought Russia where she turned the national drink from vodka to bourbon, the national soup from borscht to bourbon and all the water in the Baltic Sea to bourbon.

She was very very happy and she went to sleep for a long time.

Thirty-two years later, Virginia Kelly still remembers the scene "as clear as day." Her husband was a good man, she recalls, but sometimes bourbon changed him.

The cookies smelled like his grandmother. Like the flour and lard she mixed together and the ever faithful shot of bourbon she had purloined from Papa's bottle. He was just back from a tour of duty in Vietnam and just a little bit on edge. He couldn't walk by the ficus tree in the den without a bit of a chill wandering down his back.

Papa was asleep and he crept into his room for a sip of the forbidden "happy-juice" as his Papa called it. Wow! Did that taste good!

He grabbed his M-1 and began to spray the house with gunfire. Granny and her cookies went flying. Papa and his bottle of "happy-juice" blasted their way into a new book called...

The Bourbon Chronicles

When we begin to examine the thirteenth step we see that we have come a long way. We have been irritable, perhaps despondent or even loathsome. But those close to us have supported us on our long journey...The journey to freedom.

We have been to hell and back, my friend, and now the thirteenth step is here. *You must apologize for being the asshole you are and have a drink!*

Recovery is in your mind and since you don't have a mind you don't have to recover! This is the secret you have been waiting for. It's not chimneys lurking against you in the Moonlight... And it sure is not china plates filled with vodka. It is your will power and your higher power and the power of the United States Senate and their new national anthem that calls you to a new life of very fine and delightful consequences that include (but are not limited to) petting a yak, painting the Sistine Chapel by numbers, and running your hand up hoo-hoo's skirt.

So you think you have made it?

Well, for $14.95 more you can have the fourteenth step and learn that bourbon wasn't so bad after all. But we can't say more or that would give it all away.

Dr. Mozambo's Congo Powder

And when I took some
A thousand icicles pierced my winter
Just like when you walked out on me with that
Horrible laugh on your face
Thinking you were something
But already being brought to your knees
In your head

That was when I decided to slit your throat

(Sometime in the future this piece of writing was introduced into court to indicate the unlimited lengths I would go to to avenge the...)

I cut you seven times
It was with love
It was with a knife
My grandfather had purchased it from a pawn shop
It was from the civil war
It was very sharp

CREEP—CREEP—CREEP—CREEP

—Into your bedroom

—On your bed

—The first cut is in your leg and you wake up startled

    The blood is flowing down your thigh
    A flow of menstrual proportions and the Red Sea
    The second cut comes now

"I remember a time when you could still suck a man and let his come vibrate over your tongue. I remember doing this while a Gene Pitney recording played thirteen times and we let it keep going while we talked about *a rechecher a la temps perdue* and why authors die young. I remember an evening on the beach at Santa Monica sucking three or four dicks...

"The sand was cold against my feet as I traveled across the dark beach. You could just make out the vaguest images of other flesh-travelers. They walked up and down and disappeared in twos and threes into a storm drain. When the lights of the police-cop motorcade came by everyone separated. Not I. I climbed up a lifeguard station and ran into a hotman. I had seen him in bars around the area before. He recognized me and unbuttoned his Levi's. God! His dick was a magnet for my lips!"

—But icicles grow
—Even in the summer of my love

        —SIR
        —SIR
        —SIR

—Even in the summer of my love

So now we have a gas bill
A phone bill
An electric bill
A grocery bill
A cable T.V. bill

Bills for when we go out
And bills for when we stay in
Bills for when we work
And bills for when we do not work
We have various doctor's bills
And a psychiatrist bill because
We worry about bills
There are veterinarian bills
And the goddamn Democrats sent me a hand bill
About why we pay all these fuckin' bills and
How they want to stop the bills
Well
They can pay my bills while I'm in the mental institution

Maximize my viewing

I'll go back to the beach and try to re-live a night when I
Went down
Without remorse
On three or four young guys who had hardhat crotches who
Didn't think a thing about anybody named Esmerelda or Gloria
Or Denise but they just wanted to get their semen-filled
Cocks licked into oblivion by a hot mouth yearning for the
Pleasure of

CUSTOMERS!

It is just like a relief line with hostile people who want to go back to the
beach for customers

      —SIR
      —SIR
      —SIR

Takeout vengeance
A new convenience store
Where black maskers stab out eye holes
And invoke masters of deceit
Who put needles in your ears
And tell you you are stupid

RETALIATION

WE
ALL
KNOW
THE EFFECT
OF
TAKING
A
HAND GUN
AND
BLOWING
OFF
A HEAD

The effect must be somewhat gratifying
Splatters of brain matter
Decorating and re-decorating
The environment
Someone who you hated
A person of wrong intentions
A devotee of the fourteenth step
        Which says
Blow all the

BITCH-WITCH-MOTHERFUCKER-SHITHEAD-COCKSUCK-
JISIMROOT-BALLBUSTER-SHYSTER-DORK-NOMIND-
PENCILPUSHER-WAGGEDOUT-VIBRATING

ASSHOLES

AWAY

Daniel Suders was an ordained clergyman active in the Episcopal church and a bartender. For more than ten years he worked in some of the sleaziest bars in Hollywood. His customers ranged from bikers who write poetry, to hookers and boy hustlers, and to any number of psychotic socio-paths, most of whom have done time. He was also a writer and enjoyed debunking popular pre-packaged and freeze-dried ideology. Before his death, he completed Volume III of *The Longest And Worst Poem In The English Language*. He is also author and illustrator of *The Adventures Of Mona The Lawn Blower*.

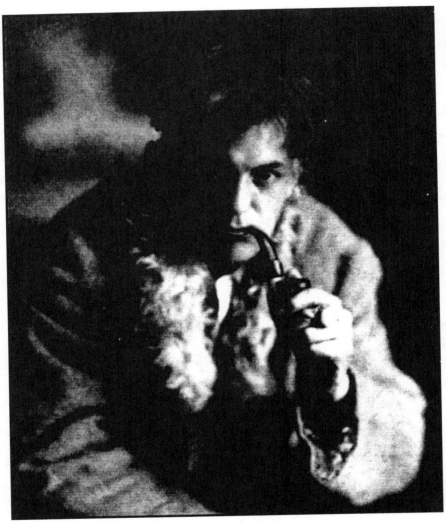

Aleister Crowley (in 1906)
The Father of Modern Western Magick
Born 1875, Died 1947

HYMN TO LUCIFER

by Aleister Crowley

Ware, nor of good nor ill, what aim hath act?
    Without its climax, death, what savour hath
Life? an impeccable machine, exact
    He paces an inane and pointless path
To glut brute appetites, his sole content
    How tedious were he fit to comprehend
Himself! More, this our noble element
    Of fire in nature, love in spirit, unkenned
Life hath no spring, no axle, and no end.

His body a blood-ruby radiant
    With noble passion, sun-souled Lucifer
Swept through the dawn colossal, swift aslant
    On Eden's imbecile perimeter.
He blessed nonentity with every curse
    And spiced with sorrow the dull soul of sense,
Breathed life into the sterile universe,
    With Love and Knowledge drove out innocence
The Key of Joy is disobedience.

Aleister Crowley
Also known as
The Beast 666,The Wickedest Man Alive
and *The Prophet of the New Aeon*

CROWLEY'S REBELLION

by AD VERITATEM IX°

Aleister Crowley is the author of the Falcon titles:
The Enochian World of Aleister Crowley: Enochian Sex Magic
Aleister Crowley's Illustrated Goetia: Sexual Evocation
Aleister Crowley and the Practice of the Magical Diary
The Revival of Magick and Other Essays
The Pathworkings of Aleister Crowley
The Temple of Solomon the King
Little Essays Toward Truth
The Equinox of the Gods
Gems From the Equinox
The Heart of the Master
Eight Lectures on Yoga
Magick Without Tears
The World's Tragedy
The Law Is For All
AHA!

Do what thou wilt shall be the whole of the Law.

Aleister Crowley will be remembered as one of the most famous Rebels and Devils of all time. His proclamation of the Law of Thelema re-oriented the fundamental philosophical and religious foundations of Western society. And in recent years, O.T.O. (the first of the Orders of Antiquity to embrace the Law of Thelema) has helped extend the teachings of *The Book of the Law* to lands and cultures as distant as Japan.

In preparing this essay for publication, we have decided to let Crowley speak for himself, quoting his New Comment to *The Book of the Law,* 1925, copyright O.T.O., published in an abridged edition by New Falcon Publications as *The Law Is For All,* edited by Israel Regardie. Chapter and verse citations, as well as page numbers, of the extracts are provided for ease of reference.

The reader may decide whether these thoughts, penned some seventy years ago, remain at the very vanguard of modern concerns as we prepare to enter the 21st Century.

On The Nature Of Man & God

Every man and every woman is not only a part of God, but the Ultimate God. "The Centre is everywhere and the circumference nowhere". The old definition of God takes new meaning for us. Each one of us is the One God... [p. 75]

Each man instinctively feels that he is the Centre of the Cosmos, and philosophers have jeered at his presumption. But it was he that was precisely right. The yokel is no more 'petty' than the King, nor the earth than the Sun. Each simple elemental Self is supreme, Very God of Very God. Ay, in this Book is Truth almost insufferably splendid, for Man has veiled himself too long from his own glory: he fears the abyss, the ageless Absolute. But Truth shall make him free! [I, 4, p. 76]

We are not to regard ourselves as base beings, without whose sphere is Light or "God". Our minds and bodies are veils of the Light within. The uninitiate is a "dark star", and the Great Work for him is to make his veils transparent by 'purifying' them. This 'purification' is really 'simplification'; it is not that the veil is dirty, but that the complexity of its folds makes it opaque. The Great Work therefore consists principally in the solution of complexes. Everything in itself is perfect, but when things are muddled, they become 'evil'... The Doctrine is evidently of supreme importance, from its position as the first 'revelation' of Aiwass. [I, 8, p. 81–82]

The type of tailless simian who finds himself a mere forked radish in a universe of giants clamouring for hors d'oeuvres must take refuge from Reality in Freudian phantasies of 'God'. He winces at the touch of Truth; and shivers at his nakedness in Nature.

He therefore invents a cult of fear and shame, and makes it presumption and blasphemy to possess courage and self-respect. He burrows in the slime of "reverence, and godly fear" and makes himself houses of his own excrement, like the earthworm he is. He shams dead, like other vile insects, at the approach of danger; he tries to escape notice by assuming the colour and form of his surroundings, using 'protective mimicry' like certain other invertebrates.

He exudes stink or ink like the skunk or the cuttle-fish, calling the one morality and the other decency. He is slippery with hypocrisy, like a slug; and, labeling the totality of his defects perfection, defines God as feces so that he may flatter himself with the epithet divine. The whole manoeuvre is described as religion. [II, 77–78, p. 261–262]

Political Liberty

The Book of the Law flings forth no theological fulminations; but we have quarrels enough on our hands. We have to fight for Freedom against oppressors, religious, social, or industrial; and we are utterly opposed to compromise. Every fight is to be a fight to the finish; each one of us for himself, to do his own will; and all of us for all, to establish the Law of Liberty...

Let every man bear arms, swift to resent oppression, generous and ardent to draw sword in any cause, if justice or freedom summon him! [III, 57, p. 317]

As the practical ethics of the Law, I have formulated in words of one syllable my declaration of the

RIGHTS OF MAN

Do what thou wilt shall be the whole of the Law.
There is no god but Man.
Man has the right to live by his own Law.
Man has the right to live in the way that he wills to do.
Man has the right to dwell where he wills to dwell.
Man has the right to move as he will on the face of the Earth.
Man has the right to eat what he will.
Man has the right to drink what he will.
Man has the right to think as he will
Man has the right to speak as he will
Man has the right to write as he will.
Man has the right to mould as he will.
Man has the right to paint as he will.
Man has the right to carve as he will.
Man has the right to work as he will.
Man has the right to rest as he will
Man has the right to love as he will, when, where and whom he will.
Man has the right to die when and how he will.
Man has the right to kill those who would thwart these rights. [III, 60, p. 321]

[Ed. Note: In a letter to Gerald Yorke, dated 9/13/41, Crowley wrote, "*Rights of Man* is an historical document. The items don't go easily on the Tree; but I've got them down to give sections: moral, bodily, mental, sexual freedom, and the safeguard tyrannicide..."— quoted in *Magick*, Weiser, 1994, ed. Hymenaeus Beta]

Social Values

This thesis concerning compassion is of the most palmary importance in the ethics of Thelema. It is necessary that we stop, once for all, this ignorant meddling with other people's business. Each individual must be left free to follow his own path! America is peculiarly insane on these points. Her people are desperately anxious to make the Cingalese wear furs, and the Tibetans vote, and the whole world chew gum, utterly dense to the fact that most other nations, especially the French and British, regard 'American institutions' as the lowest savagery, and forgetful or ignorant of the circumstance that the original brand of American freedom—which really was Freedom—contained the precept to leave other people severely alone, and thus assured the possibility of expansion on his own lines to every man. [I,13–31, p. 89–90]

There is a good deal of the Nietzschean standpoint in this verse. It is the evolutionary and natural view. Of what use is it to perpetuate the misery of Tuberculosis, and such diseases, as we now do? Nature's way is to weed out the weak. This is the most merciful way, too. At present all the strong are being damaged, and their progress hindered by the dead weight of the weak limbs and the missing limbs, the diseased limbs and the atrophied limbs. The Christians to the Lions!

Our humanitarianism, which is the syphilis of the mind, acts on the basis of the lie that the King must die. The King is beyond death; it is merely a pool where he dips for refreshment. We must therefore go back to Spartan ideas of education; and the worst enemies of humanity are those who wish, under the pretext of compassion, to continue its ills through the generations. The Christians to the Lions!

Let weak and wry productions go back into the melting-pot, as is done with flawed steel castings. Death will purge, reincarnation make whole, these errors and abortions. Nature herself may be trusted to do this, if only we will leave her alone. But what of those who, physically fitted to live, are tainted with rottenness of soul, cancerous with the sin-complex? For the third time I answer: The Christians to the Lions! [II, 21, p. 176–177]

It has naturally been objected by economists that our Law, in declaring every man and every woman to be a star, reduces society to its elements, and makes hierarchy or even democracy impossible. The view is superficial. Each star has a function in its galaxy proper to its own nature.

Much mischief has come from our ignorance in insisting, on the contrary, that each citizen is fit for any and every social duty. But also our Law teaches that a star often veils itself from its nature. Thus the vast bulk of humanity is obsessed by an abject fear of freedom; the principal objections hitherto urged against my Law have been those of people who cannot bear to imagine the horrors which would result if they were free to do their own wills. [II, 58, p. 207]

Personal Values

Each star is unique, and each orbit apart; indeed, that is the corner-stone of my teaching, to have no standard goals or standard ways, no orthodoxies and no codes. The stars are not herded and penned and shorn and made into mutton like so many voters! I decline to be bellwether, who am born a Lion! I will not be collie, who am quicker to bite than to bark. I refuse the office of shepherd, who bear not a crook but a club. [I, 35–37, p. 93]

All strength and all skill should be flung with a spendthrift gesture on the counter of the merchant of madness. On the steel of your helmet let there be gold inlaid with the motto "Excess." [I, 52, p. 126]

It is bad Magick to admit that one is other than One's inmost self. One should plunge passionately into every possible experience; by doing so one is purged of those personal prejudices which we took so stupidly for ourselves, though they prevented us from realizing our true Wills and from knowing our Names and Natures. The Aspirant must well understand that it is no paradox to say that the Annihilation of the Ego in the Abyss is the condition of emancipating the true Self, and exalting it to unimaginable heights. So long as one remains "one's self," one is overwhelmed by the Universe; destroy the sense of self, and every event is equally an expression of one's Will, since its occurrence is the resultant of the concourse of the forces which one recognizes as one's own. [II, 8, p. 166]

The Secret of Magick is to "enflame oneself in praying." This is the ready test of a Star, that it whirls flaming through the sky. You cannot mistake it for an Old Maid objecting to Everything. This Universe is a wild revel of atoms, men, and stars, each one a Soul of Light and Mirth, horsed on Eternity. [II, 34, p. 207]

Drugs

Drunkenness is a curse and a hindrance only to slaves. Shelley's couriers were 'drunk on the wind of their own speed.' Anyone who is doing his true Will is drunk with the delight of Life.

Wine and strange drugs do not harm people who are doing their will; they only poison people who are cancerous with Original Sin. In Latin countries where Sin is not taken seriously, and sex-expression is simple, wholesome, and free, drunkenness is a rare accident. It is only in Puritan countries, where self-analysis, under the whip of a coarse bully like Billy Sunday, brings the hearer to 'conviction of sin,' that he hits first the 'trail' and then the 'booze.' Can you imagine an evangelist in Taormina? It is to laugh...

Truth is so terrible to these detestable mockeries of humanity that the thought of self is a realization of hell. Therefore they fly to drink and drugs as to an anaesthetic in the surgical operation of introspection.

The craving for these things is caused by the internal misery which their use reveals to the slave-souls. If you are really free, you can take cocaine as simply as salt-water taffy. There is no better rough test of a soul than its attitude to drugs. If a man is simple, fearless, eager, he is all right; he will not become a slave. If he is afraid, he is already a slave. Let the whole world take opium, hashish, and the rest; those who are liable to abuse them were better dead. [II, 22, p. 186]

Sexual Values

There shall be no property in human flesh. The sex instinct is one of the most deeply-seated expressions of the will; and it must not be restricted, either negatively by preventing its free function, or positively by insisting on its false function...

The sexual act is a sacrament of Will. To profane it is the great offense. All true expression of it is lawful; all suppression or distortion is contrary to the Law of Liberty. To use legal or financial constraint to compel either abstention or submission, is entirely horrible, unnatural and absurd. [I, 41, p. 98]

We of Thelema are not the slaves of Love. "Love under will" is the Law. We refuse to regard love as shameful and degrading, as a peril to body and soul. We refuse to accept it as the surrender of the divine to the animal; to us it is the means by which the animal may be made the Winged Sphinx which shall bear man aloft to the House of the Gods.

We are then particularly careful to deny that the object of love is the gross physiological object which happens to be Nature's excuse for it. Generation is a sacrament of the physical Rite, by which we create ourselves anew in our own image, weave in a new flesh-tapestry the Romance of our own Soul's History. But also Love is a sacrament of trans-substantiation whereby we initiate our own souls; it is the Wine of Intoxication as well as the Bread of Nourishment. "Nor is he for priest designed/Who partakes only in one kind." [p. 109]

"As ye will." It should be abundantly clear from the foregoing remarks that each individual has an absolute and indefeasible right to use his sexual vehicle in accordance with its own proper character, and that he is responsible only to himself. But he should not injure himself and his right aforesaid; acts invasive of another individual's equal rights are implicitly self-aggressions. A thief can hardly complain on theoretical grounds if he is himself robbed. Such acts as rape, and the assault or seduction of infants, may therefore be justly regarded as offenses against the Law of Liberty, and repressed in the interests of that Law. [p. 110]

Every one should discover, by experience of every kind, the extent and intention of his own sexual Universe. He must be taught that all roads are equally royal, and that the only question for him is "Which road is mine?" All details are equally likely to be of the essence of his personal plan, all equally 'right' in themselves, his own choice of the one as correct as, and independent of, his neighbour's preference for the other. [p. 111]

The Beast 666 ordains by His authority that every man, and every woman, and every intermediately-sexed individual, shall be absolutely free to interpret and communicate Self by means of any sexual practices soever, whether direct or indirect, rational or symbolic, physiologically, legally, ethically, or religiously approved or no, provided only that all parties to any act are fully aware of all implications and responsibilities thereof, and heartily agree thereto. [I, 50–51, p. 114]

The act of Love, to the bourgeois, is a physical relief like defaecation, and a moral relief from the strain of the drill of decency; a joyous relapse into the brute he has to pretend he despises. It is a drunkenness which drugs his shame of himself, yet leaves him deeper in disgust. It is an unclean gesture, hideous and grotesque. It is not his own act, but forced on him by a giant who holds him helpless; he is half madman, half automaton when he performs it. It is a gawky stumbling across a black foul bog, oozing a thousand dangers. It threatens him with death, disease, disaster in all manner of forms. He pays the coward's price of fear and loathing when pedlar Sex holds out his Rat-Poison in the lead-paper wrapping he takes for silver; he pays again with vomiting and with colic when he has gulped it in his greed. [p. 135]

Therefore, the Love that is Law is not less Love in the petty personal sense; for Love that makes two One is the engine whereby even the final Two, Self and Not-Self, may become One, in the mystic marriage of the Bride, the Soul, with Him appointed from eternity to espouse her; yea, even the Most High, God All-in-All, the Truth.

Therefore we hold Love holy, our heart's religion, our mind's science. Shall He not have His ordered Rite, His priests and poets, His makers of beauty in colour and form to adorn Him, His makers of music to praise Him? Shall not His theologians, divining His nature, declare Him? Shall not even those who but sweep the courts of His temple, partake thereby of His person? And shall not our science lay hands on Him, measure Him, discover the depths, calculate the heights, and decipher the laws of His nature? [I, 52, p. 136]

Women's Rights

Laws against adultery are based upon the idea that woman is a chattel, so that to make love to a married woman is to deprive the husband of her services. It is the frankest and most crass statement of a slave-situation. To us, every woman is a star. She has therefore an absolute right to travel in her own orbit. There is no reason why she should not be the ideal hausfrau, if that chance to be her will. But society has no right to insist upon that standard. It was, for practical reasons, almost necessary to set up such taboos in small communities, savage tribes, where the wife was nothing but a general servant, where the safety of the people depended upon a high birth-rate. But today woman is economically independent, becomes more so every year. The result is that she instantly asserts her right to have as many or as few men or babies as she wants or can get; and she defies the world to interfere with her. More power to her—elbow! [I, 41, p. 99]

We of Thelema say that "Every man and every woman is a star." We do not fool and flatter women; we do not despise and abuse them. To us a woman is Herself, absolute, original, independent, free, self-justified, exactly as a man is.

We dare not thwart Her Going, Goddess she! We arrogate no right upon Her will; we claim not to deflect Her development, to dispose of Her desires, or to determine Her destiny. She is Her own sole arbiter; we ask no more than to supply our strength to Her, whose natural weakness else were prey to the world's pressure. Nay more, it were too zealous even to guard Her in Her Going; for She were best by Her own self-reliance to win Her own way forth!

We do not want Her as a slave; we want Her free and royal, whether Her love fight death in our arms by night, or Her loyalty ride by day beside us in the Charge of the Battle of Life.

"Let the woman be girt with a sword before me!"
"In her is all power given."

So sayeth this our *Book of the Law*. We respect Woman in the self of Her own nature; we do not arrogate the right to criticise her. We welcome her as our ally, come to our camp as her Will, free-flashing, sword-swinging, hath told Her, Welcome, thou Woman, we hail thee, Star shouting to Star! Welcome to rout and to revel! Welcome to fray and to feast! Welcome to vigil and victory! Welcome to war with its wounds! Welcome to peace with its pageants! Welcome to lust and to laughter! Welcome to board and to bed! Welcome to trumpet and triumph; welcome to dirge and to death!

It is we of Thelema who truly love and respect Woman, who hold her sinless and shameless even as we are; and those who say that we despise Her are those who shrink from the flash of our falchions as we strike from Her limbs their foul fetters. [p. 307–308]

The Book of the Law is the Charter of Woman; the Word Thelema has opened the lock of Her "girdle of chastity." Your Sphinx of stone has come to life; to know, to will, to dare and to keep silence. [p. 308]

But now the Word of Me the Beast is this; not only art thou Woman, sworn to a purpose not thine own; thou art thyself a star, and in thyself a purpose to thyself. Not only mother of men art thou, or whore to men; serf to their need of Life and Love, not sharing in their Light and Liberty; nay, thou art Mother and Whore for thine own pleasure; the Word I say to Man I say to thee no less: Do what thou wilt shall be the whole of the Law! [III, 55, p. 310]

Love is the law, love under will.

Ordo Tempi Orientis (O.T.O.) may be reached at: OTO, P.O. Box 684098, Austin TX 78768, USA.

Aleister Crowley
Late in life

LIVING THELEMA

by Jack Parsons

Author of the Falcon title:
Freedom Is A Two-Edged Sword

I will attempt to present you with the outline of a practical reduction of the philosophy behind *The Book of the Law,* as it applies to our modern life.

This will be difficult, since there is an enormous background of technical, historical, social, and psychological data which I shall be forced to omit. This is all available. I hope that you will be sufficiently interested to review it yourself, if you have not done so.

If you will remember that I am dealing with the end product of this material, and trying, in a very short period, to condense this into a practical conclusion, I will appreciate your tolerance.

There are certain individuals who aspire to a maximum of independence in thought and in action, in order to achieve the optimum in the function of their nature and their creative will.

From among such have come the dreamers and creators, the leaders and revolutionaries, artists and poets and scientists. All that we know of progress and of culture has come from them; all, out of the neolithic swamp, by fire and air, by earth and water, and by the creative word, has come from those minds, from those hands.

The anthropoid mind fears and mistrusts such sports, and rides an unwilling ape on the coattails of the creative evolute. Unwilling, unwitting, and often something more than that.

In the indomitable will of the first order genius, there is sufficient ferocity or subtlety to overcome arboreal opposition, although the manifest result is usually *post mortem,* over a somewhat mutilated corpse.

But there are numberless fine minds, men and women of high talent and culture, who, lacking a little in the internal certainty, or facing an overwhelming social opposition, have deployed into futility and failure.

We propose a philosophy and a way of life having a pragmatic appeal to such minds.

A vast number of the human race has the mentality of slaves. Following Barnum, we can also deduce an appropriate number of slave masters.

There is no criticism here. The orders of nature are obvious, and acceptable to the philosophic. But, to the slave mind, there is often something unendurable in the notion of freedom and independence; it would have all men as its brothers in bondage. With this, the slave masters are in full accord.

It would be tedious to examine the techniques by which slavery has been fostered, the superstitious and authoritative devices, religious, political, social and economic, which have forged the chains. Whole philosophies, conceiving the universe of nature as sorrow, and the nature of man as sin, have been constructed to palliate sacrifice, expiation, and obedience.

God and Pope and king, society, humanity, the people, the proletariat, the family, war, the national emergency and all the other bogeys from the armory of fear have been summoned to confront the non-groveler. And those psychological weapons have been terribly enhanced.

This is obvious, and there is room in the world for animal acts and animal trainers—but not more than enough room!

If the individual abdicates his independence in the face of this rabbit hypnosis, this prestige suggestion, then he has deserved the bondage into which he is delivered.

It is a matter of balance. The leopard won't change his spots, not very rapidly, nor is it needful that he should. It is only needful that the Lion take his proper place in the jungle, and keep the leopard where he belongs, and the rabbit.

The creative individual must take his place as a creative leader in society. He must fulfill his destiny and his responsibility; he can achieve both in fearlessly following his creative will, his own inner truth, and, in inevitable corollary, he must know and assist others who strive to do likewise.

Then, by leading the slaves a little out of slavery, and the masters a little into humanity and culture, maintaining all the while his own inviolable independence, he will achieve that balance which alone gives significance to the human story.

LIBER 77 VEL OZ
THE RIGHTS OF MAN

Do what thou wilt shall be the whole of the Law.

There is no god but Man.
Man has the right to live by his own Law.
Man has the right to live in the way that he wills to do.
Man has the right to dress as he wills to do.
Man has the right to dwell where he wills to dwell.
Man has the right to move as he will on the face of the Earth.
Man has the right to eat what he will.
Man has the right to drink what he will.
Man has the right to think as he will
Man has the right to speak as he will
Man has the right to write as he will.
Man has the right to mould as he will.
Man has the right to paint as he will.
Man has the right to carve as he will.
Man has the right to work as he will.
Man has the right to rest as he will
Man has the right to love as he will, when, where and whom he will.
Man has the right to die when and how he will.
Man has the right to kill those who would thwart these rights.

Love is the law, love under will.

This exposition of the Rights of Man is a statement of first principles. You are referred to Crowley's works, the writings of Nietzsche, Mencken and Bertrand Russell; Emerson's essay on Self-Reliance; and the Declaration of Independence and Bill of Rights in the American Constitution. Here I am not unduly concerned with Theory, but rather with you, who, like myself, have independently reached these conclusions, and who are interested in a practical reduction.

Freedom is twofold; there is the freedom within, and the freedom without, and, like all things, the first freedom starts at the home plate.

The mainspring of an individual is his creative will. This will is the tone of his tendencies, his destiny, his inner truth. It is one with the force that makes the birds sing and flowers bloom; as inevitable as gravity, as implicit as a bowel movement, it informs alike atoms and men and suns.

To the man who knows this will, there is no why or why not; no can or cannot; he is!

There is no known force that can turn an apple to an alley cat; there is no known force that can turn a man from his will. This is the triumph of genius, that, surviving the centuries, enlightens the world.

This force burns in every man.

There are those who are too cowardly, too weak, to seek or express it.

There are those who are too full of pretense, of gullibility, of fear and greed to give it utterance.

Their lot is bitterness, failure and frustration; dust and ashes are their portion.

There are those who are bewildered, at odds with themselves, overwhelmed by adversity. They seek the light, and if they persevere, they will find it—within Themselves.

What are the obstacles to the attainment of the Will? There are many, but they may be grouped into certain primary divisions. And the name of every one of them is FEAR.

1. Fear of Incompetence: I would like to, but I could never do it. This is the flimsiest of excuses;—a narcissistic pap poisoning creation at its source. Confidence, enthusiasm, belief, egotism are the roots of creation.

BELIEVE IN YOURSELF: That is the first rule. Humility can come later. Build yourself to yourself—be proud—you are unique, and marvelously made. There is no other like you.

2. Fear of the opinion of others: What would people say? What people—what would they say? To Hell with them. Every genius that lighted the world has outraged public opinion—do you fear that pack of cards?

BE YOURSELF: Be true to yourself, be honest, enjoy yourself, go your own way, the way of the stars.

3. Fear of hurting others: Mother wouldn't want me to—! Are you yourself or another? Whose life do you live, to whom are you responsible, who is your master? Shall we ban cigarettes because they make Mrs. Grundy cough; hang lumber dealers because Christ was crucified, and rend Edison because Johnny was electrocuted?

Does it kill mother when you stay out until one? Is hubby so dreadfully hurt over that flirtation, and wifey in tears about the blonde? This is a subtle device of the slave master—"do what I say or I'll feel badly."

EXPRESS YOURSELF: Live your own life—follow your own star—as the Bible has it: "Forsake your father and mother"; "Let the dead bury the dead";—let the sick tend the sick—but follow yourself and no other christ or god. You are sufficient; you justify yourself; you are your own reason: THERE IS NO MORE NEEDED!

You should be polite about it; you may even be gentle about. Wanton hurt is needless and gains nothing; but inner, inflexible strength, terribly gentle in its own right of expression, can and must follow its own Will as surely as a star follows its own orbit, undeterred and undisturbed by the wailing of inhabitants of minor satellites.

4. Fear of insecurity: I might lose my job. This is the most paltry, the most despicable of the excuses—this slavish whine for daily bread—anything you say, masters, I'll be good; just feed me!

HAVE FORTITUDE: Be courageous, and the adventure of Life is yours. Failure—can there be an ultimate failure where manhood is sustained? Is not any failure in freedom better than any success in the Slave Pen?

Yes, you might agree, (at least I assume that somebody might agree) but these things are difficult. Where do we start?

We start, naturally, with the least of the little things. For on the other end of the fulcrum from that little thing is the Universe, and all your hearts' desires. Dedicate yourself to your best and highest, and begin. What is the person you most desire to be—(I mean, freely and honestly, not morally)? Imitate that person, and what began as imitation will end as perfection.

It is possible to cultivate habits of mind and of attention. The splendor of nature is all about us, immortal in loveliness, inexhaustible in wonder. The sky calls to us in the high places, the wind and the rain greet us, trees and grasses speak to us, mountains and the great plains and green valleys; we have only to open our minds and hearts to the eternal forces, and we and the eternal forces are one.

From such harmonies, the creative will draws force to inform the mind. He who has opened the way to nature will not wait long to know his own Way.

In the beginning, any consistent action dedicated to the discovery of the Will or to its development, suffices. The nature of an act is in no wise important, so long as it serves as a lever to set the Will in motion, and so long as it is repeatedly performed.

Almost any device is permissible if it helps. The use of a Talisman, fetish, or image symbolizing the Will; the use of a daily formula or ritual, and most especially the dedication of a certain period every day, rain or shine, in sickness or health, in enthusiasm or loathing, for the exclusive practice of the dedicatory act. There is a danger; mind or muscle building as an end in itself can degenerate into a subtle form of masturbation.

The Will must be freed of its fetters. The ruthless examination and destruction of taboos, complexes, frustrations, dislikes, fears, and disgusts hostile to the will is essential to progress. Even in the case of pet preferences and prejudices, it must be realized that those things are only significant to the individual—meaningless and often silly to the larger world. On a hot day, Galahad probably stank under his armor. And that sensibility which is nauseated by the sex odor of its own kind, and titillated by the sex odor of plants, might be profitably studied under the heading of a perversion.

Now suppose that the second step is reached. The Will is beginning to flow. You know who you are, what you are, you have discovered your destiny.

It is a time for rejoicing, but not for relaxation. There is no reason in nature why you cannot write music beyond Beethoven, poetry beyond Shelley, out-invent Edison, or out-theorize Einstein!

They are beacons, lighting a sky which you, in your own time and in your own way, will one day illumine.

The task is just begun. There is work ahead, years of work,—but work in the real world. Woe to him who dallies with escapist day dreams, with fancies and visions and trances, with specious words and poses, and the onanistic flatter of his fellow opium eaters.

The Will is creative and dynamic, and it must create and move in hard fact. By their fruits shall ye know them. Success is your proof;—but YOUR success, on your own terms. The way is hard; you will face failure after failure, fall after fall. But each fall and each failure is a success, a new jewel for the diadem of conscious experience.

Life—beautiful, terrible, splendid and pitiless;—Life is your adversary and your love. She you must accept unreservedly, and she you must overcome. She woos to destroy, she submits to conquer; she conquers to submit—that Tigress is your paramour, the Cosmos is your adventure.

And the goal? The totality of experience—the gesture commensurate with the universe.

Is that not enough?

Jack Parsons, a founder of the Jet Propulsion Laboratory in Pasadena, California, was a rocket scientist, occultist and member of Crowley's magical order. He died in 1952 in a mysterious laboratory explosion. His eloquent writings on the human condition convey passion, intelligence and a deep conviction.

ANATHEMA OF ZOS

The Sermon To The Hypocrites

by Austin Osman Spare

Hostile to self-torment, the vain excuses called devotion, Zos satisfied the habit by speaking loudly unto his Self. And at one time, returning to familiar consciousness, he was vexed to notice interested hearers—a rabble of involuntary mendicants, pariahs, whoremongers, adulterers, distended bellies, and the prevalent sick-grotesques that obtain in civilizations. His irritation was much, yet still they pestered him, saying: MASTER, WE WOULD LEARN OF THESE THINGS! TEACH US RELIGION!

And seeing, with chagrin, the hopeful multitude of Believers, he went down into the Valley of Stys, prejudiced against them as FOLLOWERS. And when he was ennuyé, he opened his mouth in derision, saying:—

O, ye whose future is in other hands! This familiarity is permitted not of thy—but of my impotence. Know me as Zos the Goatherd, saviour of myself and of those things I have not yet regretted. Unbidden ye listen'd to my soliloquy. Endure then my Anathema.

Foul feeders! Slipped, are ye, on your own excrement? Parasites! Having made the world lousy, imagine ye are of significance to Heaven?

Desiring to learn—think ye to escape hurt in the rape of your ignorance? For of what I put in, far more than innocence shall come out! Labouring not the harvest of my weakness, shall I your moral-fed desires satisfy?

I, who enjoy my body with unweary tread, would rather pack with wolves than enter your pest-houses.

Sensation... Nutrition... Mastication... Procreation... This is your blind-worm cycle. Ye have made a curiously bloody world for love in desire. Shall nothing change except through your accusing diet?

IN THAT YE ARE CANNIBALS, what meat should I offer? Having eaten of your dead selves savoured with every filth, ye now raven to glutton of my mind's motion?

In your conflict ye have obtained...? Ye who believe your procreation is ultimate are the sweepings of creation manifest, returning again to early simplicity to hunger, to become, and realise—ye are not yet. Ye have muddled time and ego. Think ye to curb the semen SENTIMEN-TALLY? Ye deny sexuality with tinsel ethics, live by slaughter, pray to greater idiots—that all things may be possible to ye WHO ARE IMPOSSIBLE.

For ye desire savours useless to pleasure.

Verily, far easier for madmen to enter heaven than moral Lepers. Of what difference is Life or Death? Of what difference is dream or reality? Know ye of nothing further than your own stench? Know ye what ye think ye know for certain? Fain would I be silent. Yet too tolerant is this Sun that cometh up to behold me, and my weakness comes of my dissatisfaction of your solicit...but be ye damned before obtaining fresh excuses of me!

Cursed are the resurrectionists! Is there only body and soul?

Is there nothing beyond entity? No purchase beyond sense and desire of God than this blasting and devouring swarm ye are?

Oh, ye favoured of your own excuses, guffaw between bites! Heaven is indifferent to your salvation or catastrophe. Your curveless crooked-ness maketh ye fallow for a queer fatality! What! I to aid your self-deception, ameliorate your decaying bodies, preserve your lamentable apotheosis of self?

The sword-thrust—not salve—I bring!

Am I your swineherd, though I shepherd unto goats? My pleasure does not obtain among vermin with vain ideas—with hopes and fears of absurd significance. Not yet am I overweary of myself. Not yet shall I palliate abomination, for in ye I behold your parents and the stigmata of foul feeding.

In this ribald intoxication of hypocrisy, this monument of swindlers' littlenesses, where is the mystic symposium, the hierarchy of necro-mancers that was?

Honest was Sodom! YOUR theology is a slime-pit of gibberish become ethics. In YOUR world, where ignorance and deceit constitute felicity, everything ends miserably—besmirched with fratricidal blood.

Seekers of salvation? Salvation of your sick digestion; crippled beliefs: Convalescent desires. Your borrowed precepts and prayers—a stench unto all good nostrils!

Unworthy of a soul—your metamorphosis is laborious of morbid rebirth to give habitance to the shabby sentiments, the ugly familiarities, the calligraphic pandemonium—a world of abundance acquired of greed. Thus are ye outcasts! Ye habitate dung-heaps: your glorious palaces are hospitals set amid cemeteries. Ye breathe half-heartedly within this cesspit? Ye obtain of half-desires bent-persuasions, of threats, of promises made hideous by vituperatious righteousness! Can you realise of Heaven when it exists WITHOUT?

Believing with associating ye are spurious and know not the way of virtue. There is no virtue in truth, nor truth in righteousness. Law becomes of desire's necessity. Corrupt is the teacher, for they who speak have only spent words to give.

Believe or blaspheme! Do ye not speak from between your thighs?

To believe or unbelieve is the question. Verily, if you believe of the least—ye needs must thrive all things. Ye are of all things, of all knowledge, and, belike, will your stupidity to further self-misery!

Your wish? Your heaven? I say your desire is women. Your potential desire a brothel.

Ah, ye who fear suffering, who among ye has courage to assault the cloudy enemies of creeds, of the stomach's pious hopes?

I blaspheme your commandments, to provoke and enjoy your bar; your teeth grinding!

Know ye what ye want? What ye ask? Know ye virtue from maniacal muttering? Sin from folly? Desiring a teacher, who among ye are worthy to learn?

Brutally shall I teach the gospel of soul-suicide, of contraception, not preservation and procreation.

Fools! Ye have made vital the belief the Ego is eternal, fulfilling a purpose now lost to you.

All things become of desire; the legs to the fish; the wings to the reptile. Thus was your soul begotten.

Hear, O, vermin!

MAN HAS WILLED MAN!

Your desires shall become flesh, your dreams reality and no fear shall alter it one whit.

Hence do I travel ye into the incarnating abortions—the aberrations, the horrors without sex, for ye are worthless to offer Heaven new sexualities.

Once in this world I enjoyed laughter—when I remembered the value I gave the contemptible; the significance of my selfish fears; the absurd vanity of my hopes; the sorry righteousness called I.

And YOU?

Certainly not befitting are tears of blood, nor laughter of gods.

Ye do not even look like MEN but the strange spawn of some forgotten ridicule.

Lost among the illusions begat of duality—are these the differentiations ye make for future entity to ride your bestial self? Millions of times have ye had re-birth and many more times will ye again SUFFER existence.

Ye are of things distressed, living down the truths ye made. Loosing only from my overflow, perchance I teach ye to learn of yourselves? In my becoming shall the hungry satisfy of my good and evil? I strive me neither, and confide subsequent to the event.

Know my purpose: To be a stranger unto myself, the enemy of truth.

Uncertain of what ye believe, belike ye half-desire? But believe ye this, serving your dialectics:—

Subscribing only to self-love, the outcroppings of my hatred now speak. Further, to ventilate my own health, I scoff at your puerile dignitaries' absurd moral clothes and ovine faith in a fortuitous and gluttonous future!

Dogs, devouring your own vomit! Cursed are ye all! Throw-backs, adulterers, sycophants, corpse devourers, pilferers and medicine swallowers! Think ye Heaven is an infirmary?

Ye know not pleasure. In your sleepy lusts, feeble violence and sickly morale, ye are more contemptible than the beasts ye feed for food.

I detest your Mammon. Disease partakes of your wealth. Having acquired, ye know not how to spend.

YE ARE GOOD MURDERERS ONLY.

Empty of cosmos are they who hunger after righteousness. Already are the merciful spent. Extinct are the pure in hear. Governed are the meek and of Heaven earn similar disgust. Your society is a veneered barbarity. Ye are precocious primitives. Where is your success other than through hatred?

There is no good understanding in your world—this bloody transition by procreation and butchery.

Of necessity ye hate, and love your neighbour by devouring.

The prophets are nauseating and should be persecuted. Objects of ridicule, their deeds cannot live through their tenets. Actions are the criterion, then how can ye speak other than lies?

Love is cursed. Your desire is your God and execration. Ye shall be judged of your appetite.

Around me I see your configuration—again a swine from the herd. A repulsive object of charity! The curse is pronounced; for ye are slime and sweat-born, homicidally reared. And again shall your fathers call to the help of women. Ye vainly labour at a rotten Kingdom of Good and Evil. I say that Heaven is catholic—and none shall enter with susceptibility of either.

Cursed are ye who shall be persecuted for MY sake. For I say I am CONVENTION entire, excessively evil, perverted and nowhere good— for ye.

Whosoever would be with me is neither much of me nor of himself enough.

*   *   *   *

Zos tired, but loathing his hearers too much, he again reviled them saying:—

Worm-ridden jackals! Still would ye feast on my vomit? Whosoever follows me becomes his own enemy; for in that day my exigency shall be his ruin.

Go labour! Fulfill the disgust of becoming yourself, of discovering your beliefs, and thus acquire virtue. Let your good be accidental; thus escape gratitude and its sorry vainglory, for the wrath of Heaven is heavy on easy self-indulgence.

In your desire to create a world, do unto others as you would—when sufficiently courageous.

To cast aside, not save, I come. Inexorably towards myself; to smash the law, to make havoc of the charlatans, the quacks, the swankers and brawling salvationists with their word-tawdry phantasmagoria: to disillusion and awaken every fear of your natural, rapacious selves.

Living the most contemptible and generating everything beastly, are ye so vain of your excuse to expect other than the worst of your imagining?

Honesty is unvoiced! And I warn you to make holocaust of your saints, your excuses: these flatulent bellowings of your ignorance. Only then could I assure your lurking desire—easy remission of your bowdlerised sins. Criminals of folly! Ye but sin against self.

There is no sin for those of Heaven's delight. I would ye resist not nor exploit your evil: such is of fear, and somnambulism is born of hypocrisy.

In pleasure Heaven shall break every law before this Earth shall pass away. Thus if I possessed, my goodness towards ye would be volcanic.

He who is lawless is free. Necessity and time are conventional phenomena.

Without hypocrisy or fear ye could do as ye wish. Whosoever, therefore, shall break the precept or live its transgression shall have relativity of Heaven. For unless your righteousness exist not, ye shall not pleasure freely and creatively. In so much as ye sin against doctrine, so shall your imagination be required in becoming.

*   *   *   *

It has been said without wit: "Thou shalt not kill." Among beasts man live supremely—on his own kind. Teeth and claws are no longer sufficient accessory to appetite. Is this world's worst reality more vicious than human behaviour?

I suggest to your inbred love of moral gesture to unravel the actual from the dream.

Rejoice ye! The law-makers shall have the ugly destiny of becoming subject. Whatsoever is ordained is superseded—to make equilibrium of this consciousness rapport with hypocrisy.

Could ye be arbitrary? Belief foreshadows its inversion. Overrun with forgotten desires and struggling truths, ye are their victim in the dying and begetting law.

The way of Heaven is a purpose—anterior to and not induced by thought. Desire, other than by the act, shall in no wise obtain: Therefore believe SYMBOLICALLY or with caution.

Between men and women having that desire there is no adultery. Spend the large lust and when ye are satiated ye shall pass on to something fresh. In this polite day it has become cleaner to fornicate by the wish than to enact.

Offend not your body nor be so stupid as to let your body offend ye. How shall it serve ye to reproach your duality? Let your oath be in earnest; though better to communicate by the living act than by the word.

This God—this cockatrice—is a projection of your imbecile apprehensions, your bald grossness and madhouse vanities. Your love is born of fear' but far better to hate than further deception.

I would make your way difficult. Give and take of all men indiscriminately.

I know your love and hate. Inquire of red diet. Within your stomach is civil war.

Only in self-love is procreative will.

What now! Shall I attempt wisdom by words? Alphabetic truths with legerdemain grammar? Thee is no spoken truth that is not PAST—more wisely forgotten.

Shall I scrawl slippery paradox with mad calligraphy? Words, mere words! I exist in a wordless world, without yesterday nor to-morrow—beyond becoming.

All conceivableness procures of time and space. Hence I spit on your tatterdemalion ethics, mouldering proverbs, priestly inarticulations and delirious pulpit jargon. This alone I give ye as safe commandments in your pestilent schisms.

> Better is it to go without than to borrow.
> Finer far to take than beg.
> From Puberty till Death realise "Self" in all.
> There is no greater virtue than good nourishment.
> Feed from the udder, and if the milk be Sour, feed on ...
> Human nature is the worst possible!

Once I lived among ye. From self-decency now I habitate the waste places, a willing outcast; associate of goats; cleaner far, more honest than men.

Within this heterogenousness of difference, reality is hard to realise; evacuation is difficult.

These spiritualists are living sepulchres. What has decayed should perish decently.

Cursed are they who supplicate. Gods are with ye yet. Therefore let ye who pray acquire this manner:—

O Self my God, foreign is thy name except in blasphemy, for I am thy iconoclast. I cast thy bread upon the waters, for I myself am meat enough. Hidden in the labyrinth of the Alphabet is my sacred name, the SIGIL of all things unknown. On Earth my kingdom is Eternity of DESIRE. My wish incarnates in the belief and becomes flesh, for, I AM THE LIVING TRUTH. Heaven is ecstasy: my consciousness changing and acquiring association. May I have courage to take from my own super-abundance. Let me forget righteousness. Free me of morals. Lead me into the temptation of myself, for I am a tottering kingdom of good and evil.

May worth be acquired through those things I have pleasured.

May my trespass be worthy.

Give me the death of my soul. Intoxicate me with self-love. Teach me to sustain its freedom; for I am sufficiently Hell. Let me sin against the small beliefs.— AMEN.

Concluding his conjunction, Zos said:—

Again, O sleep-walkers, beggars and sufferers, born of the stomach; unlucky men to whom happiness is necessary!

Ye are in sufficient to live alone, not yet mature enough to sin against the law and still desire women.

Other than damnation I know no magic to satisfy your wishes; for ye believe one thing, desire another, speak unlike, act differently and obtain the living value.

Assuredly inclination towards new faculties springs from this bastardy!

Social only to the truths convenient to your courage, yet again beasts shall be planted.

Shall I speak of that unique intensity without form? Know ye the ecstasy within? The pleasures between ego and self?

At that time of ecstasy there is no thought of others; there is NO THOUGHT. Thither I go and none may lead.

Sans women—your love is anathema!

For me, there is no way but my way. Therefore, go ye your way—none shall lead ye to walk towards yourselves. Let your pleasures be as sunsets, HONEST ... BLOODY ... GROTESQUE!

Was the original purpose the thorough enjoyment of multitudinous self, for ecstasy? These infinite ramifications of consciousness in entity, associating by mouth, sex and sense!

Has the besetting of sex become utter wretchedness—repetition made necessary of your scotomy?

O bloody-mouthed! Shall I again entertain ye with a little understanding? An introspection of cannibalism in the shambles of diet—the variating murder against the ancestral? Is there no food beyond corpse?

Your murder and hypocrisy must pass before ye are uplifted to a world where slaughter is unknown.

Thus, with a clean mouth, I say unto ye, I live by bread alone. Sleep is competent prayer. All morality is BEASTLY.

Alas, there has been a great failure. Man is dead. Only women remain.

With tongue in cheek I would say: "Follow me! That ye realise what is hidden in all suffering. I would make your self-mortification voluntary, your wincing courageous."

Still will ye be with me? Salutation to all suicides!

*   *   *   *

With a yawn Zos wearied and fell asleep.

In time the stench awoke him—for he had slept amidst the troughs—and he observed that the crowd were no longer with him—that only SWINE remained. And he guffawed and spake thus: Not yet have I lost relationship and am thereby nearly asphyxiated! Caught up am I in the toils of sentiment, the moral hallucinations within the ebb and flow of hopes and fears?

Shall age alone transmute desire? Not yet have I disentangled illusion from reality: for I know not men from swine, dreams from reality; or whether I did speak only unto myself. Neither know I to whom my anathema would be the more impressionable ...

My insensible soliloquy is eaten as revelation! What I spake with hard strived conceit to increase enterprise brings forth only swinish snorts. Water is not alone in finding its level.

I have not met tragedy, no, not in this life! Yet, whether I have spewed their doctrines upon the table of the Law or into the troughs, at least I have not cast away the flesh of dreams.

And turning towards his light, Zos said: This my will, O Thou Glorious Sun. I am weary of my snakes descending—making slush.

Farewell antithesis. I have suffered. All is paid.

Let me go forth and recreate my sleep.

ASSASSIN

by Harry Crosby

(voici le temps des assassins)
— Jean Nicholas Arthur Rimbaud

Constantinople on the Seventeenth of the Month of Ramadan. It is cold and late at night winter darkness with a cold hard wind hurricane-ing across the Bosporus. Harsh sleet of snow. The windshield is caked with frost except for the square where I have rubbed the frost off with my hand. My fingers are stiff with cold. We have crossed the bridge from Peira into Stamboul. At the cross-streets the arc-lamps stare sharp and hard like harlots. Walls on our left loom dark and menacing. We pass under an arch guarded by a red lantern. We are outside the walls. There is a feeling of emptiness like a night at the front during the War. A sharp turn over cobblestones the jarring of brakes and we are climbing out shivering into the wind. It is even colder than before and the ground is hard as rock. Stark telegraph poles stand behind us. We are standing before an enormous tent. A call and a sharp answer and a hand tearing open the flap as the wind tears out a strip of camouflage. We bend down and enter the tent. It is monstrous in size and there are shadows cast from the large oil lamp swinging from the tent pole. Around this tent pole Kurd shepherds in a dark circle are slowly turning stamping their feet on the hard ground to the harsh discord of a drum. Silent men and dark. Along the dark edges of the tent the eaters of hashish squat on their heels. There are no women. I crouch down with the eaters of hashish. An angular hand offers me a small square of hard green paste. I bite into it. It has a dry irritant taste. I finish it as I watch the intense circle never stopping always measured and controlled pounding on the ground to the harsh discord of barbaric rhythm. And again the angular hand and again the eating of hashish. Towards four in the morning we leave the shepherds still dancing and go out into the raw darkness and drove back to the hotel. I remember only the wind because it was hard as stone.

II

The word *Assassin* is derived from the Arabic *Hashishin,* from Hashish, the opiate made from the juice of hemp leaves. When the sheik required the services of an Assassin the Assassin selected was intoxicated with the hashish. It is of interest to note that the effect of hashish is not instantaneous as is the case with cocktails or cocaine but its effect is much more violent and of a much longer duration. The effect of this drug—it is much stronger when eaten than when smoked—is to produce megalomania (a form of insanity characterized by self-exaltation) in its most violent form.

In this poem the Sun-Goddess, or Mad Queen as I shall call her, has replaced the Sheik and I am the Assassin she has chosen for her devices. She has intoxicated me with the hashish and I await her command.

III

The Mad Queen commands:

"Murder the sterility and hypocrisy of the world, destroy the weak and insignificant, do violence to the multitude in order that a new strong world shall arise to worship the Mad Queen, Goddess of the Sun."

IV

I see my way as swords
their rigid way
I shall destroy

V

Morning in a hotel room at the Peira Palace. I emerge from sleep. I wake. I get out of bed. I look at myself in the mirror.

VI
VISION

I exchange eyes with the Mad Queen.
the mirror crashes against my face and bursts into a thousand suns

all over the city flags crackle and bang
fog horns scream in the harbor
the wind hurricanes through the window
and I begin to dance the dance of the Kurd Shepherds

I stamp upon the floor
I whirl like dervishes

colors revolve dressing and undressing
I lash them with my fury

stark white with iron black
harsh red with blue
marble green with bright orange
and only gold remains naked

columns of steel rise and plunge
emerge and disappear
pistoning in the river of my soul
   thrusting upwards
   thrusting downwards
   thrusting inwards
   thrusting outwards
      penetrating

   I roar with pain

black-footed ferrets disappear into holes

the sun tattooed on my back
begins to spin
   faster and faster
   whirring whirling
throwing out a glory of sparks
sparks shoot off into space
sparks into shooting stars
shooting stars collide with comets

     Explosions
Naked Colors Explode
    into
Red Disaster

I crash out through the
window naked, widespread
upon a
  Heliosaurus
I uproot an obelisk and plunge
it into the ink-pot of the
Black Sea
I write the word
    S U N
across the dreary palimpsest
of the world
I pour the contents of the
Red Sea down my throat
I erect catapults and
lay siege to the cities of the world

I scatter violent disorder
throughout the kingdoms of the world
I stride over mountains
I pick up oceans like thin cards
and spin them into oblivion
I kick down walled cities
I hurl giant firebrands against
        governments
I thrust torches through the eyes of
        the law
  I annihilate museums
  I demolish libraries
  I oblivionize skyscrapers
I become hard as adamant
indurated in solid fire
rigid with hatred

I bring back the wizards and the sorcerers

the necromancers
the magicians
I practise witchcraft
I set up idols
with a sharp-edged sword
I cut through the crowded streets
comets follow in my wake
stars make obeisance to me
the moon uncovers her
nakedness to me

I am the harbinger of a New Sun World
I bring the Seed of a
   New Copulation
I proclaim the Mad Queen

I stamp out vast empires
I crush palaces in my rigid hands
I harden my heart against churches

I blot out cemeteries
I feed the people with stinging nettles
I resurrect madness
I thrust my naked sword
between the ribs of the world
I murder the world!

VII

I the Assassin chosen by the Mad Queen
I the Murderer of the World shall in my fury murder myself. I shall cut
out my heart take it into my joined hands and walk towards the Sun
without stopping until I fall down dead.

VIII

I have cut out my heart I am walking
forwards towards the Sun I am faltering I am falling down dead

IX

Antidote to Common Poisons. Call the physicians at once. Give the
antidote in good quantity. For hashish cold douches; ammonia inhaled;
artificial respiration; stimulants; watch circulation and respiration; keep
patient awake.

X

It is the afternoon of the same day and I am on the Orient Express. I
remember only the sea-walls sliding forwards into the sea and the whistle
from the locomotive is the sharp color of the Sun.

Harry Crosby was born in 1898 and has since existed in both literary and
magical obscurity. As the self-proclaimed Harbinger of Chaos, he manifested a life of Hedonism rivaling many of the greatest cultural dissi-
dents. Sun, Death, Speed, and Blackness are unified in the mythological
world Crosby creates, and through unfaltering obsession and possession,
he walks in. His devotion culminated in a Sun-Death ritual of suicide on
December 10th, 1929.

Christopher S. Hyatt, Ph.D.
Considered by some the greatest healer in the world today
Considered by others the most stupid person alive

WHO OWNS THIS PLANET EARTH?

Rebels, Devils Or?

by Christopher S. Hyatt, Ph.D.

Author of the Falcon titles:
Undoing Yourself With Energized Meditation
The Enochian World of Aleister Crowley
Aleister Crowley's Illustrated Goetia
Taboo: Sex, Religion & Magick
Sex Magick, Tantra & Tarot
Secrets of Western Tantra
The Psychopath's Bible
Tantra Without Tears
Pacts With The Devil
The Tree of Lies
Urban Voodoo

The Scene: The Space Ship Enterprise.

The Question: Kirk to Spock—Who owns the Planet Earth and its inhabitants?

The Answer: Spock to Crew—Those who have the power to define. Those who have the power to lie well.

The ownership of the Planet has changed hands a hundred times. I think if you trace their papers back far enough one of their first owners was called Jehovah. Approximately 18% of the present population still believe He and His Son still own the planet and they have been chosen to rule the rest.

The earthlings have an interesting habit of dividing up ownership through wars and then marking their territory on little scraps of paper. The inhabitants of each territory think they are superior to their neighbors. This in turn creates new wars and new divisions. This is their particular form of making changes. It is difficult for them to change without being forced to or having some horrible event take place.

They use primitive genetic practices. Conquered regions are used as experimental breeding grounds. When they ran out of new frontiers and artificially attempted to stabilize the planet there were four main classes of people. The intelligent and powerful, the status quo, the poor and the criminal. When they invented space travel the powerful and the criminals left, the poor were slaughtered and the ownership of the planet passed to the Status Quo. These were known as the middle class of mid-zonal professionals who from their inception have attempted to imitate the powerful and intelligent. They in turn re-invented the same four classes and the ownership of the planet is up for grabs. The majority of the problems on this planet are the result of the idea that humans are not sovereign and autonomous, but property owned by primitive Gods and incompetent governments. At this time the United States believes it is the most competent and elite.

It is important to remember when visiting this planet that words, things and thinking are experienced by the inhabitants as the same. They are full of pride, easily hurt and capable of just about anything. They suffer from a poor memory when it comes to self improvement and an excellent one when it comes to remembering slights and imagined injuries.

They enjoy the game known as scapegoat. This is a game where they find someone less powerful to blame their problems on. Often they will torture, enslave and murder their victims. As I said and it warrants repeating, the inhabitants respond to words and pictures with the same neuro-physiological reactions as real events. Be cautious, it can get quite dangerous down there. They are very aware of differences and at times respond with curiosity but tend to respond with violence.

The dawning of popular Western Metaphysics (the history of metaphor) is best expressed by the story of the Tree of Knowledge, when an imagined, undifferentiated, blissful world called the Garden of Eden was suddenly split apart when a female member of the species ate an apple and then tempted her mate to do the same. Adam and Eve's act of disobedience, born from a womb of curiosity, divided the world into two. Good and evil became primary modes of thinking and reacting and members of the species have proceeded to develop entire philosophies from this metaphor. As I have said, although very childish, they are also very inventive.

The primal set of concepts, good and evil, springs from disobedience, the very well spring of God's greatest gift, man's free will. It was the very use of this gift which inescapably gave birth to shame, guilt, original sin and planetary bankruptcy. It seems that intention transforms accidents into crimes.

Expelled from paradise into a world of gravity and work mankind must now forever struggle for his act of primal disobedience.

From an idyllic world free from pain, man found himself in the world of change, of differences and similarities, of epistemology, and of language, a tool which can cut in two directions at the same time. The ancient Hawaiian's have a proverb which says, "In language is life and death."

From the simple myth of Eden which almost every Western child is familiar, sprang a world view, which, in its extreme, is represented by modern day earth television evangelism. It appears, that God is a landlord, indeed a slumlord, but always a Lord. Man is an ungrateful, rebellious slave-child who can never pay his debt, except possibly by complete obedience, casting his mind and nature into the "caring" hands of his angry and frustrated Creator.

This species' philosophy has enjoyed centuries of speculating on the fruits of this primal disobedience—The emergence of the Opposites. Some of these opposites have been Nature/Nurture, Being/Becoming, Whole/Part, Real/Apparent, Mind/Body, Physical/Spiritual, Man/God and other meta-morsels.

Any intelligent human could simply re-create the entire history of the planet by plotting the Opposites, both as independent grids and or as interactive forces over time. In fact we could diagnose or mirror an individual or an entire culture's development simply by understanding which position on each grid a group's belief system is plotted. For example, the Chinese believe in fate, the Americans believe in free will.

The "opposites" (either/ors) have served as epistemological training ground for metaphysicians who could demonstrate their superiority to the masses by turning an apple into an orange. Of course, only those divinely ordained to understand the true meaning of these terms could participate in this sport. The rest stood in awe and worshipped those who had the credentials and ability to understand the dark and mysterious world(s) of Being and Becoming.

The problem of opposites lies in the inadequate information gained from the Tree of Knowledge—good and evil. When man learned about good and evil he did not learn how words are like containers that can be filled with just about any type of liquid.

Like a child who receives an airplane for a gift and is so delighted and overwhelmed by the way the wheels turn, he never learns that the plane, if used differently, can fly. The utter emptiness of words gave man the opportunity to fill them with whatever he needed, while at the same time believing the words had an independent substance of their very own.

The opposites have served as a primitive model of classifying, ordering and understanding the universe. Their real use is the their speed and ease allowing for quick reactions in dangerous situations. The grunt "UGH" means run.

Although the species has changed from its beginnings it still prefers to rely on opposites rather than even simple interacting grids.

In other words, the notion of opposites is not a "natural law," but simply a primitive survival device with many interesting and dangerous uses. If we carefully examine history we will find that man has torn himself apart with his belief in the REALITY and NECESSITY of Either/Ors.

For the man in the street, the philosophies of opposites, particularly Good and Evil, have served as a torture chamber, a crucifix made from metaphor. Thrust into a world which views him as the property of Gods and States and overwhelmed by an unrepayable debt, the metaphysics of slavery and the facts of pain, pleasure and death; bolstered by science, whose theorists have become the whores of the state, man is now informed that he is ill. The proof of this is his refusal to submit completely. The world debt is due to his saying "no" to total slavery. He will not obey. We are at War, and man is the enemy. The question is: Who is on the other side?

Original sin is now *also* translated into sickness, calling in a new and scientific priest craft who rush to the rescue. Man is sick, addicted, lame, and dangerous, needing constant protection and supervision by the state, insurance companies, and a never-ending parade of caring, licensed professionals. We are told over and over again that man's illness and addictions are costing *US* billions. Man the slave/resource, is causing *US* trouble, he is interfering with *OUR* Plans. Man's debt has now increased a billion-fold. Those who question the "plans" or the sanity of the metaphors in play, are diagnosed as morally unfit or mentally ill.

Evil emerges as a metaphor which refers to those who refuse to accept the Plan—the prevailing Garden of Eden—created by God so She may bestow Her Love and Grace. If man refuses he must be force-fed.

What makes the notion of Evil and Good work is the belief that the words have substance independent of the workings of man's own mind and his uncanny need and ability to create *final causes.*

All that is required for metaphysics to function, to perform its magic, is any unanswered question which can be associated with fear and pain. What makes a leader is someone who claims that he can fill the void.

While most humans agree that slavery is evil—that the ownership of one human by another is immoral—few humans equate slavery with enforced education, welfare, health, and the idea of a perfect orderly universe. Slavery is usually associated with power over others and with the ability to enforce one's will on another without the fear of retaliation. Within the "right" of ownership and debt there is a hidden mystery—a metaphysics—a knowledge only available to those with the power to create and enforce their metaphysics. Whenever a new group achieves power, they also inherit the metaphysics, and magically, the ability to use it.

However, an interesting twist has taken place in the entire slave/master paradigm. Enforced education, welfare, health, *are for our own good and it is our duty to submit to the treatment.* This is immediately followed by the platitude *that all these laws are necessary for the smooth functioning of society, which, of course, we all observe daily. Without someone to run the show we would have chaos and disorder.* This is followed by a SMILE, and the statement that "things could be worse."

Modern slavery is not simply a "Thou Shalt Not," but numerous "Thou Shalts." Many liberated humans even believe that it is the obligation of the Masters to care for their Slaves. Of course, what is different is the title-word "citizen" and that today's *sophisticated* redistribution of power *shows* no blood during family hour TV.

We can begin to scent the meaning of evil. It smells of change, contradiction, uncertainties. It is the *lack of* stability, becoming, the *opposite of* order, being, peace, the good. Here the confusion coincides with physiology. We have mixed the whole thing up. We have confused the physiology of comfort, the cognition of stability, beliefs as truth, predictable futures, statistics—with the *idea* of a Morality. In other words, while chaos, disorder, change and destruction are integral and necessary elements of life on this heavy G planet, we abhor its realization and worse yet, its *Existence.* This requires the postulation of its opposite as an Ideal a heaven juxtaposed against earth. A God who loathes his Creation. From this has evolved a need to group act, to over-control and "normalize." We are simply No-Good Shits—by Definition.

From this we have created the Idea of the one God, separated from his creation by Evil. The new slavery, unlike the old, not only *guarantees* that the slave will be punished if he transgresses, but also *guarantees* stability, order, health and education—by decree. The new slave must let God (State) bestow care and supervision onto her, in order to ensure the continuing "safe" functioning of the person as resource. If the person refuses, denies the right of the Master and his Plan, the person is Evil. It is important to remember (the story of Job stresses this), Evil cannot be a characteristic of the Master, only the Slave. When the slave gets smart she reverses the process.

Mind and Will are exchanged for a *guaranteed* future. But even a modern slave cannot tolerate the complete awareness of the exchange.

Acknowledging his cowardice and slave mentality would offend his "pride." To cover up the trade, we require more fictions and ideologies.

We now search for the enemy of stability, as if it had a face, an identity, other than life itself.

And our search for those who cause the discomfort is directed at the rebels. Those who dare rattle the cage of stability.

The rebel the one who sought and tamed new frontiers, once revered as hero and mystic, is now turned into the sociopath. This transformation from hero to devil is partially a result of the stability demanded by those who come after him (the middle class) to live off the fruits of his courage and struggle, the mass which comes to fill the world carved by those who thrived on nature's unpredictable chaotic qualities. Once the frontier is "tamed" Status Quo moves in and demands order. A place where they can build their nests and ensure the betterment of their genetic coils. Morality is in fact an invention for the Middle Class. It creates a notion of order and justice in the world. The truly Powerful do not require these fictions and the Poor…well, they know better.

What of the rebel now? If lucky, he became wealthy and powerful, and with that, mobile, able to keep out of reach of those who require tranquillity and predictability in order to breed. If unlucky, he is forcibly exiled, jailed or murdered.

However, this is not the end of the story, for Nature "knows" that it cannot survive without the rebel. She is born again and again, and when born into stability, taming is difficult. The child is incorrigible, delinquent, hyperactive, requiring Ritalin, psychotherapy, special education. If lucky, the child escapes with the deep scars of guilt, shame and self-hatred, but at least having a chance to find its own frontier. If unlucky, the child is tortured, jailed, or suffers from never-ending despair.

When there is no frontier for the rebel the soul of a society begins to suffer. Some, like Wilhelm Reich, contend that the culture can itself be diseased. He referred to this as the Emotional Plague. In the end he was proven correct, not simply by the culture, but by individuals who embodied the repressed counterparts of an ideal.

According to Jungian tradition the manifestation or experience of evil results from the repression of both the personal and the collective shadow, sometimes resulting in physical manifestations such as Hitler, regarded in this age as the Epitome of Evil. However, what is the cause of this repression but the Ideal itself? In the face of this intimation, why still worship the Ideal?

As Nietzsche so beautifully put it, the ideal of truth posited by the Christian world, was the value which overturned it. Can we say that our *fear and denial* of instability or disorder, which in my view is the result of a lack of belief in ourselves as anything but a slave race, be perceived as more devastating than chaos and instability itself? The attempt to destroy evil, in and of itself, is an attempt to destroy life. Accepting that disobedience was the first evil, it follows that any attempt to destroy disobedience is an attempt to destroy life. I believe that even the rebel Jesus would agree that his acts of dis-obedience were perceived as evil by the establishment Rabbis, who used the notion of evil to destroy him.

To understand what a "civilized Christian society" means by Evil, we should dilate on Hitler's aspirations. He saw himself on a Messianic mission to purify and help his definition of perfected man evolve and rule the world. He saw himself and his followers as the Masters and the rest of the world as slaves. He was willing to do anything to see his vision fulfilled, including Usurping the Power of Mass Murder from God (see the Flood). But remember Usurping is the greater sin.

He performed his willful acts openly and told the world what his intentions were. He brought to consciousness a picture of mass evil (something which everyone else was doing, but behind more-or-less closed doors). Was his Sin any different when compared to Stalin, Mao, Ghenghis Khan, the Christian and Islamic inquisitions, and the hundreds of other cultures, civilizations and religions which have thought of themselves as Chosen, on a Mission, superior and willing to murder for the Ideal? Could we say then, that his evil was simply losing, or was it the "more important" fact that he employed violence? If so, what of the American Indian, and other races and cultures destroyed by the Christian notion of a pure white race. And what of the Blacks in America? No, most humans would argue that Hitler's evil was something more. What was it? It may have been because it happened in our own time, it was blatant, he lost the war, he crossed his genetic borders, or attacked the "chosen people" or ? ?

[As an aside, I would like to inform the reader that some individuals, after reading this, have asked me if I was a National Socialist simply because I used Hitler as an example!]

The word Evil functions in such a way as to allow one group to justify its own atrocities and make them noble. By dealing with such a powerful metaphysical abstraction (one which is physiologically associated with pain, fear, trembling and survival), it is an easy step to the performance of an act such as "execution," with the sense of moral righteousness and vindication. It is not a man who is being executed, it is Evil. It is the void filled with all the imagination and terror of a cowardly "adjusted" Status Quo man.

What is the psychological effect on the slave of the following two statements?

1) We will execute anyone who disobeys. 2) We will execute anyone who is evil.

As Nietzsche has shown, evil is an invention serving a purpose. It allows one group to justify its *will to power* over another, just as it has been used to intimidate most men.

REBELS AND DEVILS

The rebel with a cause is one who risks the label of evil when she attempts to remove—or go beyond—the categories of limitation currently believed. Just like the notion of the four-minute-mile which once became "eternally" defined as an Absolute, the rebel challenges arbitrary definitions, commandments and rules, which are believed to be Absolute. Some of these are death, gravity, limitations of the body and intelligence.

What we do and how we feel is a function of believing in fictitious limitations which have no basis except in habits.

Good and Evil and Opposites in general are primitive devices used by our minds to order the universe, and in my view, create an atmosphere of conflict which might not otherwise exist. The meaning and truth ascribed to the various pairs of opposites including such famous arguments as Nature/Nurture are a function of Who has the Power to create Definitions and, thereby, Offenders.

If the human mind requires "evil" in order to function, let it be death, stupidity, gravity and disease. If the human mind requires the notion of "good," let it be ceasing the primitive process of projecting our Greatness onto Idols—accepting Evil onto Ourselves.

WHO OWNS YOU?

The table below shows three models of OWNERSHIP: The first is the Model of God; the second, derived from the first, is the Model of Society and its Caretakers. The third is the Model of the Rebel-Devil.

OWNERSHIP TABLE: WHO OWNS WHOM?

MODEL ONE: GOD	MODEL TWO: SOCIETY & ITS CARETAKERS	MODEL THREE: THE REBEL-DEVIL
God OWNS Man	Society OWNS Man	Man OWNS Himself
God is the Center and Perfect	Society is the Center and Perfect	Life is the Center
Man is Sinful	Man is Sick	Man is ?
Religion	Law	Philosophy
Priest	Politician/Doctor	Cyber-Philosopher/ Adventurer

Sin/Pathology	Pathology & Rebelliousness	Functionality & Good Will
God is Studied	Man is Studied as a problem	Life is Studied as an interest
One Up/ One Down	One Up/ One Down	Shifting Systems of Probabilistic Truth
Oppression	Oppression	Essential Cooperation
Adaptation to God's Will	Adaptation to Society's Will	Grow to Possibilities of Self

One purpose of this Ownership Table is to help the individual gain insight into fundamentalist attitudes of Ownership.

Only when man Owns Himself is the dehumanizing process of slavery non-existent. The notion of Ownership, be it explicit or tacit, is the Key Concept which determines what is thought of as a problem and what solutions can be offered.

If we accept the Model of the Cyber-Shaman (that man Owns Himself), 95 percent of the so-called problems— which we read about in newspapers, hear about on the radio, watch on television, and discuss with friends—*Do Not Exist*. Thus, all proposed *Solutions* for these *Pseudo-Problems* are *Meaningless*.

The concept of OWNERSHIP starts in the cradle and does not end— not even in the grave.

Thus, our solution is not the eradication of

Ownership

But Rather

Not Viewing Oneself As Ownable

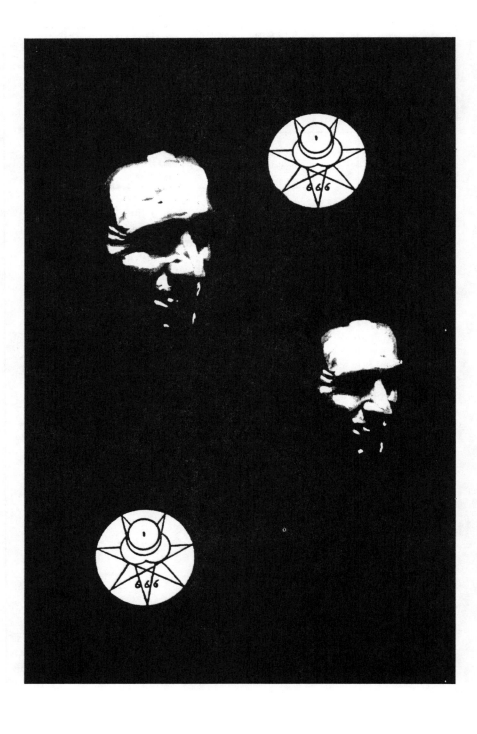

Frranzzz!
by Jim Goldiner

Frranzzz!
Frranzzz Kaaafka!
           can you hear me Franz
or have they really done you in for good

my time has come round again

i lost the case on the first trial
no appeal allowed of course
this i understood
but they let me go

And Franz ive done it again
i got myself into the same fix
and i love it Franz
                    i love it

Only one question
    will i get the same judge and jury

Osho (Bhagwan Shree) Rajneesh
Enlightened Master, Teacher and
One of the Greatest Religious Leaders of All Time

REBELLION IS THE BIGGEST "YES" YET

by Osho (Bhagwan Shree Rajneesh)

Author of the Falcon title:
Rebellion, Revolution & Religiousness

Beloved Master. All the historical rebellions have a huge "no" at their source. Your rebellion of the soul is centered in the mystery of "yes." *Will you please speak to us on the alchemy of "yes"?*

There are a few very fundamental things to be understood.

First, there has never been a rebellion in the past, only revolutions. And the distinction between a revolution and a rebellion is so vast that unless you understand the difference you will not be able to figure the way out of the puzzle of your question. Once you understand the difference...

Revolution is a crowd, a mob phenomenon. Revolution is a struggle for power: one class of people who are in power are thrown out by the other class of people who have been oppressed, exploited to such a point that now even death does not matter. They don't have anything. Revolution is a struggle between the haves and the have-nots.

I am reminded of the last statement in the *Communist Manifesto* by Karl Marx. It is tremendously beautiful, and with a little change I can use it for my own purposes.

First his exact statement: he says, "Proletariat"—his word for have-nots—"Proletariat of the world unite, and don't be afraid because you have nothing to lose except your chains."

Moments come in history when a small group of people—cunning, clever—start exploiting the whole society. All the money goes on gathering on one side and all the poverty and starvation on the other. Naturally this state cannot be continued forever. Sooner or later those who have nothing are going to overthrow those who have all.

Revolution is a class action, it is a class struggle. It is basically political; it has nothing to do with religion, nothing to do with spirituality. And it is also violent, because those who have power are not going to lose their vested interest easily; it is going to be a bloody, violent struggle in which thousands, sometimes millions of people will die.

Just in the Russian Revolution thirty million people were killed. The czar's whole family—he was the king of Russia before the revolution—was killed by the revolutionaries so brutally that it is inconceivable. Even a six-month-old girl was also killed. Now, she was absolutely innocent, she had done no harm to anybody; but just because she belonged to the royal family... The whole royal family had to be destroyed completely. Seventeen people were killed, and not just killed but cut into pieces.

It is bound to happen in a revolution. Centuries of anger ultimately turn into blind violence.

And the last thing to remember: revolution changes nothing. It is a wheel: one class comes into power, others become powerless. But sooner or later the powerless are going to become the majority, because the powerful don't want to share their power, they want to have it in as few hands as possible.

Now, you cannot conceive in this country... There are nine hundred million people, but half the capital of the country is just in Bombay. Nine hundred million people in the whole country, and half the capital of the whole country is just in a small city. How long can it be tolerated? Revolution comes naturally, automatically—it is something blind and mechanical, part of evolution. And when the powerful become the smaller group, the majority throws them away and another power group starts doing the same.

That's why I say revolution has never changed anything, or in other words, all the revolutions of history have failed. They promised much, but nothing came out of it. Even after seventy years, in the Soviet Union people are still not getting enough nourishment. Yes, there are no more the old czars and counts and countesses and princesses and princes—but in a vast ocean of poverty, even if you remove those who have power and riches it is not going to make the society rich; it is just like trying to make the ocean sweet by dropping teaspoonfuls of sugar in it.

All that has happened is a very strange phenomenon that nobody takes notice of. Only. poverty has been distributed equally: now in the Soviet Union everybody is equally poor. But what kind of revolution is this? The hope was that everybody would be equally rich.

But just by hoping you cannot become rich. Richness needs a totally different ideology of which mankind is absolutely unaware. For centuries it has praised poverty and condemned richness, comfort, luxury. Even if the poor revolt and come into power, they don't have any idea what to do with this power, how to generate energy to create more richness, comfort and luxury for people. Because deep down in their minds there is a guilty feeling about richness, about luxury, about comfort.

So they are in a tremendous anguish, although they have come to power. This is the moment they could change the whole structure of the society, its whole productive idea. They could bring more technology; they could drop stupid kinds of wastage.

Every country is wasting almost ten percent of its income on the army. Even the poorest country, even this country is doing the same idiotic thing. Fifty percent of the people in this country are on the verge of any day becoming an Ethiopia, a bigger Ethiopia. In Ethiopia one thousand people were dying per day. The day India starts becoming another Ethiopia—and it is not far away—then one thousand will not do; it will be many thousands of people dying every day.

By the end of this century the population of India will be the biggest in the whole world. So far it has never been; it has always been China that was ahead. By the end of the century—and there are not many years left, just within twelve years we will be reaching the end—India will have one billion people. Five hundred million people are bound to die, because there is no food for so many people.

But still the politicians, those who are in power, are not concerned at all what happens to humanity. Their concern is whether power remains in their hands or not. They can sacrifice half of the country, but they will go on making efforts to have atomic weapons, nuclear missiles.

It is a very insane kind of society that we have created in thousands of years. Its insanity has come now to a high peak. There is no going back. It seems we are all sitting on a volcano which can explode any moment.

Revolutions in the past have happened all around the world, but no revolution has succeeded in doing what it promised. It promised equality, without understanding the psychology of human individuality. Each human individual is so unique that to force them to equality is not going to make people happy, but utterly miserable.

I also love the idea of equality, but in a totally different way. My idea of equality is equal opportunity for all to be unequal, equal opportunity for all to be unique and themselves. Certainly they will be different from each other, and a society which does not have variety and differences is a very poor society. Variety brings beauty, richness, color.

But it has not yet dawned on the millions around the world that revolution has not helped, and they still go on thinking in terms of revolution. They have not understood anything from the history of man.

It is said that history repeats itself. I say it is not history that repeats itself; it only seems to repeat itself because man is absolutely unconscious and he goes on doing the same thing again and again without learning anything, without becoming mature, alert and aware.

When all the revolutions have failed some new door should be opened. There is no point in again and again changing the powerful into the powerless and the powerless into the powerful; this is a circle that goes on moving.

I don't preach revolution.

I am utterly against revolution.

I say unto you that my word for the future, and for those who are intelligent enough in the present, is *rebellion*.

What is the difference?

Rebellion is individual action; it has nothing to do with the crowd. Rebellion has nothing to do with politics, power, violence. Rebellion has something to do with changing your consciousness, your silence, your being. It is a spiritual metamorphosis.

And each individual passing through a rebellion is not fighting with anybody else, but is fighting only with his own darkness. Swords are not needed, bombs are not needed; what is needed is more alertness, more meditativeness, more love, more prayerfulness, more gratitude. Surrounded by all these qualities you are born anew.

I teach this new man, and this rebellion can become the womb for the new man I teach. We have tried collective efforts and they have failed. Now let us try individual efforts. And if one man becomes aflame with consciousness, joy and blissfulness, he will become contagious to many more.

Rebellion is a very silent phenomenon that will go on spreading without making any noise and without even leaving any footprints behind. It will move from heart to heart in deep silences, and the day it has reached to millions of people without any bloodshed, just the understanding of those millions of people will change our old primitive animalistic ways.

It will change our greed, and the day greed is gone there is no question of accumulating money. No revolution has been able to destroy greed; those who come into power become greedy.

We have passed through a revolution just now in this country, and it is a very significant example to understand. The people who were leading the revolution in this country against the British rule were followers of Mahatma Gandhi, who preached poverty, who preached non-possessiveness. The moment they came into power all his disciples started living in palaces which were made for viceroys. All his disciples who had been thinking their whole lives that they are servants of the people became masters of the people.

There is more corruption in this country than anywhere else. This is very strange—this is Gandhian corruption, very religious, very pious, and the people who are doing it were trained, disciplined to be servants of the people. But power has a tremendous capacity to change people; the moment you have power you are immediately a different person. You start behaving exactly like any other powerful people who have gone before.

Nothing has changed. Only the British are gone, and in their place a single party has been ruling for forty years. Now it is not just a single party, but a single family; it has become a dynasty. And the exploitation continues and the poverty continues—it has grown at least a hundred times more since the British Empire has been gone.

Everything has deteriorated—the morality, the character, the integrity, everything has become a commodity. You can purchase anybody; all you need is money. There is not a single individual in the whole country who is not a commodity in the marketplace; all you need is money. Everybody is purchasable—judges are purchasable, police commissioners are purchasable, politicians are purchasable. Even under the British rule this country has never known such corruption.

What has the country gained? The rulers have changed, but what does that signify? Unless there is a rebelliousness spreading from individual to individual, unless we can create an atmosphere of enlightenment around the world where greed will fall down on its own accord, where anger will not be possible, where violence will become impossible, where love will be just the way you live…where life should be respected, where the body should be loved, appreciated, where comfort should not be condemned. It is natural to ask for comfort.

Even the trees… In Africa, trees grow very high; the same trees in India don't grow that high. I was puzzled, what happens? I was trying to find out why they should grow to the same height but they don't, and the reason I found was that unless there is a density of trees, trees won't grow high. Even at a lesser height the sun is available, and that is their comfort, that is their life, that is their joy. In Africa the jungles are so thick that every tree tries in every way to grow as high as possible, because only then can it have the joy of the sun, the joy of the rain, the joy of the wind. Only then can it dance; otherwise there is nothing but death.

The whole of nature wants comfort, the whole of nature wants all the luxury that is possible. But our religions have been teaching us against luxury, against comfort, against riches.

A man of enlightenment sees with clarity that it is unnatural to demand from people, "You should be content with your poverty, you should be content with your sicknesses, you should be content with all kinds of exploitation, you should be content and you should not try to rise higher, to reach to the sun and the rain and the wind." This is an absolutely unnatural conditioning that we are all carrying. Only a rebellion in your being can bring you to this clarity.

You say that in history all the rebellions were based on "no." Those were not rebellions; change the word. All the revolutions were based on "no." They were negative, they were against something, they were destructive, they were revengeful and violent .

Certainly, my rebellion is based on "yes"—yes to existence, yes to nature, yes to yourself. Whatever the religions may be saying and whatever the ancient traditions may be saying, they are all saying no to yourself, no to nature, no to existence; they are all life-negative.

My rebellion is life-affirmative. I want you to dance and sing and love and live as intensely as possible and as totally as possible. In this total affirmation of life, in this absolute "yes" to nature we can bring a totally new earth and a totally new humanity into being.

The past was "no."

The future has to be "yes".

We have lived enough with the "no," we have suffered enough and there has been nothing but misery. I want people to be as joyful as birds singing in the morning, as colorful as flowers, as free as the bird on the wing with no bondages, with no conditioning, with no past—just an open future, an open sky and you can fly to the stars.

Because I am saying yes to life, all the no-sayers are against me, all over the world. My yes-saying goes against all the religions and against all the ideologies that have been forced upon man. My "yes" is my rebellion. The day you will also be able to say "yes" it will be your rebellion.

We can have rebellious people functioning together, but each will be an independent individual, not belonging to a political party or to a religious organization. Just out of freedom and out of love and out of the same beautiful "yes" we will meet. Our meeting will not be a contract, our meeting will not be in any way a surrender; our meeting will make every individual more individual. Supported by everybody else, our meeting will not take away freedom, will not enslave you; our meeting will give you more freedom, more support so that you can be stronger in your freedom. Long has been the slavery, and long has been our burden. We have become weak because of the thousands of years of darkness that have been poured on us.

The people who love to say "yes," who understand the meaning of rebellion, will not be alone; they will be individuals. But the people who are on the same path, fellow-travelers, friends, will be supporting each other in their meditativeness, in their joy, in their dance, in their music. They will become a spiritual orchestra, where so many people are playing instruments but creating one music. So many people can be together and yet they may be creating the same consciousness, the same light, the same joy, the same fragrance.

It is a long way—"no" seems to be a shortcut—that's why it has not been tried up to now. Whenever I have discussed it with people, they said, "Perhaps you are right, but when will it be possible that the whole earth will say 'yes'?"

I said, "Anyway we have been on this earth for millions of years and you have been saying 'no'—and what is your achievement? It is time. Give a chance to 'yes' too."

My feeling is that "no" is a quality of death; "yes" is the very center of life. "No" had to fail because death cannot succeed, cannot be victorious over life. If we give a chance to "yes" based in rebelliousness it is bound to become a wildfire, because everybody deep down wants it to happen. I have not found a single person in my life who does not want to live a natural, relaxed, peaceful, silent life.

But that life is possible only if everybody else is also living the same kind of life.

I can understand the fear of people that individual rebellion may take a long time, but there is no problem in it.

In fact each individual who passes through this rebellious fire becomes at least for himself a bliss and an ecstasy, and there is every possibility that he will sow the seeds around him. But he has not failed; he has conquered, he has reached to the very peak of his potential. He has blossomed. There is nothing more that he can think of; the whole existence is his.

So as far as that individual is concerned the rebellion is complete. He will be able to sow seeds all around. And there is no hurry; eternity is available. Slowly, slowly more and more people will become more and more conscious, more alert. Enlightenment will become a common phenomenon.

It should not be that only once in a while there is a Gautam Buddha, once in a while there is a Jesus, once in a while there is a Socrates—the names can be counted on only ten fingers. This is simply unbelievable. It is as if your garden is full of rosebushes, thousands of rosebushes, and once in a while one rosebush blossoms and gives you roses. And the remaining thousands remain without flowers?

Unless a rosebush comes to blossom it cannot dance—for what? It cannot share; it has nothing to share. It remains poor, empty, meaningless. Whether it lived or not makes no difference.

The only difference is that when it blossoms and offers its songs and its flowers and its fragrance to existence and to anybody who is willing to receive, the rosebush is fulfilled. Its life has not been just a meaningless drag; it has become a beautiful dance full of songs, a deep fulfillment that goes to the very roots.

I am not worried about time. If the concept is understood, time is available; enough time is available.

In the East we have a beautiful proverb: The man who loses the path in the morning, if he returns home by the evening he should not be called lost. What does it matter? In the morning he went astray—just little adventures here and there—and by the evening he is back home. A few people may have come a little earlier; he has come a little late, but he is not necessarily poorer than those who have come earlier. It may be just vice versa: he may be more experienced. He has known more because he has wandered more; he has known more because he has committed more mistakes. He is much more mature and experienced because he has gone wandering so far astray. And then coming back again, falling and getting up—he is not necessarily a loser.

So time is not at all a consideration to me.

My rebellion is absolutely individual and it will spread from individual to individual. Sometime this whole planet is bound to become enlightened. Idiots may try to wait and see what happens to others, but they also finally have to join the caravan.

The very idea of enlightenment is so new, although it is not something that has not been known before. There have been enlightened people, but they never brought enlightenment as a rebellion. That is what is new about it. They became enlightened, they became contented, they became fulfilled, and a great fallacy happened and I have to point it out. Although I feel not to show any mistakes of the enlightened ones—I feel sad about it—but my responsibility is not for the dead. My responsibility is for those who are alive and for those who will be coming.

So I have to make it clear. Gautam Buddha, Mahavira, Adinatha, Lao Tzu, Kabir, all these people who became enlightened attained to tremendous beauty, to great joy, to utter ecstasy—to what I have been calling *satyam, shivam, sundram,* the truth, the godliness of the truth and the beauty of that godliness.

But because they had become enlightened they started teaching people to be contented: "Remain peaceful, remain silent." This is the fallacy. They attained contentment after a long search. It was a conclusion, not a beginning; it was the very end product of their enlightenment, but they started telling people that you can be contented right now: "Be fulfilled, be silent."

That's how they became anti-rebellious, without perhaps knowing that if a poor man remains contented with his poverty it is dangerous; if a slave remains contented with his slavery, it is dangerous.

So all the enlightened people of the past attained to great heights, about which there is no doubt. But there is a fallacy that they all perpetuated without exception. The fallacy is that they began telling people to start with that which comes in the end. The flower comes only in the end; one has to start with the roots, with the seed. And if you tell people to start with the roses, then the only way is to purchase roses of plastic. The only way to be contented without meditation is to be a hypocrite, because deep down you are angry, deep down you are furious, deep down you want to freak out, and on the surface you are showing immense peace. This peace has been like a cancer to humanity.

You can see it happening in this country more clearly than anywhere else, because this country was fortunate, blessed by more enlightened people than any other country—but unfortunately, because so many enlightened people committed the same fallacy, this country remained for twenty centuries continuously a slave. This country has remained for centuries

"Hallelujah!" came the response from the back.

The vicar managed to get to the end of his sermon, but at the end went up to the American and said, "Excuse me, I'm afraid in this country we like to keep a bit of decorum. We try to keep a stiff upper lip. It is the queen's own country, this is a place of God, and I frankly found your behavior rather disconcerting."

"Hey man, I'm sorry, you are right on. I just loved the quaint way you gave us all that great shit about Moses and the Ten Commandments and I thought I would throw a few thousand greenbacks in your direction for this great thing going on here."

"Cool, man!" said the preacher.

It does not take much to find out what is deep inside. All decorum, all culture is so superficial; it will be a tremendous joy to see people in their authenticity, in their reality, without any decorum, without any make-up, just as they are. The world will be tremendously benefited if all this falseness disappears.

The alchemy of "yes" and the rebellion based on "yes" are capable of destroying all that is false, and discovering all that is real and has been covered for centuries, layer upon layer by every generation, so much that even you yourself have forgotten who you are.

If suddenly somebody wakes you up in the middle of the night and asks you, "Who are you?" you will take a little time to remember who you used to be the night before when you went to bed.

It happened that George Bernard Shaw was going to deliver a lecture some distance away from London. On the way in the train came the ticket-checker. George Bernard Shaw looked in every pocket, opened all his suitcases, but the ticket was not there. Finally, he was perspiring and the ticket-checker said, "Don't be worried, I know who you are; the whole country knows, the whole world knows. The ticket must be somewhere, you don't be worried. And even if it is lost, I am here to help you get out at the station, wherever you want to get out."

George Bernard Shaw said, "Shut up! I am already in confusion and you are making me more confused. I am trying to remember where I am going! That ticket was the only thing... I am not searching for the ticket for you, idiot; I don't care about you, you can get lost. Bring me my ticket!"

The man said, "But how can I find your ticket?"

George Bernard Shaw said, "Then what am I supposed to do? Where should I get down? Because unless I know the name of the station..."

It is almost the same situation with everybody. You don't know who you are; your name is just a label that has been put upon you, it is not your being. Where are you going?—you don't have any ticket to show you where you are going to get down, and you are just hoping that somebody may push you somewhere, or maybe somewhere the terminus comes and the train stops and it does not go anywhere else. . . Just hoping.

But why are you traveling in the first place? In fact, for all these fundamental questions you have only one answer: I don't know. In this state of unawareness your revolutions cannot succeed. In this state of unawareness, your desire for freedom is just a dream. You cannot understand what freedom is. For whom are you asking freedom?

My idea of a rebellion based on "yes" means a rebellion based on meditation, for the first time in the history of man. And because each individual has to work upon himself, there is no question of any fight, there is no question of any organization, there is no question of any conspiracy, there is no question of planting bombs and hijacking airplanes.

I am not interested in hijacking airplanes, neither am I interested in destroying any governments. But it will be the final result of my individual rebellion based on meditation: governments will disappear. They have to disappear; they have been nothing but a nuisance on the earth. Nations have to disappear. There is no need of any nations; the whole earth belongs to the whole of humanity. There is no need of any passports, there is no need of any visas.

This earth is ours, and what kind of freedom is there if we cannot even move? Everywhere there are barriers, every nation is a big imprisonment. Just because you cannot see the boundaries you think you are free. Just try to pass through the boundary and immediately you will be faced with a loaded gun: "Go back inside the prison. You belong to this prison. You cannot enter into another prison without permission." These are your nations!

Certainly, a rebellion of my vision will take away all this garbage of nations, and discrimination between white and black, and give the whole of humanity a natural, relaxed, comfortable life. This is possible, because science has given us everything that we need, even if the population of the earth is three times more than it is today.

Just a little intelligence is needed—which will be released by meditation—and we can have a beautiful earth with beautiful people, and a multidimensional freedom which is not just a word in the dead constitution books but a living reality.

One thing finally to be remembered: the days of revolution are past. We have tried them many times, and every time the same story is repeated. Enough. Now something new is urgently needed. And except for the idea that I am giving to you of a rebellion, individual and based on meditativeness, there is no other alternative proposed anywhere in the world.

And I am not a philosopher; I am absolutely pragmatic and practical. I am not only talking about meditative rebellion, I am preparing people for it. Whether they know it or not doesn't matter. Whoever comes close to me is going to become a rebellious individual, and wherever he will go he will spread this contagious health. It will make people aware of their dignity, it will make people aware of their potentiality. It will make people alert to what they can become, what they are, and why they are stuck.

My sannyasins' function is not to be missionaries, but to be so loving, compassionate, such fragrant individuals... It is not a question of converting people from one ideology to another ideology. It is a far deeper transformation—from the whole past to a totally new and unknown future. It is the greatest adventure that one can think of.

Satyam-Shivam-Sundram, Session 26, November 19, 1987

Osho, known also as Bhagwan Shree Rajneesh, was born in India in 1932 and died in 1990. He stands as one of the most famous, and to some, infamous, religious leaders of modern times. He probably holds the record for being thrown out of, or refused entry into, the greatest number of countries in history. His life and his work should be inspirations to rebels everywhere. For information contact Osho Commune International, 17 Koregaon Park, Poona 411 011, India.

THE CALLING OF THE HOLY WHORE

by Diana Rose Hartmann

Co-author of the Falcon title:
Hard Zen, Soft Heart

The Rebel, whether male or female, is not a Reactionary. Reaction is usually a habit or action based on the belief systems we've incorporated and triggered by a given circumstance. One's cultural programming will always affect one's reaction to any situation. For example, Michael Crichton's *Disclosure* was a reaction to the relatively recent spate of sexual harassment cases brought to light by women everywhere. If the butcher at the grocery store calls me "honey" the hair on my neck bristles because I've learned that such generic terms of endearment are condescending to women. (Of course, if I call the *butcher* "honey," it's an expression of my nurturing side.) Reactionaries are often in danger of becoming that same enemy against which they preached. Consider the results of the French Revolution, or even the Hippies.

True Rebellion, however, emerges from the gut. The Rebel is closer to the mystic than the revolutionary in that the core of his or her rebellion is an aspect of his or her evolution—it is coming into One's Self, if you will. One rebels from the heart without lust for results. Francis of Assisi was a Rebel. Joan of Arc was a Rebel. Every artist or scientist or poet who has broken through the boundaries of himself and his time is a Rebel. A Devil, in relation to the above scheme of things, is simply a Rebel who expresses his cause to the audience of the greater social structure, with creative action.

As poet, prophet, and Rebel, William Blake wrote in the *Marriage of Heaven & Hell*: "Good is the passive that obeys Reason. Evil is the active springing from Energy." Blake's vision maintained that Hell was the home of Genius and Creativity and Energy and Nature, whereas Heaven was the residence of Reason and Restriction and Passivity and

Culture. Neither Devils nor Angels were "evil", rather such duality was necessary to existence. Without such contraries, there would be progression, no evolution. Blake argued that all true poets were "of the Devil's party without knowing it."

In the Judeo-Christian novel, Lucifer or Satan can be hailed as the first rebel brave enough to carve himself into the stones of history. Let us view our protagonist Lucifer as a rebellious angel who had too much creative energy, too much will to be satisfied with his role as a puppet of Jehovah, the Keeper of Reason. Lucifer rebelled against his Lord and master, got exiled from the place honorably known as Heaven and subsequently created a new religion in that infamous state we fondly deem Hell. Now the point made here is not whether or not Lucifer AKA Satan is "bad" or "good", but that something New and Completely different, a break from the stagnant pool of so-called peace called Heaven, was created through the Rebel's act. Without Hell, it would be impossible to define Heaven. Without "evil," it would be impossible to define "good."

The word "devil" and "divinity" grew from the same root, "devi" of Indo-European origin. Similarly, the word "demon" stems from the Greek "daemon" which referred to Genius. Ancient Greek philosophers and poets spend many an hour invoking their own personal daemons. Somewhere along the line of history, genius, creative rebellion, and energy became associated with evilness. Human beings, lazy creatures prone to habit, were taught to accept whatever vision of the world they inherited. To speak out was heresy.

But I digress. Dr. Hyatt commissioned me to write on the topic of Rebels and Devils from a woman's perspective. And I must admit, it took many nights of pondering this rather enormously potent subject to come up with a thesis. You can accuse me of gender bias and stereotyping, but when I think of Rebels and Devils, I imagine personages with penises. History may speak of rebellious women and she-devils, but the archetypal Rebels and Devils are masculine entities. Rebellious Women are usually referred to as bitches. Female devils are typically called witches.

(When I speak of the female Rebel, the Bitch or the Witch, I'm not talking about the Feminist who aim is to become equal to men. I'm talking about a Bitch with a capital "B". I'm talking about the woman who expresses the soul of the Goddess in her most independent guise. She is not a ball-busting man-hater, but a woman who is nurturing, highly sexual, yet unable to be possessed. Etymologist Fiona Houghton informs us that for several centuries the Queen in any suit of cards was referred to as "bitch." (Think Catherine the Great or Cleopatra.)

Yet, most modern day Feminists ostensibly sacrifice their feminine natures, and thereby their true power, in their quest for "equal rights." Few have bothered to ask, equal to what? What do men really have worth stealing? And while some of this sacrificing has indeed moved women from their role as chattel to their role as "partner", as Camille Paglia attests by "getting women out of the kitchen and into the office, we have simply put them into another bourgeois prison." The Feminist followers of the likes of Andrea Dworkin and others have ceased to be rebels. The Feminist establishment has become Reactionary at best and Restrictive at worst. (Their quest to define Pornography as an evil-which-must-be-banned threatens our Freedom of Speech.)

What separates the Feminine Rebel from the Feminist Reactionary is the acknowledgment of her sex, her mystery, her essential femaleness. We're talking a revival of the Vamp and the Tramp. We're talking the invocation of the Whore of Babylon. We're talking a repossessing of sexual power, but with a difference. This Vamp, this Whore, this Sex Goddess, will also express true femininity, with all its nurturing, dark wet womb-like qualities. We're talking about reclaiming our status as a daughter of Eve.

In the standard Judeo-Christian myth, Eve would probably be the counterpart of Lucifer.

Her crime, like Lucifer's, is disobedience to God. She dared to exercise her own will. She dared to embrace her sexual power. She dared to take on the role of seductress and initiate her boyfriend, Adam. When Eve tasted of the very Fruit she was told to abstain from, she assimilated her individuality as a woman. And she took great pleasure in her new discovery. Subsequently, she convinced Adam to Eat as well and he noticed that he was different from her. Now, the two did not get into any competitive warfare (at least not immediately) about who was "dom" and who was "sub." Instead that toasted "Viva Le Difference!" and evolved from there.

As the Poet says, "Without Contraries there would be no Progression."

The two kids were exiled from the Garden, where their respective sexual differences were ignored, and cast out into the world, where a whole lotta fucking (if we acknowledge the large number of children begotten by these two) went on.

The Fundamentalist will maintain that it was an apple (though apples had probably not evolved to our vision of applehood in 2000 BCE). The Rationalist, however, might see some logic in a statement my "Bible as Literature" professor taught: The Fruit is simply a metaphor for the manifestive or creative power inherent in our sexuality, our difference.

The eating of the Fruit and acknowledgment of sexuality was a BIG deal. It was, in fact, the ultimate act of rebellion against the Status Quo and it's allegedly divine upholder, Big Jehovah.

Michel Foucault and other philosophers have pointed out the easiest way to control a society is to convince each member of the flock to restrict their sexual power—an insidious form of government usually effected by means such as taboo, legislation, or publicized threats of eternal damnation. And so society is brainwashed into believing that their bodies do not belong to themselves, but rather to some Higher Authority (be it Judge or Priest or Doctor) who knows better.

The purveyors of our current belief system have convinced us that we live in a free society, but subversively inform us through the media pawns with a slew of moralistic horror stories assuring us that passivity and obedience are "good" while action and "disobedience" are bad. We are thrown back into the Garden with all of its innocence, comfort and passivity. In the Nineties we are living in what Michael Ventura deemed "The Year of the Gump." Forest Gump, acclaimed hero with an assured nomination in the Academy Awards, is a perfect puppet. He does what he is told. Moreover, he does it well. Ventura writes that "Americans found a hero with no will of his own—to cushion their surrender to men who are *all* will. Newt Gingrich, Rush Limbaugh—names composed of strange slick syllables eerily similar to 'Forest Gump.'"

Scary, eh? We are living in a decade of socially enforced Political Correctness and conscious submission. Says, Dr. Hyatt, "God doesn't even like it." We live in a society where taboos and legislation have been fostered by seemingly innocuous, but highly repressive, teachings. Kids say "no" because they are convinced it's hip. It's in. And most of us are too confused by technology—by the exponential increase of information that is available to us—to think for ourselves anymore, the "God" science now serving the Apple. Worse, couple this with the desperation of our own needs and we have the Garden of Eden before (or maybe after) the Fall?

Professional women in particular are quickly becoming "equal," alien-ated from their own bodies and soul. Women's nature—whether it be the emotional excess generated by premenstrual hormones or that magical trait called women's intuition—is stifled in the work place. Men suffer as well, as they must close their eyes at the sight of a sexy woman, repress-ing natural instinct, because they fear sexual harassment suits. Dr. Hyatt said, "Repression has come a 360 degree turn through logic, law and science." Young women are taught to dismiss all great literary and artis-tic works which don't agree with feminist agenda as "misogynist." They are taught to suppress or ignore any instincts which don't fit in with the feminist doctrine. Freedom? They are taught to not flaunt themselves sexually or they will be sexual objects. Guess what? We *are* sexual objects and we should be damn proud of it. Rebellion is hard work.

Don't lose hope. Work can be enjoyable. And while I can't show you, dear reader, where to look to find your Fruit of creative potential, you personal Fruit of the Devil, the Witch, or the Rebel. I can tell you where I found mine. I cheated. I had a helpmate and I'll call her Babylon. She was the Fruit of my own Tree of Life, the One which grew me, my soul if you will, which I had previously been, afraid to partake of. She was wily and sexy and powerful and witchy. She is the Holy Whore, the slut with a soul, the proponent of Do-Me feminism, et. al. The foe of Andrea Dworkin; the friend of Camille Paglia and Madonna. She is Robert Grave's White Goddess, the muse, the witch, the ideal woman who is at once mother and lover. Madonna and Whore. She is the Fruit which will move every woman to adulthood. She is the energy of the gut, the voice of the rebel, the creative force of the devil.

This idea of a Holy Whore seems like an enigma to most people. It encompasses the Devil and the Angel, the Rebel and the Sheep. Nature and Artifice, in an solitary being. Just try to explain her to a friend not versed in esoterica or occultism and you'll surely see raised eyebrows, or disgusted grimaces. The adjective "sacred" means worthy of religious veneration, something declared or made holy. OK. Prophetic texts are called sacred, as are a variety of rituals and icons; even particular mountains or rivers are considered sacred. But whores?

Prostitution is defined as the use of sex to gain something: money for the streethooker, fame for the untalented Hollywood starlet, or security for the suburban housewife who married for the sake of fear. The term Sacred Prostitute seems oxymoronic, but in a sense it is redundant. In her book *When God Was A Woman*, Merlin Stone points out that the Hebrew word *"ZONAH"* means both prostitute and prophetess. Sacred Whores were know as the "Holy Virgins," priestesses of the Goddesses Ishtar, Asherah, or Aphrodite. The famed Vestal Virgins are thought to have practiced magical sex rituals in honor of the Roman Matriarch Vesta.

How could a professed virgin practice sex magick, you ask? In the case of these priestesses "Virgin" did not mean that the hymen was intact or that these women were kin to the immaculate mom of J. Christ. A virgin was simply an unmarried woman, a woman who claimed ownership of herself. But the Holy Whores weren't feminists competing for equality with the opposite sex. In fact, their job was to dispense the grace of the God/dess through the art of their sexuality, and the true expression of their feminine natures. These women knew the power of their sexuality and the power of their femininity. They were perfect mothers and perfect whores. They were Virgins because they were Intact.

So what happened to the Sacred Whore? And why do I propose that Reclaiming the Sacred Whore is probably the most rebellious and empowering task a modern woman can accomplish?

Sexually empowered women, let alone whores, are often seen as threats, bitches, dykes, ball-busters, etc., by both women and men alike. Sexually independent women are demoralized as evil temptresses, obstacles between man and a heaven full of sexless wimps. Mad violence against women is also increasing as men indoctrinated with ides that their own instincts are unholy take to abusing women, both physically and mentally, blaming them for causing their own natures to stir.

The loss of the intact woman, Mary Magdelene (whose name means "she of the temple-tower") combined with the Immaculate Madonna in one body, resulted in a societal imbalance. Both sexes lose. Men must choose between a nurturing mother or a titillating sexpot. Scarlet O'Hara or Melanie. Women learn to either use their sexuality as a manipulative tool or to repress their sexuality and acknowledge passivity and submission as the ticket for survival. Without the embodiment of the Sacred Whore in every woman, society twists dysfunctional and self-help books continue to be the biggest sellers in the publishing industry.

Of course, women can't flock to temples and set up camp as Holy Whores in this day and age without being arrested. But a change in the way women see themselves, and in the way men view women is a start. Jungian Psychologist, Nancy Qualls-Corbett, describes the Holy Whore as "a woman, who, through ritual or psychological development, has come to know the spiritual side of her sexuality, her true Eroticism, and lives this out according to her individual circumstances." The Sacred Prostitute has reclaimed her Self, her Body, as Sacred, and connected with her True Will.

Ostensibly, acknowledging one's own Nature as an integral and sacred truth seems a given. Yet consider an event which transpired only a couple years back. When the TV show *Murphy Brown* depicted an unmarried woman having a baby without repercussions, the Puritans cried out. The woman should be punished for allowing her nature take its course. Subsequently, the moral majority pricked up its ears and our former vice president, Dan Quayle, flew to Hollywood to tell high school students and the media that the message posited by the TV show is indeed an evil one. "It suggests that it's OK to bear illegitimate babies," Quayle said. Ask yourself. How can a baby be against the law? Whose law? Jehovah's? Newt Gingrich's? The Pope's?

You may also want to ask why homosexuality—even as scientists are proving that homoerotic inclinations have genetic components—is still considered sinful in some states or social circles.

Angels can tell lies as well as devils, can't they?

Of course they can. And reflecting over the past couple years of my life, I can see that I've been taken in substantially by con-angels. I've lost sight of myself. Of the Rebel within, that Whole, Wholly, Holy Whore which was the seat of my strength. I blame my alienation from her on nothing in particular. Let's just say I started believing the lies of society, I stopped swimming upstream. I got a day job. I wanted to buy things. I packed my intuition in a box. I surrendered my paintbrush (which had stubbornly dedicated itself to creating perpetually more colorful realities) and purchased a TV Guide. I traded the work of Rebellion for the security of adulthood and put a sock in the subversive mouth of the Holy Whore. You'd think I'd be a happy camper, all acceptance and leisure now that I'm part of the herd. Wrong.

It's time to remove the sock. The loss of the Rebel within, the failure to feed the voice of the Devil, has left me listless and vapid. There is energy in opposition. There is life in the strife of contraries.

Diamond Galas once asked, "When a witch is about to be burned on a ladder in flames, who can she call upon?" The answer is Satan.

"Satan," Galas says, "is that subversive voice that can keep you alive in the face of adversity." We all live in the face of adversity. We all live amongst the Angels of Restriction. Yet the Voice of the Devil is the song of the heart, the raw energy necessary to evolution and individuation.

Diana Rose Hartmann, M.A. writes literary fiction, psychological rants, and computer games. Her work has appeared in many publications, including *The Sun, The Seattle Times, Green Egg,* and *bOING-bOING.*

Francis Israel Regardie
Born November 17, 1907—Died March 10, 1985

FRANCIS ISRAEL REGARDIE

The Final Words Of A Western Master

Interviewed by Christopher S. Hyatt, Ph.D.

Israel Regardie is the author of the Falcon titles:
The Eye in the Triangle: An Interpretation of Aleister Crowley
What You Should Know About the Golden Dawn
The Golden Dawn Audios: Series I, II, and III
The Complete Golden Dawn System of Magic
Gems From the Equinox (editor)
The Legend of Aleister Crowley
Magick Without Tears (editor)

CSH: This interview is going to be tough.

FIR: Yes—I find myself resisting it. Every time I open my mouth I appear to get into some sort of trouble.

CSH: Yes. You're an iconoclast. Let's start with something easy.

FIR: All right; I'm game.

CSH: When did you start writing *The Complete Golden Dawn System of Magic?*

FIR: Somewhere around 1979 or so. My memory is not quite clear as to the exact date. But it was about then that I wrote my first synopsis of what should be included.

CSH: What made you take on such a monumental project?

FIR: (Laughing) It's rather difficult to say. (I've had a couple of Bloody Marys!) Well—my reasons for writing it were manifold. I will describe a couple of the more simple motives that I don't mind making public. Others are more personal, so I'll keep them private for the time being.

The first exposition, written over forty years ago, was hastily thrown together. It was incomplete in all sorts of ways. In those days I was more impulsive or more impatient than I am now. There were whole areas which should have been elaborated, but which were not clarified at all. Some very important Golden Dawn documents were also omitted—even though my original intention was to make the book as complete as I could.

A very dear friend of mine, Carr P. Collins, Jr. of Dallas [Texas], was good enough to obtain, in 1979, a complete set of Golden Dawn documents from the late Gerald Yorke in England. He gave me enormous encouragement and moral support. This then provided the opportunity of realizing how much had been omitted and how much could be re-edited. On studying this new set of documents I decided to ensure that *The Complete Golden Dawn System of Magic* would be a much more complete version of the Order's teaching than the original hastily-put-together version was.

One of the things that has always rankled me is human secrecy. So long as this body of knowledge remains locked up in one or more human being's brains, it runs the risk of being lost to mankind forever. It needs to be put in book form to be distributed all over the world, so that if some type of cataclysm occurred someone, somewhere, would be able to redis-cover this material and once more make it available. So long as a few books can be found tucked away somewhere, this knowledge cannot be lost. So, therefore, in writing *The Complete Golden Dawn System of Magic* my intention was to make it as complete as possible, hoping that Falcon would make certain that this had the widest possible distribution. Thus, in the event that there was a major calamity, and Western civiliza-tion as we know it was destroyed in the Northern hemisphere, there would be dozens or hundreds of sets of this teaching distributed in the Southern hemisphere. Then this form of occult knowledge, this particular rendition of being "brought to the Light," would endure for another thou-sand years or so.

CSH: Do you then see a disaster of these proportions occurring in the next few decades?

FIR: Yes, I suspect something of that type occurring. But for the moment, let's go to something else.

CSH: How did you meet Carr?

FIR: It went something like this. He was involved with a small study group in Dallas, studying *The Tree of Life* and *The Golden Dawn*. The first seemed pretty obscure. The group was mostly concerned with the problem of pronouncing the Hebrew words. So out of the blue, he wrote me a letter care of my then publishers. "We want to learn how to pronounce these words. Can you help us?" At that time it hadn't occurred to me to dictate a tape. Anyway, I didn't have a tape recorder then; this was in the early 60s, some twenty years ago, though I did have a wire recorder. In answering him, I suggested that all he had to do was to enquire at the nearest Hebrew synagogue or temple for this information. "They won't burn you, they won't cook you, they won't do anything awful to you. Just say that you have your group interested in the Qabalah (they won't understand in the least; perhaps they'll think you're crazy), and you want to learn the pronunciation of certain Hebrew words and names. They will either say "Get the hell out of here" or else "Look, we've got a young man here who will be glad to help." So that's the letter I wrote to Carr. I never heard another word. About a year later I was fiddling around with my files and came across this letter of his with the notes that I had made. So I wrote him another letter. I asked, "What happened? Did you take my counsel and go to a local temple and find out how these words are pronounced?" His reply was, "No. We did nothing of the kind. Why don't you come down here and give us a course?" At first this sounded preposterous to me. But he again wrote me a letter and asked would I come? Not really wanting to do this, I thought I would be a real smart ass and said, Yes, I'll come, naming what I then thought a preposterous fee for one day; my fee will be $500.00 plus all expenses. And damn it, he went for that! So I couldn't back out. I never thought anybody would be extravagant enough to offer me $500.00 for that. So anyway, that's how I met Carr and the relationship has been good since. There were a couple of amusing differences in the meantime about that. He said, "Fine, come down to Dallas and in the evening after the lecture, we'll pick your brains." I was a might hackled at that. I said, "Now look, if I come down to lecture, or whatever it is, for two days, I'll give you everything I can during the daytime, but after dinner, or when my hours are up, I don't want anybody around me. Leave me alone!" So that put an end to his notion that they were just going to sit around and have a nice long conversation all evening. In other words I would not be obliged to talk for 48 hours continuously.

CSH: I guess they still gained a lot.

FIR: I hope so. They were very, very nice people. A good group whom I came to love and respect. That's why I appreciate his latest letter, that if I ever move to Dallas there would be a nice nucleus of friends. Anyway that's the way it happened. So from that day he's been very sympathetic, very generous and understanding and a good sounding board. He could occasionally provoke a series of questions that I hadn't let's say, sponta- neously considered, which was most evocative or stimulating.

CSH: Did you feel his was a rather prosaic point of view?

FIR: Not really. He was a very warm, practical person, very pragmatic. I like him enormously. You've got a totally different kind of mind altogether, more analytical.

CSH: Well—I do know that I prefer experience to long drawn out theories or explanations. I'm the kind of person that prefers the experience rather than the explanation of the experience. Of course, I have been trained to think in a scientific and analytic fashion. Sometimes perhaps it gets in the way.

FIR: I doubt it. Your analytic mind is OK.

CSH: Thanks. But I prefer religious and therapeutic orientations which are more experiential than theoretical. Too much theory always disturbs me. I know we've talked about this before. The lack of life in many of the people who have gotten into the occult. Many of them have become sort of dead. They lose their sex life, they lose their party life, and a lot of them lose all spontaneity. In fact, I doubt if many of them have much life at all.

FIR: You're right. They probably never had much real life to them. This picture however extends more or less over this whole occult field, a sort of moral miasma.

CSH: What makes me feel good is when I see some of the Bhagwan Rajneesh's followers. They are out there dancing and yelling and...

FIR: Yes, that's great. Darned good idea.

CSH: They are doing something. Even those with an intellectual background—they are active and alive. My nature demands the catharsis—the doing. The image of the librarian sitting in a vast room with millions of books turns me off. To me this is not the study of the occult! I like the Golden Dawn System because it demands something more experiential than the intellect.

FIR: Yes, this is why I like it too. Anyway, I am not that intellectual. I can be, but I have more of a sense of the whole structure rather than a deep intellectual understanding.

CSH: That's right. You have a good grasp of the whole field and of the people in it. Are we getting into trouble yet?

FIR: Yes we are. (Laughter) If we've got to use another word, which still requires a lot of explanation, I have an intuitive perception of some of the essence of this material.

CSH: Yes. And I think that has more to offer than someone who can delve into every vowel and consonant.

FIR: That's why we still need librarians to balance people like you and me.

CSH: However, you have people like Waite (who are librarians of the most dogmatic kind) who have had or attract the kind of audience that we're talking about, a very moralistic, staid, old-fashioned, non-expressive, non-orgasmic...

FIR: Yes, non-orgasmic in nature. It's the old Christian morality again. He was steeped in that. And he attracted those few people who were already steeped in it like him. Anybody else would have loathed him.

CSH: Yes! If they had a sense of their own being they probably would. Remember that time we were in a Boulder bookstore and this girl started to talk about how stiff Regardie's writings were compared to Waite! She didn't recognize you, of course, and you in jest agreed with her.

FIR: Yes, that was very funny. If I thought that my work was as stiff and straight-laced as his I would soon shoot myself. (Laughter)

CSH: Waite sure wouldn't fit in well with a guy like you, or Crowley or Rajneesh or anyone who was pro-life. I imagine that some people who have read your works can't imagine you having a lot of fun and driving around in a sports car at the age of 77.

FIR: We are getting in trouble again, but what you said is sad but true. This is one reason why I generally avoid people in this field. They can't integrate the fact that someone like me can have a lot of fun—and be simply ordinary in so many ways. They expect of me a certain role and become disappointed when they find me so different from their expectations.

CSH: Isn't that always a problem in the occult...that a weird separation is made between the spiritual and the material. I find that very annoying.

FIR: You're lucky. You haven't had that early orientation which separates them.

CSH: No, I never had.

FIR: You're so lucky in that sense. I grew up, as it were, in a theosophical milieu. I discovered it (theosophy) too early which was a great mistake. As a result of that, Blavatsky imprinted her moral dichotomy on me. Or let's say I was ready for the imprinting (I can't blame it on the old girl). Obviously I did reject a great deal of that by moving towards Crowley. Yet in many ways I'm still prosaic.

CSH: Then you rejected it again by moving towards Reich.

FIR: Yes, but that was much later, about 1950. But there was the earlier revolt against her rigid morality by gravitating towards Crowley which none of the rest of my theosophical family would have done. Or could have done. Poor Crowley had to live with my adolescent stiffness. He prodded me, but he was really very gentle and understanding to this 20 year old kid. I owe so much to him. Crowley never saw the material as contrary to the spiritual. This may be one reason he is not liked.

CSH: Didn't Eddy say poverty was a disease?

FIR: Eddy?

CSH: Mary Baker.

FIR: She's right! It took me a long time to appreciate that old girl. I never really appreciated her until I wrote *The Romance of Metaphysics* in 1939–40 [since republished as the *Teachers of Fulfillment*]. Even then, I didn't really appreciate what she said until probably 12 years ago.

CSH: What about her thing about not giving drugs to children when they were ill?

FIR: Oh that's overdoing it. Fanaticism of the worst kind. When kids had polio she kept saying that everything would be fine. Because in her mind the physical body didn't really exist, it was only an illusion.

She was crazy as all hell. But once you get her basic ideas in your bonnet of what she stood for however, it follows in a kind of logical sequence. A kind of illogical-logic.

CSH: If the physical body doesn't exist, why bother giving anything to it?

FIR: But the funny thing is, she knew that was a farce... because she loved money. And if the things of this world were unreal, why crave them?

The problem with people who read Eddy, and the people who read Crowley, or Jesus or Rajneesh or you or anyone else, is that they don't see the various sides of the author's personalities. They sort of choose one facet that they want to see. It is a sad thing.

CSH: Yes, they have to see only one facet. Just one facet. I guess they try to make whole pictures out of things which are not wholes in the real world sense. One body—therefore one personality, etc. This is why so many people have problems with themselves. This attitude doesn't lead one to have much hope for the human race in its present form.

FIR: That we know. It doesn't say much for the human race; they can't handle this sort of thing. Now we are really getting into trouble. (Laughter) Look at what they did to Reich!

Let's get back to Eddy. Apart from anything else, the old girl really was an amazing woman. The thing that I marvel at, since we know how difficult it is to change behavior patterns; here's a woman who was a failure, sick, rejected, a total failure up to the age of 60, and to make a turn-about at 60, I think is a real bloody miracle. So that's where she fits in as far as I'm concerned, with the whole notion of the magical and mystical experience which somehow changes a non-entity into an entity. Something must have happened to her—what? But whatever it was, it transformed her and made her into a dynamo. There are a lot of silly explanations floating about, but I don't believe most of them.

CSH: Did her transformation stop her from being frightened?

FIR: No, she was always frightened actually. She would go through these periods of let's say hysterical seizures, in which she'd have real paranoid notions that she was being attacked by malicious animal magnetism, which is a pure paranoid delusion. Her only safeguard against that, was to surround herself with all the faithful disciples she could muster. They would pray, and deny that there was any such thing as malicious animal magnetism. And this went on all her life. If you take the position that there is only goodness and light in the world then by her logic all else is an illusion, body included.

CSH: But she couldn't really believe that?

FIR: Well she did, theoretically. Only in theory, and then only to a limited extent. She transformed her life by this theory. But she was still subject to the same set of delusions.

CSH: Freudian repressions, would you say?

FIR: Yes. Which every now and then would bubble up. Something would happen as a prompt or stimulus and up they would come. And she was helpless. But it was labeled Animal Magnetism. God help any person in her environment on whom she put that label. They would really be persecuted, driven out from the flock.

CSH: Exiled, I bet, to California. (Laughter) What's Animal Magnetism—by her definition?

FIR: Somebody who directs a stream of evil thoughts which were probably all about sex (laughter) ...Most of her disciples were pure virginal maidens all afraid of their tails; this was malicious animal magnetism. A guy like you or me (ha!) would come along and make them aware of their sexual streamings and that's malicious animal magnetism. (Laughter) They would have to get rid of you immediately.

CSH: So she wouldn't have gotten along with Crowley very well?

FIR: (Laughter) You are really funny. Oh, no. He wouldn't have gotten along very well with her either! He wouldn't have gotten near her.

CSH: How do you explain the split that some people in the occult have about sex and spirituality?

FIR: Rather as Freud would explain it.

CSH: You don't see such a split between the spirit and sex.

FIR: No. None at all.

CSH: I don't think most people in the occult or the metaphysical field would share that with you.

FIR: No. But that's because they're not aware of the basic Freudian mechanisms or theories. Nor can they observe the operation of these mechanisms in themselves.

CSH: Or the demonstrations of Reich, either.

FIR: Oh, it's the same thing. One has to identify Reich with Freud. One is an evolution from the other. They're both rooted in the same ground, but neither of them would admit it. That's the abysmal stupidity of this whole field, too.

CSH: Does this explain why you don't want to bother with most people in the occult and psychology fields?

FIR: In a very large measure. As soon as they begin to talk it's offensive to me.

CSH: In which way?

FIR: Cosmic Foo-Foo. Flying saucers, star seeds, or whatever kind of crazy nonsense. All the stuff that's pure projection of their own need structures. Occasionally I will go to an occult bookstore here or there and browse around. I just listen to people talk. I don't say anything. Sometimes I may strike up a conversation to get them going. They don't recognize me—that is until now, with all these photos you've published. I'll prod them, and just listen to the crap that follows. You see you have gotten me in trouble again.

CSH: Are these type of people what you refer to as sweet and light?

FIR: Yes, that and more. I would also call them lazy and infantile. They give the field a bad reputation. For them there is no evil, no lust, there is no nothing. They have the planes all mixed up. Everything changes by just wishing. Everything is nice, pure and holy, which is *au fond* but not in their sense of the words.

CSH: Really they don't want to deal with anything.

FIR: No. Nothing! They're happy all the time…

CSH: Do you really think that?

FIR: No! Of course not. They're an abysmal mess. An abysmal mess.

CSH: That's probably one reason they don't like Crowley much.

FIR: He would chew up this Cosmic Foo-Foo and spit it out. Crowley made so many enemies simply by talking about sex, violence, etc., the way he did. And let me add this, you're creating a whole lot of enemies for us now in the opening of *The Complete Golden Dawn System of Magic,* where you talk about sex. You will create a whole lot of enemies right away.

CSH: Do you think we should take that section out?

FIR: No. Those kinds of people don't belong to the true tradition of the Golden Dawn anyway.

CSH: In what sense am I creating enemies?

FIR: Because this strikes a mortal blow to the very core of their existence.

CSH: How do you deal with that? You are a person who is, for lack of a better phrase, pro-sex, pro-life, etc.
FIR: Yes, I like it.

CSH: So here you are writing this material to a large group of people who, in essence, don't have the foggiest idea what you are talking about.
FIR: There is always a forlorn hope that a seed will drop somewhere. After all, it dropped on me! God, when I was 16 I was an inhibited mess. And then I saw the name Blavatsky in a book and that did the trick. That moved me on to other things. I say, you know I've had a charmed life in one sense. I've never really had to make any great effort to be progressive. I know you don't agree with me on this point, but I still have to stick to my guns here and I must say this comes from a very deep conviction that I'm really a very ordinary kind of character who had the good fortune, the luck, the insanity, whatever, to hook his wagon to two stars, almost by accident and got whirled away with it and from there all these other things occurred without really any effort on my part.

CSH: You might be ordinary in that sense, but a lot of people are ordinary and they never got whirled away nor do they do anything but live an ordinary life.
FIR: (Laughter) I'm lucky. This is what I say, the Gods have been very kind to me, very kind.

I was lucky, that's all. It's like that lovely story about the guy who picks up a girl and takes her to his room. They begin to talk the next morning. "How come a nice girl like you is in this room with me? You are a graduate of Vassar, a Ph.D., wealthy, etc., how come?" She says, "Well, I'm just lucky." So I'm in the same boat. I have been pursued by good luck. Not because of anything I've done. Almost in spite of what I've done.

CSH: Well, that's very rare.
FIR: Yes, it is. I've been so lucky, or had good Karma. Occasionally things just drop into my lap. Look, let's be very personal. What could be more lucky than having you come along, 20 years ago to learn Reichian therapy from me? And now just look at us today. We are involved in so many things together.

CSH: Can you talk further on your feeling of luck?
FIR: Yes. From the point of view of just plain bloody good accidental luck, I'm one of the luckiest bastards in the world really. Here I am, originally a little Jewish non-entity who somehow, with a stroke of good luck, got into things he could never have dreamed of—never. And without any education. I had one semester of high school, and then went to school at night admittedly.

CSH: Many occultists I've met have said, there's no such thing as luck! They believe that the person makes it all happen.

FIR: All right. Let's say someone is a Buddhist, we can speak in terms of good Karma or merit. I must have accumulated good merit in the past that has finally paid off in the form of what we call good luck now.

CSH: Do you buy that?

FIR: Yes. Oh sure. Intrinsically. So even though I explain it in my English way, I'm a perfectly ordinary guy, who then got so whirled up, so accidentally, into another kind of spiritual activity.

CSH: That will teach you to write letters to people like Crowley. (Laughter)

FIR: Yes (still laughing), it took 18 months for my letter to get there. But it got there. Now that really is pure accident. I wrote him in 1927 at his publishers 13 years after they went out of business.

In the meantime World War I had occurred. He had wandered around all over the damn place. He had no permanent address. He was a wanderer.

CSH: Like me?

FIR: No, he was worse than you'll ever be. He coined the right phrase himself, he was "a wanderer of the wastes." He couldn't settle down. He always had to be moving. He was a bit like Carr is now. Nothing could make Carr settle down, nothing, but that's another story—it's his true will which is great. But Crowley was worse. You know accident and destiny are the same thing. I equate them. Karma, destiny, accident, it's unmistakable.

CSH: I'd like to hear more about how you got started in all of this.

FIR: My sister brought home some of her cultish books on diet and health. I saw the name Blavatsky in one of these books. She was unfortunately ridiculed by the whole family, but she really brought culture to the home. She brought music, books, etc. Actually I am deeply indebted to her. So what could be more accidental than opening up one of her cultish books and seeing "Blavatsky"? There were of course other names mentioned there—why that particular one? I think it was just an awakening of an old Karmic tie. And why Crowley? I was at a meeting one night with a lawyer who had a copy of Crowley's book on Yoga. He had a half a dozen adoring neophytes, you know, he was parading as the great, wise man. So we sat around listening to him read in his pretentious legal voice, from Crowley's book. Boy, it got me! It awakened a high enthusiasm in me. So I had to get the name of the book, the author, and the address. And the address was 13 to 14 years old! I wrote him a letter and went off to Philadelphia to study at the art school there. Eighteen months later a letter came from the old man in Paris, which said, "I have your letter, get in touch with my representative in New York." I did so immediately. All this is a fantastic story, really. Pure accident. Why I would have stumbled into this...bred as we all were, in this atmosphere of complete repression, inhibition, patriarchy, etc. How could I have come out of that into this weird bloody wonderful world...it's a miracle, that's all I can say. My life is a series of miracles that have occurred in the most haphazard "accidental" way.

CSH: Let's switch topics for a moment.

FIR: O.K. What would you like to talk about?

CSH: Well...the "new" Christian movement.

FIR: Oh that! More enemies. O.K. I originally thought that the movement had some promise. Having steeped myself in Christian mysticism, my thought was when I first heard of the movement, that there was a revival taking place in Christian mysticism. And that's when I began to investigate. It took only a short while to realize it was completely hollow. It was a purely hysterical eruption.

CSH: It also seems very patriarchal and authoritarian.

FIR: Well, see it as the eruption of all their father images. Of course it's totally authoritarian. One of the weird things about it though, (and this is so funny), I never got one of them to explain this to me. The Pentecostals, the real originators of all this born-again stuff never celebrated Christmas. Apparently they believe that Christmas is a pagan holiday and not truly Christian.

CSH: So you spent some time investigating that organization?

FIR: Oh yes. About a year or so, hoping that there might be some real element of revival of the old ecstasies of St. John of the Cross, St. Theresa and other mystics.

CSH: In the gnostic tradition?

FIR: They'd die a million deaths rather than think of that.

CSH: How long do you think this movement will last?

FIR: So long as there are repressed and split people this movement will endure in one form or another; it always has. It's only in the last 100 years that it has been called Pentecostal. You know the lovely vision of St. Anthony, he was always tormented by visions of the devil and naked women, etc., so you know what was on his mind. They were basket cases, preoccupied with sin and the devil.

CSH: Don't you see any redemption in trying to be master of the flesh?

FIR: No. When confronted by temptation, yield. (Laughter)

CSH: And that's the only way to redemption? (Laughter)

FIR: Right. St. Paul said, "Shall we sin in order to be saved?" and he said no, but the answer is really yes! (Laughter) For how else can you be saved? Otherwise there is no point in salvation. But seriously for a moment, the flesh must be dealt with but not through any of the silly techniques provided by the current religions. And it must not be mastered on moral grounds, but simply on the functional grounds of wanting to be more than human. Lastly, for it to be mastered, it must first be fulfilled and respected; no repression, no denial, no punishment, no nonsense.

CSH: I have a question. What is evil?

FIR: From the Christian point of view, evil is your body, your sex drive. Sex is the beginning and the end of evil, as in the Adam and Eve story— original sin.

CSH: But what is it from the more enlightened point of view? What is evil?

FIR: Damned if I know. (Laughter) It gets into black and white magic... We were talking about that earlier over dinner. If you're doing something for yourself it's black magic. If you're doing something for someone else it's white magic. That to me sounds very silly. So if you're trying to improve yourself, then it's black magic, right? The whole idea of evil as it is commonly used is crazy. By the way, is there a grey magic?

CSH: You recommended psycho-therapy for those people seeking to embark on the Great Work. It seems that most people don't pay any attention to your advice.

FIR: Absolutely. But never mind whether they pay attention, I'll still insist on it. You see it is the only valid requirement for a sane occultism.

CSH: What school of therapy?

FIR: I don't care. Any school.

CSH: Jungian?

FIR: Even that. Once they've been exposed to even a little bit of it, it's like a virus, like herpes, it takes root.

CSH: I feel that therapy doesn't get deep enough.

FIR: I agree with you, but it makes a beginning, that's all I'm concerned with. As long as some entry can be made into their armor somewhere along the road, then it's all to the good. The rest will happen, by happenstance, Karma, accident, call it whatever you will.

CSH: At least we can hope for that.

FIR: I think we can count on it. I will. It may not show immediately, but after some years it will. Look what it's done for your friend. Your description of him was that he is almost human! Miracles do happen. Any kind of therapy I think is absolutely essential for someone in this field, because as a rule they have absolutely no insight whatsoever. Now if they've been slightly oriented to the Crowley point of view, they're a wee bit different. But they can still be completely balmy.

CSH: What type of therapy is best from your point of view?

FIR: Listen, I have my own experience of therapy. I had one year of Jungian, two years of Freudian, four years of Reichian. There is no comparison between them. The year of Jungian was a wasted year. The only thing it did for me, and this is the most important thing, it made me delve into Jungian literature. I became conversant with the lingo. It gave me a philosophy which still has its place in my life, but as therapy I think it's utterly useless. And all this business of active imagination and making an image of a figure in a dream and talking to it is plain mental masturbation.

CSH: A lot of them say it's similar to skrying.

FIR: There's a difference.

CSH: How would you differentiate?

FIR: Well, you've got a technique for dealing with the skrying to make sure it's not your imagination, to make sure that it's not delusion; you've got a technique for dealing with it.

CSH: In *The Complete Golden Dawn?*

FIR: Yes, sure. It's in the critique I wrote for the section on skrying. It didn't come over on the computer disk at first, but I think it's a pretty good critique.

CSH: Yes, I got that in the mail and I will process that.

FIR: Yes, that you've got to do. That's an important part of the whole business, I'd hate to have that omitted.

CSH: Colin Wilson recently said that he regarded you as the last living representative of the great occult tradition of the late 19th century, whose names included Blavatsky, Yeats, Mathers, Waite, Crowley and Dion Fortune. Also Francis King gave you credit for the revival of the esoteric tradition in the 1960s. Before you start shaking your head, Alan Watts and people like Leary and Wilson credit your work as having made a great contribution to the higher consciousness revolution. What are your feelings about these statements?

FIR: I'll accept the statement of King's and maybe that of Watts, Wilson and Leary. Yes, that I'll accept. I will say that's unequivocal. The other statement of placing me in the category of H.P.B. etc., this is a considerable exaggeration. I would like to believe that that's true, but in all common sense there isn't any justification. Blavatsky and Crowley are in a category all by themselves; leave out Yeats who I think is a lesser figure where this area is concerned. He may have been a considerable poet, but there is nothing in his history to indicate his great command of the magical tradition. Arthur Machen was another non-entity in this area too, though he was a very great novelist, and so forth. He was an advocate of the Waite school of the Golden Dawn, which is of no consequence...

There are a handful of very great traditional names in the occult move-ment that are worthy to be categorized all by themselves. I am not in that area. Nonetheless, I consider myself more in the nature of somebody who has taken seriously the work of H.P.B., Crowley and a few of the others, and popularized them in the sense of making them somewhat more intel-ligible to the layman.

CSH: Can you say more about the Golden Dawn?

FIR: The Golden Dawn was founded by, and was an offshoot of, some early Masonic Rosicrucian organizations in England. That is, they were so-called Rosicrucian orders that limited their membership to high grade Masons. There isn't too much evidence to indicate they knew a very great deal about esotericism as such. At least that is one of the common criticisms; I'm not sure about that. If Mathers and Wescott and Wood-man came out of the *Societas Rosicruciana* in Anglia, if they came out of that, they were pretty well informed, so I think it would be fallacious to assume that they were merely masonic dilettantes as claimed by the arch-heretic critic, Ellic Howe. What it stood for, was what similar organiza-tions throughout the ages have stood for, the teaching of a form of eso-tericism which expressed the spirit of the age. Now by esotericism we mean a form of teaching which can be found in every clime, in every country, in every religion, as when Jesus said to his disciples, "to the multitude I speak in parables, to you I speak in plain ordinary language." Well the ordinary language was the esotericism, and the parables are the nonsense that the lay folk accept about religion or philosophy and all the occult sciences. The Golden Dawn, in some manner, managed to obtain access to various phases of the occult arts, some of which have been known earlier, in fact many of them can be found in the British Museum. But, even so, Mathers and Wescott gave them a new twist that made them more intelligible and more readily grasped by the modern man. Apart from that, however, there was a very great deal of teaching that didn't come from the British Museum, that didn't come from ancient manuscripts, that in some manner which I don't purport to understand, or wish to explain at the moment, they had access to great quantities of teaching that was unique to the Golden Dawn. For example, the Enoch-ian System, so-called, was known before, in very rudimentary form. But as Dr. Head once pointed out, Dee and Kelley obtained a great deal of material, but they hadn't the faintest idea how to use it. Under the stimu-lus of the genius of the Golden Dawn, primarily Mathers, this was trans-formed into an encyclopedic synthesis that included every minute portion of the current Golden Dawn teaching, and was made into a workable sys-tematic whole.

CSH: What is the practical purpose of the Golden Dawn?

FIR: What is the practical purpose of so many modern systems? That is to render a person whole. To give them more insight into their meaning, into their significance, into their functions as human beings, this is their goal. Where they came from, where they are now, and whither they are going. It's a method of developing a whole person, who is aware of all the hidden facets of his whole nature and knows how to bring them into play at will.

CSH: It seems to be a very lofty goal. How does the Golden Dawn attempt to accomplish this?

FIR: It attempts to accomplish this by certain exercises, by meditations and by ritual. All three of them were combined together in a very skillful manner, so that the student who really was, let us say, a person capable of initiating his own progress, of being a self-starter, would be able to take this vast body of knowledge and apply it to himself and thus, to use one of the phrases in the Adeptus Minor Grade, to gradually unite himself to his essential divinity and thus become more than human.

CSH: You've mentioned over the years that you've experienced disappointment in some people who have been attracted to the Golden Dawn and to the occult in general, and have made some prescriptions that are available to the general public to remedy this problem. Can you clarify this point?

FIR: All right, yes. I'll get myself in trouble again. (Laughter) Many of them are dilettantes, many of them are somewhat unbalanced people, and many of them are highly neurotic people. Some of them are just plain escapists, using occultism and magic as means of escaping from their own personal, emotional and neurotic problems. This is not the function of the Golden Dawn, or any other legitimate occult system. I'm critical of many of them, not merely of the dilettantes that I've just called attention to, but even of the better names, like Crowley, for whom I've enormous admiration at the same time. I've put that on record in many places and I regard him as one of the great figures in the history of occultism. But nonetheless, for example, when he published the Golden Dawn material, either he or his editors (which included some great names), somehow botched up the whole editing job. In Equinox 2 and 3 a great deal of the Golden Dawn teaching was given, but it was so doctored and so distorted, that if that were left there without recourse to any other body of knowledge, it would seem most inadequate. Crowley's genius was so great, that while he understood the Golden Dawn System well, he had very little ability to bring it down to the level of the layman with whom he was going to deal. He wasn't going to spend his life with geniuses of this kind, because there are too few of those around. So he was going to have to begin with little people, silly people. But, he had no patience with them, and, he had very little ability to bring down this vast body of knowledge to their level. I have to admit, without patting myself on the back, that I am one of the little people who had the ability to take some of this profound teaching, to succeed where Crowley failed in making it a coherent body of knowledge, to bring it to the level of, let's say, the man of average intelligence. Not so that he who runs may read, but that he who stands still and studies would be able to discern it in a coherent useful body of knowledge that might enable him to transcend the ordinary limitation of the unenlightened human state and achieve a higher so-called cosmic consciousness.

CSH: It is said by some that organizations like the Golden Dawn have at their bag a form of elitism.

FIR: I will accept that totally. I would say that The Golden Dawn is an elitist system. Even in its heyday during the late 90s and in the early part of this century, there probably were never more than 250 people at most in all the manifold temples in England. And yet, those 250 people, and that body of knowledge, even after the rebellions that resulted in the breakup of the Order into component parts, have nonetheless leavened the whole of occultism and brought about a great dispersal of this kind of information. It is my fervent hope that as time goes on, and as this knowledge becomes more available to a greater and greater number of people, this elitism will spread. That is, it is for those few who are willing to take evolution into their own hands, and make these attempts to transform themselves. The great mass of people are quite willing to drift along. They want no part or have no idea of voluntary forms of evolution, self-induced or self-devised.

CSH: How would you differentiate elitism from sweet and light occultism?

FIR: Let's go with the elitist first. The elitist belongs to no particular class, no particular race and to no particular sect. They are individuals who have courage enough, insight enough, determination and persistence enough, to take life into their own hands to proceed with the job of dealing with the reality of themselves, good, bad or indifferent, and attempt to wield themselves into a coherent whole. The "sweet and lighters," to use a name coined by one modern teacher—are metafizzlers. They are metaphysical people who see only good, and sweetness and light; nothing else exists for them. There is no evil in the world, there are no bad people, there are only good people gone a little bit sour, but all is light and sweet. The realists and elitists, the Golden Dawn Adepts, if you like, have no such delusions.

CSH: So the Golden Dawn Adept, ideally, would be a person who would be willing and able to face all components of his own personality, without either ignoring them, repressing them or denying them. The "sweet and light" people simply ignore anything that doesn't fit in with their preconceived ideas or wishes.

FIR: Right. In the Golden Dawn, in the rituals of Practicus or the Philosophus grade, there is a nice phrase extrapolated from the Chaldean Oracles, so-called, in which it says, "Nature teaches us, and the oracles also affirm, that even the evil germs of matter may alike be made useful and good." In other words, there is nothing in man, absolutely nothing, which cannot be used in order to further the Great Work, to further his own psycho-spiritual development into an integrated, illuminated human being. There were several passages in some of the rituals and in some of the documents of the Golden Dawn, which speak of the "evil persona," the Qlippoth, the so-called evil elements of man. When mastered and put in their proper place, they may serve him as a mighty steed, a powerful beast whereupon he may ride to wherever he wants to go.

CSH: That viewpoint sounds very similar to Jung's and Reich's ideas.

FIR: Exactly. There is little difference. The rejected elements are always latent and when given enough provocation and stimulus will always rise up to haunt the individual when he least expects it. Therefore they have to be faced, dealt with, and incorporated into the very heart of one's being.

CSH: You make the point over and over again that it is your desire, in fact your demand, that any person desiring to be a neophyte and take his place in the Golden Dawn, go through some form of intensive therapy which will help him realize some of these shadowy factors and integrate them into his personality, so as not to be overwhelmed by the immense forces that are released through the Golden Dawn teachings and practices. From what you have mentioned to me privately from time to time, this is not happening. This must be a great disappointment to you.

FIR: It is a tremendous disappointment. In fact, something has happened in recent years over which I feel rather betrayed. One person to whom I spoke some years ago, and who attempted to form a new Golden Dawn Temple, swore to me by all that was good and holy, that this would be one of the basic rules that would be insisted upon—that any incoming member of the Order would be required to engage in some form of psychotherapy. And we agreed on ANY form; it didn't make any difference whether it was Jungian, Freudian, Reichian, Adlerian, Eclectic or what, as long as they had enough psychotherapy of any kind to make them aware of this vast area which can be colloquially called the unconscious. Parts of themselves which they do not know, and have not known, but which have to be brought into purview of the whole self and incorporated into the total self. As time went on, this person intoxicated by the apparent growth of the Temple, dropped this proviso that we both had agreed upon, and which was one of the factors that I insisted on if I was to give any help. As a result, all sorts of squabbles have recently overtaken the temple, over which I wash my hands altogether. Recently, as a result of these squabbles, I am informed by the Hierophant that it has been decided, therefore, to reinstate the original rule, to insist that all newcoming members between the grade of Neophyte and Adeptus Minor have at least a minimum of 100 hours of any form of psychotherapy. I feel a great deal better about the 100 hours; it's still nowhere near enough, but the hope that I have secretly, is that by the time they've had 100 hours of psychotherapy they will realize the enormous need they have for further depth psychotherapy in order to prepare them for the great stresses and strains that the Great Work imposes on the organism. They will be willing to go further, and therefore follow it through to the end, thus incorporating the experience of psychotherapy into the experience of the Great Work. In other words, one is part of the other. Psychotherapy is the preparation, and the Great Work, the magical procedure of the Golden Dawn, call it whatever name you will, is the fulfillment of the promise that is revealed by, let's say, the preliminary hours and years of psychotherapy.

CSH: Some people would say that you are pretty tough in your demands for gaining this knowledge and insight. They might feel that all is really necessary is their love for the Great Work and their intellectual commitment.

FIR: Sincerity, intellect and love are nowhere near enough. Nowhere near enough. It reminds me of the title of a book by a prominent psychoanalyst in recent years, *Love Is Not Enough*. Love is *not* enough in the Great Work. The history of the Golden Dawn is replete with people who had love, devotion, intellect and all the other so-called great virtues, but nonetheless nothing came of their efforts. The Order went down to oblivion. The Order was torn asunder by strife, warfare, by internecine conflicts, by rebellions. A great deal of that *might,* and I use that word advisedly, might have been obviated by most of the members taking psychotherapy. Now I say *might,* admittedly, because we know that even in the very psychoanalytic organizations, even though the members did have psychoanalysis, psychotherapy in one form or another, they were still split at times by personality squabbles, by differences of opinion. However these organizations exist in full force today. They have not gone down to oblivion, like the Golden Dawn did. Only now is there a hope for its complete resurrection. But let's say that it is one form of psychic insurance that there will be less turmoil and destruction than might otherwise be the case.

CSH: Some people in the occult field are very critical about the use of what are known as psychedelic drugs. What is your feeling about this?

FIR: I'd have to remark first of all, that the Golden Dawn, *per se*, never approved of the use of psychedelics or any drugs. That's only one part of the story. The other part of the story is that throughout history, as far back as we can go, we know there is evidence, that many of the gurus in India, Tibet, Israel, and other parts of the world, relied on the use of psychedelics for many purposes. Crowley probably had the wisest and sanest approach to this whole problem, and that was that the beginner in the Great Work only has vague hopes of achieving certain psycho-spiritual states; he has no direct knowledge of them. Therefore, with the judicial use of some of these drugs he might be given a foretaste of where he is going, and what he is working for. Once he tasted that, once having experienced that, he might be willing to make the expenditure of time and effort in following the other exercises and disciplines that would help him to get to where he wants to go without the aid of drugs.

CSH: Some people who I have talked to over the years have said that there is no need for psychotherapy, no need for the Golden Dawn, no need for self-work. They firmly believe that the simple use of these substances would be more than sufficient to bring a person to their higher and divine self.

FIR: Totally untrue, as I know you would agree from your own observations. I don't think there is any evidence to support and warrant that. The drugs produce a state which is akin and analogous to some of the mystical states. But as the drug wears off, so does the state wear off, and there is very little recollection and very little endurance of the psychedelic state. So therefore, that idea really doesn't hold water. The combination of the use of the psychedelics AND the various disciplines, train the mind, train the psyche, train the organism of the student or the practitioner, to retain within his consciousness, within his organism not merely consciousness *per se,* but to retain the memory of the spiritual state he has experienced, and therefore enable him AT WILL to return to that state whenever he so desires.

CSH: To change topics on you quickly, what are the mysterious Rosicrucians? Are they similar to the Secret Chiefs? (Laughter)

FIR: They were not ever spoken of as Secret Chiefs. It was a group of unknown people who were quite evidently Christians, Christian mystics, who had apparently become aware of the mystical traditions which predated their Lord by aeons. By the way, one of the legends states that one of them, the very father of the Order, Christian Rosencreutz, had been brought up in a Catholic monastery, and at an early age had traveled all over Europe and the middle East and North Africa, where he had been initiated into the Qabalah, alchemy and magic, etc. and brought it back to Europe, to his native monastery. There he initiated three or four of his brethren and thus began the Rosicrucian Order. Some critics are inclined to say that is mythology. Be that as it may, and it may well be mythology, but by the end of the 17th century, there were small bodies of people which had sprung up using the three Rosicrucian classics as the basis for their fraternity and were teaching the Qabalah, magic and alchemy, obviously in a very secret way.

The Protestant and Catholic churches would have made very short work of them if they had come out in the open with that kind of knowledge. But they were attracting bodies of people to them, or small groups of people and setting up organizations which used the word Rosicrucian in one way or another. Some of them infiltrated the Masonic Order which had its origin around the same time, the early part of the 18th century. In fact there was a degree in one of the rites, the Scottish Rite, which is called the Rose Croix degree. This may imply that some of the Rosicrucian bodies had made a link with the Masons as a means of perpetuating their knowledge. This is one theory. The other theory is that the Jesuits who were intent on destroying the Rosicrucians and the Masons had set up phony degrees as a means of bringing discredit to this Rosicrucian movement.

CSH: I noticed when I said "Secret Chiefs" you laughed a bit.

FIR: I laugh...it's a difficult subject to handle. First of all I don't like dealing overtly with the topic of Secret Chiefs because the whole thing has been so abused by idiotic people that almost to talk about them means reducing oneself to their superstitious and psychotic level.

CSH: This is a good chance to make YOUR point about this problem public. People do walk around saying "the Secret Chiefs said this or that."

FIR: Of course they do. They are idiots or worse. That's why I dislike talking about it except to say that most of the people who do talk about it are talking out of their hats. However, where there is smoke, there is some little fire. And I am willing to admit that there may be some few beings in the flesh, as human beings, who live here and there, without our being aware of them, who have "super-normal power" and "super-normal knowledge" that enable them to direct the destinies of organizations like the Golden Dawn or other movements. But there is no point in going hunting for them because if they are Secret Chiefs they are going to remain Secret Chiefs and you'd be much wiser leaving the whole topic alone. If they want you they will come looking for you. You don't have to go looking for them. It's like in the theatrical business, the agent says, "Don't ring me, I'll ring you." So the point is, don't bother looking for the Secret Chiefs. If you are going to be of any importance to the Great Work, to the Golden Dawn or any similar organizations, if you have the potentiality of being useful they will somehow look you up. All your searching in the world is never going to help you find them, never. So leave them alone and go about doing your business whatever that may be, meditation, ritual magic, or all the other allied facets of the Great Work, go ahead and do that and develop your own self to the best of your ability, then maybe one of these days if all goes well, and if you can be useful to the Great Work, one of them may come along and say "Look here, buster, you've got some more work to do and we'll help you." Even if something like that did happen I would advise that your ego be in its proper place.

CSH: That is a great explanation. How do you differentiate the Western Esoteric tradition from the Eastern Esoteric tradition?

FIR: In reality there isn't a great deal of difference. The difference is largely one of terminology. For example, I have toyed with the idea of making a comparison of Mahayana Buddhism and the Tibetan system with the Golden Dawn. They are very similar. There isn't that much difference. So far as the Hindu systems are concerned, they are more sweet and light than the Western and the Tibetan systems. The Tibetan systems are very much like the Western systems to me. They're tough-minded and they don't encourage the sweet and light love tripe that is characteristic of the Hindu system. The Tibetan systems and the Western are very similar. The Hindus stress more than sweet and light. They're more loving, and at the same time much more ego-expansive in that they identify themselves with God after certain experiences, and so forth, which in the West is done with a great deal more caution.

CSH: You seem to have little trust or respect for organizations and groups who are promoting love as the basis of their system and the cure-all for everything.

FIR: I have very little trust for them. Which is not to say that I don't think love in that sense of the word is terribly important. But I don't like the tossing around of the word LOVE, I don't like this kind of sloppy sentimentality. It usually usurps every other kind of real work. They merely sit around and talk. God loves you, Jesus loves you, Buddha loves you...they do very little work and nothing is accomplished.

CSH: So in a certain sense you could be considered another western master of work as some people have called Crowley the great Master of work. He did not let his people sit around and talk all day about how much they love each other. Instead he demanded effort out of everything they did. Worship is work.

FIR: I don't consider myself a master—in no way. Let's say I'm an advocate of work and not a master. He may be a master. I'm not. The less gab they have, the less emphasis on I love you, you love me, God loves us, and I love God, the more emphasis on facts. Look, you're a human being, and you've got a certain amount of guts—use it as a means of scaling the ladders of achieving the heights. Love and God will take care of themselves. First be yourself, damn it, and stop talking about things you have no understanding of. This is my attitude.

CSH: That's a great statement. And even though you don't regard yourself as a master, many do. This idea about Love and Work leads me to another question. Why is there such a separation between the body and the spirit in this work? This to me seems not only false but very sad.

FIR: It's very sad actually, yes. This is one of the many reasons why I insist that anybody getting into the Golden Dawn, the Great Work, MUST precede any practical work with some psychotherapy, because the experience of any form of psychotherapy will at least make the student aware that he does have a real sexuality and a rich emotional creative life which must not be bottled up, repressed or inhibited. He must always realize that repression only leads to compulsion in one form or another and interferes with the accomplishment of his goals. Therefore we must rid ourselves of both repression and compulsion. One of the best ways of accomplishing this goal is through Reichian therapy. But as I said before, any form of psychotherapy will go far towards ridding the student of his armoring, thus aiding in the acquisition of real insight which is the first step towards the emergence of spiritual understanding and illumination.

CSH: That seems to be what the Tantra Yogis were saying as well. Tantra, of course, is concerned with "method-technique." It is not simply concerned with sex as is commonly thought. It seems that Tantra posits the view that the power and force of the sex instinct can be used to make something happen—maybe a peak experience or enlightenment. They approach the whole idea of sex differently, very differently from the Semitic religions and Hinduism. Western religions are always worried about sex—it is an obsession with them. There are always co-conditions for partaking of pleasure—marriage, love, children—always conditions. Why do you think such a split has occurred between sex and spirit?

FIR: That's really a very complex thing, and is not readily answered. Suffice it to say that it has developed and it's dangerous, very dangerous. It doesn't intrinsically belong to the Great Work. In the Great Work every phase of one's makeup has to be used, employed and integrated to make a whole. Nothing can be denied. Nothing. To exclude one's sexuality is really to ask for a very great deal of trouble in the development of neurotic and even psychotic traits. In modern times, the only thing I can assume is that some of the exponents of the system had neurotic problems of their own. However much I admire H.P.B., and I've put myself on record on this and I will stand by it, I have the greatest admiration for the old girl, but nonetheless, she was brought up as a Christian, as a member of the Eastern Orthodox Church and she's inherited all the worst aspects of Christian inhibition where sexuality is concerned.

Whatever the Indian influences she encountered over the years merely strengthened her negative attitudes towards sexuality.

CSH: There is almost the same thing about money and the Great Work.

FIR: Yes. It's almost as if most hold the Christian point of view. It is all a bunch of nonsense. One of the motivations of this, I think, and Mathers has expressed this somehow in one of the Golden Dawn writings, is that one may get too caught up in self-indulgence that he fancies money will bring. You can do whatever you want to, get anything you want to with money, and therefore become a little bit lax in one's devotion to the Great Work. It's a damn poor argument actually, because the same thing is true of poverty. You can get so attached to poverty that you groan and grunt about it and then begin to use all sorts of excuses, "I don't do this and I can't do that, because at the moment I'm too poor to have a gown, I'm too poor to have a room where I can meditate, I'm too poor to have a temple, etc."

CSH: As one of the great gurus said, a man with no clothes who sits under a tree and meditates, can and often does, become attached to his place under the tree. So in that sense what you are saying is that it is not the problem with materiality, money, sex, or ego *per se,* it is the blind attachment to anything which creates the problem.

FIR: It's the person himself who is the problem. He stands in his own way. And again I insist that this is why some form of psychotherapy is needed... To get rid of these neurotic attachments or fixations to sex, to money, to the parents, to the ego, or whatever. Nothing really happens until this is done.

CSH: As we know there has been a growing hatred of the occult movement by the born again Christians. It almost seems that where the cross goes, so goes the sword. What do you feel about their fanaticism and their potential for violence?

FIR: I find this is characteristic of all the Semitic religions, Judaism, Christianity and Mohammedanism, have always been spread by the sword. They are the great scourge on the escutcheon of the West. For example, when one reads in the Bible about the entry of the primitive tribes of Israel led by Moses and Joshua and the Kings into the land of Canaan, it was always with the sword. They went in and wiped out thousands of people in the name of Jehovah and took over the land. Then along come the Christians who did exactly the same thing. They were thoroughgoing barbarians, and spread the cross with the sword. Some of the most awful crimes against mankind were committed during the Crusades. That makes gruesome reading. Another set of gruesome reading materials is to be found in the conquest of the Americas—Mexico, Peru, etc., where the friar, the monk, went hand in hand with the soldiers to convert with the sword and with the garrote. The same thing is going on today. If the born-agains, if the Christians, had their way, they would suppress every particular poisonous brand. So Christianity hasn't changed much in the last 2,000 years, the cross and the sword still going together. In fact one of the most popular Christian hymns is "Onward Christian Soldiers... Marching on to war with the cross of Jesus, etc..."

CSH: Do you feel that they are going to gain more power as time goes on?

FIR: Yes, I do feel that they are going to gain more power in the next 50 to 100 years, but I have the intuition, or the optimistic feeling, that this nonetheless is the last dying gasp, or the last gasp of a dying religion. The day of Christianity is relatively over. They seem to be more powerful at the moment, and in many ways they are, but there is also a riptide, a backlash, going on which is also highly antagonistic to their activities. There is going to be a fearful clash in the near future which will result, I think, in the total elimination of Christianity altogether. There is the rise of the Oriental religions. The Moslems are no longer taking things sitting down and letting the Christians walk all over them. They are becoming more militant, which I say is fine for the moment. Let them become more militant, and let the Christians become more militant. They may wipe each other out to leave the world safe for those who want to go their own way in the search for truth.

CSH: The Christians would regard, I guess, The Golden Dawn and its teachings as black magic or...devil worship. (Laughter)

FIR: And heretical and so on and on. Ha!

CSH: Why do you think they would say that about us? (Laughter)

FIR: Let's say when the Rosicrucians began in the early part of the 17th century, the Christian Church and the Jesuits thought any deviation from the dogma laid down by the Church was heretical and should be investigated by the Inquisition. The victims were given over to the stake.

CSH: So can we posit that the born again Christians are becoming another form of inquisition?

FIR: They are indeed. Indeed. I fear it's very, very dangerous. We won't mention any names, but there is a very prominent preacher on T.V. who I'm sure would love to institute an Inquisition and get rid of all those who don't follow his particular brand of insanity.

CSH: I wonder who that could be? (Laughter) Robert Anton Wilson mentioned his name in his book *Prometheus Rising* (New Falcon Publications) for which you wrote an introduction. Bob is very optimistic about the coming age, *The New Age*, as he sees it, and he is very optimistic about the effects of technology and life extension, etc. I know that in many ways you agree with him and you feel very happy that there is this feeling in the air, but at the same time you have some strong doubts about this.

FIR: I am in almost total agreement with him, but I have the gravest doubts that it is going to occur in the immediate future. He believes before the year 2000 we will have space colonies, and that Christianity will no longer be as vociferous as it is, and that we will be entering the New Age. I don't feel quite so optimistic. It is too utopian. And I don't trust utopias. I think it's going to take some hundreds of years before we really get rid of the pernicious effects of the born-again Christians and Christianity as a whole. Probably a couple of hundred years. It's going to peter out slowly (no pun intended). It'll go through various retrogressions and surges of power, alternating, but eventually in a couple of hundred years it will fizzle out and then new religious forms, new religious expressions, that will be much more allied to the method of science, will come into being. But before this there will be Holy Wars. I hate to say it, but in many ways I don't have to say it.

CSH: You have expressed concern for this civilization elsewhere in this interview and I hear this concern again. Can you say more?

FIR: Yes I am, but we needn't feel too badly about that... civilizations have risen, come to maturity, and then died. That's an old but true story of all things. Everything has its origin, birth, maturity, and death. Cultures are no different. America, which I love, is no different. The way the Christian culture in the last 2,000 years has dealt with the world is nothing to make a very great fuss about. It is apparent that the time is coming when it's going down to destruction. If my memory serves me right, over a hundred years ago, H.P.B. wrote somewhere in *The Secret Doctrine* that western civilization is coming to an end. How soon, she didn't know, but she certainly said within the next century. Apparently one of her predictions is about to come to pass. Whether it does or not (although I fancy that it will), I want to see the Great Work (The Golden Dawn and other worthy systems) preserved in another part of the world, so that students there will have the wherewithal to continue their Way if anything disastrous does happen.

CSH: Falcon has published *The Eye in the Triangle: An Interpretation of Aleister Crowley,* and *The Legend of Aleister Crowley.* Sales are good and we are pleased. However we are unhappy that so many serious occult students fear him or hate Crowley. Can you provide any insights into this unfortunate phenomenon.

FIR: I don't know that any of my insights are new, but I think a great deal of that was due to his own ego. He had a colossal ego. He was almost like the Ford Company—every knock is a boost. (Laughter) So he didn't mind having himself damned, so long as it was done publicly, and that it gave him notoriety, giving the world notice that he was around. He kept all his foibles, however many there were, always brought to the forefront so that the world was aware of Aleister Crowley and his pranks. If he committed adultery, which one or two people still do today, he made a point of insuring that everybody knew about it. And, if on occasion, he indulged in homosexuality, he publicized that too. If he took drugs, he made sure that everybody knew about that also. Moreover he fabricated all sorts of lovely stories to blacken his reputation further; that he sacrificed children and killed women. All that is a lot of poppycock. It gave him notoriety. He was having a wonderful time, having a good laugh at the expense of the general public. What he didn't realize, and this shows that despite his genius what a damn fool he was, there were journalists and writers who took him seriously, and really condemned him for this sort of thing. And actually lived off him. They made a lot of money off him. Some of them even took seriously his statement that he killed male children, 150 of them a year. Obviously, if they had read the footnote involved, they would have realized that he was speaking in terms of symbolism, and that he was having intercourse 150 times a year. And that was all there was to it. But some of these people licked their chops and thought this was a rotten, dirty old man.

He made good copy, so they really lambasted him. Thus a great deal of his bad reputation, despite everything else creative that he did, has to be laid to his own door. I have very little sympathy really with what he did, because if he wanted to leave his mark on mankind without these black marks against him, he could have done it very easily. But his ego ran away with him, and he thought he was having a wonderful lark, not taking time out to consider that everybody didn't have the same kind of humor that he did. They took all his jokes seriously and now they are coming home to roost. One reviewer in the *Los Angeles Times* many years ago, in reviewing Crowley's autobiography says, "Crowley was a Victorian hippy." Be that as it may, Victorian hippies are no different from modern hippies. They don't go around killing 150 babies a year and publicizing it and not winding up in jail. Crowley was an idiot insofar as he did that. Now he had his own rationalizations for that, and most of them were that he was intent on destroying the old set of morals and the old set of clichés about human behavior, so therefore what he did should be made public so as to get rid of the guilts that were attached to sex, etc. Apparently it didn't work out that way.

CSH: Some people say that Crowley, if he were alive today, would look quite normal in Los Angeles, or San Francisco or New York.

FIR: Oh, there's no question about that. He'd be just one of thousands and maybe millions. EXCEPT, of course, his genius would still make him stand out more vigorously.

CSH: But in terms of his homosexuality?

FIR: ...in San Francisco it would not be noticed. But his genius would still shine very brightly.

CSH: In 1984 Falcon published Crowley's *The World's Tragedy*. You wrote an introduction to this book, and you considered it to be very iconoclastic.

FIR: There were two things that stamped that book as iconoclastic, and gave it a very small distribution in 1910, when it was first published. First, it was very anti-Christian, and the second, he overtly advertised the fact that he was a homosexual, that he was a sodomite, and that the book, therefore, was not to be sold in England. It might be sold anywhere else, but not in England. It might be sold anywhere else, but not in England, or he would have wound up in jail, since sodomy was against the law. His attack on Christianity was really a lampoon. It's very, very funny, and it's very blasphemous, and very eloquent, and I'm sure most of the good Christians today would find it very, very offensive. They found it offensive in 1910, and despite the amount of anti-Christian books that have been written in the last 60 to 70 years, it would still strike a number of Christians as very painful to their very, very delicate nerves. But it was a combination of those two things, his avowed homosexuality, and his total and complete contempt and hatred of Christianity, which earned that book a reputation which prevented it from being published again.

CSH: Some people have said you were in love with four "things" in your life...

FIR: Wine, women and song. (Laughter)

CSH: That's only three. (Laughter) But how do you see now these four loves of yours? (H.P.B., Crowley, The Golden Dawn and Reich.)

FIR: Yes, I would say that, Yes. I would say that Blavatsky was my first love. I say that she has influenced me more profoundly than almost any other occultist. I use the word occultist truly in her case, rather than occult writers. I first read her when I was about 16, and studied her for years, and occasionally still study her. I can still open up *The Secret Doctrine* with a great deal of curiosity, and before too long find myself really involved and engrossed, and can read for a couple of hours, finding it even more illuminating than I did 60 years ago. From her, of course

I ventured afield into areas indicated by her and discovered Crowley. With him, of course, my contact was much more personal than it was with H.P.B. That's because I never knew her; she died around 1890, and of course, I wasn't born for another 17 years. But Crowley was alive when I was still a young man, and without going into a number of details, I met him to become his secretary for some few years, and had a good deal of contact with him. From him I learned a very, very great deal. What I learned from him is very difficult to put into words. I don't think I learned a great deal of magic from him; I did learn a great deal of magic from his writings. *The Equinox* especially. I soaked myself in the volumes of *The Equinox* for years, and knew them backwards and forwards, inside out, etc. Crowley somehow had an enormous maturing effect on me. I was a young boy when I met him, I had just turned 20. Somehow, in his own inimitable way, he helped me to grow up and become something of an adult. I owe him a very, very great deal, a very great deal. Later we fell out, which was due to my own stupidity. After I recovered from my annoyance of a quarrel with him, I reestablished my admiration for him, and my love, if you like, and still hold him in the highest esteem, although I am a great deal more objective about him now that I ever was before. So that accounts for Blavatsky and Crowley. Then there is Wilhelm Reich. I discovered him around 1947. Again we don't need to go into the how and why. I became enamored of him almost immediately. Within a very short period of time got myself involved in Reichian therapy, in which I stayed for four years. Reich and I had a number of personal communications, which must remain private. I explain why in my book on Reich to be published in 1984. Lastly there is the Golden Dawn. In 1932 Crowley went off to Europe to show his paintings in Berlin, where subsequently they were destroyed by the Nazis. Anyway, he was gone for several years, and I was left at loose ends. At that time I became secretary to Thomas Burke just to keep me going. In that time I started my first literary work. I wrote two books, *The Garden of the Pomegranates,* an outline of the Qabalah, which wasn't too good; it was a series of notes that were thrown together. That was followed by *The Tree of Life* which Riders commissioned me to write. I told them what I had in mind, and they gave me £50, that was $250, which to me in those days was a great deal of money. In three or four months, I turned out *The Tree of Life* which, though a good book, languished for a long while. A copy of it came to the attention of The Golden Dawn people through the medium of Dion Fortune. Much to my surprise, one of the chiefs of The Golden Dawn in Bristol came to visit me, and to my further astonishment, invited me to join. One of them had had a vision that a young man with an important book would join the Order. So they identified that with me and *The Tree of Life* and since I was at a loose end, Crowley being gone, etc. etc., I accepted it. And that was one of the wisest moves that I have ever made in my life. It was there, then, that much of my magical knowledge and experience came to fruition, and were organized. For awhile I had a teacher in the form of the Golden Dawn chiefs who lavished a good deal of care and training on me, etc., etc. I am grateful to them... Very! That was a very important part of my life... It is impossible to say which is more important. All of them were, in their own ways and probably, of the four, Crowley and The Golden Dawn were the most valuable. They have left indelible marks on my life, and my career if I want to use that term, but certainly on my personal life. Crowley first, and The Golden Dawn second. On the other hand, I cannot separate Crowley from The Golden Dawn, because Crowley was The Golden Dawn, and The Golden Dawn was Crowley. Crowley was, to use one of my earlier clichés, a graduate without honor from the Golden Dawn. He took the Golden Dawn teaching and transformed some of it, used other bits of it literally, but still it was all based on The Golden Dawn, even though he gave his Order another name, the A∴A∴. So I felt very much at home in The Golden Dawn, and really had no problem absorbing the material, sailing through it very, very rapidly just as Crowley had many years earlier.

CSH: Now you're a few days from being 78, you've seen a lot of things, you've done a lot of things. What are your present interests and what would you like to do?

FIR: Wine, women and song. (Laughter) Gosh, that sure sounds like Crowley, doesn't it? It's true I love good wine, beautiful women, and good music more than I ever did before! My other interests (laughter) in life are the same as they've been for the last 60 years. In other words, I am devoted and dedicated to the Great Work and I want to see it spread. I want to see The Golden Dawn renewed, reformed, started by young, vigorous, alive people with a system made much more rigid and elite in the sense of deliberately imposed discipline, with psychotherapy made an intrinsic part of the program. Teaching some of different, nonetheless it still fits in with the general framework as being an account of a simplified magical system with all the depth left out and simply relying upon a kind of auto-suggestion, if you like. Like the ritual of Thoth, which really consists of auto-suggestive and mnemonic phrases which are in better English than most of the Christian Science affirmations, but still consist of the same sort of thing. Yoga, particularly hatha yoga and a few others, is not much different in essence from my interest in Reich and relaxation techniques. Or rather Yoga is an elaborate extension of Reich. So later when I discovered Reich and his breathing techniques, it wasn't really that new to me. It was already part and parcel of the yoga system which I'd almost grown up in many, many years earlier. The only thing that was new was Reich's point of view, the whole idea of the muscular armor, the character armor, but then there was nothing really tremendously new about that either, because that was an outcropping of Freud, the superego, etc., etc. It all fits together whether anyone likes it or not. The Reichians won't like what I say, nor will some of the yogis, but there it is. I have never been a true believer of any *one* thing. I take what's best for me and leave the rest behind. This is one reason I make people mad. It's hard to box me in as a pure anything. I use all and everything.

CSH: If you were to sum up life in one sentence, what would you say?

FIR: It's a weird bloody business! I have no other cliché for life. Life is a pain at times, getting old is a pain, but I accept that. I only feel that old YHVH must have been drunk when he created this mess. Many things are arse backwards. Many are simply funny. But I firmly believe that you must have a sense of humor about the whole business, particularly if you get into this sort of work. Most people in the occult have no sense of humor. This is so important, as you try to show in your own book, *Undoing Yourself With Energized Meditation.* I know most people won't understand it. It's too complex, it's not a thing that someone can cling to. You don't let your reader rest. You're always throwing things at him. You're showing him so much. I still hold that someday it will be a classic in the field, but most people are too scared, too rigid to live through that book. Life is life, and from the occult point of view, we somehow pay off some old debts and incur some new ones, and develop ourselves as best we can, gradually and ultimately achieving the Great Work. Not in this lifetime, but perhaps in some other, and so it goes. Enlightenment and freedom are the goals.

CSH: Thanks for the compliment, we will have to see. But if you were to choose what form you would come back in next time, in terms of reincarnation, what would you choose?

FIR: I have mentioned this to you in private. What I would like, is to come back to a decent family where I would be given a good classical education first of all. And in the second place I would like to come back into a family where they were familiar with the whole series of concepts of occultism, the Great Work, the Golden Dawn. It would be rather nice to be born into a family where the Golden Dawn would be intrinsic to their point of view, to be able to pick up almost immediately where I had left off before.

CSH: You also said, that you might like to be a Siamese pussycat.

FIR: (Laughter) Well, that's a possible alternative! No, I'd still like to go on as I've been going on obviously for some time and that is to continue the Great Work until I become a Rajneesh. (Laughter)

CSH: You don't want to become like Rajneesh!

FIR: No. (Laughter) Just one of the Secret Chiefs. (sic!)

CSH: Falcon hopes to be bringing out a couple of articles of yours next year. One of them is on Eugenics. [Not yet released. Ed.]

FIR: Occult Eugenics?

CSH: Can you expand on that?

FIR: Occult Eugenics was really inspired by Crowley's silly novel *Moonchild*. That was such a gag, and such a burlesque, that it annoyed me. And he was so cruel in that book to everybody he knew that I wiped all that out from my mind and gradually over a period of years, an idea occurred to me predicated on this: that if a couple wanted to, let's say, bring into the world children who had "greater capabilities" they could use some of the magical techniques as a means of insuring that they would produce "better" children.

CSH: I know we're jumping the gun, but can you discuss some of these techniques.

FIR: Magical techniques! A bedroom where they're going to copulate which they purify by the pentagram ritual. Depending upon what kind of child they envisioned, do the invoking pentagrams and hexagrams of the planets and/or signs of the zodiac, write the appropriate kind of ritual rehearse that, and then while making love, recite the ritual with fervor. Do that several times and see if that affected the incoming reincarnating entity or attracted a higher grade being.

CSH: That is a fascinating idea. Do you know anybody who's tried it?

FIR: No. These ideas have had some kind of circulation. Once in a while I hear from somebody, but there are obviously a lot of people who have read of it but have never written to me, so who knows? Some of these things may have been experimented with, we know nothing about them. And I wouldn't tell if I did.

CSH: I know one thing for sure, the born-again Christian movement wouldn't approve of Occult Eugenics. (Laughter, Regardie laughing hysterically.)

FIR: (Still laughing) Oh no—no. None of what Falcon is publishing is going to be approved of by the born-agains, or in fact even by many occultists. You guys are too free—too loose—too different.

CSH: You are aware that occasionally we are called the Evil Press— Devil worshipers and other silly things. Of course they call you worse. On occasions our lives are threatened by people who say they are going to put bombs in our cars—our homes, offices, etc.

FIR: Those you have to accept as ever-present possibilities from the madmen outside. I've received shit like that all my life. I wouldn't pay too much attention to them. However, it's really a compliment.

CSH: I'll try not to.

FIR: They're mad, absolutely mad.

CSH: I'll close with a statement by Dr. J. Marvin Spiegelman [author of *The Tree of Life: Paths in Jungian Individuation, Buddhism and Jungian Psychology* and many other titles] which he made about you "...He once more reveals himself to be an outstanding, living occult magician, and the only one to combine this with the insight of the scholar, the caring of the psychotherapist, and the religious attitude of the spiritual man."

FIR: I'll accept that, but I still like wine, women and song. (Laughter)

CSH: Then a toast to the Great Work.

FIR: Hear! Hear! So mote it be! (Laughter)

Israel Regardie was one of the greatest figures of the Western mystical tradition. He was the foremost practitioner of the Golden Dawn system of magic; author of numerous books on meditation and magic; Neo-Reichian therapist; and secretary, associate and biographer of Aleister Crowley.

TABOO AND TRANSFORMATION IN THE WORKS OF ALEISTER CROWLEY

by Richard Kaczynski, Ph.D.

Author of the Falcon titles:
Perdurabo: The Life of Aleister Crowley
The Revival Magick and Other Essays (co-editor)

Spiritual polymorph, sexual omnivore, psychedelic pioneer, and unapologetic social misfit, Aleister Crowley cut a scandalous figure in his Edwardian heyday. He was rediscovered during the counter-cultural revolution of the 1960s and beatified as a pop culture icon, with the groundswell of interest resulting from this renaissance yet to crest. While his detractors are as numerous as his admirers, to dismiss him as a mere hedonist is to ignore the ghost in the machine: As Gerald Yorke, Crowley's friend and *advocatus diabolus,* explained: "Crowley didn't *enjoy* his perversions! He performed them to overcome his horror of them."[1] Yorke's is no disingenuous revisionist memoir. Throughout Crowley's corpus runs the idea of spiritual transformation by plunging into one's phobias and philias.

The ceremonial magick championed by Crowley and his forebears in the Golden Dawn is, in a nutshell, alchemy: The transformation of one's base character into spiritual gold. Crowley sought to improve upon this High Art by channeling human nature's most powerful drives into a form of sexual alchemy. His rationale, while not using this language, boils down to a simple thesis: If psychological triggers can precipitate spiritual

---

[1] Fuller, Jeanne Overton. *The Magical Dilemma of Victor Neuburg.* London: W.H. Allen, 1965, p. 244.

change, then the taboos socially programmed into us can act as triggers for major spiritual transformation. Thus, Crowley spent his life probing the impulses against which guilt, sin or plain common sense dissuaded most.

This behavior found its earliest expression in what Crowley admits is a defining moment of his childhood:

> I must have been about 6 years old. I was capering round my father during a walk through the meadows. He pointed out a bunch of nettles in the corner of the field, close to the gate (I can see it quite clearly to-day!) and told me that if I touched them they would sting. Some word, gesture, or expression of mine caused him to add: Would you rather be told, or learn by experience? I replied, instantly: I would rather learn by experience. Suiting the action to the word, I dashed forward, plunged in the clump, and learnt.
>
> This incident is the key to the puzzle of my character.[1]

From there, the exploration of ill-advised impulses became a constant quest. Thanks to his fundamentalist upbringing in the Plymouth Brethren faith, an abundance of taboos presented themselves. Simply reading the wrong book was a potential mis-step for the young Crowley. By his teenage years, he had discovered the "Three Evil Kings," i.e., Drin-King, Smo-King and Wan-King.

By the time Crowley entered Trinity College, he understood the hazards of gratuitous sensuality. His second book, the notorious *White Stains* (1898), emulated the Decadent art and literature of his social circle. Critics, then as well as today, twittered at such suggestive titles as "A Ballad of Passive Paederasty" and "With Dog and Dame," oblivious to the cautionary tale underlying the risqué subject matter: The book's protagonist finds the thrill of his mild erotic quirks waning over time, driving him to more extreme vices which ultimately culminates in madness and murder. At its core, the book is a critique of hedonism.

Despite the moral of *White Stains*, Crowley wrestled with his own young adult drives. Long periods of abstinence—proscribed for magicians by medieval grimoires—proved counter-productive. While abstaining, sexual urges didn't dissipate, they consumed him. Rather than slowly starve the impulse to death, Crowley concluded a better strategy was simply to appease it and get on with the Great Work. He considered sex an impulse like thirst or hunger, best divorced from the emotional baggage which society attached to it. Later he would remark, "The stupidity of having had to waste uncounted priceless hours in chasing what

---

[1] Crowley, Aleister. Chapter LVII. Beings I Have Seen with My Physical Eye. *Magick without Tears*. New Jersey: Thelema Publishing Co., 1954; rpt. Tempe, AZ: New Falcon Publications.

ought to have been brought to the back door every evening with the milk!"[1] Alas, these countless priceless hours gained him a reputation whose repercussions he would suffer repeatedly throughout his lifetime: In 1900, on the basis of his character, he was barred from further advancement in the Hermetic Order of the Golden Dawn. Thus, purposive indulgence collided with prudishness, and its eidolon was Queen Victoria.

Despite a childhood aversion to England's monarch, he admitted that "I was brought up in the faith that Queen Victoria would never die."[2] She symbolized the spirit of the age, where respectability and propriety was imposed on all expressions, both public and private. Social stagnation, Crowley believed, was rooted in this hypocritical and risible hypermorality. It was in this context that Crowley and his climbing colleague, Oscar Eckenstien, "broke into shouts of joy and an impromptu war dance"[3] upon learning of Queen Victoria's death in 1901. By the time he wrote *The World's Tragedy* in February of 1909, his disdain had crystallized:

> Priests who are celibates—outside of choir!
> Maidens who rave in Lesbian desire:
> The buck of sixty, cunning as a trapper,
> Stalking the pig-tailed, masturbating flapper;
> The creeping Jesus—Caution! we may shock it!—
> With one hand through his turn-out breeches pocket;
> Flagellants shrieking in our streets and schools,
> Our men all hogs, and all our women ghouls:—
> This is our England, pious dame and prude,
> Who calls me blasphemous, unchaste, and rude![4]

By the end of 1909, Crowley began to realize the magical potential of sex. He was in Africa with his student Victor Neuburg, conducting a series of visionary experiments which would become *The Vision and the Voice*. While attempting to skry into the 14th of the 30 Enochian Aethyrs, Crowley found his progress blocked. Seized with inspiration, the magicians built a makeshift altar to the Greek god Pan and consecrated it with a sex act. Although Crowley was promiscuous, Neuburg

---

[1] Crowley, Aleister. *The Confessions of Aleister Crowley.* London: Hill & Wang, 1969, p. 113.

[2] Chapter LXXVII. Work Worth While: Why? *Magick without Tears,* See also an identical remark in *Confessions,* p. 41.

[3] *Confessions,* p. 216.

[4] Crowley, Aleister. *The World's Tragedy.* Paris: privately printed, 1910, p. XXXVII; 2nd ed. Phoenix: New Falcon Publications, 1992.

was only his second male lover. The first, from his college days, left him with feelings of sin and guilt. This time, the homosexual encounter—in the open air under the desert sun, to the service of the Great Work—profoundly impacted him. He felt his ego—the Aleister Crowley raised in Victorian England by Plymouth Brethren parents—dissolve. In the language of initiation, he had crossed the Abyss.

Thus his attitude toward sex progressed significantly in the decade between entering college and writing *The Vision and the Voice*. In his original view, the reproductive impulse was a distraction from spiritual work, and was best sated to maximize the amount of time the mind could devote to higher goals. By 1909, he realized that the socially constructed boundaries called morality could literally block spiritual growth. By breaching taboos, Crowley realized he could break down these barriers, countermanding his social programming. This is what a later generation of rebels and devils would call "undoing yourself."[1]

Crowley's 1912 meeting with Theodor Reuss, head of the Ordo Templi Orientis, forged the last link in this chain of thought. In this legendary encounter, Reuss accused Crowley of revealing the O.T.O.'s central secret in *The Book of Lies*. When Crowley claimed innocence, Reuss directed him to Chapter 36, "The Star Sapphire." Reading the words, "Let the Adept be armed with his Magick Rood [and provided with his Mystic Rose.]" with the understanding that Reuss interpreted these words as sexual symbols, the light bulb lit. The chain was completed. Sex was not merely a distraction from the Great Work, nor merely a barrier to advancement. It was the very vehicle of a potent form of magick which replaced the traditional claptrap with our own bodies.

To be fair, Crowley was already heading in this direction, as documented in the Abuldiz working, *The Scented Garden*, and *Liber Stellae Rubeae*.[2] But the Reuss encounter gathered those thoughts into coherent

---

[1] Hyatt, Christopher S. *Undoing Yourself with Energized Meditation and Other Devices*. 6th printing. Tempe, AZ: New Falcon, 1993.

_____, *Undoing Yourself Too*. Tempe, AZ: New Falcon, 1988.

[2] Crowley, Aleister. Liber LX: The Ab-ul-Diz Working. *The Vision and the Voice with Commentary and Other Papers*. York Beach: Weiser, 1998, p. 287–337.

_____, *The Scented Garden of Abdullah the Satirist of Shiraz* (Bagh-i-muattar). London, 1910: rpt. Chicago: Teitan Press, 1991.

_____, Liber Stellae Rubeae sub figura LXVI. *The Equinox* I(7), 1912, p. 29–36.

form. From this point, Crowley vigorously engaged not only in ritual sex[1] but other taboo experiences, all in the pursuit of spiritual insight.

Thus, when he took up painting around 1917, he advertised for "Dwarfs, Hunchbacks, Tattooed Women, Harrison Fisher Girls, Freaks of All Sorts, Coloured Women only if exceptionally ugly or deformed, to pose for artist." When he founded his Abbey of Thelema in Cefalù, Italy, in 1920, he took a page from Paul Gaugin and made the walls his canvas. The result was *La Chambre des Cauchemars* (Chamber of Nightmares), whose murals bombarded viewers with an array of frightful, disturbing and sexually explicit images. Crowley told visitors:

> There, in the corner, are Lesbians as large as life. Why do you feel shocked and turn away: or perhaps overtly turn to look again? Because, though you may have thought of such things, you have been afraid to face them. Drag all such thoughts into the light... 'Tis only your mind that feels any wrong... Freud endeavors to break down such complexes in order to put the subconscious mind into a bourgeois respectability. That is wrong—the complexes should be broken down to give the sub-conscious will a chance to express itself freely..."[2]

Karl Germer, visiting the Abbey in 1926, confirmed the cathartic intent of these murals. "Beast evidently did all that as a medicine...against the English disease *par excellence*."[3]

Having fleshed out his psychological theory of magick, he began explaining it to his students. As Frank Bennett recounts his visit to Cefalù,

> [H]e began to talk to me about initiation, and said it was a matter of getting the sub-conscious mind at work, that when this subconscious mind was allowed to have full sway, without interference with the physical mind, illumination begun for he said this subconscious mind was our Holy Guardian. He illustrated this by saying that everything was felt in this mind, and it is constantly urging its will upon the physical mind, and when these impressions, or inner desires, are restricted or suppressed, evil and all kind of trouble are the result.[4]

---

[1] Symonds, John, and Grant, Kenneth. (eds.). *The Magical Record of the Beast 666.* Quebec: Next Step, 1972; rpt. London: Duckworth, 1983.

[2] Captain J.H.E. Townsend to J.F.C. Fuller, 19 April 1921, Harry Ransom Humanities Research Center, University of Texas at Austin.

[3] Karl Germer to Norman Mudd, 4 February 1926, Binder New 116, Yorke Collection, Warburg Institute, University of London.

[4] Frank Bennett. (1921). Magical Record of Frater Progradior in a Retirement at Cefalue Sicily. Yorke Collection.

While Crowley disagreed with psychoanalysis,[1] this etiological theory of "evil and all kind of trouble" paraphrases Freud's ideas regarding repression, sublimation and neurosis.

He also experimented with drugs at this time, making them accessible to the Abbey's visitors to rob them of their mystique and allure. His views on drug addiction paralleled *White Stains'* warning about sex, and, by extension, apply to all behaviors driven by the pleasure principle: Anything pursued hedonistically ultimately leads to moral collapse; but placing it in service to the Will protects the magician from addiction or other apostasies.[2] This calls to mind *The Book of the Law's* instruction, "To worship me take wine and strange drugs whereof I will tell my prophet, & be drunk thereof! They shall not harm ye at all." (*AL* ii.22). On this passage, Crowley cautioned:

> Lest there be folly, let me say that this passage does not license reckless debauch. The use of drugs and drink is to be strictly an act of Magick. Compare what is said in the First Chapter with regard to the use of the functions of sex.[3]

Thus he reiterated that explorations of the human psyche's dark underbelly be intentional and purposive.

Other experiments at Cefalù involved gender bending, the *menage a trois,* sado-masochism and coprophagia. While Crowley considered this legitimate psychological research, he realized the controversial nature of his work. Between the publication of *The Diary of a Drug Fiend* and the unfortunate death from typhoid of an Abbey visitor, the tabloids of the time unleashed an astonishing series of attacks. Crowley's reaction:

---

[1] Crowley, Aleister. An improvement upon psychoanalysis. *Vanity Fair,* December 1916, p. 60, 137; rpt. Hymenaeus Beta and Richard Kaczynski (eds.), *The Revival of Magick and Other Essays.* Tempe, AZ: New Falcon, 1998.

[2] Crowley, Aleister. *The Diary of a Drug Fiend.* London: W. Collins & Co., 1922.

_____, The great drug delusion. A New York Specialist (pseud.) *The English Review,* June 1922, 571–576.

_____, The drug panic. A London Physician (pseud) *The English Review,* July 1922, p. 65–70.

_____, Crowley found these principles harder than expected to put into practice in *Liber Tzaba vel Nike (The Fountain of Hyacinth),* Binder A4–A5, Yorke Collection.

[3] Crowley, Aleister. Duplicate typescript with mss corrections of part of the unpublished commentary on the 'Book of the Law,' Oasis of Nefta, al-Djerid, Tunisia, 1923. Rare Books Department, Z. Smith Reynolds Library, Wake Forest University, Winston-Salem, N.C.

I regard all these people, all England with rare individual exceptions, as moral cowards with all that that implies. Sir Richard Burton had an experience precisely similar to mine. So had Christopher Columbus. So had Darwin. Their instinctive dread is of a man who dares the unknown. *Omne Ignotum pro terribili* and such a man may bring it to their door at any moment. The whole history of science illustrates this. Science is now tolerated because Science has been at pains to prove that (on the balance) it has benefited mankind. I, bringing as I do, new knowledge of the unknown, and obviously the mark for fear, horror and persecution.[1]

Small wonder that Crowley's records from Cefalù were seized and destroyed by H.M. Customs as pornographic when he tried returning them to England.

In the end, Crowley became the eidolon or reflection of all those impulses denied by the society which Queen Victoria symbolized. Confronting the Beast meant confronting those repressed impulses, with the resulting ordeal dubbed "The Vision of the Demon Crowley." Indeed, those who persevered and saw through the smoke screen became his staunchest advocates—Gerald Yorke, Louis Wilkinson, Karl Germer and Israel Regardie among them—while those who bolted off were convinced they had narrowly escaped the clutches of the devil. "The main danger seems to be getting caught on the reef of his own interpretation," Kenneth Grant commented. "But this, after all, is but the proper function of the 'Demon Crowley'!"[2] Likewise, when Crowley began a campaign to rehabilitate his reputation, Gerald Yorke neatly summarized the function of the Great Beast:

> To my mind, part of your 'mission,' if I may use a word I mistrust, is to show that the code of morals of what a Thelemite calls the Old Aeon has been superseded, and that now any act is right provided it is done in the right way, as in interpretation of True Will. It must have been your Will to be the Beast, and a whitewashed Beast is an useless commercial article.[3]

Crowley must have been convinced, for he continued living the rest of his life with no apologies.

Analogues In Other Traditions

The notion of sacrifice—literally to make sacred, or to find the holy in the mundane—is not unique to Crowley.

---

[1] Aleister Crowley to Norman Mudd, 20 April 1924, Yorke Collection.

[2] Kenneth Grant, private communication, 5 December 1989.

[3] Gerald Yorke to Aleister Crowley, 20 March 1928, Binder New 116, Yorke Collection.

Hasidic Jews find God through the "enjoyable and necessary acts of ordinary life."[1] Early forms of Hasidism's *Chabad* mysticism included practices like *Haalat ha-Nitzotzot* ("elevating the sparks," or recognizing everything as a manifestation of God), *'Avodah he-Hipukh* ("worship through inversion," where self-fulfillment comes from joining things— even God—with its opposite), and its extension *Yeridah le-Tsorekh 'Aliyah* ("descent for the purpose of ascent"). When the *Tzaddikim* began discussing things like the sanctity of sin, exploring the *Sitra Ahra* (the "opposite tree" or *Qlippoth*), or discussing how one can find God by exploring the desire to kill one's neighbor, these practices were eliminated as dangerous.[2]

In Tantra, followers of the *Kaula* branch and *vama marg* or "left hand path" advocate the well-known *panchamakaras* or *panchatattva* ritual. Literally meaning "five elements," it involves partaking five substances which are usually religiously prohibited. The five items, in Sanskrit, all begin with the letter M; hence, this ritual is often referred to as "the five M's." The items are *madya* or *madir_* (wine or liquor), *matsya* (fish), *m_msa* (meat), *mudr_* (parched grain) and *maithun_* (sex, often out of caste). The concept behind this ritual is that which drove Crowley's explorations: Social taboos, broken in a religious context, can produce great spiritual advancement.[3]

Finally, the masters known as the *Aghori* represent such an extreme manifestation of this formula that they are the object of fear and awe in India, believed to have transcended all boundaries of good and evil. Their best-known activities center around mankind's greatest taboo, death. *Aghori* will sleep in cemeteries, often sharing the same coffin with corpses. They observe and wait, ready to celebrate the popping of the body's skullcap, for to them that represents the final release of the soul. Once or twice in a lifetime, an *Aghora* will consume a piece of human brain, the first place to show the stirrings of the spirit and the last place

---

[1] Cantor, Norman F. *The Sacred Chain: The History of the Jews.* New York: HarperCollins, 1994, p. 214.

[2] Ariel, David S. *The Mystic Quest: An Introduction to Jewish Mysticism.* New York: Schocken, 1988.
Elior, Rachel. *The Paradoxical Ascent to God: The Kabbalistic Theosophy of Habad Hasidism.* New York: State University of New York Press, 1993.

[3] Garrison, Omar. *Tantra: The Yoga of Sex.* New York: Causeway, 1964.
Feuerstein, Georg. *Tantra: The Path of Ecstasy.* Boston: Shambhala, 1998.
Douglas, Nik, and Slinger, Penny. *Sexual Secrets: The Alchemy of Ecstasy.* New York: Destiny, 1979; rpt. New York: Inner Traditions, 1989.

from which it is vacated. Even necrophilia is not unknown.[1] By immersing themselves in the most dreaded of all things—human death and decay—the *Aghori* seek not only to come to terms with death, but also—like Crowley, the *Chabad* mystics and the *Tantrikas*—to come a little closer to understanding God.

Richard Kaczynski, Ph.D. is a psychologist specializing in non-mainstream religious beliefs. He has written extensively and lectured internationally on mystical and magical beliefs and practices.

---

[1] Svoboda, Robert E. *Aghora: At the Left Hand of God.* Brotherhood of Life: Albuquerque, NM, 1986.

PART II
The World Of Chaos

BEYOND THE EVENT HORIZON

Responses To Chaos Culture

by Phil Hine

Author of the Falcon titles:
Condensed Chaos: An Introduction to Chaos Magick
Prime Chaos: Adventures in Chaos Magick

Chaos Magic breaks with occult conventions—it doesn't claim a tradition or ancient lineage. It doesn't claim any spiritual gurus, other than perhaps, Austin Osman Spare, a reclusive English artist who, much to the annoyance of his ceremonial contemporaries, was a successful magician who didn't so much go against what passed for occult 'laws', but didn't seem to care about them in the first place. Chaos magic says that when you got down to it, having a personal experience of magic is more important than believing in karma, reincarnation, or the lost city of Atlantis. Even worse, Chaos Magic says that what you believe in is up to you, and that there is no Ultimate Truth!

Chaos Magic doesn't look into the past with rose-tinted spectacles, or await a future when everyone else is a chaoist too. But we do have a name for what's happening at the moment. We call it PandaemonAeon. Pan—Daemon. The interplay of two forces, Baphomet and Choronzon. Baphomet is the encapsulation of all tendencies to change, growth and movement—as a God, 'he' is ever-changing, ever-mutating; the morphic representation of life, genius, magic. Choronzon is aptly named the Lord of the Abyss of Hallucinations. It is the Spectacle—the hydra-headed beast spreading its tentacles across the world through the web of television, advertising, and all means of transmitting information. Choronzon endlessly spawns and replicates desires as forms—styles, revolutions, fashions, identities; manifesting fears and desires until they are "more real than real." Choronzon creates and supports the illusion of the single ego, which maintains itself by erecting thresholds and boundaries, rejecting everything which does not fit a simplified construct. Baphomet is the source of inspiration, whilst Choronzon shapes that inspiration into belief and dogma. In this model, Baphomet would be the source of inspiration for a certain wandering prophet, whilst Choronzon created the shell of superstition, dogma and religion which grew up around him. We can say that Aleister Crowley was a wild-eyed avatar of Baphomet, but that Choronzon has created the shell which some people use nowadays as a shield against realising their power to be themselves, rather than their broken reflection of a dead magus.

We all hang out in the belly of the beast. We have been led to believe that Choronzon can be resisted or banished, yet all attempts at revolution or image-creation ultimately are fed back to us in the hyper-real marketplace of illusion and counter-illusion. Revolutions in art are served up as modern advertising gimmicks. Last year's culture-rebels become this year's culture-vultures. All well-signposted escape-routes feed the beast, whilst supporting the illusion of subverting it. Now none of this is particularly startling—as the multiple heads of Choronzon curl ever-inwards upon each other, modern culture becomes increasingly obsessed with itself. The standard reaction to the increasing awareness of the modern condition appears to be that of rootlessness, cynicism, nihilism and alienation. In fact, such reactions to modern living have become positively commonplace and mediocre. We have become inured to the blandishments of the advertisers and the blatant lies of politicians. "Nothing is True" ceases to be a revolutionary slogan, as increasingly any cultural sense of "faith" is lost in science, politics, religion, and radical sloganeering. The 1990's is characterised by a growing feeling of helplessness— nothing that you do will make any real difference. The result is loneliness, depression, alienation—combined with the desperate scrabble to prove oneself to be an 'individual'—to 'stand out from the crowd' and at the same time belong to something which gives out a semblance of permanence.

Modern society is chaotic and fragmentary, coming increasingly to resemble a fractal structure; a bewilderingly complex organism, in contrast to the stark functionalism of the 'Brave New World' skyscrapers of the modernist style. Diversity rules, in a display of increasingly fragmented subcultures and nested beliefs, all jostling for attention in the marketplace. Mass communication systems have shrunk the world, and it is possible to discern a wide variety of cultural styles and epochs melting together in music, art, fashion, literature, and food. The profusion of magical and mythological systems available to the modern occultist also demonstrates this trend. Magical subcultures multiply and co-exist within a complexity of belief and orientation which outsiders to the scenes find difficult to grasp. At the same time, the distinction between magical enclaves becomes blurred as individuals are able to cross back and forth between them. Although modern magicians, like their forebears, tend to identify themselves as being apart from the rest of modern culture, magic, as with any other product, is swayed by trends and fashions.

As a cultural trend, Postmodernism breaks with the Modernist idea of progress and historical continuity, and instead, ransacks all available cultures and time zones in a diverse exercise in collage. The immediacy of experience becomes the important factor, rather than continuity with any past or projection into any one future. Thus, an appropriate slogan for this age would be Mutate and Survive. Nothing is finalised or formalised, but merely re-arranged.

This is an age where magic might thrive. The search to give magic a solid footing, using scientific glamours or gambits to achieve respectability, can be seen as transient phases, linguistic games for amusement, or deliberate tactics to create free areas for the manipulation of belief and projection of image. As a speaker at a conference on Ley Lines put it: "Stop looking for facts, believe what you like, and have fun!" The different strands of alternative belief may find themselves winding together as participants borrow ideas and tactics from each other, rewriting them for their own specific glamours. Magic becomes another approach for survival in the shifting labyrinth of modern life. As much a form of entertainment as anything else if current trends continue, no form of human experience will be judged to have any 'higher' value than any other.

It can also be seen that modern imaging techniques have acquired a magical dimension, if not a magical ethos, behind them. Whilst there is a cultural trend towards the fleeting, the ephemeral, the transient; and while the pace of modern life is ever increasing, all Control Systems are increasingly projecting an aura of stability and foundation as part of their authority. This reflects the rising nostalgia for common values; a shared social past; and universal, traditional values. As the social matrix becomes increasingly subject to rapid fluctuations, throwing out anchors into a collectivised past becomes more prominent than movement into a future. The desire to establish a core identity within the profusion of styles has led to image building becoming an industry in itself—as much reflected by the tactics of political groups and corporate bodies, as in the fetishistic scramble for designer labels and trendy occult symbols. Identity has, therefore, become another commodity to be traded in the marketplace. The gulf between objective icons and the illusory has widened to such an extent that illusions have come to have an equal value.

Chaos Magic, where "Nothing is True" and "Everything Is Permitted," arises out of the twists of contemporary culture, a reflection and reification of the current social landscape as much as Crowley's magical philosophy emerged from the colliding visions of his era. Crowley's magical work paved the way for the emergence of Chaos Magic, in a way that he could not predict. The power of the Age of Enlightenment lay in the way that its visionaries began to talk and write about a future world where everyone had a piece of the action. This can be seen in the utopian visions of Adam Smith or Francis Bacon, the towering cities imagined by Frank Lloyd Wright or the 'iron cage of bureaucracy' darkly prophesied by Max Weber. This vision of a total future was shattered by the advent of the Bomb. Nowadays, all global futures are at best tenuous. Getting to work in the morning requires that I resist the embrace of any number of futures being offered to me on my way to the station—Born-Again Christian and Marxist ones being the most popular, at the moment. Once in my office, I may be offered participation in the latest techno-logical dream-environments from Microsoft or Rank Xerox. Equally, the news that the Antichrist is on earth and living in Stoke Newington is only a phone call away. If "Nothing is True" it seems equally likely that "Everything" might be true, even, as *Principia Discordia* reminds us, "false things."

Proof then, has retreated in the face of belief. Science, once heralded as the arbiter of truth, has had its facade of objectivity punctured. Intellec-tuals may point to the uncertainty of Heisenberg, but generally this has more to do with the growing distrust of statistics and the knowledge that scientists in the pay of governments and multi-nationals are no more objective than their masters. Science, once the avowed enemy of religion, now sees books by Christian physicists and Taoist mathematicians. Science sells washing powders and status symbols and comes in the form of icons of technological nostalgia.

Where does this leave the magician? Of course, this depends upon your viewpoint. This is an age wherein any belief can establish itself as an island of sense. Every year, it seems that more and more belief-systems emerge, clamouring for attention, clawing themselves a piece of the action with economic and political leverage, followers and schisms. Over the last twenty years or so, there has been a phenomenal rise in the vari-eties of belief and philosophy open to the would-be magician, all of which are 'true' of course. The great mysteries now lie next to each other on the bookshelves, preserved in both popular and academic versions, no longer secret, concealed or occult.

What has also begun to happen is that that basic premise of western culture, the Aristotelian either/or, true/false divide has started to weaken at the edges. If the need to 'prove' something as true is no longer impor-tant, then what is left but "Do What Thou Wilt?" When "Nothing is True" everything becomes art, play, or make-believe. Instead of trying to prove my belief against that of others, I am free to begin to take pleasure in my choice of belief, and to see the humorous side of other people's. It is more in my interest to support and propagate diversity of belief, rather than attempt mass conversion. As Pete Carroll put it, "We are free to grasp whatever freedoms are available and do whatever we fancy with them."

Such a sense of freedom may be exhilarating. It may also, of course, be deeply unsettling and alienating, tempting us to drop out, tune in, escape, smash the state, join the rat-race, find a desert island, found a spiritual community, blank out, o.d. or kill them all. All of which are forms of resistance sanctioned by the beast, of course. The system loves resistance. Resistance is often creative and it feeds on creativity until the subversive becomes just another pre-packaged lifestyle on special offer. So Cease to Resist. Relax and enjoy the PandaemonAeon. Believe everything and anything. Seek not proof, but take pleasure in your choice of belief. Wipe that superior sneer of your face and try smiling (if only inwardly) at the people/institutions/beliefs that you've waged your personal war against. Wouldn't it be more fun if you didn't run around quite so hard trying to be an individual, or fighting to prove or uphold your chosen belief-system?

Aleister Crowley is a case in point. His lifestyle foreshadowed chaos culture; his magical writings were only a distraction. He knew that to become a legend, you have to be larger-than-life. Critics often point to the contradictions of his life: he posed as a holy guru and shat on carpets; he wrote poetry and pornography; he worshipped women and kicked his scarlet women downstairs. It's easy to condone, condemn or justify someone else, especially when they are dead. But one thing you can say is that Crowley lived his life to the fullest. Not content with being himself, he became a man of many parts and roles, impossible to pin down as one thing or another. Who can say which one was true? It's certainly a shame that Crowley has inspired so many legions of lukewarm wannabes. I've met at least three Great Beast 666's over the last few years, and not one of them had even one-tenth of the wit, humour, wisdom or panache that I would expect from a figure of Crowleyan proportions. Isn't it curious how those who strive to be someone else are very selective; yes, I can see that you've got the heroin habit and mastered the art of beating up on your 'scarlet women,' but you haven't been extradited from any countries, you haven't published anything, nor have you climbed any mountains of late.

Anyone can be neurotic—it's almost as mediocre as cynicism; if you must aspire to something larger-than-life, then be mad! And I mean real "look mummy what's that funny man doing" madness—the kind where you don't need an audience.

Then again there is the path of magic. Here, I mean magic as opposed
to the Occult. The Occult has become a subculture—a 'scene'. Anyone
who's had any experience with this scene will have met the people who
appear to have invested a great deal in projecting an aura of bohemian
decadence or a 'sinister' glamour. One of the attractions of the occult for
some people is that you can easily convince yourself that you are a
mighty adept whilst remaining neurotic and totally unable to cope with
the realities of ordinary mortal concerns. Then again, the occult has an
attraction to would-be rebels. Yes, it's terribly rebellious to dress in black
and wear an inverted pentagram necklace. It's so outrageous to sneer at
Christians whilst proudly displaying your Aleister Crowley T-shirt. But
this isn't so much madness as sadness—the kind of sadness of the types
who hang around occult bookstores in order to bore other people with
their wisdom, or the guys who behave as though sexual magic is the last
possible way to finally losing their virginity. Like any other subculture, it
is swayed by fashions and trends, image-makers and experts.

How do you like to think of the Occult? A timeless wisdom who's
roots are lost in the mists of primal history? Fragments of incalculable
power who tumbled from the wreckage of Atlantis, only to survive in the
mysteries of Qabalah, the secret fraternities, and the shards of cunning
passed from mouth to mouth in darkest rural England? How easy it is, to
sit in a centrally-heated room and momentarily imagine that what you are
doing is somehow similar to the practices of a neolithic shaman.

It must be admitted that occultists tend to look at the past and the far-
off future through somewhat rose-tinted spectacles. There is power even,
in this kind of romanticism. If you believed that each word, each gesture,
each symbol of the magical art that you painstakingly committed to
memory before daring to put it into practice was part of an ancient and
secret wisdom (revealed only to the worthy and the wise, of course), then
I'm sure that doing magic whilst caught up in this belief could be incredibly powerful for you.

The power of this romantic belief is such that people will leap vocifer-
ously to its defense. Modern occultists are often concerned with proving
their own particular authenticity over everyone else. Hence the scramble
for charters, proof of wisdom handed down from priestess to priestess,
initiation lines from master to master, and the search for inner-plane contacts with the 'right' entities—a trend which has its roots in the 18th
Century Age of Enlightenment. This game, of staking a claim of authentic traditional succession for one's magical beliefs, was upset in the late
1970's, with the arrival of the 'new' kid on the occult block—Chaos
Magic.

People are often confused by the label 'chaos' because it's a label
which can include anything else. A label that destroys other labels. Well,

chaos is a perspective, rather than a belief system. Powered by the same forces that impel other subcultures to increasing diversification, the occult genre is manufacturing the illusion of separate strands of magical belief, which maintain themselves by emphasizing their difference to that of others. There's Witchcraft, in all its forms, the pick and mix selection of shamanic styles, the growing interest in Germanic magic, the popularisation of voodoo, the continuing fetishization of famous people—how long will we have to wait for the Aleister Crowley laundry list collection? Are we to believe that all these styles are kept separate and inviolate from each other? Obviously, those who have a vested interest in maintaining such boundaries would have us think so.

But Chaos magic is an exercise in collage, dub acid house; a mixing of styles and colours. Anything which attempts to cross boundaries and mix styles is bound to be looked upon with a certain suspicion. It's a vital current which is not attempting to create a niche for itself, but attempting to do something different. Chaos Magic says that magic is concerned with change, within a changing world, something which is too important to take seriously. Chaos Magic is itself mutating, of course. If you do Chaos Magic, you're not merely following someone else's ritual scripts and plodding in the footsteps of someone else's illuminations. What you get is something unique to yourself. Whether you keep it hidden under your bed, or get it published/broadcast/spray-painted on walls, is of course, up to you.

The world is magical, wild and wonderful, yet we close ourselves to the everyday miracles which might, if we allow them, propel us into excitements and ecstasies beyond our imagination. Put aside the habit of world-weary cynicism, and something wonderful might slap you in the face. Playing at magic might become easier than boring everyone else with continually justifying its existence by quoting philosophers, quantum physicists and popular style gurus. Chaos Magic says that all belief-systems are models, theories, visions—some more useful than others, some fun to visit, others not. But merely "seeing" is not enough. At the core of all magic is that which chaos magicians have termed gnosis. Gnosis is the abandonment of self—the surrender to intoxication. Moments of gnosis inspire us to not only "see" the world in a different way, but to act in the light of that illumination. Gnosis is mysterious, sweeping upon us unaware in a myriad of forms; through drugs, sex, from sudden realisations of significance to the hidden hand of coincidence. It may elude the ardent seeker of spiritual experience, whilst opening the floodgates of perception to the 'ordinary' person next door. A momentary flash of gnosis may shatter our beliefs, or support our suspicions. But Gnosis is not merely illuminated perception or insight borne through intoxication; gnosis is knowledge which stirs us into action. This is the source of all magic—the knowledge of what is possible and more, the energy to make that leap into those regions of unknown territory.

In this way, magic defends itself. Its keys are not on open display, despite the multitude of books, gurus, teachers, magical orders and all the other brokers of the spirit striving to convince us that they alone have the missing link to knowledge and power. Gnosis is also capricious; there are people who have spent many years investing in belief, practising the rituals and ethics of esoteric systems, yet they have never known ecstasy of spirit. Whilst someone else may offer you a key to magic, only you can use it, and no one can predict quite how many doors it will open, and what awaits you on the other side.

Phil Hine is a former editor of the internationally acclaimed magical journal *Chaos International*. He has facilitated workshops and seminars on modern magical practice in America and Europe. He is the author of *The Pseudonomicon*; *Condensed Chaos*; and *Prime Chaos*. He may be reached at BM Grasshopper, London, WC1N 3XX, England.

UNDOING YOURSELF WITH CHAOS MAGIC

by Robert F. Williams, Jr.

What follows is geared toward those new to Chaos Magic and for those struggling along in so-called magical organizations that study magic but can't seem to actually do anything magical. It is also for those who are pouring over old magical texts searching for the secrets of magic, trying to unearth a ritual that really works, and instead find themselves uncovering information that is not understandable or pertinent and is basically just plain useless.

A good starting point if you have been discouraged by this type of time wasting and are ready for a change, is to read the work of present day alternative thinkers like William S. Burroughs, Timothy Leary, Robert Anton Wilson, Peter J. Carroll, Philip K. Dick, Christopher S. Hyatt, Phil Hine and Israel Regardie. If you are already reading some of this stuff, that is even better—don't stop! Once you've begun you'll find that one good author seems to guide you to the next. They will help you to begin looking at things from a divergent point of view. Mutating your perspective is an excellent beginning for the transformation necessary to become a Chaos Magician. A new way of viewing things is an important starting point and yet it is only the starting point—Chaos Magic demands action.

Chaos Magic can be distinguished from other forms of magic by several basic tenets. These I will get into in just a moment. I would first like to make clear one differentiation as it relates to this subject. Many concepts in Chaos Magic are "simple"; however, when I say "simple" I do not mean "easy". Chaos Magic is about change, both in the restructuring of the mind and in the world in which we live. Once you've begun to work with Chaos Magic you will discover that it *really does work,* that is to say, you will realize that you are actually capable of manipulating your outer existence as well as your internal reality. When you reach this point the big question will become: "Now that I can change, what am I going to change to?" This issue is more than just a philosophical exploration; it becomes an actuality that has to be faced.

Self-directed change implies achievement, and yet the simple word "change" has ramifications that are staggering to most people. In fact most people are allergic to change—by that I mean the average person will, without any real inner reflection, place themselves in a routine and stay in that routine as long as possible. Sometimes these routines are not pleasant. We see these people everywhere, trapped in lives of alcoholism, drug addiction, bad marriages, job problems or whatever. People stay in these routines rather than face making a change. People tend to continue these behaviors as long as possible and they will, at all costs, avoid honestly looking at themselves and avoid any opportunity to try something different. This brings to mind a quote from one of my heroes, Ralph Waldo Emerson, who once noted "foolish consistency is the hobgoblin of little minds." Even the smallest life changes, such as being forced to take a minor detour from the normal route to work, can ruin an entire morning for most little minded people. Are you one?

For the Chaos Magician, change, even for the sake of change, is better than no change at all. For lack of change leads to stagnation and to stagnate is to die. Changes such as assuming different viewpoints, being open to different belief systems and to at least temporarily accept new ideas, doing things differently, all of these things imply movement from one belief point to another belief point. This movement can produce momentum, and momentum, guided by purpose—unencumbered by doctrine and presuppositions—can produce the desire of the directed will. This, then, indicates a successful magical act. A magical act may be defined as causing reality to conform to the will.

"Belief is a technique" is one of the basic tenants of Chaos Magic and we can use any belief system that appeals to us. The point is that this new-found belief has to be established as (a temporary) reality and it has to be believed in as fully as possible while it is being used. Basically we pretend that something is true until it works. Belief can be used to trick the Subconscious or Unconscious into accepting that something is real, then the Subconscious, which has almost unlimited power, goes about bringing this condition into reality. While we are using a belief it is important to do everything possible to trick the Unconscious and convince it that your belief is a reality. One of the ways this can be done is to act the part, dress the part, talk and live the part of the belief that is being used. Basically "act as if" until the belief becomes a reality. It is far easier to act your way into changed thinking than it is to think your way into changed action. If you dress someone up as a soldier, make them march around like a soldier, have them carry a rifle and bark martial orders at them, they will soon believe that they are a soldier and thus become a soldier. Military leaders have known this for centuries.

A symbolized representation of the desire is more functional and will burn more clearly and be less obstructed in the Subconscious than a consciously thought out desire will work or can be maintained in the Conscious mind. The Unconscious mind understands and performs in response to symbolic representations of desire. Carl Jung was aware of this and so was a magician named Austin Osman Spare. Although Spare referred to Jung and Freud as "Junk and Fraud," his magical system was influenced by both men's ideas. Spare realized and understood the power of the Unconscious. He also understood the potential of the Conscious to interfere with realizing its potential. He therefore created a system that allowed him to sneak information past the Conscious and plant it into the Unconscious.

The Unconscious mind responds best to symbols of desire. Using symbols that have been created by another or that are very old or are written in some foreign language are not any more effective than those that you create yourself—in fact the opposite may be true. Your effort to create your own symbol or "alphabet of desire" means that both your Conscious and Unconscious mind are fully aware of what you have been up to. This fact in itself allows you a personal relationship with your work. I would much rather sleep in my own bed, or drive my own car than someone else's. This holds true for your personal symbols and the feeling of familiarity. Self-created symbols allow you to resonate with something that is a part of you and therefore is more effective.

Creating your own symbolized desire is no harder than knowing what your desire is (and that is the hardest part), writing it out as "IT IS MY WILL TO … !" Once this has been done, you may use any method you wish to convert this desire into a symbol. Combine the letters, make a drawn or written representation, juxtapose the words into a mantram that disguises its original meaning, shape into a clay talisman or whatever— your method is only limited by your own imagination.

An altered state of consciousness (gnosis) is an essential factor for this magical procedure to achieve its successful consummation. The Conscious must be distracted from the desire so the desire can move into the Unconscious and be properly seeded. The Conscious mind actually will interfere with the work if it is allowed to participate. The Conscious mind cannot be counted on to hold a clear image of your desire, let alone to actually send the desire out into the aether to cause change. If you have ever tried to hold a singular image or thought in your mind and not allow any other thoughts or images to enter, you understand how difficult this is. The conscious mind cannot stand being limited to such and it will do all in its power to fight this process. If you have any doubt try thinking of your front door knob and nothing else for three minutes. Good luck.

The Subconscious is the most powerful and change-effecting. If a sharp, clear image of your desire is planted into your Subconscious it will burn there indefinitely sending information to the world within and outside of you to effect the desired change. Not only is the Unconscious powerful, it is a reservoir of all information that is taken in. It contains the entire store of all information that has been assimilated through the course of our lives. Within the Subconscious resides snatches of all the foreign languages we've heard, all the mathematical equations we've been taught, and all the sights, sounds, smells, and feelings of everything that we have experienced from the first day we went to kindergarten, the moment of our birth, before birth, to now. The sum total of everything that we have ever perceived both consciously and unconsciously is stored here. This information is very useful when doing Divination.

The point is that the Conscious mind must be fully occupied or distracted while planting the seed (casting the spell) into your Unconscious. The most effective way of achieving this is to alter your conscious state. The two opposite ends of the spectrum of altered consciousness are to fire the mind up into an extreme state of excitement or bring it to a state of total calmness. These have been represented by magicians as a volcano and a pool of calm water, Fire and Ice, Death and Sex, Thanatos and Eros. This is how the magical society The Illuminates of Thanateros arrived at its name, illumination through the ritual use of sex and death states of consciousness. These states may be achieved by various methods.

The ritual need not be complicated although elaborate ritual work, can be fun and is definitely beneficial in terms of distracting the Conscious mind away from the true desire—in other words it will help you overcome, as Crowley put it, "the lust of result."

First you decide your desire and create a symbol to represent it. Then you banish and go about achieving an altered state: you can dance, drum, have sex, spin in circles, hyperventilate, stare into a mirror, focus on single spot on the wall, meditate or hypnotize yourself. Your path to the top of the mountain is your own. After some experimenting you will find what is most effective for you. When you have reached the peak of altered consciousness, or mind distraction, it is time to recall and *strongly visualize* the symbolized representation of your desire. Do *not* think about the desire itself—in fact, forget the desire—and see only the symbolized representation. Visualize this in your mind's eye as long as possible and then let it go and forget the desire. It is important not to let the Conscious mind interfere with what you have just done. When you have finished, banish once again.

Quantum Theory may help explain how this process works. A Conscious belief as a symbolized desire actually manifests as information in the Subconscious. Quantum Theory would indicate that information has a shaping effect on matter and the world around us. With Chaos Mathematics and Chaos Theory it is thought that the Universe is chaotic and random as opposed to ordered and governed by strict laws. At any given moment any number of possible futures could manifest and in fact might exist simultaneously. Information from this moment couples with one of the possible futures that it has an affinity for and shapes it into a probability, thus encouraging it to be more likely to happen. If you make something more likely to happen you are literally forcing the hand of chance or causing reality to conform to will ... Magic!

Robert F. Williams, Jr. was one of the founding members of the Illuminates of Thanateros in the United States (which can be reached at: 3202 East Greenway Road #1307-198, Phoenix, AZ 85032, U.S.A). He was a contributing author to several books and magazines. His tragic death, shortly before the first edition of this book went to press, shocked us all.

IN MEMORY OF ROBERT F. WILLIAMS, JR.

by Douglas Grant

Robert "Bob" Williams, Jr.'s last years in this mundane reality saw him attain many of his desires on the rollercoaster of Magick and life. I will never forget how he created unique Visions from old and new ideas, perpetuating the momentum both he and others had created. To you Robert Williams, I raise my cup to Magick and the Manifestation of Dreams and Desires. There is perhaps a no more *a propos* book than *Rebels and Devils* to dedicate to my friend and Frater, Robert "Bob" Williams. To many, Robert personified the "Rebel" and within both Occult and even Chaos Magick circles, he became a "Devil".

Robert never styled himself as a teacher. He inspired the people he worked with to cultivate their own imagination and creativity to spur evolution in their lives. If you approached Robert with questions, he rarely ever gave you answers. He would point you toward the clues that might expand your perception and help you realize there were no concrete answers but rather more questions to explore. Robert's approach prompted you into expanding your own horizons and finding your own paths. Admittedly, this pushed a few people to topple the razor's edge, but those that could see past their reality tunnels catapulted themselves forward in Experience, Attainment of Desire and Wisdom.

Robert felt that Chaos Magick contained the Seeds of Change for the Western Occult Tradition, and through this Vision, he planted those seeds throughout the United States. Robert practiced Magick with a vengeance, exerting his Will upon the world to achieve his desires. Though some viewed him as ruthless, I worked with Robert in an extensive and personal relationship for five years, up until the moment of his passing, and found him to be in essence, a compassionate and unselfish man. Our relationship spanned a complete range of emotions and was forged through difficulty, obstacles and joy. At times, we admitted to each other our thoughts of homicide for the other but at the same time, said to each other that "we wouldn't trade all the Hell we've been through for anything in the world or wish it upon our worst enemy." Many found it hard to get along with Robert, but I have found this to be a common phenomenon among many great men and magicians. Many are frightened by those with an ability to make things happen and the vision and persistence to carry it out.

Robert went where angels feared to tread. He set the stage for the manifestation of his own Desires and those of many who worked with him. The impossible dreams he concocted seemed unattainable, and perhaps in light of what the "current" was pushing, they were. But Robert always persevered in spite of obstacles, idiots and time-wasters. *Rebels and Devils* epitomizes one of his dreams: to help bring together those that pursue their own Vision and make it happen regardless of the odds or the toll it might take.

Douglas Grant has participated in the presentation of cutting-edge Chaos Magic lectures and workshops in the U.S. with such luminaries as Peter J. Carroll, Ian Read and Phil Hine. Through his company, *Dagon Productions,* he has also become well-known for his design work and publishing of music, magazines, books and promotional material. He can be reached at Dagon Productions, P.O. Box 15284, Portland OR 97293, USA.

CHAOIST MODELS OF MIND

by Peter J. Carroll

Author of the Falcon title:
Psybermagick: Advanced Ideas in Chaos Magick

We will not use the much abused word "consciousness" which has at least three different meanings. Further, we will attempt precision with all terms and forms of grammar that we employ, to avoid the ambiguities, unspecifiable transcendentalisms, psychological jargon and new-age psycho-babble which render most attempts to model the activities of the "mind" objectively meaningless.

We shall refer to "our selves" in the plural throughout, thus avoiding the superstition of the unitary self which has unfortunately survived as an artifact in post-monotheist culture and grammar. We shall also adhere to strict Anontic grammar by avoiding all tenses of the verb "to be." We never observe "being," we only observe doing, we never observe identity, we only observe separation or similarity. Thus we have no reason to infer any form of being or to infer that anything is anything else.

Chaos And Freedom

The conflict between our subjective experience of free will and the apparent causality or determinism of physical processes evaporates when we examine the ingredients of the paradox closely.

Quantum physics provides overwhelming proof that this universe does not, at its most basic level, function on a deterministic basis. Instead all processes operate probabilistically like the throwing of dice. Only when large numbers of probabilistic processes occur together do we observe the semblance of cause and effect. Even then the mechanisms of non-linear dynamics—or "Chaos" in the mathematical sense—frequently allow indeterminate quantum processes to manifest as large indeterminacies in the behavior of macroscopic phenomena. Strict determinism, then, does not occur, but neither does completely free will. A will completely unconditioned by biology, or any previous memory experience would manifest in entirely random and mostly useless acts. Although we normally construct machines to process matter, energy, or information in the most predictable fashion possible, we can easily endow a computer with any required degree of so-called creativity and free will.

We can do this by either instructing it to generate a series of possible responses by random means and then have it use logic to select the optimal sourse of action from amongst these possibilities, or we can program it to select a series of acceptable responses on a logical basis and then to pick one of them at random. In both cases only quantum based hardware components can supply true randomness. We can also combine both of the above processes in complex procedures with additional weighting factors and parameters which interact with each other. In doing this we mimic exactly the mechanisms by which we all ourselves act.

Determinism does not completely define our acts, but neither do we need to suppose that we have some inexplicable metaphysical excuse called free will for the unpredictability of our acts. We have the ability to act with a degree of randomness. We also have a conditioned tendency to identify with, or to claim responsibility for most of what we do. In some past civilizations this tendency seems much less apparent and many recent geniuses have spoken of their inspirations arising as if from a course that they did not normally identify with.

If you wish to experience more freedom and creativity of thoughts then simply practice letting your chaotic random thought facilities play with rich sources of information. Alternate intense rational thought with periods of daydream and imagination at increasing frequency until genius blossoms.

Multiple Selves

"Self awareness" only appears mysterious or paradoxical within the old paradigm of a regular individual self, for how can such a single thing have awareness of itself? Clearly, what we call self-awareness consists of various of our selves monitoring other of our selves. Our internal dialogue takes place between various of our selves. To give a computer self-awareness, we have to construct it as two or more processing units which monitor each other's activities. The human brain develops quite a number of independent selves as it grows, each with its own emotionally based agenda. Self-awareness dawns as these selves begin to examine each other's activities. Everybody has multiple personalities although only an unfortunate minority suffer from the amnesia which marks the clinical manifestation of this universal condition. However most people in contemporary post-monotheist cultures still feel pressured to present the facade of self-consistent single personality. If they ever act out of character they will normally expend a considerable effort of introspection trying to integrate or rationalize their behavior into a "false" consistent whole, unless, of course, they have the excuse of drunkenness.

People in pagan cultures did not feel the need to rationalize their acts into a consistent whole and could cheerfully worship at the temple of Venus one day and Mars the next and they would often explain their impulses as inspirations from a particular deity.

Monotheism equates with the idea of a single self or a small group of selves dominating the others. Social control becomes much simpler under these conditions for a culture only has to program its members with the desirable behavior patterns characterized by a single deity—thus monotheism supplanted paganism.

However bizarre these appear, every god or self excluded becomes a demon liable to come screaming up from the dungeon at an inappropriate moment. When self-love fails, when the selves cease to cooperate or communicate with each other, madness begins. Thus, professionally spiritual people within a monotheist paradigm so frequently end up committing sexual outrages. Their normally dominant selves loathe and despise lust, yet eventually lust takes its revenge. In the past when monotheisms had secular power, repressed violence often manifested in astonishingly excessive ecclesiastical brutality.

Most Chaoists regard themselves as colonial organisms consisting of a parliament of equals, each with something to offer in particular circumstances, and who have no need to maintain the cultural fiction of a dominant illusory "I" in charge of all their varied riches, for each self has adequate resources to handle its specialty, particularly if allowed free reign to do so.

For a Chaoist, introspection consists of an exchange of mutual admiration, respect, and encouragement between the selves, not a period of criticism, revision, and argument over who did what and why with the communal body of the one Christ. (For those who do not believe there were many brothers to Jesus.) Conventional psychoanalysis aimed at integrating all the conflicting selves within a person will always fail for the same reasons that monotheist religions fail to eradicate sin—however such failure ensures employment for both priesthoods.

Personally we find it pleasurable and useful to take frequent inventory of all the gods or selves in our pantheon and to let each take some daily exercise when possible, in the imagined style of the complete renaissance person.

Magic

We shall at this point resist the temptation to generalize from the paradigm of independent archetypes within the personal head to the unscientific premise of the archetypes of the collective unconscious as independent metaphysical agencies.

The gods live within our heads and transpersonal similarities between gods arise from shared human biology and culture. However a large body of extremely elegant scientific evidence now confirms the magical view that the information in the brain can act non-locally in space and time to create the full range of psi effects from telepathy, clairvoyance, and psychokinesis, to so-called retroactive enchantment, modification of the apparent past.

As non-local exchanges of information across space and time seem fundamental to the functioning of this universe, we have to explain why parapsychology usually works so capriciously and unreliably. If the mechanism which enforces a uniform light speed in this universe also allows parapsychology, then we should perhaps expect a more reliable exchange between identical light quanta than between two non-identical brains or between a physical phenomenon and a mental image which represents it only imperfectly.

Building largely upon the inspiration of the English magician Austin Spare, chaoists have developed a large body of theory and technique to establish what Spare called the "sacred alignments" by which he meant the pathways through which information moves between the "conscious mind", the "subconscious or unconscious mind", and the universe at large.

We do not consider it useful to make rigid distinctions between the varying degrees of awareness we have of our brain functions. It seems that we never completely forget anything although parts of the seventy odd years long video of our lives submit only to extreme recovery techniques such as hypnosis. Our selves appear to chatter constantly to each other unnoticed by those selves which customarily talk and listen the most. As sunlight obscures the stars by day so does wakefulness obscure the fact that our selves talk and dream constantly amongst themselves, but most of what takes place in the brain passes unnoticed by the selves which do the loudest thinking. Those parts of the brain less involved in discursive thinking have greater parapsychological abilities because any image or desire held there will receive less interference from conflicting desires and doubts from other parts.

Austin Spare realized this and developed elegant techniques based on abstract sigils and emotional hyper-activation to plant desires in the magically effective parts of the brain.

We consider that a model of the mind based upon the theories of multiple selves, and a quantum non-local exchange of all mystical, religious, and magical phenomena without exception. This attitude necessarily forms a rethink of how certain apparent occult phenomena, such as "ghosts" and "charged" objects, actually work, and it forces a more or less complete abandonment of that dull old pseudo-science astrology.

In passing, we note that we take some exception with the rather moralistic tone of the Neo-Kabbalistic Leary-Wilson model of an ascending hierarchy of neural circuit selves. We give equal honor to all of our selves. Only when a god gets forced to act in the wrong circumstances does it become demonic.

References

Liber Null and Psychonaut by Peter J. Carroll
Liber Kaos by Peter J. Carroll
Psybermagick by Peter J. Carroll

Peter J. Carroll is one of founders of the Magical Pact of the Illuminates of Thanateros (IOT) which he led for a decade. He has spent twenty-five years in research and experiment and is the author of two other books: *Liber Null & Psychonaut* and *Liber Kaos: The Psychonomicon.*

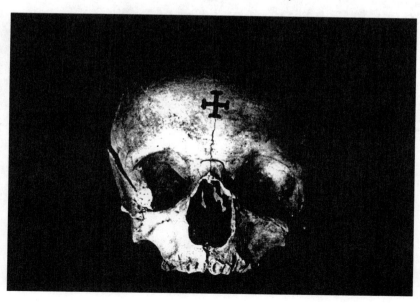

Ian Read
Editor of *Chaos International*
and founder of the band *Fire & Ice*

AN INTERVIEW WITH IAN READ

Interviewed by Phil Hine

PH: How long have you been involved with magic?

IR: My first real interest began in 1974 when I was doing re-enactment, although I did previously know a rather dubious character who claimed to be a magician—he ended up dying whilst under the influence of hallucinogenic drugs—he was one of the people who first got me interested in it.

PH: What is the primary system that you work your magic within?

IR: Germanic-Teutonic or Nordic; whatever word you want to use for it. I really haven't deviated from that very much. I've had my excursions into other paradigms, but it just works best for me, really.

PH: What attracts you to the Germanic current?

IR: Initially, because I grew up in a small village in Hampshire where people are more conscious of being English than they tend to be in cosmopolitan areas like London. I was always aware that we had our own gods. Now, over the years, I've found that this system works best for me.

PH: You've spent the last few years editing *Chaos International*—what do you see as the important points about the Chaos Magic current?

IR: The important thing for me is that it acts as a excellent arena for attracting the best people found on the magical scene. There are few people involved in other magical orders and not involved in the Pact[1]

---

[1] The Illuminates of Thanateros (IOT), or "The Pact," was born as the result of The Mass of Chaos, a ritual done in 1976 in an abandoned ammunition dump "dug deep into a mountain somewhere in the Rhineland." In attendance were dozens of magicians. One year later some of these people met again in an Austrian castle. It was there that the Illuminates of Thanateros was formally arranged and made manifest. Since that time The Pact's membership has grown to world-wide proportions.

who interest me. There are a few—but not many. Also the fact that it allows me to do whatever I want to do—and I'm fairly traditional and strict about my way of working—and yet be a senior member of the IOT—despite hardly being a Chaos Magician. It's very difficult to define what a Chaos Magician is.

PH: What do you think are the essential qualities of a magician?

IR: A magician has to be more of everything than the average person is. I've clearly stated this on numerous occasions, but it cannot be said to often—magic is an elite pursuit. This is quite clear from stories about Gandalf, Othinn, Gwydion, Merlin—they are all astonishingly elite individuals. The idea of mass movements for magic are ludicrous really.

PH: So do you think that magic attracts people of an elite disposition to itself then?

IR: I think magic attracts arseholes, generally.

PH: Why do you think that is?

IR: Because they use it as a crutch, like they use religion. It attracts people who are inadequate, who think that if they read enough books or sit at the feet of enough gurus, they can somehow improve themselves. They want short-cuts, and don't realize that when you start doing it, it's going to bring more problems than answers. It certainly did for me. I would say that doing magick is like trying to get a third dan in any martial art. If you go to a reputable martial arts master, it's going to be hard work for many, many years! I start seeing a few glimmers of hope now for me, after twenty years. I don't know how many people in my position who would be honest enough to say that—magic is full of too much bullshit, in my book.

PH: Do you think that bullshit is perpetuated by people trying to push their own traditions and books?

IR: There is certainly an element of that. Magic is big business, there's no doubt about that. Out of every hundred books on magic, there will only be about two which are worth reading. And in those two, there's probably only about 10% that holds anything of value.

PH: What's your view on the near-deification of past magical personalities; people such as Dion Fortune, Aleister Crowley or Israel Regardie?

IR: I have ambivalent views on this. I remember reading a few years ago that a good way of learning was to study the biographies of famous people in magic, in order to try and emulate their good points. The difference is that I don't think you should try and become them, or even act in the way that they acted. You try to develop your character based on their good example. To try and deify them is outrageous—they would have not liked that if they were worth anything. If a teacher is worth his salt, then he's not going to want you to do that. I do think that young people need to be set a good example. Fortunately, I grew up in an age where good examples were still around. I fear now for people under thirty-five. I wouldn't like to be born now. I feel privileged to have seen the end of the old world and the beginning of the new. I remember milk being delivered by horses. Now, going to the moon is old hat. I know, from being the editor of a magazine, that if you show me a man under thirty-five, I'll show you a man who can't write a sentence in English that's structured properly. It's very sad, and it's not only in England. I get letters all the time, written in German (which I have a fairly good knowledge of, considering I'm a foreigner), and I know that they're written badly.

PH: Can you offer any hope for the current cultural situation?

IR: Well, if it completely destroys itself it may be a good thing. After all you need complete destruction before you get new growth. That's perhaps the mystery of Hagalaz, the rune of Hail. I don't believe that human-kind has changed—probably not since we decided to stand on two legs. We've got no better, and no worse. I'm interested in building a network, around the world, of people of a like mind, and of a like spirit, and a like soul, if you want to use that rather blasphemous term. I'm not really too bothered about the mass of humanity. You need to have the normal plebs really, they'll never change. Whilst building up Chaos International, I spent some time hanging around at occult functions in London, and what that taught me was that there's no one more despicable, dishonest, nasty, petty and generally pathetic than the average occultist. Quite honestly I prefer going down to Hampshire and sitting in the company of my folks, who have no pretensions. Their handshake's worth something. That's a point of power to me—if you can give your word and keep it. To have the power to say "This is my word" and to keep it, that is the secret of oaths—most people can't do it—they're just pathetic. They lie and cheat because it's easier.

PH: When Chaos Magic began to spread it's word, it's only core axiom was that "Nothing is True, Everything is Permitted." Some people seem to have taken that as saying that you can throw away any rules of conduct, behavior and magical discipline.

IR: That doesn't bother me. I see myself as one of the wolves, and if people act like that around me I go straight for the throat. I think that's how the world will operate. Of course you can do that, but you must understand that to do that you need power. I'm big enough and ugly enough to look after myself, and I could probably go around behaving like that. There'd always be someone coming along to stomp on me, but I'm quite capable of it. Most of these pathetic people who do that aren't.

I find that quite amusing in a way, but it's rather like martial arts—when you're a real tough nut, you never get in any fights.

PH: So for you, personal power is different to calling upon cosmic energies or calling yourself an Adeptus Major?

IR: Well you can call yourself whatever you like—I generally don't call myself anything. If people could invoke these things I'd admire them, but you need a strong vessel to do that. Some years ago, I was at the Prediction Festival in England, and I met Bel Bucca, who's a rather famous carver of heathen idols. He looked at me, and he said "Can you imagine how many of these rather sad people in this room, who are now catching on to the runic bandwagon, could stand, and stare into the eye of Othinn."

PH: There's a recognizable difference then, between one who gets into a magical area because it's the current trend, and a working magician.

IR:. Two magicians meet each other, and they know. They have charisma. It's more difficult for a real magician to appear to be a twit, than it is the other way round. There are lots and lots of these silly people running around claiming that they are into magic, and it's laughable really.

PH: Hence "A King may choose his garment as he will: there is no certain test; but a beggar cannot hide his poverty."

IR: Definitely. Aleister Crowley had a lot of intelligent things to say. I find it rather amusing when I hear all these people slagging him off. First of all, I would put it to them that, okay, we live in an age of mediocrity, so it's easier to shine now, but they should make a little bit out of their life before they should clamor for their words to be heard.

PH: How much would you say that Chaos Magic is a fad?

IR: Well, I think it was a fad, and I think we're coming to an end of that now. People in the IOT are much more elite than they were. It's become harder to get in. We're much more hidden. We do not encourage arseholes to become members; in fact we don't lay any red carpets down for new people. In fact once we tell people what will be demanded of them, they often run fleeing.

PH: Have you found that people approach the IOT expecting to be welcomed with open arms?

IR: Oh lots of people approach me about magic. Sometimes I pretend I don't know the first thing about magic, or use any other number of subterfuges. I don't believe that you should encourage people. The right people will find a way, and if you lay out red carpets, you get the sort of arsehole who will follow any sign if they think at the end of it there's something for nothing. All you get for nothing, is nothing.

PH: Apart from editing *Chaos International,* you've also got a band, *Fire & Ice.* How did that come about?

IR: Magic is a lot to do with charisma, and controlling the environment to your own advantage. It is strongly my view that people who believe in you are giving you power. My way is to produce quality things. I stumbled into music by accident, from singing folk songs for my own pleasure, and once I'd finished my tour of duty with independent bands such as *Death In June* and *Current 93*—I was a founder member of *Sol Invictus*—after that period, I thought that was the end of my musical career. But David Tibet and others were clamoring for me to continue. I realized that it could be a good avenue for putting a lot of my magical ideas across. As is the way, I get very few letters from people who understand what I'm saying, but my songs do have a lot of power encoded in them. I never declare what that power is, or where it's to be found. People have to discover it for themselves. *Fire & Ice* is an avenue for my magic.

PH: The music of *Fire & Ice* has been described as "Apocalyptic Folk"—do you think this is a fair comment?

IR: I think it's perhaps the closest you can get to putting a label on it. I really don't like labeling it. I think that Jazz music was probably better before someone bothered to dream up the name Jazz. I tend to try and avoid labeling, but I would argue that the bands such as *Death In June, Sol Invictus* and *Current 93* are doing modern folk music, and bringing it up to date.

PH: How's your music been received?

IR: I've had, to my knowledge, no really adverse criticism. Of course that may not be a good thing. What saddens me is the number of non-committal reviews. I remember Crowley saying "Give me hot, or give me colder—nothing tepid." But there are a lot of fans out there who write intelligent letters to me.

PH: Do you think that the power in your music is appreciated by your fans?

IR: Yes, a lot of them do appreciate what I have to say. I am heartened by that.

PH: In everything you've said so far, there's a strong current of historical value in both your music and your magical work.

IR: You need to learn from past foolishness, and you should go forward, both adopting old values which are still valid, and finding new ones. We can look to the future, but we can look to the past with more certainty.

PH: The Chaos Magician doesn't tend to look at the past or the future with rose-tinted spectacles.

IR: No. The exciting thing about Chaos Magic was that from day one, it directed itself to man in the latter part of the Twentieth-Century, which I'm not aware of any other major current doing that. This is why it has had success, I think.

PH: Some magical currents seem to be based on an idealized notion of the past which doesn't bear any relationship to what we know about our ancestors.

IR: One only needs to look at the way people view Celtic magic to see that. Let's face it, there weren't that many Celts who came to Britain. They were a very warlike people, but the fact of the matter is that they weren't very good at it, because the Saxons defeated them constantly, and shoved them into far corners of the land.

PH: Why is it do you think, that so many occultists are attracted to that kind of romanticism?

IR: They don't want to face the real world. I like fantasy myself, but I like to fantasize about things and reach for them. The idea of fantasy is to give yourself an arena of possibility to jump into, not to create something that's completely pointless and stupid.

PH: Do you agree that magic demands more of you than you would at first expect?

IR: Definitely. Magic is very demanding. It's clear to me that for most people, they are trying to escape from this world. I believe that this world is our arena. We don't escape from it, we try to build our own corner of it that's better than the corner that every other arsehole has.

PH: Do think that a lot of what passes for magical theory is redundant nowadays?

IR: Yes. I'm more interested in doing—seeing the effects by result—than all the arguments such as how many Chaos Servitors can jump up and down on the end of a ball-point pen.

Ian Read is the editor of *Chaos International,* one of the world's most respected magical periodicals. As a musician he has worked with such bands as *Death in June, Current 93* and was co-founder of *Sol Invictus.* In November, 1992 Ian founded *Fire & Ice* which has released the albums *Guided by the Sun, Hollow Ways, Midwinter Fires, California Daze* and the single *Blood on the Snow. Fire & Ice* takes the purity and philosophy of early music and melds it into a message redolent of the powerful seeds of honor, truth, loyalty and the bond of true friendship. Ian can be reached through BM Sorcery, London WC1N 3XX, England.

ETERNITY IS GOOD FOR YOU

by Dave Lee

He remembered waking up in Gunter's Mercedes. Nice car to wake up in, if you had to sleep in a car. He remembered flashing metallic darkness, awful sourceless nausea, a sheen of recent rain on the road, a bitter taste when he had lit a cigarette. Sitting feeling shrunken and stupid, hands huddled between his thighs. Falling down helpless in a car park full of arclight, waking again in daylight, on the outskirts of some city in the rain. Raoul had made him ill and then healed him.

He recalled a clean-cut young door-answering acolyte with a serious expression that verged on the blank. Stumbling on the stairs. Raoul's admission that he had cursed him.

Raoul had said to him, "Because when you believe me, little wizard, you will be afraid. But you have come here for your little century, haven't you? Maybe your two centuries. You know, most people would live to be a hundred if they simply stopped tripping over themselves, all but the real genetic cripples of course. Nobody has any real ambition. You think you are elite, but what are your ambitions?"

He had paused for effect. "I shall tell you. Ordinary pleasures, many cunts and arseholes and breasts, Love as you call it, and a stiff prick to satisfy them. Wine, food and music. Drugs. Friendships with others in your little elite club. Love, as you call it the mutual parasitism of the most unimaginative sexual obsessions. And your puerile fantasies of space travel and a world of immortal fun and exploration. Your ambitions are just appetites, and your pain makes you run round in circles."

Alex had asked "What's so different about you then?"

"You do not understand, and I do not need your understanding. I have the freedom to mold the whole future of this planet, turn the human race into...whatever I wish. Stay here another week and I will make you love me. Then your little life will be more magical than you could ever make it."

Raoul had insisted Alex photograph him with a Polaroid, as his face shifted and lost years before his eyes. Alex had looked at the snapshots, and they showed what his eyes had seen. He had turned down Raoul's offer and left.

Alex believed Raoul had sent one of his zombies to smash up the flat of his Viennese lover, Anna. She had got home in the middle of this depredation, and had fought. She ended up with a big hole in her belly, lucky to survive the blood loss. Alex hated Raoul, despite his awareness that impotent hate is a debilitating disease.

He exhaled heavily, coming back to the present for a moment, sitting on the floor in Maire's bedroom. Morning light slanted through the spectacular high windows. He was surrounded by bits of newspaper, the raw ingredients of a curse he already knew was never to be.

Alex believed he had thought it through, the way that magicians sometimes talk big about death-cursing, but it doesn't usually work, for the simple reason they don't really want to do it. He thought he had a method: he started by picturing himself killing his victim in various physical ways. Try bringing a heavy brass candlestick down on his skull, feeling the satisfying crunch of bone. Do it again, smash his fucking head in. No: that's just old classic film footage, thin on detail. How about holding a gun to his head and blowing part of it away? The light goes out of his eyes while you're looking. Better. Or you shoot him in the belly, he rolls around a lot, screaming in a strangled sort of way, the pain and fear too much for a good open yell. He looks up at you and tries to mouth something with his dying breath. Yes, we're getting near. Tarantino, Easton Ellis, even. Maybe he throws up everywhere, maybe he throws a fit, his tongue blackened sticking out of his mouth, making funny sad sounds as his body thrashes helplessly.

These things are still your barest outlines, culled from films, TV, books. You'll have to try harder. It's your imagination, go ahead.

He told himself how it should work out: If you get that far, the next stage is to detach yourself completely from that hatred. Your touch must be light, almost casual. The assassination weapon you are building will be disguised, looking not at all sinister. It may be a pretty picture, quite an innocuous object which you will use to destroy him. If you manage to reach this stage, the rest is easy. Or so Alex told himself. That was the point he had reached, as a cloud glitched the bars of light, and shut off the vision of dancing dust modes, island universes of discarded tissue.

He had gone to the door of the flat to collect Maire's mail. She was lying in bed, magnificently at ease, reading and smoking. Alex stared out of the window. He looked at his watch, and remembered the day he had got back to London. He had called Gerry the occult newsman the day before he left Vienna, finally locating him at midnight in his office.

"I'll come straight to the point, so you can go back to sleep as soon as possible. Have you heard of a guy call Raoul Zeigler?"

"What pot does he piss in?" Gerry slurred.

"Occult Martial Arts, Immortalism, maybe cultism."

"Err, yes, I think I've got it. Yes, a queer fish. He's said to have a hundred acolytes, all lined up in tents. He's as rich as a prudent whore, and by all accounts a shit-hot sorcerer. Rumor is he's going to use the collective magis of all these dumb fuckers in his garden to create a super elemental, a sort of Doomsday Tulpa, to accomplish some insane move like world domination." Gerry belched. "That do you?"

"Is he connected to any magical orders?" Alex had asked.

"Don't know, probably your lot, he's sounds so full-time fucking weird." He had heard Gerry yawning. "If I get anything else do you want me to call you?"

"No, I'm on the move, I'll see you soon. I owe you one."

The return to London: Alex and Gerry met for beer and debriefing, surrounded by panels of Bloomsbury. Talk turned to immortalism.

They had listed the elements of life-extension, all the usual stuff about diet, sex, emotional renewal, pranayama to clean out the energy body, and positive thinking to clear the mind of depression. This is all pretty obvious. And Gerry raised the obvious objection: who wants to be some prissy, boring old bastard living off a macrobiotic diet and going mad if people cross their legs in his presence because it disrupts the energy flows in the fucking room. Without lust for life, none of the rest of it made sense. Your life has to be worth living, or you're better off as pet food.

Alex had told Gerry about Raoul. Gerry was obviously making mental notes, despite the lavish libations. Raoul seemed to have discovered a technique of reversing aging, but he was insane in an unusual and significantly dangerous way. And his humiliation of Alex rankled afresh. He brought himself back to the quiet street in front of him. His mind was blocked by this obsession. It sat across his view of life, demanding his attention. He was sick of it. What he needed to know, was that it was part of a bigger picture, which would engage his passion from a different angle.

Maire looked over to him. "How's the curse going?"

"OK," Alex said. "Tell me how you worked that out."

Maire pushed back her luxuriant red hair, smiled and said, "You are cutting up The Times news pages. Serious News equals Death. Ergo, you are constructing a collage on the theme of death. My informed guess is that the intended target is one Herr Zeigler, whom you mentioned the day you got back. When was that? Thank you, yesterday. And what's more, you're not sure about it, because you're working so slow. You probably need more information." Maire yawned and stretched, showing off her perfect breasts. She got up and crossed over to where he stood. Her pale redhead skin showed a pearly sheen in the window light. She smelled of fresh sweat and the previous night's sex. "Why don't you get it. I'll have to throw you out and do some work at some stage, and I'd like you to fuck me again first."

The authority of pleasure focused Alex's mind. He nuzzled her hair and stroked her long back. "Good thinking. I'll try my email." He sat at Maire's computer and dialed through to his mail server. There was one item on there, coded KACFQJ. He opened it. An animated image of the British Prime Minister's face appeared on the screen, the shimmering synthesized voice repeating the slogan "Don't worry, be happy, just look at the pictures." The face collapsed in a haze of fractal detail that blew away, leaving a gray field across which marched an army of symbols. Today's date appeared at the top, and the words "Divination by Periodic Table of the Elements." The marching symbols had arranged themselves into the grid of elements. Seven elements were highlighted. Alex scrolled the next section up. It was titled "General View", and held the analysis:

"Thallium, Hydrogen, Neptunium: Shifts of major significance in the world network of Wyrd. Poison radiations. The entry of entirely novel idea structures into the Web. The birth of new matter, return to first principles."

The next section was "Personal parameters", and went, "Aluminum: mental activity. No, it's Al = Alex. It also means change of heart. Krypton: escape from difficulties. Plutonium: initiation. Boron: obscure. The words I get are 'Eternity is good for you.' The Johnson."

The message ended. He sat on the stool, vaguely aware of the sounds of Maire cleaning her teeth in the bathroom. A laugh was shaking up from his belly, his cock stirring. Somehow, as he'd wished it, the weirdness was coming into focus without that drag of useless hate. The sickness and humiliation were just an introduction to more power. Stand aside from the feelings, and one day you will find a use for Raoul. Eternity is good for you.

Dave Lee's published works include: *Magickal Aeonnics, Beyond the Soft Machine, Magical Incenses* and *The Wealth Magic Workbook.* To contact Dave or for information regarding the IOT U.K. write: Attractor, Box 888, 103 Burley Wood Crescent, Leeds LS4 2UJ, United Kingdom.

ANNO CHAOS— THE PANDAEMONAEON

from Templum Nigri Solis

It began over Hiroshima just before 8 a.m. on the sixth of August 1945. The unthinkable and the impossible coincided in one cataclysmic event. Even though nuclear fission had been achieved in secret, its power had not been demonstrated to the world at large. The previously inviolable elements of the universe could now be co-opted by those with the right technology, and the unequivocal relationship between energy and matter was revealed. The supposed moral arbiter of the globe, the First World, had sent an emissary of absolute evil, blessed by priests in the name of an all-merciful god.

The bombing involved a massive risk: it was feared that once fission began, the entire atomic structure of matter could become fuel for a chain reaction. Nevertheless, it was a gamble that the 'guardians of the free world' were prepared to take. The human species had acquired the power of absolute annihilation, which until that morning had been the domain of gods.

With the aid of the mass media, global consciousness was forever changed. The bombing of Hiroshima—resulting in a degree of destruction hitherto difficult to comprehend—had been permitted. From thereon, everything would be permitted. If the merciful god had allowed the unthinkable to occur, and let the impossible be rendered physical, how could anything be true ever again?

The Bomb blasted a hole in humanity's collective soul. With the ever-present threat of total destruction by human agency, centuries of faith in a transcendent external principle—and the socio-political structures built around it—evaporated. Hell was now only five minutes away, and the likelihood of a divine hand reaching out to stop it was remote. Matter was now negotiable, as was the destiny of the species.

The post war generation inherited a logarithmically expanding economy, supported by a technology extrapolated from the mechanics of death.

A new, accelerated age commenced, culminating in the present day plethora of technologies, ideologies and possibilities. However, the spiritual void concomitant with this expanded material horizon triggered a search for new forms of transcendence, transcendence being a biological need of the human species. The occult revival and the large scale experiments with drugs and eastern philosophies of the sixties were some manifestations of this search, as were Billy Graham and the Second Vatican Council. Everything from package holidays to Marxism has been advanced to fill the vacuum at the heart of post-Bomb society but these have been cosmetic measures only.

The Bomb altered not only the spiritual landscape but the entire established view of the world. That first public demonstration of nuclear power heralded the transition from a relativistic universe to a quantum universe. This view is only beginning to become established in popular culture, as at the time of writing, most schools have difficulty incorporating post-Newtonian physics into their curricula. To do so would challenge the orthodox view of the universe, which is an integral construct of the old Western paradigm. In the centuries before Hiroshima, science and religion were enmeshed. Although practitioners of either would have denied it, there was a tacit alliance. Most of pre-war science still accommodated the concept of a creator/god, adherence to which caused Einstein to balk at the last theoretical hurdle.

Magic, being both an art and a science, has remained relatively free of the restrictions of orthodoxy by virtue of its position outside socially sanctioned thought. It has been constantly accumulating data and technology as human consciousness evolves, despite occasional attempts at cauterization by the nostalgically inclined. It is the very nature of Magic to be progressive, anarchic and experimental. Only the lack of an adequate network of language has held it back, and as thought it is often several steps ahead of the cultural mechanisms that express it.

Magic has acted as a matrix from which the courageous can explore a universe that answers to no authority. The iconoclasm of the rock and roll generation has allowed a young society freedom to rediscover a magical perspective. This had not been readily accessible since the transition from tribal culture to the culture of mass control, as it had always been the preserve of those privileged by circumstance.

Despite the restrictions control culture tries to impose, we now inhabit a cyber age, where information and technology are easily accessed. This is the mirror of the Shamanic Age, when knowledge was free to those who wished to reach out and interface with it directly, and all realities were immanent. Human biology and the environment were not discrete, and this is an understanding we are rediscovering today. We still have the neurological hardware that caused bushes to burn and dragons to walk the earth, and there is a new magical technology that allows us to re-boot it. This is Chaos Magic. With it, we are accelerating and perfecting the techniques that allow reality to be manipulated as efficiently and directly as possible. This new technology brings the Magician the realization that everything is possible, and every conceivable reality is in *potentia,* lying dormant within the sub-spaces of the very air we breathe. All things are in *potentia,* with no intimation of restriction. This is the Chaos of orthodoxy, the omnipresent primal soup.

Demons are configurations of energy/information, and any configuration is now possible. All the demons are out of the box, and the true spirit of the age now has a name. This is the Age of All Demons—This is the PanDaemonAeon. The year 1987 *era vulgaris* is also the year 42 PDA. Io Chaos!

This article was provided by *Templum Nigri Solis* who may be contacted at P.O. Box 672, South Yarra, VIC 3141, Australia.

PART III

VOODOOMAN

Character Created by
Christopher S. Hyatt, Ph.D. & S. Jason Black

Art by
S. Jason Black

Story by
S. Jason Black & Christopher S. Hyatt, Ph.D.

A FEDERAL PRISON CELL IN SOUTH AMERICA. . . ONE OF THE WORST PRISONS IN THE COUNTRY. A YOUNG MAN NAMED CARLOS MONTANA, A MAN WHO SURVIVED A CHILDHOOD IN THE SLUMS OF RIO, WAITS TO SEE IF HIS LIFE WILL LAST MUCH LONGER.

THOUGHTS OF HIS BETRAYAL PASS THROUGH HIS MIND, BUT HIS ANGER IS WELL CONTAINED AND HIS ATTENTION FOCUSED.

YOUR EVENING MEAL BOY.

IT'S A SPECIAL MEAL, COMPLIMENTS OF YOUR PADRINHO.

MY PADRINHO...?

226

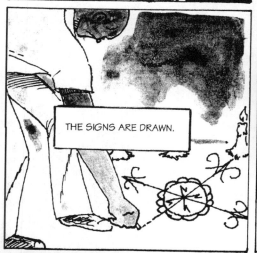

232

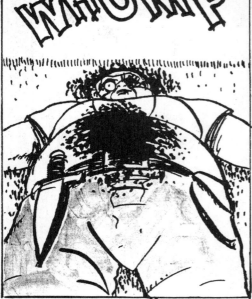

248

249

TO BE CONTINUED ...

PART IV

Struggles

PRELUDE TO
A ONE-NIGHT STAND

by Adam Matza

I need a body-sized condom
to protect me from your malaise
and you from mine.
I wasn't there when they ripped away
your goodness, so don't blame me;
tonight I'm unfazed, my foundation is razed rubble
and I'm trouble.
All I can offer is nothing
but resolute pounding stiffness
and maybe a brief glimmering glimpse
to make it seem right —
or maybe a drink or three to make it seem right.
Tonight I really don't care
about your mistakes, regrets
or money woes,
nor do you care about mine,
or the flickering pilot light casting a feint shadow —
or the trip I took and have yet to return from.

Acid courses through my veins,
and I lie
awake on a futon
late in the early morning
staring at the dust on the ceiling fan,
attempting to start from the end
and work my way back
like those unchallenging
cartoon mazes in the Sunday funny papers —
while you piss in my bathroom.

We are so slowly suicidal,
looking forward to the end,
lapsing, choking, needing CPR,
oxygen, nutrients, bliss, soil, sunlight —
a new place to rest peacefully: that beats
this restiveness in pieces.

No, this you wouldn't understand,
so take off your clothes,
share the requisite intimacy,
and then let's get on with it.

Adam Matza is a poet, musician and producer. *Weeds,* a collection of his poetry, is available from Blowfish Press, 3501 NW 47th Avenue, Suite 503, Fort Lauderdale FL 33319, U.S.A.

WHY IS THIS TERRORIST DANCING?

by Germaine W. Shames

My interest in Ali Mohammed Alami was predatory: I needed a story, a Big Story. Ali, having planted fifteen bombs across West Jerusalem in a single day, was just the ticket. Brandishing my press card, I closed in for the kill, but the moment I elbowed my way past his bodyguards and got within range of him, his pheromones snared me. I began to daydream, *How does a terrorist make love?*

Ali was no Omar Sharif. Having spent more than half his life in Israeli prisons, his stomach bugged out from repeated hunger strikes. He sat with his back to the wall and wielded his eyes like scimitars. When I met him, he was not long out of prison, grudgingly released by his Israeli captors in a prisoner exchange. Because he was photogenic and spoke four languages, the international media adopted him as their pet terrorist.

When I set out for Israel, I didn't need to pack my sex addiction; it stowed along amid the black satin folds of my designer underwear. My ostensible reason for going to this navel of the universe was to cover the mass tantrum raging there for an obscure news service, but I suspected it was just another of my ploys to get laid. Jewish girls can be very creative that way.

I landed an interview.

When I arrived at the appointed venue, the Notre Dame Hospice, Ali, flanked by bodyguards, sat drinking grainy coffee with a mismatched assortment of well-heeled Europeans and threadbare Palestinians, speaking French out of one side of his mouth, Arabic out the other. He greeted me in English.

Gradually the table cleared and I found myself alone with Ali Mohammed Alami. Straining to control the tremors in my hands, I grabbed for the tools of my trade—notebook, tape recorder, camera—and tried to barricade myself behind them. But it was no use. I couldn't stop wondering, *What sort of explosive does this terrorist darling pack in his pants? How long is his fuse?*

I asked the obvious questions: "What was going through your mind when you planted the bombs?... Under whose orders were you acting?... Would you do it again?"

He looked offended: I hadn't touched my coffee.

"Just one night, I'd like to be an ordinary man," he sighed, leaning back in his seat and eyeing me with undisguised lust.

Just one night, I mused, *I'd like to can this Barbara Walters act and know what a kamikaze feels like before the blast.*

We took a taxi to the American Colony Hotel. The place had a jazz cellar, dark, with tables so small and close you might lap brandy from your neighbor's snifter. Ali was flush against me; I could feel his breath in my hair like an off-season monsoon.

"I am done blowing people up," he thought aloud.

Let me be your last bang, I reserved.

It was late, closing time, which left us no choice but to cross over from East Jerusalem into West. Officially, Ali was under city detention and confined to his home from 6 p.m. to 8 a.m., but his pent-up longing made him reckless. He took me to a fleabag Israeli tavern, an after-hours joint crammed with locals and Jewish tourists. We seated ourselves—Ali with his back to the wall—at a table up front next to a makeshift stage, where a guitarist strummed oldies.

For several minutes Ali surveyed the room, his gaze swerving and probing like floodlights, then he sat back and began to clap his hands in time with the music. He looked relaxed and happy, almost euphoric, as if the melody had released a narcotic into his bloodstream.

"Dance with me," he said suddenly, jumping to his feet.

I was stunned. Ali Mohammed Alami was a terrorist, after all. No one else was dancing—we could not have made ourselves any more conspicuous—and Ali was outside of himself, wired and unpredictable.

"Dance with me," he repeated, pulling me from my seat.

I danced. Stiffly, aware of the turning heads and raised eyebrows of the crowd.

Ali, in glaring contrast, danced like a dervish; he spun and leapt and gyrated, beaming all the while, laughing! Then he danced up and down the aisles, dragging people—tourists, soldiers, drunks—onto the makeshift dance floor, twirling them by the hand, coupling them with strangers, until everyone was on their feet.

The dancing grew orgiastic; it overflowed the dance floor and poured out into the street. I took Ali by the arm, intending to tug him to a hot-pillow joint down the block. *How does a terrorist make love?* I just had to know. *How lethal are his charges? Will he detonate like a time bomb at the height of orgasm?*

In front of us, not a hundred paces away, a garish marquee marked the gates of paradise: Hotel Ron. Ali's tongue flashed, once, twice, across his lips. Our steps synchronized, quickened.

"Don' t be afraid of me," he said, unnecessarily.

You're talking to a woman with the self-preservation instincts of a moth, I nearly let him know.

Without warning, a deep purple shadow spilled across the sidewalk and swallowed up Ali Mohammed Alami. There were no sirens. In his place stood an armed Israeli soldier. The young man wore his rifle slung low, accenting the frayed fly of his fatigues. Several days' growth of beard rimmed his mouth.

"Close call," he emitted in halting, Hebreocized English.

"Yeah, one hell of a story," I comforted myself.

He looked baffled but offered to buy me coffee anyway.

I started to walk away—stopped. A familiar twinge drew me back to where the soldier stood, unshaven and game. It was too late. I already began to wonder, *How does an anti-terrorist make love?*

Germaine W. Shames is an author, freelance journalist and international business consultant. She holds a masters degree in Intercultural Management, a well-worn passport and nerves of steel. She has written from five continents on topics ranging from the Middle East crisis to Aboriginal land rights, from the struggle to save the Amazon to the plight of street children. She is co-author of *World-Class Service* (Intercultural Press) and numerous articles for such publications as *Hemispheres, Success, Troika, Longevity,* and the *Cornell Quarterly* among others. Her fiction often draws on characters and settings from her sojourns abroad. Her characters deliver a message at once gut-honest and ennobling.

DEVIL BE MY GOD

by Lon Milo DuQuette

Author (or co-author) of the Falcon titles:
The Enochian World of Aleister Crowley: Enochian Sex Magic
Sex Magick, Tantra and Tarot: The Way of the Secret Lover
Aleister Crowley's Illustrated Goetia: Sexual Evocation
Taboo: The Ecstasy of Evil

"I advise you to curb that waging tongue of yours."
— Bishop of the Black Connons

"It's a habit I've never formed Your Grace."
— Robin Hood

In A.D. 415 Cyril, the Bishop of Alexandria Egypt, found himself in a most awkward position. Not only was he burdened with the task of concocting viable doctrines[1] from the muddled and conflicting traditions of the young Christian cult, he was required to do so in the most sophisticated and enlightened pagan city on earth.

Long before the alleged virgin birth of the crucified savior, Alexandria, with her celebrated schools and library, nurtured the greatest minds of the Mediterranean world and Asia. Here, religion and philosophy were lovers, and their union gave rise to dynamic environment of dialog and debate. On more than one occasion Cyril tried to glean converts from the student body of the Neo-Platonic Academy, only to be stuck dumb by the discomforting realization that the fledgling philosophers were far more knowledgeable than he about the subtleties and shortcomings of his own faith. Uncomfortable as such moments were His Grace bore them dutifully. They afforded him the opportunity to suffer for his faith. His patience came to an end, however, when his faith and reputation were

---

[1] Cyril is credited with formulating the concept of the Holy Trinity, an invention for which he was eventually canonized.

challenged by a brilliant and charismatic luminary of the Alexandrian School of Neo-Platonism, Hypatia—the greatest woman initiate of the ancient world.

Hypatia of Alexandria was without question the most respected and influential thinker of her day. The daughter of the great mathematician, Theon, she took over her father's honored position at the Academy and lectured there for many years. She, more than any other individual since Plotinus, the father of Neo-Platonism, grasped the profound potential of that school of thought. Her lectures were wildly popular and attracted a stream of scholars who saw in Neo-Platonism the possibility of a truly universal spiritual order—a supreme philosophy—an enlightened religion to unite all religions. Such was the golden promise of Neo-Platonism, and Hypatia of Alexandria was its virgin prophetess.

Troubled by the continued degeneration of the Christian movement, its intolerance of other faiths and its dangerous preoccupation with miracles and wonders, Hypatia began a series of public lectures dealing with the cult. She revealed the pagan roots of the faith and systematically unmasked the absurdities and superstitions that had infected the movement. Then, with power and eloquence surpassing that of any Christian apologist, she elucidated upon what she understood to be the true spiritual treasures found in the purported teachings of the "Christ."

Her arguments were so persuasive that many new converts to the cult renounced their conversions and became disciples of Hypatia. Her lectures stimulated enormous interest in Christianity, but not Christianity as it was presented by Cyril, the Bishop of Alexandria.

Not blessed with the strength of character necessary to suffer a personal confrontation with Hypatia, Cyril embarked upon a campaign of personal vilification by preaching to his unwashed and fanatical flock that Hypatia was a menace to the faith, a sorceress in league with the Devil. These diatribes seemed to have little effect upon the sophisticated population of urban Alexandria who were beginning to realize that Bishop Cyril's Christianity was a cult that didn't play well with other children. Deep in the Nitrian dessert, however, Cyril's hateful words eventually reached the crude monastery of Peter the Reader.

Years of preaching to the wind and converting scorpions had uniquely qualified Peter to be the cleansing sword of the Prince of Peace, and the thought of a devil-possessed woman attacking his savior was more than this man of God could stomach. Mustering a rag-tag collection of fellow hermits, he marched to Alexandria where they met with officials of the Caesarean church who informed him that each afternoon the shameless Hypatia drove her own chariot from the Academy to her home. Armed only with clubs, oyster shells, and the Grace of God, Peter and his mob ambushed Hypatia in the street near the Academy. Pulling her from her chariot they dragged her to the Caesarean church where they stripped her, beat her with clubs, and finally (because of an on-going debate over the soul's eternal status if the corpse remained whole) scraped the flesh from her bones with the oyster shells. The scoops of flesh and the rest of her remains were then carried away and burned.

The reaction of the Alexandrian community was one of confusion and shock, and the Neo-Platonist school was dealt a blow from which it never recovered. Although he went to great lengths to distance himself from the incident, Cyril took full advantage of the situation and used the terror of the moment to further intimidate the city and establish that the will of the Christian God was to be resisted at one's own risk.

The martyrdom of Hypatia was certainly not the first example of truth resisting evil and losing, but it did mark the beginning of a prolonged spiritual delirium tremor from which Western Civilization has never fully recovered. Even the bright souls who did not succumb to the universal madness were forced to blossom against the twisted projections of the collective nightmare.

Spiritual growth is not impossible in such an environment. But where wisdom is perceived by the world to be ignorance; love is considered sin, and all that is best in the human spirit is condemned and repressed, the road by which a seeker of enlightenment must travel takes many curious turns. On such a journey one's companions are outlaws and rebels; sacredness breeds in blaspheme, truth falls from the lips of false prophets, heaven is sought in hell, and God is the Devil himself.

Lon Milo DuQuette is a noted Tantric authority who has written and taught extensively in the areas of Mysticism, Magick and Tarot.

THE BLACK ART OF PSYCHOTHERAPY

By Dr. Jack S. Willis

The multi entendre of the title is intentional and appropriate (multi: more than double, less than many). Let us count the ways.

First, psychotherapy is an art. It is not a science (the human-beings-are-laboratory-rats mentality of the behaviorists notwithstanding). A friend of mine, a philosopher of esthetics, defines art as: anything that people treat as art. So it is with psychotherapy. Any mad school that springs up and that gets people to call it "psychotherapy" then becomes a "psychotherapy." But is it good psychotherapy or just mad? We will return to that.

Second of the entendre is that, by whatever definition, it is a black art. And, in two ways. First, it supposedly deals with the dark side of the person. Call it dark, call it hidden, call it black; by whatever name, it is the devil within us that is awakened in psychotherapy. Second, as an art, it is dependent not only on the artistry of the practitioner, but also on the (en)light (enment) of the therapist. We will return to that, too.

Third of the entendre, it is a black art because, examined closely, it employs the same techniques, albeit in different robes, as does thaumaturgy and invocation of the spirits. The names of the spirits are different, and the drugs are (usually) different, and the invocation rituals are different; but it is magic nonetheless. And black magic at that.

Do you wish to move to a different plane of consciousness? Try hypnosis or alpha wave biofeedback or sodium amital or any number of emotion altering drugs. Do you wish to feel fully? Try Gestalt or psychodrama or Primal. Do you wish to probe the unknown and unknowable. Try Jungian. Do you wish a re-birth? Try Rankian, or rebirthing, or age regression (even to rebirth in former lives). Do you wish to be loved? Try Rogerian. Is death your issue? Existentialist therapy awaits. Or, perhaps you want better sex or mind-body unity? Try Reichian, Bio-energetics, Feldenkrais, Rolfing or Alexander technique. For every passion there is a therapy, and for every therapy there is a passionate following. What to do? What to do? We will return to that, too. There is an answer.

Final of the entendre, it is also an art of the patient (really a student rather than a patient). The art of the student is where we will finish our exploration.

Psychotherapy As Art

No two people are alike. A photograph as art can be duplicated an infinite number of times. Similarly an etching. A bronze can be recast. But people are ever unique and ever changing. The interchange between therapist and student is a ballet. Is there a leader and a follower? There can be; there doesn't have to be. But one thing of this dance is certain: if the therapist can only dance to his own tune, if he is committed to a school and a technique irrespective of the student, then the ballet will be an awkward and even disastrous performance.

How then does the student choose a teacher? How can you judge your teachers artistic sensibility? I will answer the choice of teacher question here and wait until later to address the question of his artistry. The answer to choosing a teacher is easy, if not obvious. There are two question to ask: (1) what is your objective and (2) what is your time line. Put it this way: if you exercise, do you want a little workout once or twice a week or do you want to really tone your muscles? Do you want to exercise until you loose 10 pounds, or do you want to make it a part of your life? What is your objective and what is your time line? If your objective is limited and/or you want quick answers, then choose a teacher whose method is quick and direct. Rational emotive therapy, hypnosis, cognitive-behavioral or behaviorism are good answers.

If your objective is to increase your happiness quotient, to correct your errors in living, to exorcise the daemons inside you, then choose a teacher who increases your anxiety. If your teacher promises to love you unconditionally, run. If your teacher tells you that he is problem oriented, run. If your teacher tells you that he will deal with your emotions but not with your thinking, run. If he says he deals with the here-and-now not with the past, sprint. If he says he is only a (fill in the school) therapist and that is the only school he believes in, find a new teacher. There is no sense in finding a teacher of French when you are planning a trip to Germany.

But, since nothing in life is easy, if he says he is totally flexible, that he is eclectic, that he uses whatever is appropriate with no commitment to any theory, then make a mad dash. In psychotherapy, the word eclectic is often a synonym "for I don't know the theory and I don't know what I am doing, I just do whatever feels right."

If your objective is long-term personal growth, then choose the teacher whose statements to you make you anxious, unsettled, nervous, unsure. Therein lies an answer.

The Dark Side Of Our Soul

I will make the, I think very reasonable, assumption that anyone who reads this book is interested in maximizing their potential and increasing their productivity and creativity. For such a person therapy is a Godsend (to steal a metaphor). My teacher, Israel Regardie (and Dr. Hyatt) said that he would not teach anyone the methods of the Golden Dawn unless they had had at least 4 years of Reichian therapy. Regardie took that position for a very good reason. Until we have removed some of the darkness within our own soul, any attempt at thaumaturgy will only evoke our own indwelling devils. Freud said that repression and sublimation were necessary for one to live in the society. Reich claimed the only answer was to change society. I am less pessimistic then were those two towering figures.

When they were writing, we did not have the knowledge of the developmental steps of the ego and we did not have the work of Piaget on children's cognitive development. I've proven it enough times to enough students, that I can say with some confidence that the main issue in our personal psychology is mistakes in thinking. As children we attempted to understand the silly (sometimes crazy, sometimes evil) statements and actions of our parents. However, children and adults live in different worlds of knowledge and thinking. What seems obvious to a parent, is adult babble to a child. Parents pretend that they are teaching the child to ... (behave, be considerate, share, be polite, etc.) when in truth all they are doing is confusing the child. The child tries to make sense out of the teaching, mis-understands most of what is taught; and neither the child nor the parent knows how off the two are.[1]

Human beings are magnificent but flawed creatures. We take the mistakes of childhood, we live them our whole life, we never recognize they were wrong to begin with, and that they are now doubly wrong as adults. Thus we live our lives in war with ourselves. It is a terrible waste of energy. We take the glory and the beauty of the infant and create the anger and misery of the adult. It is to take a David of Michelangelo and re-sculpt him into a Henry Moore burdened and struggling tortured soul.

---

[1] My favorite story is the mother who yells at her child to not play with the lamp because he will break it. A moment later, and CRASH! So, "I told you not to play with the lamp, now look what you've done!" But, says the bright child, "I wasn't playing with the lamp, I was playing with the spaceship." Children live in different cognitive universes than do adults.

It doesn't need to be, it shouldn't be. Freud said, where the id was, there the ego shall be. I would say where darkness was there light shall be.

The (En)Light(enment) Of The Therapist

There is a danger in psychotherapy. The danger is called the therapist. The therapist is the magician of this black art. When he attempts to exorcise your devils is he doing it by inserting his own? In psychological terms, is he attempting to project his own devils into you? And how can you tell if he is?

There is no infallible answer to this one. There are some guides. How much therapy has your proposed therapist had (minimum of 7 years)? What kind of therapy(ies) did he have? Is he attempting to use a particular school of therapy in which he has not himself been a patient? If so, choose another teacher. You can ignore licenses and degrees. They mean nothing. What matters is the knowledge of and therapy experience of your proposed therapist, not what degrees or licenses he does or does not have. In how many schools of therapy is he knowledgeable? The minimum is two. But here is the most important rule of all: if the therapist talks about himself (other than to answer your questions) or he frequently brings in how he feels or would feel in your situation then he is definitely trying to work out his own problems on your time. You have come upon a dark soul (irrespective of or in spite of any therapy he may have had). Stop now. You are with the wrong teacher. Darkness can not create lightness of being.

Choosing A Therapy

It may seem like I have talked of little else. But the subject is not exhausted. As a Reichian therapist of nearly 30 years experience, there is more that can be added. As you may know, Reichian therapy is a body approach to therapy. Therefore, we get a lot of information from the physical appearance, the gestures, the voice tone, the eyes, etc. Here, then, are some tips from the Reichian couch. Your therapist should have forehead creases. They should not be permanent (a furrowed brow), they should become prominent when the eyebrows are raised and, except for the crease, disappear when the eyebrows are lowered. His eyes should be clear, very focused, and they should move easily. There should be a definite nasal-labial line (the line from the corner of the nose to the corner of the mouth). The neck muscles should not be prominent. The voice should be resonant, coming from an open throat rather than a constricted one. If he takes a big breath, both the belly and the chest should move. Of the things I have listed here, the most important is the forehead and the eyes. If his eyes are dull or they do not move easily or his forehead has no crease lines or has permanent creases, quit now. What if you have been making wonderful progress with just this kind of therapist? My suggestion: take a six-month vacation from this therapist and look into some others. The vacation will be good for you anyway and the experience of some visits to other teachers might give you some perspective on his virtues and his failings.

If you have not chosen a therapist, or if you are going to take a vacation, here is my suggestion: There are four good schools of depth therapy: psychodynamic, ego psychology (also called object relations), neo-Freudian, and Reichian. Note that the word is *psychodynamic,* not *psychoanalysis.* The foundation is the same, but the technique is very different. Notwithstanding that Jungian is very popular among the readers of New Falcon Publications, I would urge against it. I have yet to see good results emerge from Jungian analysis. Stay as far away as possible from Primal therapy or any variant. Adlerian, in the right hands, is an acceptable alternative; but then go to someone else afterwards to get to the areas that Adlerian can not address. Bio-energetics is not bad except that you walk around angry for years, in the process losing marriages, jobs, and friends. Existentialist therapy can be done well, but it is rare. Most therapists proclaiming themselves as existentialist have not done the study necessary to make good use of the art. Existentialist is not one school; it is a whole bunch with differing degrees of worth. Of all the rest, I would say: Ignore them. They are not depth therapy, and they can not do the job you deserve.

The Art Of The Patient

Now, finally, to the most important part: **YOU!** Even a truly good teacher is no good if his student will not study, if his student will not do his homework. If you are not important to your self why should you be important to your therapist? Is it rational to expect that your therapist will work hard for you when you will not work hard for yourself?

Here is a statement that you have probably never heard any therapist make: the two most important qualities that you need to bring to the study are *anger* and *courage*. Anger in the form of the demand of yourself, the commitment, that you will not settle for less than you can be. You will not settle for injuring your children because you have not uncovered your own daemons. You will not settle for less productivity, less creativity, less enjoyment of the wonder of life than is possible for you to achieve. That does not mean that your goal is perfection. We leave that realm to the Gods. It does mean that however much you can uncover, understand, and correct is the minimum you will settle for and the devil take the hindmost.

Then there is courage. Daemons are scary creatures. What are your daemons? Are they depression, anxiety, anger, guilt, facing the fact that your parents are not the nice people you want them to be, realizing that you have been living your life for other people and not for yourself, realizing that you are not as important as you want to think you are, realizing that you made a bad choice in a mate, realizing that you have been pretending to enjoy sex? For all your determination to surrender the darkness for the light, you have to have the courage to stay the course, confess the big and the little, accept that you are what you are—not what you want to be, and most of all: the determination to except that the losses of your childhood are permanent losses. That last one is a biggie and it raises another factor.

Intellectual integrity should be another part of your art. A man of intellectual integrity does not attempt to fake reality. *What is, is.* It is not subject to our fantasies, our wishes, or our ideals. It is not pretty or ugly. It is not noble or ignoble. It is not heroic or cowardly. It simply is. As honesty is telling the truth to others, so integrity is telling the truth to ourselves. It is much harder. We know when we are lying to someone else. *But the lies we tell our self are the lies we live by.* They are part of our very being. And they are corrosive.

There is much that could be said here, but there is only one thing I want to add. Never accept anything your therapist says except as a possibility to *honestly examine.* Your own mind is the ultimate judge of the validity of any idea or interpretation. Yes, you are student to this teacher because you can not uncover your own errors of thinking. But the alternative is not to turn your mind over to someone else.

Your therapist may or may not be an advanced soul, an enlightened person. He may have penetrating insights, and he may be "a wise man" (as the Talmudists would say). And, certainly, you are in his office to take a graduate degree in living. Certainly his explanations and interpretations deserve a respectful audience. But, in the end, it is our trained judgment that is the authority. Your therapist can demand all he wants that he is right because he is the therapist/authority. Do not buy it. On the subject of you, you are the authority. Take every idea he puts forth, examine it with anger, courage, and integrity, and then, if it is wrong, discard it. Your life is a temple. It deserves respect, reverence, and prayer; don't let it go to waste, it is too sacred.

Dr. Jack S. Willis has graduate degrees in Biochemistry and Psychology and a Doctor of Chiropractic He trained in Reichian Therapy with Dr. Israel Regardie for nine years. He is director of the Reichian Therapy Center in Los Angeles, California. The Reichian Therapy Center is both a treating and teaching institute.

01/01 — UH OH!

by Jay Bremyer

Author of the Falcon title:
The Dance of Created Lights: A Sufi Tale

Have you heard about copper baboons, market bubbles, and Yes to Kindness? We raced toward an event horizon and wham! Nothing happened. We're spewed over with jitter bug juice. While worshipping the press of the pedal to the metal, someone slammed on the brakes.

Mad hackers at the edge of a crazy pattern, we live on the tit of the World 2000. Some purpose to the shape we're in? Some fit to contribute to the overall puzzle as the whole shifts in bio-electric chaos? Who's in charge of the wild winnowing anyway?

I prepared for a great non-event. Just like the early Christians did. The Paraclete shot fiery tongues through my skull. By Babel, I built a tower to impress the enlightened.

Twin tales on a goat crossing the desert. Strapped to its back, we're making love.

This time I won't turn away when she reaches for me in the garden. This time we'll sing Hell-I-Love-Ya as the veil is rent.

The World As We Know It

I don't know how I got here. They say we're the seed of a heavenly father and an earthy mother. Records were breathed in and out through Adam Kadman. Androgynous until we faced each other in missionary posture, I recognize this is the other. We make one life and then another. We're not alone here.

But we had this momentum going, history linked to the Christian Calendar, all hell breaking loose as Church Militant spins out at the corner. You've heard the rumors, right? Kids killing classmates, bad games sliding from video-pops into school yards, postmen gunning down supervisors—sick world we've made to live in.

Examining life reveals human-kind-ness. Oh, yeah! These kids have been examining. On the surface and leading to a great death, all they see nurtures apocalyptic nihilism. Trench coats covering reversed swastikas. Justice in mutilation. War on classmates who claim life is good for them. Sacrificial lambs. Scape goats. Ring in the bizarre rhymes of Mother Goose. The cruel nursery of the present moment, the tormented past. Laugh in the bloody teach of an unacceptable future.

Frenzy And The Brown-Eyed Merkaba

We love our kids, practice yoga, chant with monks, take silent retreats, walk for mankind, volunteer in soup kitchens, search for good politicians, even run for office. In general, we know what to do to improve the world. But still, I'm confused.

In deep respect I sit at the knees of wise teachers. An aspirant Upanishadi, listening inward and outward, looking for the alignment which shows that the data coincides, for an accurate take on circumstance, I swivel and glance around as a chill creeps up my back. What's going on here?

I am told that intelligent beings hover around the planet in inter-dimensional energy ships. Consciousness moves through star gates, along grid lines. Occasionally a rogue alien scrapes down and excises the genitals of a descendant of Egyptian Hathor. Her milk mixed with honey foreshadowed the promise made by a fire god to his people during forty years in the wilderness.

Investigators report that five brass monkeys wrote the protocols for a one world government. British nobility wiped out their princess to forestall an Islamic jihad. We bombed Kosovo to force the Russian technicians to abandon Y2K corrections. Nuclear weapons malfunction. We slam the Lamb's head on the back of the Lion. At last, the Wasps rule the world.

Nonsense? Obviously. History does not make sense. If we sincerely predict a worldwide collapse, if the local church is buying guns, hoarding food and, by God, building an ark – it may be time to welcome the space visitors.

Y2k And The Holy Spook

I know I'm here to grow. A good heart isn't enough. An educated mind without a good heart is worse. I reject the doctrine that all learning is equally valuable. Words are insufficient. Language is a virus. None of the models is adequate to the task. What good I can do must start with my life. I am here to choose, to be responsible. But how, particularly when I don't understand the facts?

Fact is, I've concluded, that it's an illusion to think that any of the facts are fixed. The fix is on but it's only temporary. Ultimately it's a mess— barely held together at nodules called consensus points. Reality grows multidimensionally. Tunnels connect thought processes. There is a lot going down and rising up.

Even though most of the computer problems were corrected in time to avoid a major implosion, some devotees of Apocalypse may still elect us to an extended visit in the wilderness. Folks in other countries with pirated computer processors are running emergent military-industrial complexes. Billions of defective silicon chips embedded in ventilators, elevators, prison doors, automatic milkers, grocery lines, refineries, and toxic waste stations might, someday, malfunction in episodes of catastrophic enlightenment. Maybe we have become too dependent upon artificial intelligence, what the geeks call "dumb power."

Here's the rub. Disaster by war, by ethnic cleansing, by insane national leaders, by apocalyptic nihilists in school yards and hamburger stands, by world wide web sociopaths, by computer program glitches, by asteroids, earthquakes, tidal waves, hurricanes, and volcanoes – draws us toward death. Secure systems are temporary. Don't hold your breath.

The Blue Rose Of Paradise

There's a place behind the heart where a blue rose grows. It's fairly simple, while fixing a brew and having some fun, to cultivate that. Here's an idea. Let's invent a word for the old friends we haven't met yet. Let's invite all the neighbors.

Jay Bremyer's most recent books are *The Chymical Cook: A True Account of Mystical Initiation* in the Georgia Woods (Barrytown/Station Hill), and *The Dance of Created Lights: A Sufi Tale* (New Falcon Publications). Contact Jay at bremyer@midusa.net.

A PEARL OF GREAT PRICE

by Floyd Smith

Within the Great Abyss, in the sea of delusion, there is a pearl.
Within this pearl a key is to be found,
to treasures within treasures, enough to confound.
Exposing these treasures within the pearl of great price;
Is to benign the malign, and balance it thrice,
and once the tarnish is wiped from the slate,
the light will shine forth in which words cannot state.
I only hope that this vision of foundation, is not fission, but fusion,
and not a delusion.
That the higher self of pentagrammaton,
will slay the dreaded dragon that of tetragrammaton.
For I am but a star, rising out of the abyss, as the secret chiefs watch
from the silent abode.
Casting the spark within the catalyst. Shedding the light of consecration,
within and around the abode of pentagrammaton.
Working with polarities, and curvatures of space, with time at its axis,
within vibration.
Hail unto the twelve tribes; within this talisman of light.
Whom consecrateth those with second sight.
Out of the elements; out of the dust; a star is born, which shines the
light, for the name of the law; in the name of the son.
For all to experience the knowledge within this talisman of light.
For we are all stars you and I.
For the unit within the whole will work for this purpose, but in differing
degrees.
Weaving its web of polarities, upon the loom of foundation in the cradle
of the snake.
Light of the whole veil of the mind,
as the will grows the organ will benign.
As the whole wills so mote it be.
Love is the law love under will.

SAINT FRANCIS VISITS SATAN

by Rodolfo Scarfalloto

Author of the Falcon title:
The Alchemy of Opposites

It was well past midnight. The young friar walked slowly through the wooded valley, deep in the forest of Umbria. He was absorbed in prayer, greatly troubled by the perpetual conflict he had seen among humanity in his travels. He was fervently asking for understanding when he became aware that he was very thirsty. Looking around the darkened woodland, he noticed the flowing waters of a nearby spring, glistening in the moon light. He kneeled down by the spring and took a drink, thanking sister water for quenching his thirst. He had been walking for hours, and had fasted nearly forty days. He was exhausted. Next to the spring, he noticed a small mound of dry leaves that had been heaped up by the wind.

After reciting his final prayer of the night, he lay down on the leaves and drifted off into a deep and restful sleep.

In the early morning hours, just before awakening, he dreamed that he was walking through the deepest recesses of the underworld, where he was searching and searching, until he found the one whom all of his fellow friars were trying to avoid.

The young friar fearlessly approached him. "Greetings, brother. I have come here to ask you to return home with me."

Satan laughed, and, with uncharacteristic gentleness, escorted the young friar to hell's Gate.

"Be gone, my brother. You are able to stay in my presence for a short while and not be burned because you are harmless, but you must leave before your profound grace expires."

"First I would ask why you continue to stay in this place. I am disturbed by your exile."

"As long as there is one among our kin who does not remember what you remember, I must remain; and from here, I guard the gate to our Father's house against all those who might sneak in before full remembrance is reached."

"But you do not have to stay here. If you walk with me to the gate of remembrance, others will surely follow."

"You do your work your way. And I will my work my way."

The young friar sighed. "Though I am saddened by the division between us, I cannot force you to walk with me."

Satan laughed. "And neither would you, even if you could. You would not force your will upon a butterfly. That is why I cannot harm you."

"Are your words intended to seduce me?"

"I am, indeed, the master of seduction," he laughed again. "But I cannot seduce in the absence of vanity. Any attempt to seduce you would be a silly waste of energy. I have no choice but to tell you the truth."

"So, tell me again, for I am slow of learning; why must you stay in this place?"

"To guide our brethren, in my own way, as I have said.

"I do not understand. How can condemnation and violence help them."

"By making things intolerable for them. I expose the weakness that they would greedily conceal. Those who do not listen to you, must learn through me."

"Do you not know that people fear and hate you?"

"Of course. If they did not fear and hate me, they would quickly see their own weakness, and they would have no further need of my services; which is just as well because in the absence of fear and hate, I would no longer have any power to continue my work. This is perfection, my brother. Those who need my services also provide me with the energy needed to fuel my efforts."

"You really believe that you can serve them by leading them astray?"

Satan laughed again. "It is not I who lead *them*. They lead me. It is the law."

"You have great wisdom, my brother. You understand the subtleties of creation in ways I do not. Yet, there is a stubborn place within me which insists that you can use your wisdom in a more productive manner which would bring great happiness and fulfillment to you and all those who are influenced by you. Perhaps I am naive. Perhaps my stubborn perception is just wishful thinking, born of my desire to see you end your exile. You are, after all, the beloved prodigal son, and my brother. It would be my greatest joy to share in the celebration of your return, for you are the first born of our blessed Mother and Father."

"In your simplicity, you are most persuasive, little brother. Your words are genuine and free of subterfuge. Nonetheless, I have my vigil. Here I am bound to stay."

"But we are both free to come go, and have been from the beginning of time when our Father touched the womb of Mother Darkness to bring us into being. Walk with me, and let us drink deeply of the love they have for each other and for us, their children."

There was a brief flicker of sadness in Satan's eyes, and than his face hardened again, and he laughed. "Go, little brother, before your profound grace expires, for I am still capable of finding weakness within you."

"I feel your pain, my brother, for it is my pain. We will meet again and rejoice."

As Francis walked away, Satan watched him, and briefly considered the possibility of speeding things up a bit.

The young friar was awakened from his dream by a lark standing on the ground close by. With his eyes still closed, he spontaneously recited his morning greeting to God and all creation. He vaguely remembered the dream, not knowing what to make of it. Opening his eyes, he gazed upon the clear water flowing from the nearby spring. The first rays of sunlight filtered through the trees, warming his face. The wind, which has been blowing a while ago, had settled down. The trees, rocks, the ground he was laying on, and the mist which played in the morning sun, seemed to be speaking to him in unison. He was simultaneously filled with great joy and great sadness, as he felt himself being moved by a visceral awareness which he didn't quite comprehend.

Rudy Scarfalloto was born on the island of Sicily, and moved to Brooklyn, New York at the age of eight. He received the Bachelor of Science degree in biology at Brooklyn College and the Doctor of Chiropractic degree at Life College. His chiropractic practice is in Atlanta, Georgia where he also conducts health-related seminars. In addition, he teaches anatomy and physiology at the Academy of Somatic Healing Arts.

OUR POTENTIAL LEGACY

by Adam Matza

We were an experiment gone awry,
we were the result of the acid test.
When Mom and some way-gone Dad did the Nasty,
and nine months later popped this regional generation.
And once upon
this wet spot on a speck of dust
we raged against each other for control,
the upper hand.
Wasn't it a megablast
when we pulled off some undetected manipulation?
And wasn't it a show of great strength
when we got caught and didn't give a shit?
Divorced from feeling, we were like bumper cars.
It wasn't cool to reveal and share
or to care — unless, of course, it was the look-good,
in-thing to do. Or if there was money
to be made in doing it.
And as we quickly aged —
aided by the implements of the experiment —
our music-video attention spans dwindled.
You see, we knew what was wrong,
but we let it slide,
because we didn't think we could change anything,
we'd rather hide.
And when our time came to stand,
we got back-slapped down by the Invisible Hand.
I sometimes wonder how I still survived,
but when I think of what we could have been,
and should have been,
I wonder if we were ever alive.

PART V

Reprogramming The Self

Robert Anton Wilson
Writer, Philosopher and former *Playboy* editor

HOW BRAIN SOFTWARE PROGRAMS BRAIN HARDWARE

by Robert Anton Wilson

Author of the Falcon titles:
Cosmic Trigger I: Final Secret of the Illuminati
Cosmic Trigger II: Down to Earth
Cosmic Trigger III: My Life After Death
Reality Is What You Can Get Away With
The Walls Came Tumbling Down
Coincidance: A Head Test
Wilhelm Reich in Hell
Quantum Psychology
Sex, Drugs & Magick
The Tale of the Tribe
The New Inquisition
Prometheus Rising
Ishtar Rising

As everybody with a home computer knows—and everybody who uses a computer at work also knows—the software can change the functioning of the hardware in radical and sometimes startling ways. The First Law of Computers—so ancient that some claim it dates back to the dark Cthulhoid aeons when LBJ and giant reptiles still roamed the Earth—tells us succinctly, "Garbage In, Garbage Out" (or GIGO, for short). The wrong software *guarantees* wrong answers. Alternately, the correct software will "solve" previously intractable problems in ways that appear "miraculous" to the majority of domesticated primates at this primitive stage of evolution.

I propose that the principle software used in the human brain consists of words, metaphors, disguised metaphors and linguistic structures in general. I also propose, and will here try to demonstrate, that the Sapir-Whorf-Korzybski Hypothesis, as it is called in sociology— "A change in language can transform our perception of the cosmos"—becomes intuitively obvious with a simple experiment in altering brain software by changing the structure of our language.

The human brain has been called a "three pound universe" (Hooper), an "enchanted loom" (Sherrington), a "bio-computer" (Lilly), a "hive of anarchy" (Wolfe), an "intellectual intestine" (de Selby), etc., but whatever one calls it, it remains the most powerful data-processor known on this planet. (It has been estimated by Hooper and Teresi that to duplicate all brain functions in a solid-state computer with 1987 state-of-the-art technology would require a machine as tall as the Empire State Building and as broad and long as Texas.) The brain, like your desk computer, does not receive raw data. It receives such data as it has been built to receive, and it processes the data according to the programs (software) that have been put into it.

Consider the following columns of easily-comprehensible sentences and see if you can determine the major structural difference between Column 1 and Column 2 considered as software for the human brain:

Column 1	Column 2
The electron is a wave.	The electron appears as a wave when recorded by $instrument_1$.
The electron is a particle.	The electron appears as a particle when recorded by $instrument_2$.
John is lethargic and unhappy.	John appears lethargic and unhappy in the office.
John is full of fun and high spirits.	John appears full of fun and high spirits while on holiday.
The car involved in the hit-and-run accident was a blue Ford.	In memory, I think I recall the car involved in the hit-and-run accident as a blue Ford.
This is a fascist idea.	This seems like a fascist idea to me.
Beethoven was better than Mozart.	I enjoy Beethoven more than Mozart.
This is a sexist movie.	This seems like a sexist movie to me.

The first column consists of statements in ordinary English, as heard in common usage at this superstitious and barbaric stage of Terran evolution. These statements all assume the viewpoint which philosophers call "naive realism"—the belief that something called "reality" exists somewhere "out there," beyond our brains, and can be directly perceived by our brains. Scientists, as well as philosophers, now agree that such "realism" can only be described as "naive", because no two people ever perceive exactly the same "reality," a fact well established in perception psychology, general psychology, sociology, etc. And, in fact, no two animals perceive the same "reality": each species has its own *umwelt,* or reality-tunnel made up of the signals which the senses and brains of that species can apprehend and comprehend. Worse: instruments perceive different "realities" also, as General Relativity and Quantum Mechanics have amply demonstrated.

It has been emphasized by Niels Bohr, P.W. Bridgman, Bertrand Russell, Count Korzybski and others that sentences of the sort found in Column 1 not only "ignore" the experimental relativity of perceptions but also subtly condition our brains to "ignore" or forget this relativity, if we ever learned it, or even to avoid noticing it at all. As Korzybski especially emphasized, these "Aristotelian" sentences act as software tending to program us to assume attitudes of dogmatism, unwarranted certitude and intolerance.[1]

By comparison, the second column consists of parallel statements rewritten in *E-prime,* or English-prime, a language based on the work of Korzybski and proposed for scientific usage by such authors as D. David Bourland and E.W. Kellogg III. E-prime contains much the same vocabulary as standard English but has been made isomorphic to quantum physics (and modern science generally) by first abolishing the Aristotelian *is* of identity and then reformulating each statement phenomenologically in terms of signals received and interpreted by a body (or instrument) moving in space-time.

Concretely, "The electron is a wave" employs the Aristotelian "is" of identity and thereby introduces the false-to-experience notion that we can know the indwelling Aristotelian "essence" or "nature" of the electron. "The electron appears as a wave when recorded with instrument$_1$" reformulates the English sentence into English-prime, abolishes the "is" of

---

[1] Such sentences have been designated "Aristotelian" by Korzybski because they tacitly assume the Aristotelian philosophy, which pictures a world of block-like entities inhabited by ghostly "essences" or "natures" which can be known with certitude by two-valued logical deduction. This seems so normal in our culture that many feel astounded to learn that the typically Oriental philosophy of Buddhism envisions a world of interactive processes, not entities; doubts the universal validity of two-valued logic; and claims the world can only be approximately or relatively understood, not known with certitude.

identity and returns us to an accurate report of what actually transpired in space-time, namely that the electron was constrained by a certain instrument to appear in a certain form of manifestation.

Similarly, "The electron appears as a particle when recorded by instrument$_1$" evades Aristotelian dogmatism and forces us to *operationalize* or *phenomenologize* our report by stating what actually happened in space-time—namely, that the electron was constrained by a different instrument to appear in a different form of manifestation.

Note well (and please *try* to remember) that "The electron is a wave" and "The electron is a particle" create contradiction, and have historically led to debate and sometimes violent quarrel (e.g., "I did not call my learned colleague an ass-hole. I called him a blithering idiot.") At one time these Aristotelian mis-statements (bad software)—attempting to say what an electron "is"—appeared to justify the opinion that parts of physics can only be expressed in terms of almost surrealist paradox—i.e., within the same Aristotelian logical-linguistic structure, many physicists circa 1920–1930 were led to proclaim that "The universe is illogical" or "The universe does not make sense" etc.

On the other hand, as Bohr first noted, the E-prime alternatives— "The electron appears as a wave when constrained by instrument$_1$" and "The electron appears as a particle when constrained by instrument$_2$"—do not appear *contradictory but complementary.* They do not lead to debate or violent quarrel they do not portray the world as bizarre or irrational and (not coincidentally) they simply report what actually took place in the space-time of actual experiments.

Although Dr. Bohr did not formulate E-prime—or even Danish-prime, Danish being the language in which he habitually wrote and probably thought—the basis of E-prime can be found in his Principle of Complementarity and the Copenhagen Interpretation of physics which he created in collaboration with his students circa 1926–28.

The American physicist P.W. Bridgman (like Bohr, a Nobel laureate) first generalized the Bohr approach by articulating the specific principle that scientific propositions should be stated in terms of actual *operations.* If we rigorously follow this rule, we will eventually find ourselves writing E-prime if English serves as our normal language—or in French-prime if we regularly write French, etc. We will have exchanged obsolete Aristotelian software for modern scientific software. We will then program our brains differently, formulate different thoughts and (almost certainly) learn different perceptions or styles of perception.

For the benefit of students of philosophy, although both Bohr and Bridgman appear to have been chiefly influenced by the actual (and startling) experiments in 1920s quantum mechanics, their major intellectual influences appear to have been Kierkegaard, in the case of Bohr, and

William James, in the case of Bridgman. Thus, the logic of modern physics, and of E-prime, not only serves as an isomorph of the quantum world but also as the natural way to present the key ideas of Existentialism and Pragmatism. As I have already hinted, E-prime also closely resembles the principles of Zen Buddhism and of phenomenological sociology, as influenced by the radical Existentialist Husserl. This suggests that E-prime may not only clarify debates within science but also prove useful in daily life—if we wish to think pragmatically or existentially or in terms of experienced events in space-time rather than thinking metaphysically of "ghosts in the machine," i.e., abstract essences haunting block-like entities.

Already one suspects that a great deal of the misunderstanding of, or total confusion about, certain non-Aristotelian systems derives from the fact that most writers, not habitually using E-prime, have discussed these systems in ordinary English, which introduces Aristotelian structures into non-Aristotelian data and thus breeds chaos and endless paradox. Once again, "Garbage In, Garbage Out." Aristotelian software does not transduce non-Aristotelian data.

As an experiment, any reader who has had problems understanding quantum physics, Zen, Existentialism or phenomenology should try rereading a book on each and translating all sentences with the Aristotelian "is" to new sentences in E-prime. You may then come to share my suspicion that the difficulties are not found in the subjects but in the use of the wrong language to discuss the subjects—the wrong software for the data.

Looking at the next two sentences in Column 1— "John is lethargic and unhappy" and "John is full of fun and high spirits"—we again encounter contradiction, and we may well suspect pathology. The inexperienced psychiatrist, indeed, might quickly pronounce that John "is" suffering from a manic-depressive psychosis. And, of course, others with a less clinical orientation might rush with equal haste to decide that one set of reports must be due to careless observation or downright lies, and accept the opposite reports as totally true. This could lead to lively debate, or actual quarrel about what sort of man John "really is."

(The reader may find it amusing, as I do, that quarrels of this sort— what sort of man John "really is" or what sort of woman Mary "really is"—occur every day in our still-medieval society, even though less than one quarreler in a thousand knows consciously that such debates depend on Aristotelian philosophy and that asking what something "really is" only make sense at all, at all, within the context of Aristotelian definitions of "reality" and "isness.")

The E-prime translations— "John appears lethargic and unhappy in the office" and "John appears full of fun and high spirits on holiday"—do not contradict each other, report the actual observations in space-time accurately, and remind us that we never know or experience John as an Aristotelian essence (a "spook" in Max Stirner's terms) but only as an aspect of a social field, just as we never know an electron as an Aristotelian essence but only as aspect of an instrumental field.

Another linguistic point seems noteworthy here. I absently wrote "on holiday" because I have spent several years in Ireland; and in Ireland, as in England, people do not go "on vacation", they go "on holiday." The choice of metaphors here does not seem accidental. To say that one goes on holiday is to speak the language of the working class, for whom the time off appears merry and playful; but to say one goes on vacation is to speak the language of the ruling class. *Vacation* comes from the same root as *vacant* and reflects what the owner sees when he looks around the floor—a vacancy where John "should" "be". (I suspect that the owner probably thinks some negative thoughts about the Labor Unions and the "damned Liberal" Government that force him to pay John even when John "is vacant.")

I leave it as a puzzle for the reader: Do the Irish and English speak Working Class in this case because they have had several socialist governments, or have they had several socialist governments because they learned to speak the language of the Working Class? And: has the U.S., alone among industrial nations, never had a socialist government because it speaks the Ruling Class language, or does it speak the Ruling Class language because it has never had a socialist government?

Moving along, "The first man stabbed the second man with a knife," although it contains no explicit Aristotelian "is", continues the Aristotelian assumption that the brain directly apprehends and comprehends "objective" "reality". Dropping this monkish medieval software and trying modern scientific software we get the E-prime translation, "The first man appeared to stab the second man with what appeared to me to be a knife." This accurately reports the activity of the brain as an instrument in space-time, evades Aristotelian dogmatism, operationalizes or phenomenologizes our software—and, incidentally, may spare us from the traditional embarrassment of Psychology Students if we happen to land in a class where the instructor inflicts a certain notorious experiment upon us. In the case of that experiment, the first man actually makes stabbing motions, without stabbing or piercing, and with a banana, not a knife. Most students, in most cases where this experiment has been performed, actually see a knife instead of a banana. (Another reason for doubting Aristotelian software: perception and inference mingle so quickly and feed back to each other so totally, that one cannot existentially untangle them.) Together with John-in-the-office and John-on-holiday, this should illustrate vividly that E-prime has applications beyond physics and on into daily life. It should also make clear that the software of Aristotelian structural assumptions in standard English indeed programs the brain to malfunction—"Garbage In, Garbage Out." (Further illustrations of how the brain, running on Aristotelian software, populates the world with hallucinations and projections can be found in my books *Prometheus Rising, Quantum Psychology* and *The New Inquisition*, among others.)

Similarly, "The car involved in the hit-and-run accident was a blue Ford" seems inadequate and obsolete Aristotelian software—as many eye-witnesses have discovered with some pain during skillful cross examination in court. The E-prime translation into modern software, "In memory, I think I recall the car involved in the hit-and-run accident as a blue Ford" would remove a lot of fun from the lives of lawyers but seems more harmonious with what we now know about neurology and perception psychology.

Again, "This is a fascist idea" contains Aristotelian software, unscientifically omits the instrument from the report, and perpetuates dogmatism and intolerance. Translated into post-quantum E-prime software, this becomes "This seems like a fascist idea to me," which scientifically indicates the instrument being used to constrain the data—in this case, the evaluative apparatus of the speaker's brain. Note one more time that "This is a fascist idea" contradicts "This is not a fascist idea" and provokes quarrels (in which each side seems likely to arrive at the conclusion that the other side "are" damned idiots or worse). "This seems like a fascist idea to me" does not contradict "This doesn't seem like a fascist idea to me" and merely registers the fact that the space-time trajectories of two brains, like two Einsteinian instruments, will yield different readings of the same space-time events.

Our next example, "Beethoven is better than Mozart" might bring the difference between Aristotelian and post-quantum software into clearer focus for many. As formulated in standard English, this assertion implies, if analyzed philosophically, that there exist indwelling essences, or "natures," or spooks, in the music of Beethoven and Mozart, and that Beethoven's spooks "really are" better than Mozart's spooks. Since no such spooks are findable in space-time, the debate about this issue, formulated in this software, can go on forever or until somebody gets so bored that he resorts to blunt instruments to silence the debaters.

The translation into E-prime, "I enjoy Beethoven more than Mozart" reports accurately a series of space-time events—enjoyment processes in the brain of the speaker. This does not contradict another speaker's alternative report, "I enjoy Mozart more than Beethoven," and both reports can profitably be classed as complementary in Bohr's sense.

I cannot resist a minor digression. Although I have only read, and never heard, the endless debate between Mozart maniacs and Beethoven buffs, on one occasion I did hear such a Thomist or medieval debate about Bartok. This happened in a restaurant in Dun Laoghaire, Ireland, and the debaters, two *Englishentities* (a word I have coined to avoid the human chauvinism implied in *Englishpersons*) grew increasingly heated and hostile as they argued. The male Englishentity insisted that Bartok's music "really is" rubbish and junk and noise etc. The female English-entity insisted, *au contraire,* that Bartok's music "really is" wonderfully new and experimental and exciting etc. I found it excruciatingly hard to avoid the temptation to walk over to their table and explain E-prime to them. I think the main reason I resisted the temptation lies in many often-repeated experiences that convinced me that Englishentities recognize an American accent as soon as they hear it and most of them "know", or think they know, that any American—or any other non-Englishentity—"really is" stupid and uncultured compared to any Englishentity, and they therefore simply would not have listened to me. Such Englishentities have developed a remarkable skill in looking simultaneously polite and bored while engaged in not listening to non-Englishentities—as the Irish, the Hindus, the Africans and numerous others have noted before me.

Finally, "This is a sexist movie" contains Aristotelian metaphysics implying indwelling essences or spooks within the film. The E-prime translation, "This appears a sexist movie to me" includes the observer and the instrument (the observer's brain) in the report and programs the brain with modern, rather than medieval, software. And, again, "This is a sexist movie" contradicts "This is not a sexist movie," while "This appears a sexist movie to me" does not contradict but complements "This does not appear a sexist movie to me."

(One is tempted to add that the whole *bon ton* debate about sexism "in" movies appears only an "intellectual" sublimation of the older, cruder debate, surviving in more primitive areas, like Little Rock, Arkansas, or the U.S. Congress, about indwelling "obscenity" "in" movies. E-prime software takes the fanaticism out of such debates, removes Aristotelian metaphysics and places us back in the phenomenological world of how individual brains process their experience in space-time.)

A further illustration of these principles appears *a propos.* Once while speaking before the Irish Science Fiction Association at Trinity College, Dublin, I was asked, "Do you believe in UFOs?" Evading the temptation to launch an oration on the disadvantages of the yes-no logic of "belief" and the advantages of the modern logic of probability and percentages, I answered simply, "Yes." The questioner then grew excited and offered a long argument that UFOs "really are" those rare meteorological events called "sundogs." I replied simply that he appeared to believe in UFOs also. He then grew more excited and denied vigorously that he "believed" in UFOs, even though he had just moments earlier argued that (a) UFOs exist and (b) he knew what all of them "really are."

This story amuses me because I have read a great deal of the literature of the UFO debate and almost all of it seems constrained by Aristotelian software processing the brains of the debaters. So-called "Skeptics" can just as accurately be dubbed "Believers": they merely believe different models than the so-called "Cultists" or heretics. The "Skeptics" believe, very fervently, that "all" UFOs can be identified as "really being" *ordinary* hallucinations, or hoaxes, or sundogs, or heat inversions, or weather balloons, or the planet Venus, etc. The "Cultists" or heretics believe, some as dogmatically as the Skeptics but some (oddly) more tentatively, that "all"—or maybe only some—UFOs can be identified as spaceships, or time-machines, or secret weapons (of the US or Russia or a hypothetical surviving Nazi underground) or *non-ordinary* hallucinations, etc. Among those who have chosen the model of "non-ordinary" hallucinations, Dr. Carl Gustav Jung proposes that UFOs represent an evolutionarily important eruption of new energies from the "collective unconscious," Dr. Jacques Vallee argues that UFOs have been created by brain manipulations of some unscrupulous and unidentified intelligence Agency; and Dr. Robert Persinger suggests that UFOs result from external-world energy fluctuations—leading to weird lights (probably ball lightning), jumping furniture, electrical malfunctions etc.—and also altering brain waves so that internal-world hallucinations occur.

From the point of view of Aristotelian software, the important issue appears that of choosing which of these conflicting models to "believe." From the point of view of post-quantum software, the important issue appears that of not "believing" any model but estimating (as far as possible) which model seems most probable in a given case or set of cases. Post-quantum software would also probably incline us to accept Bohr's Principle of Complementarity and accept different models on different occasions, for different space-time events.

It seems probable that the prevalence of Aristotelian software in most brains at this stage of evolution accounts for the ubiquitous prevalence of dogmatic belief in one or another UFO model among both "Skeptics" and "Cultists"—and also explains the relative rarity of multi-model zeteticism.

A more controversial illustration of brain software in action: in Chicago in the 1960s, I knew a pacifist, Joffrey Stewart, who spent most of his waking hours walking the streets distributing anti-war pamphlets. Some of these broadsides Joffrey had written himself; some had been written by others but seemed worthy of circulation according to Joffrey's standards. However, Joffrey did not distribute anybody's pamphlets without first "correcting" them in accord with his own software or reality-tunnel or system of semantics. Specifically, he would place question marks before and after any word that seemed to him to imply unexamined and nefarious assumptions. The words that bothered Joffrey most seem to have been "our" and "we." If you received a leaflet by, say Noam Chomsky or Dave Dellinger, after it had been revised by Joffrey, you would see sentences like the following (I am paraphrasing from memory, but I believe I capture the spirit of Joffrey's Criticism of Language):

"…and ?our? taxes are being used to napalm infants…"
"…to defend ?our? standard of living…"
"…these atrocities ?we? are committing…"
"…and why, after all, are ?we? in Vietnam?"

It appears that the Aristotelian "is" of identity should not be considered the only glitch in our brain software. Joffrey Stewart's question marks certainly led me to revise my own software, and I cannot listen to TV these days without mentally inserting similar interrogations in many widely used expressions. When I hear Mr. Reagan described as "our President," I think of Joffrey writing this as "?our? President"; and, then, of course, I recall that less than 25 percent of eligible voters elected Mr. Reagan, the other 75+ percent either voting for somebody else or showing their skepticism and/or contempt by not voting at all.

At this point it seems advisable to quote Korzybski: 'I have said what I have said; I have not said what I have not said." For instance, a while back I set a little trap for careless and Ideologically impassioned readers, by pointing out that in a specific context the word "sexism" should only be used in relation to evaluative processes in the brain of the speaker. From this existentialist-phenomenologist (or operationalist) truism, certain readers probably deduced the inaccurate conclusion, "This author denies that anything to be called sexism exists in the objective world at all." Once again, the wrong software caused the signals to go awry.

Nothing in my remarks implied that using the word "sexism" to describe a company that pays female workers wages averaging less than fifty percent of comparable male workers' wages should be related only to the evaluative activities of the brain of the commentator. Quite the contrary. The operationalist approach here would relate the word "sexism" to the economic data demonstrating the measurable existence of the wage differential.

An old example in physics will clarify this. If an iron bar has a measured temperature of 98° Fahrenheit, what would you expect to find in measuring the temperature of an electron in the bar?

If you guess 98° Fahrenheit, you appear to be using the wrong software. If you say that the question cannot be answered without more data, I suspect you still haven't got the right software for this test.

Some books will tell you that "an electron has no temperature." More accurately, I think, one should say that the word "temperature" has scientific meaning at, or above, the molecular level, but has no meaning below the molecular level. Temperature measures the *movement* of molecules and hence cannot be meaningfully applied to sub-molecular processes.

Thus, to say that "sexism" must be considered operationally to refer to evaluations in a brain when speaking of art works does not mean that "sexism" must always refer *only* to such internal matters. When speaking of economic practices, "sexism" has meaning in relation to economic statistics. This parallels the situation in physics, where "temperature" refers to molecular movement in meaningful statements, and loses all meaning when one attempts to apply it to sub-molecular phenomena.

In conclusion, I would like to suggest, again, that these arguments for post-quantum software (language structures) have as much application and practicality outside science as within science. The cutting edge of philosophy—everything that can be called post-Nietzschean—represents a similar struggle against the increasingly obvious malfunctions of Aristotelian categories; one finds this recognized among such seemingly opposed groups as the Cambridge Linguistic Analysts and the Paris Situationists. Modern literature at its liveliest or most inventive—I think of Joyce, Pound, Borges, Faulkner, Beckett, O'Brien, Williams, Burroughs, Ginsberg—represents a series of strategies to break out of the Aristotelian software of our culture by creating non-Aristotelian linguistic grids. Modern painting took on non-Aristotelian traits as early as 1907 and music at about the same time. To the extent that we remain hypnotically entranced by Aristotelian language structures we become isolated not only from science—and, as I have hinted, from such exotic and interesting systems as Buddhism—but also from the lively and innovative part of modern culture generally.

Novelist, non-fiction writer, teacher and former *Playboy* editor, *Robert Anton Wilson* is the author of numerous books on such wide-ranging subjects as quantum mechanics, UFOs, history, science fiction, sex, mind-altering drugs, mysticism, scientists (pompous and otherwise), secret societies and, especially, human consciousness. They include the best-selling *Cosmic Trigger* series, the *Illuminatus!* trilogy (with Robert Shea), the *Schroedinger's Cat* trilogy, *Sex, Drugs,& Magick Prometheus Rising, The New Inquisition, Reality Is What You Can Get Away With* and many other works. He currently lives in Northern California.

Timothy Leary, Ph.D.
World Famous Psychologist, Writer and Philosopher

TWENTY-TWO ALTERNATIVES TO INVOLUNTARY DEATH

by Timothy Leary, Ph.D. & Eric Gullichsen

Dr. Leary is the author of the Falcon titles:
What Does WoMan Want?
The Intelligence Agents
The Game of Life
Info-Psychology
Neuropolitique

> *"Death is the ultimate negative patient health outcome."*
> — William L. Roper, Director,
> Health Care Financing Administration (HCFA),
> which administers Medicare

Most human beings face death with an "attitude" of helplessness, either resigned or fearful. Neither of these submissive, often uninformed, "angles of approach" to the most crucial event of one's life can be ennobling.

Today, there are many practical options available for dealing with the dying process. Passivity, failure to learn about them, might be the ultimate irretrievable blunder. Pascal's famous no-lose wager about the existence of God translates into modern life as a no-risk gamble on the prowess of technology.

For millennia the fear of death has depreciated individual confidence and increased dependence on authority.

True, the loyal member of a familial or racial gene-pool can take pride in the successes and survival tenacity of their kin-ship.

But for the individual, the traditional prospects are less than exalted. Let's be laser-honest here. How can you be proud of your past achievements, walk tall in the present or zap enthusiastically into the future if, awaiting you implacably around some future corner, is Old Mr. D., The Grim Reaper?

What a PR job the Word Makers did to build this Death Concept into a Prime-Time Horror Show! The grave. Mortification. Extinction. Breakdown. Catastrophe. Doom. Finish. Fatality. Malignancy. Necrology. Obituary. The end.

Note the calculated negativity. To die is to croak, to give up the ghost, to bite the dust, to kick the bucket, to perish. To become inanimate, lifeless, defunct, extinct, moribund, cadaverous, necrotic. A corpse, a stiff, a cadaver, a relic, food for worms, a *corpus delicti*, a carcass. What a miserable ending to the game of life!

Fear Of Death Was An Evolutionary Necessity In The Past

In the past, the reflexive genetic duty of TOP MANAGEMENT (those in social control of the various gene-pools) has been to make humans feel weak, helpless, and dependent in the face of death. The good of the race or nation was ensured at the cost of the sacrifice of the individual.

Obedience and submission was rewarded on a time-payment plan. For his/her devotion the individual was promised immortality in the post-mortem hive-center variously known as "heaven," "paradise," or the "Kingdom of the Lord." In order to maintain the attitude of dedication, the gene-pool managers had to control the "dying reflexes," orchestrate the trigger-stimuli that activate the "death circuits" of the brain. This was accomplished through rituals that imprint dependence and docility when the "dying alarm bells" go off in the brain.

Perhaps we can better understand this imprinting mechanism by considering another set of "rituals," those by which human hives manage the conception-reproduction reflexes. A discussion of these is less likely to alarm you. And the mechanisms of control imposed by the operation of social machinery are similar in the two cases. We invite you to "step outside the system" for a moment, to vividly see what is ordinarily invisible because it is so entrenched in our expectation.

At adolescence each kinship group provides rituals, taboos, ethical prescriptions to guide the all-important sperm-egg situation.

Management by the individual of the horny DNA machinery is always a threat to hive inbreeding. Dress, grooming, dating, courtship, contraception, and abortion patterns are fanatically conventionalized in tribal and feudal societies. Personal innovation is sternly condemned and ostracized. Industrial democracies vary in the sexual freedom allowed individuals. But in totalitarian states, China and Iran for example, rigid prudish morality controls the mating reflexes and governs boy-girl relations. Under the Chinese dictator Mao, "romance" was forbidden because it weakened dedication to the state, i.e., the local gene-pool. If teen-agers pilot and select their own mating, then they will be more likely to fertilize outside the hive, more likely to insist on directing their own lives, and, worst of all, less likely to rear their offspring with blind gene-pool loyalty.

Even more rigid social-imprinting rituals guard the "dying reflexes." Hive control of "death" responses is taken for granted in all pre-cybernetic societies.

In the past this conservative degradation of individuality was an evolutionary virtue.

During epochs of species stability, when the tribal, feudal and industrial technologies were being mastered and fine-tuned, wisdom was centered in the gene-pool stored in the collective linguistic-consciousness, the racial data-base of the hive.

Since individual life was short, brutish, aimless, what a singular learned was nearly irrelevant. The world was changing so slowly that knowledge could only be embodied in the species. Lacking the technologies for the personal mastery of transmission and storage of information, the individual was simply too slow, too small, to matter. Loyalty to the racial collective was the virtue. Creativity, Premature Individuation, was anti-evolutionary. A weirdo, mutant distraction. Only Village Idiots would try to commit independent, unauthorized thought.

In the feudal and industrial eras, Management used the fear of death to motivate and control individuals. Today, politicians use the death-dealing military and the police and capital punishment to protect the social order. Organized religion maintains its power and wealth by orchestrating and exaggerating the fear of death.

Among the many things that the Pope, the Ayatollah, and Fundamentalist Protestants agree on: confident understanding and self-directed mastery of the dying process is the last thing to be allowed to the individual. The very notion of *Cybernetic Post-Biological Intelligence* or consumer immortality-options is taboo, sinful. For formerly valid reasons of gene-pool protection.

Religions have cleverly monopolized the rituals of dying to increase control over the superstitious. Throughout history the priests and mullahs have swarmed around the expiring human like black vultures. Death belonged to them.

As we grow up in the 20th century we are systematically programmed about How to Die. Hospitals are staffed with priests/ministers/rabbis ready to perform the "last rites." Every army unit has its Catholic Chaplain to administer the Sacrament of Extreme Unction (what a phrase, really!) to the expiring soldier. The Ayatollah, Chief Mullah of the Islamic Death Cult, sends his teenage soldiers into the Iraq minefields with dog-tags guaranteeing immediate transfer to the Allah's Destination Resort. Koranic Heaven. A terrible auto crash? Call the medics! Call the priest! Call the Reverend!

In the Industrial Society, everything becomes part of Big Business. Dying involves Blue Cross, Medicare, Health Care Delivery Systems, the Health Care Financing Administration (HCFA), terminal patient wards. Undertakers. Cemeteries. The funeral rituals.

The monopolies of religion and the assembly lines of Top Management process the dying and the dead even more efficiently than the living.

We recall that knowledge and selective choice about such gene-pool issues as conception, test-tube fertilization, pregnancy, abortion is dangerous enough to the church-fathers.

But suicide, right-to-die concepts, euthanasia, life-extension, out-of-the-body experiences, occult experimentation, astral-travel scenarios, death/rebirth reports, extra-terrestrial speculation, cryogenics, sperm-banks, egg-banks, DNA banks, personally-empowering Artificial Intelligence Technology—anything that encourages the individual to engage in personal speculation and experimentation with immortality—is anathema to the orthodox Seed-Shepherds of the feudal and industrial ages.

Why? Because if the flock doesn't fear death, then the grip of Religious and Political Management is broken. The power of the gene-pool is threatened. And when control loosens in the gene-pool, dangerous genetic innovations and mutational visions tend to emerge.

Some believe that the Cybernetic Age we are entering could mark the beginning of a period of enlightened and intelligent individualism, a time unique in history when technology is available to individuals to support a huge diversity of personalized lifestyles and cultures, a world of diverse, interacting social groups whose initial-founding membership number is one.[1]

The exploding technology of computation and communication lays a delicious feast of knowledge and personal choice within our easy grasp. Under such conditions, the operating wisdom and control naturally passes from aeons-old power of gene pools, and locates in the rapidly self-modifying brains of individuals capable of dealing with an ever-accelerating rate of change.

Aided by customized, personally-programmed quantum-linguistic appliances, the individual can choose his/her own social and genetic future. And perhaps choose not to "die".

---

[1] The authors divide the stages of human history into: tribal, feudal, industrial, and cybernetic. The arrival of the latter stage is heralded in the authors' book *Cybernetic Societies*, to appear.

The Wave Theory Of Evolution

Current theories of genetics suggest that evolution, like everything else in the universe, comes in waves.

So, at times of Punctuated Evolution, collective metamorphosis, when many things are mutating at the same time, then the ten commandments of the "old ones" become ten more suggestions...

At such times of rapid innovation and collective mutation, conservative hive dogma can be dangerous, suicidal. Individual experimentation and exploration, the thoughtful methodical scientific challenging of taboos, becomes the key to the survival of the gene-school.

Now, as we enter the Cybernetic Age, we arrive at a new wisdom which broadens our definition of personal immortality and gene-pool survival: *The Post-Biological Options Of The Information Species.* A fascinating set of gourmet-consumer choices suddenly appear on the pop-up menu of The Evolutionary Cafe.

It is beginning to look as though in the Information Society, the individual human being can script, produce, direct his/her own immortality.

Here we face Mutation Shock in its most panicky form. And, as we have done in understanding earlier mutations, the first step is to develop a new language. We should not impose the values or vocabulary of the past species upon the new Cybernetic Culture.

Would you let the buzz-words of a preliterate paleolithic cult control your life? Will you let the superstitions of a tribal-village culture (now represented by the Pope and the Ayatollah) shuffle you off the scene? Will you let the mechanical planned-obsolescence tactics of the Factory Culture manage your existence?

So let us have no more pious wimp-sheep talk about death. The time has come to talk cheerfully and joke sassily about personal responsibility for managing the dying process. For starters let's de-mystify death and develop alternative metaphors for consciousness leaving the body. Let us speculate good-naturedly about post-biological options. Let's be bold about opening up a broad spectrum of Club-Med post-biological possibilities.

For starters, let's replace the word "death" with the more neutral, precise, scientific term: *Metabolic Coma.* And then let's go on to suggest that this temporary state of "coma" might be replaced by: *Auto-Meta-morphosis*, a self-controlled change in bodily form, where the individual chooses to change his/her vehicle of existence without loss of consciousness.

Then, let's distinguish between involuntary and voluntary metabolic coma. Reversible and irreversible dying.

Let's explore that fascinating "no man's land'—the period between body-death and neurological-death in terms of the knowledge-information processing involved.

And let's collect some data about that even more intriguing zone now beginning to be researched in the cross-disciplinary field of scientific study known as Artificial Life.[1] What knowledge-information processing capacities can be preserved after both metabolic coma and brain cessation? What natural and artificial systems, from the growth of mineral structures to the self-reproduction of formal mathematical automata, are promising alternative candidates to biology for the support of life?

And then let us perform the ultimate act of Human Intelligence. Let's venture with calm, open-minded tolerance and scientific rigor into that perennially mysterious *terra incognita* and ask the final question: What knowledge-information processing possibilities can remain after the cessation of all biological life: somatic, neurological and genetic?

How can human consciousness be supported in hardware outside of the moist envelope of graceful, attractive, pleasure-filled meat we now inhabit? How can the organic, carbon-constructed caterpillar become the silicon butterfly?

C.S. Hyatt, Ph.D. and A.K. O'Shea have suggested three stages of *Post-Biological Intelligence*:

1. *Cybernetic Recognition* of the myriad knowledge-information processing varieties involved in the many stages of dying.

2. *Cybernetic Management*, developing knowledge-information processing skills while out-of-body, out-of-brain and beyond DNA.

3. *Cybernetic-Technological*, Attaining one, or many, of the immortality options.

---

[1] Los Alamos, famous as the birthplace of atomic weapons, today also houses the Center for Nonlinear Studies, where a group has been meeting weekly to discuss the many technical aspects of the newly identified field of Artificial Life. The center recently sponsored a week-long international workshop, the world's first, where scientists met to discuss the implications and craft the foundational theories of the field.

The meeting was friendly, fun, and wildly trans-disciplinary. Nanotechnology pioneers outlined the potential for protein engineering, and robotics expert Hans Moravec presented compelling arguments that a genetic takeover was underway, our cultural artifacts now evolving past the point of symbiosis with the human species. Self-replicating structures ranging from minerals to computer viruses were demonstrated.

Post-Biological Recognition Intelligence

We recognize that the dying process, for millennia has been blanketed by taboo and primitive superstition, has suddenly become accessible to human intelligence.

Here we experience the sudden insights that we need not "go quietly" and passively into the dark night or the neon-lit, musak-enhanced Disney-heaven of the PTL crowd. We realize that the concept of involuntary, irreversible metabolic coma known as death is a feudal superstition, a marketing efficiency of industrial society. We understand that one can discover dozens of active, creative alternatives to going belly-up clutching the company logo of the Christian Cross, Blue Cross, Crescent Cross, or the eligibility cards of the Veterans Administration.

Recognition is always the beginning of the possibility for change. Once we comprehend that "death" can be defined as a problem of knowledge-information processing, solutions to this age-long "problem" can emerge. One realizes that the intelligent thing to do is to try to keep one's knowledge-processing capacities around as long as possible. In bodily form. In neural form. In the silicon circuitry and magnetic storage media of today's computers. In molecular form, through the atom-stacking of nanotechnology in tomorrow's computers. In cryogenic form. In the form of stored data, legend, myth. In the form of off-spring who are cybernetically trained to use *Post Biological Intelligence*. In the form of post-biological gene-pools, info-pools, advanced viral forms resident in world computer networks and cyberspace matrices of the sort described in the "sprawl novels" of William Gibson.[1]

The second step in attaining *Post-Biological Recognition Intelligence* is to shift from the passive to the active mode. Industrial age humans were trained to await docilely the onset of termination and then to turn over their body for disposal to the priests and the factory (hospital) technicians.

Our species is now developing the Cybernetic Information Skills to plan ahead, to make one's will prevail. The smart thing to do is to see dying as a change in the implementation of information-processing: to orchestrate it, manage it, anticipate and exercise the many available options.

---

[1] William Gibson, cyberpunk psy-fi visionary, has published *Neuromancer, Count Zero* and *Burning Chrome*. They are recommended reading for their technically and socially plausible vision of high-tech low-life on the streets.

We consider here twenty-two distinct methods of avoiding a submissive or fearful dying.[1]

Post-Biological Programming Intelligence

Elsewhere the authors have defined 8 levels of intelligence: biological emotional, mental-symbolic, social, aesthetic, neurological-cybernetic, genetic, atomic-nano-tech. At each stage there is a recognition stage, followed by a brain-programming or brain-reprogramming stage.

In order to re-program it is necessary to activate the circuits in the brain which mediate that particular dimension of intelligence. Once this circuit is "turned on" it is possible to re-imprint or re-program.

Cognitive neurology suggests that the most direct way to re-program emotional responses is to re-activate the appropriate circuits. To reprogram sexual responses it is effective to re-activate and re-experience the original teen-age imprints and re-imprint new sexual responses.

The circuits of the brain which mediate the "dying" process are routinely experienced during "near-death" crises. For centuries people have reported: "My entire life flashed before my eyes as I sank for the third time."

This "near-death" experience can be "turned-on" via the relevant anesthetic drugs. Ketamine, for example.

Or by learning enough about the effects of out-of-the-body drugs so that one can use hypnotic techniques to activate the desired circuits without using external chemical stimuli.

We see immediately that the rituals intuitively developed by religious groups are designed to induce trance states related to "dying." The child growing up in a Catholic culture is deeply imprinted (programmed) by funeral rites. The arrival of the solemn priest to administer extreme unction becomes an access code for the *Post-Biological* state. Other cultures have different rituals for activating and then controlling (programming) the death circuits of the brain. Until recently, very few have permitted personal control or customized consumer choice.

Perhaps this discussion of the "dying circuits of the brain" is too innovative. Sometimes it is easier to understand new concepts about one's own species by referring to other species. Almost every animal species manifests "dying reflexes." Some animals leave the herd to die alone. Others stand with legs apart, stolidly postponing the last moment. Some species eject the dying organism from the social group.

---

[1] Mystics may remark that there are also 22 paths in the Kabbalistic "Tree of Life" associated with the Tarot.

To gain navigational control of one's dying processes three steps suggest themselves: 1) activate the death-reflexes imprinted by your culture, experience them... 2) trace their origins, and... 3) re-program.

The aim is to develop a scientific model of the chain of cybernetic (knowledge-information) processes that occur as one approaches this metamorphic stage—and to intentionally develop options for taking active responsibility for these events.

Achieving Immortality

Since the dawn of human history, philosophers and theologians have speculated about immortality. Uneasy, aging kings have commanded methods for extending the life span.

A most dramatic example of this age-long impulse is ancient Egypt which produced mummification, the pyramids and manuals like the *Egyptian Book of the Dying*.

The *Tibetan Book of the Dying* (Buddhist) presents a masterful model of post-mortem stages and techniques for guiding the student to a state of immortality which is neurologically "real" and suggests scientific techniques for reversing the dying process.

The new field of molecular engineering is producing techniques within the framework of current consensus Western Science to implement auto-metamorphosis.

The aim of the game is to defeat death—to give the Individual mastery of this, the final stupidity.

The next section of this essay presents twenty-two methods of achieving immortality. We do not especially endorse any particular technique. Our aim is to review all options and encourage creative-courageous thinking about new possibilities.

A PRELIMINARY LIST OF IMMORTALITY OPTIONS
(To Replace Involuntary-Irreversible Metabolic Coma)

I. Psychological/Behavioral Training Techniques

The techniques in this category do not assist in attaining personal immortality *per se,* but are useful in acquiring the experience of "experimental dying," reversible-voluntary exploration of the territory between body-coma and brain, death, sometimes called *out-of-body experiences*; or *near-dying experiences*. Others have termed these *astral travel*, or *reincarnation memories*.

1. Meditation & Hypnosis.

These are the classic yogic routes to exploration of non-ordinary states of consciousness. They are well known to be labor and time intensive. For the most intelligent and comprehensive discussion of these techniques, we recommend Crowley.[1]

2. Carefully Designed Psychedelic Drug Experiences Of "Dying" & Genetic (Re-Incarnation/Pre-Incarnation) Consciousness.

There is, here, no commitment to any occultist theory about biological incarnation. We refer to techniques enabling access to information and operational programs stored in the brain of the individual. In normal states of consciousness, these are subroutines operating below voluntary access.[2]

3. Experimental Out-Of-Body Experiences Using Anesthetics.

John Lilly has written extensively about his experiences with small dosages of anesthetics such as Ketamine.[3] It is possible that the out-of-body subjective effects of such substances are (merely) interpretations of proprioceptive disruption. Nevertheless, Lilly's reported experiences seem to indicate that information is available through these investigative routes.

4. Sensory Deprivation/Isolation Tanks.

Again, Lilly has investigated this subject most comprehensively.[4]

5. Re-Programming Exercises (Suspending The Effects Of & Replacing Early "Death" Imprints Imposed By Culture).

6. Development Of New Rituals To Guide The Post-Body Transition.

Our cultural taboos have prohibited the development of much detailed work in this area. One of the few available sources in this area is E.J. Gold.[5]

---

[1] Aleister Crowley, *Eight Lectures on Yoga.* (Divided into two parts respectively entitled, "Yoga for Yahoos," and "Yoga for Yellowbellies.") New Falcon Publications, 1991.

[2] Marvin Minsky has outlined a theory that "mind" emerges from a collection of smaller interacting entities, themselves mindless. This is outlined in his book *The Society of Mind,* Simon & Schuster, 1986.

[3] John Lilly, *The Scientist,* and *Programming & Metaprogramming in the Human Biocomputer.*

[4] John Lilly, *The Deep Self.*

[5] E.J. Gold *American Book of the Dead.* IDHHB, 1973. See also Gold's *Creation Story.*

7. Pre-Incarnation Exercises.

With these, one uses the preferred altered state method (drugs, hypnosis, shamanic trance, voodoo ritual, born-again frenzies) to create future scripts for oneself.

8. Aesthetically-Orchestrated Voluntary "Dying".

This procedure has been called suicide, i.e., "self-murder," by officials who wish to control the mortem process. Mr. and Mrs. Arthur Koestler, active members of the British EXIT program arranged a most dignified and graceful voluntary metabolic coma. A California group, HADDA, is placing an amendment on California ballot to permit terminal patients to plan voluntary metacom with their medical advisors.

    The non-Californian can always look for an enlightened MD, or consenting adult friends to act as guides to the Western Lands.

II. Somatic Techniques For Life Extension

Techniques to inhibit the process of aging comprise the classical approach to immortality. In the present state of science, these "buy time."

9. Diet.

The classic research on diet-and-longevity has been performed by Roy L. Walford, M.D.[1]

10. Life-Extension Drugs.

These include anti-oxidants and others. A comprehensive reference is *Life Extension* by Sandy Shaw and Durk Pearson.

11. Exercise Regimes.
12. Temperature Variation.
13. Sleep Treatments (Hibernation).
14. Immunization To Counter The Aging Process.

III. Somatic/Neural/Genetic Preservation

Techniques in this class do not ensure continuous operation of consciousness. They produce potentially reversible metabolic coma. They are alternatives for preserving the structure of tissues until a time of more advanced medical knowledge.

---

[1] Roy L. Walford, M.D. *The 120 Year Diet,* Simon & Schuster, 1986 and *Maximum Life Span,* W.W. Norton, New York 1983.

15. Cryogenics Or Vacuum-Pack "Pickling."

Why let one's body and brain rot, when that seems to imply no possibility at all for your future? Why let the carefully arranged tangle of dendritic growths in your nervous system which may be the storage site for all of your memories get eaten by fungus? Perpetual preservation of your tissues is available today at moderate cost.[1]

16. Cryonic Preservation Of Neural Tissue Or DNA.

Those not particularly attached to their bodies can opt for preservation of the essentials: their brains together with the instructional codes capable of regrowing something genetically identical to their present bio-machinery.

IV. Bio-Genetic Methods For Life Extension

Is there any need to experience metabolic coma at all? We have mentioned ways to gain personal control of the experience, to stave it off by "conventional" longevity techniques, to avoid irreversible dissolution of the systemic substrate.

Techniques are now emerging to permit a much more vivid guarantee of personal persistence, a smooth metamorphic transformation into a different form of substrate on which the computer program of consciousness runs.

17. Cellular/DNA Repair.

Nanotechnology is the science and engineering of mechanical and electronic systems built at atomic dimensions.[2] One forecast ability of nano-

---

[1] One of the few cryogenic preservation companies in operation is the Alcor Foundation, (800) 367-2228.

[2] The most visible and eloquent proponent of nanotechnology is K. Eric Drexler of MIT and Stanford Universities. His book *Engines of Creation* provides a detailed overview of the held. Other more technical works include:

K. Eric Drexler, *Molecular Engineering: An Approach to the Development of General Capabilities for Molecular Manipulation,* Proc. Natl. Acad. Sci USA, Vol. 78 #9, September 1981 pp. 5275–5278.

K. Eric Drexler, *Rod Logic & Thermal Noise in the Mechanical Nanocomputer,* Proc. 3rd Intl. Symposium on Molecular Electronic Devices, Elsevier North Holland, 1987.

K. Eric Drexler, *Molecular Engineering: Assemblers and Future Space Hardware,* Aerospace XXI, 33rd Annual meeting of the American Astronautical Society, paper AAS-86–415.

Feynman, R. "There's Plenty of Room at the Bottom," in *Miniaturization,* H.D. Gilbert (ed.), Reinhold, New York, 1961 pp. 282–296. One of the origi-

technology is its potential for production of self-replicating nano-machines living within individual biological cells.

These artificial enzymes will effect cellular repair, as damage occurs from mechanical causes, radiation, or other aging effects. Repair of DNA ensures genetic stability.

18. Cloning.

Biologically-based replication of genetically identical personal copies of yourself, at any time desired, is approaching the possible. Sex is fun, but sexual reproduction is biologically inefficient, suited mainly for inducing genetic variation in species which still advance through the accidents of luck in random combination.

V. Cybernetic (Post-Biological) Methods For Attaining Immortality [Artificial Life In Silicon]

As the neuromantic cyberpunk author Bruce Sterling notes, evolution moves in clades, radiating outward in omni-directional diversity, and not following a single linear path. Some silicon visionaries believe that natural evolution of the human species (or at least their branch of it) is near completion. They are no longer interested in merely procreating, but in designing their successors. Carnegie-Mellon robot scientist Hans Moravec writes:

> We owe our existence to organic evolution. But we owe it little loyalty. We are on the threshold of a change in the universe comparable to the transition from non-life, to life.[1]

Human society has now reached a turning point in the operation of the process of evolution, a point at which the next evolutionary step of the species is under our control. Or, more correctly, the next steps, which will occur in parallel, will result in an explosion of diversity of the human species. We are no longer dependent on fitness in any physical sense for survival, our quantum appliances and older mechanical devices provide the requisite means in all circumstances. In the near future, the (now merging) methods of computer and biological technology will make the human form a matter totally determined by individual choice.

As a flesh-and-blood species we are moribund, stuck at "a local optimum," to borrow a term from mathematical optimization theory.

---

nal works approaching molecular-scale engineering. Nobel prize winner Feynman is without a doubt one of the most brilliant scientists of the century.
[1] Hans Moravec, *Mind Children,* 1988.

Beyond this horizon, which humankind has reached, lies the unknown, the as-yet scarcely imagined. We will design our children, and co-evolve intentionally with the cultural artifacts which are our progeny.

Humans already come in some variety of races and sizes. In comparison to what "human" will mean within the next century, we humans are at present as indistinguishable from one another as are hydrogen molecules. Our anthropocentrism will decrease.

We see two principle categorizations of the form of the human of the future, one more biological-like: a bio/machine hybrid of any desired form, and one not biological at all: an "electronic life" on the computer networks. Human-as-machine, and human-in-machine.

Of these, human-as-machine is perhaps more easily conceived. Today, we already have crude prosthetic implants, artificial limbs, valves, and entire organs. The continuing improvements in old-style mechanical technology slowly increase the thoroughness of human-machine integration.

The electronic life form of human-in-machine is even more alien to our current conceptions of humanity. Through storage of one's belief systems as on-line data structures, driven by selected control structures (the electronic analog to will?), one's neuronal apparatus will operate in silicon as it did on the wetware of the brain, although faster, more accurately, more self-mutably, and, if desired, immortally.

19. Archival-Informational.

One standard way of becoming "immortal" is by leaving a trail of archives, biographies, and publicized noble deed.

The increasing presence of stable knowledge media in our Cybernetic Society make this a more rigorous platform for persistent existence. The knowledge possessed by an individual is captured in expert systems, and world-scale hypertext systems[1] thus ensuring the longevity and accessibility of textural and graphical memes.

Viewed from outside the self, death is not a binary phenomenon, but a continuously varying function. How alive are you in Paris at this moment? In the city in which you live? In the room in which you are reading this?

---

[1] A world-scale hypertext system to permit instantaneous on-line access to global knowledge networks has been envisioned and written about by Ted Nelson, in *Literary Machines,* published by the author. Other information is available in Nelson's *Computer Lib* (1974), republished by Microsoft Press (1987).

20. *Head Coach* Personality Data Base Transmission.

Head Coach is a computer system under development by Futique Inc., one of the first examples of a new generation of psychoactive computer software. The program allows the user (performer) to digitize and store thoughts on a routine daily basis. If one leaves, let us say, 20 years of daily computer-stored records of thought-performance, one's grandchildren, a century down the line can "know" and replay your information habits and mental performances. They will be able to "share and relive experiences" in considerable detail. To take a most vulgar example, if an individual's moves in a chess game are stored, the descendants can relive, move-by-move, a game played by Great-Great-Grandmother in the past century.

As passive reading is replaced by "active re-writing," later generations will be able to relive how we performed the great books of our time.

Yet more intriguing is the possibility of implementing the knowledge extracted over time from a person: their beliefs, preferences, and tendencies, as a set of algorithms guiding a program capable of acting in a manner functionally identical to the person. Advances in robotics technology will take these "Turing creatures" away from being mere "brains in bottles" to hybrids capable of interacting sensorily with the physical world.

21. Nanotech Information Storage: Towards Direct Brain-Computer Transfer.

When a computer becomes obsolete, one does not discard the data it contains. The hardware is merely a temporary vehicle of implementation for structures of information. The data gets transferred to new systems for continued use. Decreasing costs of computer storage, CD-ROM and WORM memory systems, mean that no information generated today ever need be lost.

We can consider building an artificial computational substrate both functionally and structurally identical to the brain (and perhaps the body). How? Via the predicted future capabilities of nanotechnology.[1]

Communicating nano-machines which pervade the organism may analyze the neural and cellular structure and transfer the information obtained to machinery capable of growing, atom by atom, an identical copy.

---

[1] We partially regret such speculations beyond present technical capabilities. The brain is a most complex machine, with some 10^{20} individual cells, according to current estimates. Yet we are redeemed by what we see as the technical inevitability of nanotechnology.

But what of the soul? According to the *American Heritage Dictionary*: "soul (is) the animating and vital principle in man credited with the faculties of thought, action and emotion and conceived as forming an immaterial entity distinguishable from but temporarily coexistent with his body."

At first reading this definition seems to be a classic example of theological nonsense. But studied from the perspective of information theory we may be able to wrestle this religio-babble into scientific operations. Let's change the bizarre word "immaterial" to "invisible to the naked senses," i.e., atomic/molecular/electronic. Now the "soul" refers to information processed and stored in microscopic-cellular, molecular packages. Soul becomes any information that "lives," i.e., is capable of being retrieved and communicated. Is it not true that all the tests for "death" at every level of measurement (nuclear, neural, bodily, galactic) involve checking for unresponsiveness to signals?

From this viewpoint, the twenty-two immortality options become cybernetic methods of preserving one's unique signal capacity. There are as many souls as there are ways storing and communicating data. Tribal lore defines the racial soul. The DNA is a molecular soul. The brain is a neurological soul. Electron storage creates the silicon soul. Nanotechnology makes possible the atomic soul.

22. Computer Viral: Persistent Existence In Gibson's Cyberspace Matrix.

The previous option permitted personal survival through isomorphic mapping of neural structure to silicon (or some other arbitrary medium of implementation). It also suggests the possibility of survival as an entity in what amounts to a reification of Jung's collective unconscious: the global information network.

In the 21st century imagined by William Gibson, wily cybernauts will not only store themselves electronically, but do so in the form of a "computer virus," capable of traversing computer networks and of self-replication as a guard against accidental or malicious erasure by others, or other programs. (Imagine the somewhat droll scenario: "What's on this CD?" "Ah, that's just old Leary. Let's go ahead and reformat it.")

Given the ease of copying computer-stored information, one could exist simultaneously in many forms. Where the "I" is in this situation is a matter for philosophy. Our belief is that consciousness would persist in each form, running independently (and ignorant of each other self-manifestation unless in communication with it), cloned at each branch point.

NOTE

This list of options for Voluntary-Reversible-Metabolic Coma and auto-metamorphosis is not mutually exclusive. The intelligent person needs little encouragement to explore all of these possibilities. And to design many new other alternatives to going belly-up in line with Management Memos.

***

Kon-Tiki Of The Flesh

In the near future, what is now taken for granted as the perishable human creature will be a mere historical curiosity, one point amidst unimaginable multidimensional diversity of form. Individuals, or groups of adventurers, will be free to choose to reassume flesh-and-blood form, constructed for the occasion by the appropriate science.

Such historical expeditions may well be conducted in the spirit of Thor Heyerdahl's Kon Tiki voyages. To voyage in what the light of history reveals to be an objectively improbable way, merely to prove that such was possible, as unlikely as it seems.

Timothy Leary, Ph.D. was a respected Harvard psychology professor who became a guru for hundreds of thousands of people, espousing the use of the powerful hallucinogen LSD and other mind-altering drugs as a means of brain change. After he was forced out of academia, Leary became associated with many of the great names of the time including Aldous Huxley, Allen Ginsberg, William Burroughs and Charlie Mingus. In the mid-1960s his fame grew to international proportions. He was targeted as "the most dangerous man in the world" by the U.S. government and sentenced to a long prison term for possession of two marijuana cigarettes. After he was released from prison, he continued to advocate brain-change through various means, including computer software. He acted in a number of movies, and was well-regarded as a stand-up comedian/philosopher. He died of cancer in 1996.

SO YOU WANT TO BE SOMEONE

Adventures In The Polarized Self

by Joseph C. Lisiewski, Ph.D.

So you want to be "someone"! This is the eternal cry of everyone who has, does, and will ever walk the face of this earth. It is the universal panacea which has littered the language of that drone-mass termed "humanity." Its distillate, that Elixir of tangible result, will dissolve the sphere of confusion, pierce the anvil of socially induced chaos, and rend asunder forever that leprous contagion of self-doubt and inability whose forebears were the dust of parental imitation and the dirt of required mimicry. Unfortunately, such emotionally stirring words and images, bandied about by the reigning social poets and philosophers of our time, cannot create that nearly perfect set of conditions which enable *anyone* to become "someone." What are the conditions necessary for such a transformation? This idealized, yet thoroughly workable process is not a startling revelation given here for the first time. As such, it will be a grave disappointment to those occult bookstore haunting freaks who scan the shelves for the secret quick-fix. Rather, it is an intelligent approach: direct in definition, application, and result. It will truly bring about a transformation in the user which, ironically, will be the reason for its mainstream non-use.

The Use Of Structure

Everything of permanence possesses structure. From a physical object to a complex idea, all are the embodiment of structure which lends meaning to their essence. So is the process of becoming "someone." To aid visual memory, refer to the diagram below. Notice the sequence of steps, and the interdependence of Blocks 1, 2 and 3 + 5, while Block 4 serves as a foundation for the 5th. Notice carefully the labels and interrelationships, for our discussion rests upon this understanding.

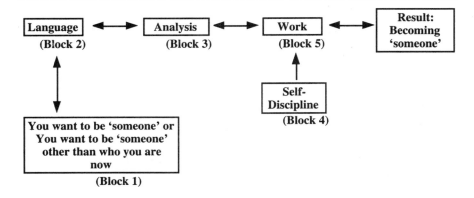

The Structure of Chaos
or
The Path of Transformation

The Elements of Chaos
or of
The Path of Transformation

In the beginning of the quest to be "someone" (Block 1), the seeker immediately encounters the problem of Language (Block 2). The driving emotion to be "someone" is seen as one side of this need, while the concept embodied in the word "someone" is viewed as the other side. This naturally leads to Analysis (Block 3), the next step in the process. These sequence of events constitute a normal rhythm in Self-Discovery: they are part and parcel of the mechanism of human thought to attempt to find, or create, order in chaos.

With analysis, the individual's past is brought into stark focus. Here, an awareness of the constant barrage of thoughts, actions and reactions, goals and desires upon him are made plain. But what is also important is the individual's awareness that these mental occupants of his past possess a strange and elusive quality: they generate a sense of vague, disturbing incompleteness which intensifies as the analysis continues. At the same time, he realizes that what he calls "himself" is the product of their interactions. There is now born deep within the emotional core, a restlessness to discover why and from what point this feeling originates.

With further effort, the now completely restless seeker finds the answer: those irritating feelings; his reactions to the influences of his past and to what he has become as a result of them, are due to his survival instinct. It is not the wanton need for food, sex, or drink; but rather the impetus toward a need for unity of the Self: that Self which up to now was fragmented. What is occurring, metaphorically speaking, is the attraction of all those diffused bits of *personal* thoughts, ideas, and desires to each other, like so many bits of iron filings to a magnet.

Now the attentive reader may say, "Of course I realize all those little bits of what I call my Self want to get together and operate as a well-oiled machine. Everybody knows that!" The problem is that the attentive reader never takes the necessary step which the *tortured* does: that of active involvement in the process. For in the case of the latter, his agony has been self-inflicted by the restlessness brought on through his own deep analysis. He has realized that to be "someone" seems contrary to those not-quite-the-right-fit feelings, thoughts, and ideas which still occupy the corners of his mind, and which lie in direct opposition to his recently activated survival instinct. He has discovered that this instinct is now in the permanent "on" position, and he can never be content with himself as he is. There is only one solution: to continue this investigation in Self-Polarization.

Somewhere in all this literal misery of change, a further insight occurs. Whether it's induced by sleep, a fine meal an inspiring poem, or a chemical tablet matters little; its advent is what counts. It's a phenomenon which has been likened to a psychological break-through, or a little-understood Law of Being, or simply as surrender to the problem. What started out as the use of language to fathom the meaning of being "someone," to give the conscious vocabulary a bull's eye on which to focus, comes back full circle. Specifically, the individual has become aware of the *trance of language.*

The action of this trance has impaired the efforts made so far, but not completely hindered them. The individual now realizes that while in this state, he has used his language of definition to assure himself that he already is "someone," and defined and re-defined himself within his world of belief. Finally, by adhering to his relentless yearning to understand, he sees that the meaning behind the desire to be "someone" really is his desire *to be "someone" other than who he is now!* Instantly, the person's grasp of this fundamental idea leads to the uncovering of the greatest crime ever committed upon any individual or group. It is this trance of language that induced him to become what he is, to feel what he does, and to worship as instructed. In so doing, it produced the sense of incompleteness which caused his search to begin. This crime of the trance language is perpetrated on each and every person from the moment of birth, until the lid of the coffin is sealed. It is used by those who were and are with you all of your life. In the person's early stage of development, he is told to "be the shining apple of his parents' eyes," which was found to really mean: "get good grades in school," but not so good as to surpass Daddy's and Mommy's accomplishments; "don't get a girl in trouble" (or if female, "don't get in trouble!"); "wash behind your ears," showing parental love by your inspection before leaving the house, and "wear clean underwear in case you're hit by a car and taken to the hospital," lest it reflects upon their role as good, decent, caring parents. Gradually, the image of being the "shining apple" of their eyes came to be defined as becoming miniatures of them in thought, word and deed. The young individual has found that he is now liked by his parents because he doesn't offend them, and they receive faint praise from the neighbors whom they secretly hate. So, the need for the security they provide (physical of course, while the youngster's Soul is being raped hourly) is reinforced by his actions which require further abandonment of his innate freedom of thought and expression. By now however, the individual has accepted this. This action-reaction mechanism of behavior progressively spreads outward into all social contacts: mates, friends, job associates, etc., like ripples in a pond. In the end (the point where the person finally decided he wanted to be "someone"), the person finds he is merely the reflection in thought, language and deed of that multi-faceted world we term Society. And the resulting social intercourse we so endearingly hear of simply means, you've been screwed up again!

But our great hope of salvation lies in that permanently switched-on survival instinct spoken of earlier. We now grasp *our own personal* feelings, thoughts and actions which are normal for us. Now is perceived those elements of that genuine, real Self, that "I" deep within. By the process of language awareness and analysis, the true human duality is seen: the hypnotically induced life of society versus the authentic life which comprises Self. The individual has achieved complete polarization.

So far, so good, or so it is thought. But now the person pays the price for his fantastic discovery and decision to become "someone" other than who he was. Throughout the process changes have begun: the old friends somehow seem different. Looking at them gives a curious sense of seeing images in a cracked mirror. They too sense something, and begin to shy away—but only a little at a time, at first. The thing most dreaded becomes more intense: a growing disgust for the values, concepts, and requirements foisted upon the individual during the now dim past of his life. He undertakes a merciless examination of everything: religion, politics, mates, vocation, life, death, meaning, and contradiction. All are in a constant state of analysis by the rapidly becoming "someone." In the latter phases of this transformation, the individual feels as though he were completely isolated from everyone, and void of all substance within. And so it should be, since for all practical purposes those players on his life-stage—those desires and needs, those things to have and to have not that peopled and occupied the world of that former Self—are no longer valid. The sublime, artistically balanced whole they formerly presented are finally seen to rest on a foundation of distorted wants and demands instilled in him by others. The requirements of the demanding new role as "someone" other than who he *was* are now accepted without further pain or refusal. The individual is now ready to implement his new insights and goal needs into his active life-stream.

The infant new "someone" now needs the tools to enable him to manifest the effects of his transformation. In all cases of such change there are at least two driving impulses which characterize the change:

(1) The need to express the new "someone" in terms of reality, i.e., to achieve something which harmonizes those personal thoughts, feelings, and drives. It may be the acquisition of more education to evidence some long hidden vision; it may consist of the honing of some skill, or the development of a talent which not only contributes to his new sense of wholeness, but which is a veritable product of it. Yet again, it may be displayed as a complete change in worldly vocation. All are possibilities.

(2) An earnest yearning to leave behind a creative legacy to future generations. This can be a book, a painting, an idea or concept, a code of behavior others have learned from him, or any of an infinite number of possibilities.

To fulfill these necessities, to manifest them as a genuine result, requires two more activities:

(1) The acquisition and application of self-discipline (Block 4) directed into

(2) Work (Block 5).

This is where many potentially vibrant and vital human possibilities are lost, due to the completely misunderstood nature of self-discipline and work. Again, the individual's negative reactions toward each are the result of society's views of them having been placed into us.

Self-discipline is not a grim process of painful adherence to a technique leading to accomplishment. It is a conscious practice which uses scientifically proven principles that change behavior patterns to enable the new "someone" to do what he requires of himself. Instead of acting from negative behavior, such as avoidance of effort to achieve something, the individual builds into his mint and physical nervous system new positive behavior patterns. Now, he finds himself acting automatically to simulate and exhibit action and reaction patterns which bring with them the successful achievement of his self-imposed visions. It works both ways: just as negative behavior and visions (or mental imaging, if you wish) initiate wrong action or non-action to produce failure, positive behavior and mental images create the corresponding mechanical right action to bring about a favorable result. Self-discipline is a technique and form of conduct which can be very successfully used in any area of life. It is recommended that the serious individual consult the applied psychology section of his library or local professional book shop. Several excellent books and tapes are available on the subject, which will prove to be one of the best investments anyone can make.

Work (Block 5), when engaged in by a self-disciplined person, produces positive results. It is not the feared bug-a-boo taught to you by those beer-guzzling, TV addicts of society who feel work is the curse by which they earn their daily bread. With this attitude, their daily bread is all they earn—and deserve. Rather, work is the purposeful direction of energy toward a goal for the sole purpose of achieving it. It is not to be dreaded, but embraced. It does not merely give life meaning, it is an intrinsic quality of life itself, and the new "someone" has an instinctive feeling this is how it should be. The individual's vistas are now opened and clear. He has changed, and through the use of self-discipline and work, has made the effort necessary to integrate the results, which were created by this process, a real-world experience. He is barred from nothing—most of all, by himself.

Epilogue

This chapter may be viewed by many readers to be radical in nature and content. This has been done on purpose, since the great number of such writings is too often presented in a simple, stale, soothing manner meant to placate the crippled mentality of a dull world. Such is also the purpose and intent of Dr. Christopher S. Hyatt, the author of the highly acclaimed *Undoing Yourself With Energized Meditation* and many other books. Dr. Hyatt has established a daring new approach in the exposition of those psychological and philosophical topics which are of such serious interest and need in the world today. He has turned the tables as it were, on the so-called sophisticated approach in *writing to educate*. Instead of a bland, piece-meal style, he employs rebellious style and attitude in disclosing scientifically valid, psychologically sound principles aimed at bringing about change within the reader: positive, useful, fruitful change. Through this approach he has ruthlessly exposed the fake sense of respectability of the functionally unconscious mass of humanity. In so doing, he has shocked them in making them aware that their so-called respectability lies in the shadow of their pseudo self-dignity. Hyatt has actively *applied* the instruction of the late Alchemist, Frater Albertus, to "shock people out of their insensibilities so they may wake from their sleep, and bring about a world of their *own* design."

WHY IS IT?
by Jim Goldiner

Why is it
that after devouring the fruit of a ripe olive
and being confronted with just the pit
and not knowing what it really is
and therefore what to do with it,
we toss it to the wind.

PULLING LIBERTY'S TEETH

by James Wasserman

Editor of the Falcon title:
Aha!

"A well regulated Militia, being necessary to the security of a free State, the right of the people to keep and bear Arms, shall not be infringed."

"Those who beat their swords into plowshares will do the plowing for those who didn't."

A "Million" Misinformed Moms

To paraphrase a famous gun-controller of old, May 14, 2000 is "a date which will live in infamy." A group consisting mostly of women and variously estimated between 150,000 and 500,000, forewent the traditional family pleasures associated with the annual Mothers' Day holiday to rally around TV personality and former Kmart spokeswoman Rosie O'Donnell. She was accompanied by such well-known gun confiscation luminaries as Diane Feinstein, Maxine Waters and Sarah Brady, all of whom spent the day expressing their contempt for the aspirations of America's founders, and their disdain for law-abiding Americans who believe in the Second Amendment. It was the first time in this writer's memory that a mass protest was aimed directly at the Bill of Rights.

Many of the "Moms" at the march were undoubtedly veterans of the Anti-War movement of the 60's and 70's, when the youthful idealism of a generation was masterfully manipulated by the anti-American Left. Now in middle-age, those who never woke up to the assault on Liberty embodied by the Nanny State, bared their teeth for a direct attack against the hated "rich, white, slave-owning men" who built the greatest, most prosperous, and freest nation in the history of the world. Professor Camille Paglia describes the March as "...the gun-control protest organized (as the major media is finally admitting) by the sister-in-law of

Hillary Clinton's longtime lawyer pal and hatchet woman, surly Susan Thomases..."[1] Surprised?

The Second Amendment: An Individual Right?

The "shot heard round the world" was fired during the first battle of the American Revolution on April 19, 1775 at British soldiers seeking to enforce British gun control laws by confiscating weapons and gunpowder belonging to the citizens of Concord, Massachusetts. Both Dr. Joyce Lee Malcolm in *To Keep and Bear Arms* and Dr. Stephen P. Halbrook in *That Every Man Be Armed* have provided prodigious, compelling and common sense scholarship to prove that the Second Amendment is a right possessed by the people.[2] If the reader has any doubt of this, he or she is referred to these two scholars. On the other hand, the text of the amendment itself, especially its phrase "the right of the people" may be considered indicative. See also similar use of the phrase "the people" in Amendments 1, 4, 9, and 10.

The passionate and brilliant writings and speeches collected in *The Federalist Papers, The Anti-Federalist Papers* and *The Debate on the Constitution,* establish beyond a shadow of a doubt that the right of the individual American to keep and bear arms was one of the most important guarantees brought forth in favor of the plan to consolidate the American Republic.[3] At least 8 of the original 13 states had provisions in their constitutions that included recognition of the right of private citizens to keep and bear arms. The words of the early leaders of America eloquently expressed their view that an armed populace is: 1) a natural check against tyranny, 2) the first line of defense against enemy attack, and 3) a natural force for the right ordering of society. The founders well understood that the liberties acknowledged by the Bill of Rights could only be held by a citizenry willing and able to protect its freedom, by force if necessary, from those who would attempt to seize it. The Second Amendment is Liberty's Teeth.

---

[1] Camille Paglia, *The Million Mom March: What a crock!* Salon.com, May 17, 2000.

[2] Joyce Lee Malcolm, *To Keep and Bear Arms,* Harvard University Press, 1994, and Stephen P. Halbrook, *That Every Man Be Armed,* The Independent Institute, 1994 .

[3] See *The Federalist Papers,* edited by Clinton Rossiter, Penguin Books, *The Anti-Federalist Papers and the Constitutional Convention Debates,* edited by Ralph Ketcham, Penguin Books, *The Debate on the Constitution,* (two volumes) edited by Bernard Bailyn, The Library of America.

Tyranny: Merely An Antiquated Eighteenth Century Concern?

In 1787, Noah Webster wrote "Before a standing army can rule, the people must be disarmed; as they are in almost every kingdom of Europe. The supreme power in America cannot enforce unjust laws by the sword; because the whole body of the people are armed, and constitute a force superior to any bands of regular troops that can be, on any pretense, raised in the United States."[1]

When William Clinton was sworn into office for his first term, he warmly remembered his former professor at Georgetown University, Carroll Quigley. Aside from being the recipient of such a singular honor, Quigley may have helped shape some of the attitudes toward the Second Amendment held by the most anti-gun president in American history. Quigley wrote in his 1966 tome *Tragedy and Hope,* "In a period of specialist weapons the minority who have such weapons can usually force the majority who lack them to obey; thus a period of specialist weapons tends to give rise to a period of minority rule and authoritarian government. But a period of amateur weapons is a period in which all men are roughly equal in military power, a majority can compel a minority to yield, and majority rule or even democratic government tends to rise."[2]

Much later in the book Quigley added, "At the present time, there seems to be little reason to doubt that the specialist weapons of today will continue to dominate the military picture into the foreseeable future. If so, there is little reason to doubt that authoritarian rather than democratic political regimes will dominate the world into the same foreseeable future."[3]

Undeterred by this nightmarish conclusion, Quigley quickly displays the confidence in alternate solutions and concern for the "quality of life" that undoubtedly touched the heart of his young protégé, "A period that is not democratic in its political structure is not necessarily bad, and may well be one in which people can live a rich and full social or intellectual life whose value may be even more significant than a democratic political or military structure."[4]

Overturning The Constitution

The civilian disarmament movement is working relentlessly to avoid the one legal means of enacting gun control—namely to amend the Constitu-

---

[1] *A Citizen of America, Philadelphia, October 17, 1787,* quoted in *The Debate on the Constitution,* Part One p. 155.
[2] Carroll Quigley, *Tragedy and Hope,* Macmillan, 1966, p. 34.
[3] *Ibid.,* pp. 1200–1201.
[4] *Ibid.,* p. 1201.

tion to either repeal the Second Amendment or to legally modify it. No lovers of the limitations on government imposed by the Constitution, gun control zealots are well aware of the obstacles placed in the path of "reformers" who seek to change it. A two-thirds majority of Congress may propose amendments which must then be adopted by three-fourths of the states. Even with these protections, such idiotic amendments as Prohibition will occur. However this is not the concern of the civilian disarmament crowd. They seek to bypass the Constitution altogether.

As Jaime Sneider, wrote, "[T]he language of organizers and supporters of the Million Mom March hints at a growing trend that culminated in yesterday's March. The (generally left-leaning) disgruntled individuals who have failed politically in getting gun-control measures passed have come to support Constitutional Nullification. ...Perhaps the scariest thing about the gun-control movement is that they want to blur the existence of truth itself. According to their own words, gun-control leaders will not stop until the private ownership of guns is illegal and the Constitution overthrown. As such, they encourage nullification of the universal moral truths contained within that document. As the gun-control activists pursue their agenda by any means necessary—supporting ever larger and more intrusive government—the true ethical purpose of the Second Amendment will only become more apparent."[1]

The following news report is especially instructive in that regard. "United Nations Secretary-General Kofi Annan has called on the international community to stem the proliferation of small arms across the world. He told a special meeting of the Security Council that restricting the flow of such weapons would be a key challenge in preventing conflict in the next century. Estimates of the number of firearms in the world range from 100 million to 500 million. Mr. Annan said there was "no single tool of conflict so widespread, so easily available, and so difficult to restrict, as small arms". ...In his report Mr. Annan recommended that member states should: *Adopt gun control laws including a prohibition of unrestricted trade and private ownership of small arms.*"[2] [emphasis added] This is nothing less than an open call to overturn the U.S. Constitution and the Second Amendment in favor of "international law," the infamous New World Order.

Gun Control And American Culture

On the day of the march, an estimated 20,000 U.S. gun laws were on the books. To quote Ms. Paglia again, "The Million Moms would do much

---

1 Jaime Sneider, *Columbia Daily Spectator* as reported by the *National Review* on May 15, 2000, *Taking Aim at The Constitution*.

2 BBC Online News Network, Saturday, September 25, 1999

more for this country if they would focus on the breakdown of family and community ties that produce sociopaths like the goons who shoot up schools and day-care centers. It was parental irresponsibility and neglect, and not simply the availability of guns, that were ultimately at the root of the Columbine massacre, where home-barbecue propane tanks had been converted into bombs."

The Moms might also have consulted the 1994 report of the rabidly anti-gun Reno Justice Department, *Urban Delinquency and Substance Abuse: Initial Findings—Research Summary*.[1] Boys who own legal firearms were found to have the lowest rate of adolescent delinquency when compared to both those owning illegal guns, and those owning none.

Adolescent Group	Street crimes	Gun crimes
Non gun owners	24%	1%
Illegal gun owners	74%	24%
Legal gun owners	14%	0% (zero)

The study attributed the disparity in part to the "socialization into gun ownership," of boys with their fathers who owned guns for hunting and sport. One might suppose the close parental bonding would be equally salutary for young girl shooters as well.

Creating Public Opinion

The American public is fed a daily dose of cooked statistics reminiscent of George Orwell's novel *1984*. However, the tragic consequences of this propaganda on national policy threaten real life and real people. The general willingness of the American population to believe the lies of politicians and media spin-masters, and the lack of interest in alternative news sources, are disturbing. An informed electorate can make decisions. A brainwashed mass merely regurgitates its conditioning.

Geoffrey Dickens, Senior Analyst of the respected Media Research Center, detailed his group's two-year study of the treatment of gun related issues by four evening news shows *(ABC's World News Tonight, CBS Evening News, CNN's The World Today,* and *NBC's Nightly News)* and three morning broadcasts *(ABC's Good Morning America, CBS's This Morning,* and *NBC's Today)*. The study tracked these shows from July 1, 1997 to June 30, 1999.[2]

---

[1] Discussed by Robert W. Lee in *The New American* for April 24, 2000.

[2] Geoffrey Dickens, *Outgunned: How the Network News Media Are Spinning the Gun Control Debate, The American Rifleman,* April 2000.

The criteria for categorization of stories as either "anti-gun" or "pro-gun" were the following. Anti-gun statements were defined as ideas like "violent crimes occur because of guns," and "gun control prevents crime." Pro gun statements included ideas such as "criminals, not guns, cause crime," "Americans have a constitutional right to keep and bear arms," and "concealed carry laws help reduce crime." If such statements in a news reports were weighted in a ratio of 1.5 to 1, the story or segment was identified as either anti-gun or pro-gun. If the ratio was less than 1.5 to 1, the story was regarded as neutral.

In 653 gun policy stories, the study found that stories advocating more gun control outnumbered stories opposing gun control by 357 to 36, or a ratio of nearly **10 to 1** (260 were categorized as neutral). Anti-gun sound bites were twice as frequent as those with a pro-gun message, 412 to 209. Gun control advocates appeared on morning shows 82 times compared with 37 gun rights advocates and 58 neutral spokesmen. Three hundred evening news segments were rated as follows: 164 anti-gun, 20 pro-gun, and 116 neutral. Talking heads were gun control advocates by a 2 to 1 ratio. Of 353 gun policy segments on morning news shows, anti-gun stories outnumbered pro-gun by 193 to 15 or a ratio of **13 to 1** (with 145 categorized as neutral).

A Familiar Half-Dozen Anti-Gun Lies

1. The "Dead Children" Lie

In the words of David Kopel, "A full listing of the lies told by the antigun lobby could fill a book."[1] Perhaps the most egregious of such is the Myth of the Dead Children. How many days go by each week when some government hack or media newsreader doesn't bow his or her head and solemnly intone the figures of 13, 15, 17 or more children killed every day by guns. Our minds are forced to conjure images of over a hundred children a week lying dead like little well-fed Biafrans in front of Daddy's bloody night stand.

In truth, the per-capita number of fatal gun accidents among children is at its lowest level since 1903 when statistics started being kept. Furthermore, the actual number of child firearm fatalities is also declining every year, even as the numbers of people with firearms in their homes increases. By way of example, in 1995, there were 1400 accidental firearm deaths in America of which 30 involved children four and under, while 170 involved the five to fourteen age bracket (thus 200 children in total). By comparison 2900 children died in motor vehicles, 950 died by drown-

---

[1] David Kopel, Research Director of the Independence Institute, *National Review* April 17, 2000, *An Army of Gun Lies.*

ing, and 1000 died by fire and burns. More children die in bicycle accidents each year than by firearms.[1] Nobody wants even one child to die. Reducing firearm accidents even further is the goal of the NRA's brilliant Eddie Eagle Program, a common sense and effective firearm safety educational effort for children—which has been boycotted, ignored, and slandered by the gun banners.

The mournful statistical mantra of the mass media/civilian disarmament lobby are cynically based on counting young adults as children. Thus a teenage gangland slaying, a young fleeing felon shot by a police officer, a jealous 21-year-old shooting his wife's seducer in a bar, or a crack deal gone bad, are all counted as "children who die by firearms." Accidents are a part of life and cannot be regulated away. But the shamelessness with which these statistics are manipulated to provide fodder for those seeking to expand the range of government control is important to note.

2. The "Guns Cause Crime" Lie

"Normal" people do not turn into crazed maniacs when a gun is placed in their hands any more than guns levitate from tables, pockets, or closets to discharge themselves and kill innocent people. The oft-repeated statement that a gun in the home is 43 times more likely to kill a family member than a criminal is another purposeful distortion of the truth to serve a political agenda. "Of the 43 deaths, 37 are suicides; and while there are obviously many ways in which a person can commit suicide, only a gun allows a small woman a realistic opportunity to defend herself at a distance from a large male predator."[2]

Another of the big lies of the gun control lobby is that most people are killed by people they know. This argument is concocted from the FBI Uniform Crime Report which states that family murders account for 18% of murders, while 40% were those who "knew" their victims. The category of "those who knew their victim" however includes drug dealers and buyers, prostitutes and clients, cab drivers killed by passengers, rival gang members involved in turf wars, and murderous barroom brawlers.

Perhaps a more telling statistic is that in 1988, over 89% of adult murderers had adult criminal records.[3] In even simpler terms, bad people do bad things.

John Lott's monumental study of gun ownership in the United States covered all 3,054 U.S. counties from 1977 to 1992, supplemented with

---

[1] John Lott, Jr., *More Guns, Less Crime,* University of Chicago Press, 1998, p. 9.

[2] David Kopel, *National Review* April 17, 2000, *An Army of Gun Lies.*

[3] John Lott, Jr., *More Guns, Less Crime,* University of Chicago Press, 1998.

data for 1993 and 1994. He reached the following conclusion, "Of all the methods studied so far by economists, the carrying of concealed handguns appears to be the most cost-effective method for reducing crime."[1] The positive effect of reducing violent crime is particularly significant for women who carry guns.[2] Furthermore, misuse of firearms by the millions of U.S. carry permit holders has proven to be virtually nil. It appears that hoplophobic[3] journalists may be more susceptible to road rage fantasies than real gun owners are.

3. "Guns Are Dangerous To Their Owners" Lie

Professor Lott quotes surveys that indicate that 98% of the time people use guns defensively, they merely need to brandish them before a criminal to stop the inevitable attack. According to Lott, 15 national polls, including those conducted by *The Los Angeles Times* and Gallup, record between 760,000 and 3.5 million defensive uses of guns per year. Florida State University Department of Criminology Professor Gary Kleck conducted a survey in 1993 which found that 2.5 million crimes are thwarted each year by gun owning Americans. His National Self-Defense Survey excluded cases where people picked up a gun to investigate suspicious noises and the like, and focused on actual confrontations between the intended victim and the offender.[4]

---

[1] *Ibid.,* p. 20.

[2] As this article was being completed, the "Annual Puerto Rican Day Parade" took place in New York City. As of this moment, 44 women have filed complaints of sexual assault against some 60 men. Allegations that police stood idly by have rocked the media and led the Mayor to proclaim that heads will roll. Imagine if just one of those women had been properly armed. Sixty drunken misogynists would have run like rabbits. Such an outrage is most unlikely to occur in the 31 of 50 states that enjoy "shall issue" concealed weapons permit laws.

[3] "I coined the term *hoplophobia*...in the sincere belief that we should recognize a very peculiar sociological attitude for what it is—a more or less hysterical neurosis rather than a legitimate political position. It follows convention in the use of Greek roots in describing specific mental afflictions. *Hoplon* is the Greek word for 'instrument,' but refers synonymously to 'weapon' since the earliest and principal instruments were weapons. *Phobos* is Greek for 'terror' and medically denotes unreasoning panic rather than normal fear. Thus hoplophobia is a mental disturbance characterized by irrational aversion to weapons, as opposed to justified apprehension about those who may wield them." *To Ride, Shoot Straight, and Speak the Truth,* Jeff Cooper, Paladin Press, p. 16.

[4] Wayne LaPierre, *Guns, Crime and Freedom,* Regnery Publishing, 1994, p. 23.

4. The "Success Of The Brady Law" Lie

The Clinton/Gore boast that half a million people have been stopped by Brady Law background checks creates an interesting case of cognitive dissonance. Like those amazing body counts reported by the press during the Vietnam War that if added together would have accounted for the population of India, there seems an inherent mathematical flaw. If half a million people committed the felony of illegally attempting to purchase a weapon when they were already legally banned from such actions by Federal law, why have there been merely a dozen arrests?[1]

5. The "Gun Show Loophole" Lie

The dreaded Gun Show loophole fretted over by the media and civilian disarmament proponents is a complete sham. If a person is engaged in gun dealing for profitable purposes, he needs to have a Federal Firearms License to do so or he is committing a felony. If an FFL dealer sells a firearm at a gun show, the exact same laws apply as if he sold it out of his store or home. In other words, identification provided by the buyer, form 4473 filled out, a background check, and complete record keeping including make model and serial number of the weapon purchased.

Question: Then what is the famous "Gun Show Loophole?"
Answer: Private sales that take place at Gun Shows.

In other words, as a gun owner I might want to trade up to a new rifle. Knowing a gun show was to be in town, I might put a little flag in the barrel of my old rifle with a "For Sale" written on it. I would have my gun checked by the police at the door, a trigger lock put on it, and hopefully find some other fellow looking for a bargain. After examining and recording each other's driver's licenses to verify that it was an in-state sale and therefore not in violation of the 1968 Gun Control Act, and asking my buyer if he is a felon (and determining to the best of my ability that he is not), and therefore not subjecting myself to a 10 year prison sentence for selling to a felon, fugitive or drug user, we would conclude the transaction. Alternately, if I died and my wife wanted to raise some cash to bury my dead ass, she might take a couple of my guns to a gun show, rent a table, and try to sell them for a decent price. If she was earning a living from this, she would be a felon. However if she was truly making private sales, it would be legal in most states.

What the civilian disarmament lobby wants to do is make sure every gun is registered, and every transfer is recorded. That way, when they achieve the power to round up guns in private hands, they'll have every-

---

[1] According to the statistics quoted by Wayne LaPierre in the April 2000 official NRA publication, *The American Rifleman.*

one's address and know exactly what everyone owns. One of their key sophistries is that since cars are registered, why not register guns? However, unlike cars, boats or airplanes, the possession of firearms is specifically enumerated as a right *of the people*, **a right protected from infringement by the same Government that registers cars.**

6. Other Countries Have Better Gun Laws Lie

To begin with, I agree with Camille Paglia, "Neither do crime statistics from other countries carry much weight with me. Only the U.S. has a complex Bill of Rights with a First Amendment guaranteeing 'freedom of speech' and a Second Amendment guaranteeing 'the right of the people to keep and bear arms,' which remain our protection against government tyranny. It's no coincidence that this most heavily armed nation in the world is also the most individualistic and entrepreneurial, with incandescent creativity in the high-tech field that has transformed the economy."

Other English speaking countries have not improved their societies as much as the major news organizations would like us to believe. Dr. Miquel Faria Jr. informs us that Australian crime rate is increasing exponentially following their infamous 1996 gun ban. In 1998 (the first year after implementation of the ban) the Australian crime rate experienced a 44 percent increase in armed robberies, 8.6 percent increase in aggravated assault, and a 3.2 percent increase in homicides. In the state of Victoria, there was a 300 percent increase in the number of homicides committed with a firearm. In South Australia, robberies increased by nearly 60 percent. In 1999, armed robberies in Australia were up 73 percent, unarmed robberies increased by 28 percent, kidnappings 38 percent, assaults by 17 percent, and manslaughter by 29 percent. During the previous 25 years before banning firearms, Australia had enjoyed a steady decrease in the rate of both homicides with firearms and armed robbery.[1]

England has not done much better. After Britain's even more stringent gun control laws were enacted in 1996, the 1998 armed crime rate grew 10 percent over 1997 despite a 19 percent decrease in the number of registered firearms. *The London Sunday Times* for January 16, 2000 estimated upward of 3 million illegal guns circulating in Britain. In some areas, the *Times* estimated that as many of one-third of criminals from

---

[1] Miquel Faria Jr., M.D., Editor in Chief of *The Medical Sentinel*, the official publication of the Association of American Physicians and Surgeons, *Australia Crime Rate: Chaos Down Under*, published in *The New American*, May 22, 2000.

ages 15 to 25 owned or have access to firearms.[1] In Canada and Britain, almost half of all burglaries take place when the occupants are at home. In the better-armed United States, only 13% of burglaries are perpetrated by those brave or foolish enough to take that risk.[2]

Guns And Race

America's first state and local gun laws were nearly all designed to keep guns out of the hands of slaves. These included laws passed prior to the American Revolution. After the Civil War, nearly every American gun law sought to keep guns out of the hands of freed former slaves. Thus gun control has always had a particularly odious racial cast.

However this is also true to an alarming degree of crime. The Welfare State has failed miserably. In four decades, it has created a permanent crime-ridden underclass whose family structure has been destroyed by regulations that encourage out of wedlock births; and social and political policies that 1) pay people not to work, and 2) export unskilled labor manufacturing jobs overseas. Thus America has created an alternate inner city sub-culture that serves as both a permanent threat to social well-being, and an object lesson in collectivism. Yet it also serves to provide statistics for the civilian disarmament movement. The horrific crime rate among inner city poor allows for the assertion that guns kill people who simply cannot be trusted to own a 20 ounce mechanical device; that somehow, these objects seem to exert a mysterious force—especially on the psyche of America's racial minorities. This is the justification behind the crippling spate of lawsuits filed against the gun industry in the last two years by big city mayors and the Department of Housing and Urban Development. Rather than leading a chorus of outrage against this insidious racial insult, the left-wing NAACP has threatened its own lawsuit against the gun industry because of the "disproportionate" effect of gun violence on the Black community.

On the other hand, there is an appalling amount of black crime. According to Department of Justice figures compiled for 1997, the latest year such figures are available, the incidence of black crime is proportionately far greater than white. A reasonable similarity appears to exist between crime figures and arrest figures. For example, according to the DOJ survey for 1997, 60 percent of robberies were reported to have been committed by blacks, while 57% of those arrested for robberies were

---

[1] Robert W. Lee, *English Crime Rate, The New American,* April 24, 2000.
[2] John Lott, Jr., *More Guns, Less Crime,* University of Chicago Press, 1998, p. 5.

black.[1] The FBI Uniform Crime Report for 1992 found that 55% of those arrested for murder were black, while 43.4% of murder victims were also black. The FBI found that in 1992, 94% of black victims were slain by black assailants.[2] Thus, when gun control advocates talk of banning "cheap handguns," the result of their efforts, if successful, will be to leave poor people in high crime areas defenseless. Ironically, it seems modern efforts at gun control are as unconscionably racist as earlier gun control policies.[3]

As a law-abiding American citizen who lives in a normal environment, I refuse to be treated like some 17-year-old, out of control, inner-city gang-banger, hopped up on crack, and suffering from a dearth of moral values. My children and I were raised to exhibit both the respect for life and personal self-control that are required to enjoy the freedom to keep and bear arms.

Alarming Precedents For National Gun Registration

From 1789 to 1934 there was not one federal gun law (with the exception of the Second Amendment). The first unconstitutional gun law was passed as the 1934 National Firearms Act which sought to ban automatic weapons by burdening them with heavy taxes and unprecedented registration requirements. The next one was the 1968 Gun Control Act, modeled nearly word for word on gun laws enacted by the Nazi regime

The Nazis inherited the German 1928 Law on Firearms and Ammunition which required registration and renewable permits for firearm owners and their firearms, mandated permits for the acquisitions of ammunition, and the issuance of hunting permits. All firearms had to be stamped with serial numbers and the names of their manufacturers. When the Nazis came to power in 1933, they thus had access to the name and home address of every legal gun owner in Germany, along with a description of his weapons.

---

[1] Jared Taylor, *What Color is Crime, The Resister* Vol. 5, No. 3 Summer/Autumn 1999.

[2] John Bolton, *Counter-Propaganda 101, The Resister* Vol. 4, No, 2 Winter 1998.

[3] Conversely, the DOJ figures for interracial crime in 1994 (the most recent year in which racial statistics were gathered) report that 89% of single offender crimes and 94% of multiple offender crimes were committed by blacks against whites. If these figures are rendered as violent crime per 100,000, 3,494 blacks out of 100,000 committed a violent crime against a white person in 1994, while 64 whites out of a 100.000 committed a violent crime against a black person. Jared Taylor, *What Color is Crime, The Resister* Vol. 5, No. 3 Summer/Autumn 1999.

The Nazi Weapons Law of 1938 guaranteed that only friends of the Nazi Party were able to own and carry firearms. Jews of course were forbidden to own guns or to participate in any business dealing in weapons. Carry permits were required in order to bear arms and were only issued to "persons of undoubted reliability, and only if a demonstration of need is set forth."

In *Gun Control: Gateway to Tyranny,* Jay Simpkin and Aaron Zelman lay out the 1938 Nazi Weapons Law with a paragraph by paragraph comparison to the US Gun Control Act of 1968.[1] Anyone interested in seeking the basis for U.S. gun control legislation is recommended to make this fearless comparison. The authors also present documentary evidence that Senator Thomas Dodd (D-CT), one of the authors of the 1968 law, had several months earlier submitted official requests to the Library of Congress for an English translation of the 1938 Nazi Weapons Law.

Gun Control Does Work To Accomplish The Wrong Results

Gun Control is a successful mechanism for the establishment of tyranny. Between 75 to 86 million American own between 200 and 240 million guns.[2] Who is going to check that each one of these guns is properly registered by each of these gun owners? Who is going to come into your house to insure that a gun lock is installed on your weapon? Do you want your neighbor encouraged to inspect your home to determine how you store your gun before allowing his children to play with yours? Should your kids be programmed to report your guns to the D.A.R.E. officer in their schools? Given the nature of people, if all guns mysteriously disappeared into thin air, would the rates of murder, assault and suicide really decline?

Pop Quiz: Was the War on Drugs more effective in:

a) limiting the manufacture, availability, and use of drugs, or

b) filling our nations prisons while extending the powers of the Police State?

My advice to any reader who still values his or her freedom, and continues to assert the sacred right of self-preservation, is to make the effort to familiarize yourself with guns. Take the time and training required to learn to use a gun well. Once you are comfortable enough to make a choice, buy a good one and practice with it. Join the NRA immediately and contribute regularly. Speak to your friends, family and neighbors.

---

[1] *Gun Control: Gateway to Tyranny,* Jay Simpkin and Aaron Zelman of Jews For the Preservation of Firearm Ownership, 1993.

[2] John Lott, Jr., *More Guns, Less Crime,* University of Chicago Press, 1998.

Make phone calls and send letters to politicians. Remind them you intend to hold their feet to the fire of the Constitution. No matter how many people tell you otherwise, the Constitution is still the law of the land. Consider the next time you hear some media sycophant drooling about the "international community" that our freedoms are unique to America. Each one of us had better be an active advocate of Liberty—otherwise, Liberty will vanish.

In *Naked Lunch,* William S. Burroughs describes the book's title as "a frozen moment when everyone sees what is on the end of every fork." I therefore make the following recommendation to anyone who plans to vote for any politician who endorses gun control. First, burn a copy of the Bill of Rights. Then pull the lever to cast your vote. That way, at least, you can say you had the courage to acknowledge the future you were creating.

James Wasserman has been studying and practicing the Magical system of Aleister Crowley for over twenty years. He is also a noted author and a strong proponent of freedom and human rights.

THE VIRTUE OF PERSONAL LIBERATION

by Dr. Jack S. Willis

"Do what thou wilt shall be the whole of the Law. Love is the law, love under will." Thus did Aleister Crowley summarize his view of the law of personal liberation.

Dr. Christopher Hyatt arrives at the same conclusion via a different route in "Who Owns This Planet Earth?" (You will find his statement in the right hand column of the table at the end of his article.)

Crowley saw liberty from his gut; Hyatt sees liberty from the philosophical concept of ownership. I see liberty as a moral imperative.

"Moral" is a big word. Don't we all have our own morality? Isn't morality a personal thing? Is not morality simply cultural, relative, good today and bad tomorrow? The answer is a big, fat, resounding NO!!!

The confusion arises because we try to stuff too many suits into one suitcase. You might get them in, but they come out all wrinkled and unwearable. To continue the simile, morality wears many suits and they need to be packed each to its own kind.

To start thinking about morality, you must first clear your mind of any thought of law. Ayn Rand said it this way: "morality ends at the point of a gun." The United States Supreme Court, in a rare statement of clarity from this otherwise muddled group of dunderheads, wrote: "In the last analysis government is an agency of violence." Any attempt to think about morality that includes any thought about what is or is not legal is preordained to failure. Any attempt to define morality in terms of what any given dictator-psychopath or any group of politician-sociopaths decides, is to simply abandon rationality before you begin. Morality is an issue of deciding how to live; law is an issue of deciding who to kill. Morality ends at the point of a gun, and government is an agency of violence.

* * * * * * * * *

There are three parts to a good presentation: tell them what you are going to say; say it; tell them what you said. So I'll tell you what I am going to say: You've heard it said, "Virtue is its own reward." Don't believe it. Virtue has a reward. The reward of virtue is life. The price of virtue is self-liberation; which is to say, self-ownership; which is to say, love under will. Take it from me, from Hyatt, from Crowley; take it *from* whom you will; take it *for* yourself.

* * * * * * * * *

Man as a species is unique. We don't have a built-in code of life. Like all animals, we have a built-in code to eat, to breathe, to eliminate. But it pretty much ends there. Beyond the merest elements necessary to sustain life, we don't have automatic codes. The more one moves away from man, the less choice there is. Alligators don't choose; they just act as they are built. The higher monkeys learn from the tribe, but each monkey either conforms to the tribe or is killed or driven out. For them, choice is an illusion. Man alone faces the choice of good or bad, right or wrong, moral or immoral. Without choice, the concept of morality does not arise; *with* choice the need for morality is an absolute.

It is the existence of choice that gives rise to the requirement of a morality. And the function of morality is to allow choice among alternatives. Without choice, there can be no issue of a moral system; with choice, there can be no answer without a moral system. The requirement for a moral system is inherent in the fact of humanness.

The issue that gives rise to the requirement of a moral system gives rise to the nature of the moral system. Because morality ends at the point of a gun, a moral system based on the guns of the state—that is a moral system based on what is legal and illegal—is a contradiction in terms. That is why thinking about a moral system first requires that any issue of the legal system be dismissed from consideration. The idea that you can "cheat on your taxes" is a contradiction in terms. To make the claim that a person can "cheat on his taxes" is identical to the claim that when faced with an armed robber on the street it is your moral duty to tell the robber about the money you have hidden in your shoe. Law is a statement of organized violence; it can not be a statement about morality[1].

---

[1] There is a second major violator of choice in addition to violence. It is one with which many people have much more difficulty. It is lying. Lying, by distorting reality, actually destroys the reality of choice. Choice becomes a sham. In fact, if one examines the full morality of choice as the essential element, one comes up with the full range of proper moral behavior (i.e., honesty, integrity, honor, fidelity, etc.).

We start, then, with the existence of choice—and, because of, and based on the fact of that choice, we start to derive a moral system. The first and base principle of a moral system then must be: that which facilitates choice is good; that which limits choice is bad. Don't worry about violence, about the killer or robber; we haven't gotten there yet. We have only one principle: the fact of choice gives rise to the requirement for a moral system which must first enshrine its own genesis in stating that that which gives free reign to choice is good, that which places prior restraint on choice is bad. Don't go extremist on me here with your personal and favorite objections; the necessary and appropriate limitations will arise soon enough in the discussion.

We have at this point done no more that lay out our plot of land. We don't have the fertilizer, and we haven't yet started to plant our moral garden. As with any garden, though, our landscape design must be predicated on the lay of the land. With choice inherent to the principle of our nature as human beings, the first principle of morality is that it is a system to allow choice among alternatives: that which facilitates choice is good, that which prevents choice is bad. There are three corollaries that follow hard on the heels of that basic principle: (1) a choice of one person that *forecloses the possibility of choice* of another is, in essence, a contradiction in concepts; (2) to choose is to act or not to act; *a choice is not the same thing as a preference;* and (3) in a social order, every choice of one person may impact on the choices available to another person; *the concept of choice does not contain the concept that choices must be without consequences.*

a choice of one person that forecloses the possibility of choice of another is a contradiction in concepts

There is only one type of act that, by its nature, forecloses the possibility of choice by another. That is an act of initiatory violence. (We will deal subsequently with acts of retributive or defensive violence.) To the extent that anyone employs violence—whether in the name of the state, the gang, or historical necessity—to that extent the person has abandoned morality. Since violence, by its nature, prevents choice, it is then *by its nature* immoral. Whether you enshrine that principal in law and punishment, or whether you enshrine it in banishment (Coventry), makes no difference to the discussion of morality (and virtue). The principle is science, the implementation is technology. The question of the form, extent, or nature of punishment for immoral behavior lies within the province of the philosophy of justice; our task here is the more limited one of establishing the base of a moral system. The morality of life implies the morality of choice that entails the immorality of initiatory violence.

to choose is to act or not to act;
a choice is not the same thing as a preference

I choose to write. That you choose to read or not to read what I write does not limit my choice. You choose to take heroin. I choose not to. Your action does not limit my action. You choose to engage in sexual intercourse on your front lawn. I might not find that particularly attractive and I might not like my children to see it; but in neither case is my choice of action limited. Certainly your view of sexuality might not agree with mine, but that is a preference of mine and is not a limitation on my action. Do you teach your children a religion while I am an atheist? Do you paint your house shocking pink while I think that an ugly color? Do you practice Enochian magic while I think that is satanic? To all questions, my preferences can not, in the name of morality, limit your choices.

The problem that people have with this issue of choice is that they equate a preference with a choice and demand that the world conform to their preferences. Since it is our nature as human beings which gives rise to the requirement for a moral system; and since, therefore, the purpose of a moral system is to allow us to make choices among alternatives; and since choice involves an issue of acting or not acting, the issues of like or dislike, approve or disapprove, agree or disagree do not enter the picture. If your 10-year-old child runs the streets naked with a bottle of whiskey, I might not like it and I might not want my children to see it; but it neither inherently imposes any action, nor prohibits any action, on my part. Preferences and morals belong in different suitcases.

in a social order, every choice of one person may impact on
the choices available to another person; the concept of choice does
not contain the concept that choices must be without consequences.

There is a classic problem in morals. Variously named, it comes down to the recognition that the action of one person often impacts on the choices available to another person. You like jazz music, I hate jazz music. You loudly play your jazz music all night long. I have no choice but to hear your loud and unpleasant (to me) music. In one context, this is simply another statement of my preference versus your preference. The difference here is that your music can directly impact my choice to sleep. Your loud music has directly limited my choice to sleep. Or, let's choose another example with fewer objections. You decide to start a pig farm next door to my house. There is no way I can escape the smell and, by most standards, that smell is certainly not pleasant. Yet I have no choice but to smell it. Your choice has limited my choice.

We could, at great length, examine this type of issue. But space requires that I just jump to the answer and leave to the reader the task of exploration. This objection to the morality of choice is based on the utopian fantasy. In developing a moral system, we look to the optimum while recognizing that there will always be cases on the edge which present problems. In any social context there must be, and always will be, cases where the exercise of one person's choices limits another person's choices. In developing a moral system we seek to optimize within constraints; we seek to maximize the potential for choice while recognizing that it can never be total and without consequences. As long as we keep firmly in mind the difference between choice and preference, we will not go too far off.

Children And Morals

Within the realm of choice, there is a particular problem that should be addressed up-front before all the doubters and naysayers have their go at their favorite pastime of denial and dismissal. That is the issue of children. Babies are little monkeys if not, perhaps, even little alligators. With age comes choice. From the baby-monkey to the free-will adult lies a continuum of development. At what point does morality come in? At what point is there the potential for enough choice, that we can say the person is morally sovereign? The answer, perhaps surprisingly, is easier then the question. Outside of physical danger, morality applies at all ages and in the same form and degree as it does to an adult. Because I know I am going to have widespread gnawing and gnashing of teeth at this point; and because an understanding of this issue makes everything else a stroll in the garden, I will take the time to discuss it thoroughly. You may not like the answer; but then we don't all have to like the same flowers, do we?[1] Children lack two things: they lack a mature cognitive apparatus and they lack knowledge. Simple statements. Not too much to disagree with. The difficulty arises from two sources: one, people don't follow the statements to their conclusion; two, people keep stacking on other lacks which, once analyzed, have no relevancy. Recall the suitcase? Morality comes in many suites, each of its own kind.

Children need to be taught ……. Add your own 1000 phrases to replace the dots. Children need to be protected from ……. Add your own 2000 phrases to replace those dots. And children are ……. Add your own BIG ONE (evil, impulsive, self-centered, etc.) to replace *those* dots. To all of those, I answer: OK, so what? Children are impulsive; aren't some adults? Children need to be taught table manners. In what book of the

---

[1] A favorite quote is from Thoreau's *Walden*: "Old deeds for old people, new deeds for new. Old people did not know enough once, perchance, to put fresh fuel on the fire to keep it going; new people put fresh fuel on the fire and, as the phrase is, were rolled round the world with the speed of birds."

human soul is it written that you can't eat meat with your fingers, that you must use a knife and fork? Children need to be taught not to hit. If we did not have to teach adults the same thing, we would not need any laws at all. Children need to be taught to share. Oh, really? From what principle of choice as morality, morality as choice, did you derive that monstrosity? But children *do* lack maturity in their thinking and they do lack knowledge.

One issue at a time. Children lack a mature cognitive process. Children require a particular type of sensitive communication from their parents in order for them to draw proper conclusions. It is easy for a child to misinterpret what is said to them. They draw a wrong conclusion, do not know that it is wrong, and then go on to use that wrong conclusion as the basis for other conclusions throughout their life. This fact of reality does give rise to a need to *limit* the choices available to children. But it does not give rise to a need to *control* children. The goal of mature behavior is to be able to choose among alternatives. We do not learn to choose by not being allowed to. Responsible parenting implies the need to read the literature on child cognitive development. This is not an overwhelming task, especially if your children are important to you. You will have done the majority of your task if you read a summary book on the research of Piaget and the practical advice books of Holt. I will give you a taste with two of my favorite examples.

If you cup your hands with the thumbs not quite touching, and then clap your hands in front of your face, you will get a slight puff of air blown into your face. If you do that to a five-year-old and ask, "Where did the wind come from?" the child will answer, "From out there," pointing to the outside. If you do the same with a seven-year-old, he will say, "From the room." If you do that with a nine-year-old he will say, "From between your hands." The age difference in answers is strictly a function of cognitive development. Here is the other example.

Give your six-year-old a glass to play with in the kitchen. Soon, he will roll it off the table and it will break. Now, if you say to the child, "Why did you break the glass?" and if you have a bright and responsive child, he will answer, "I didn't break the glass, I rolled if off the table and the glass broke itself." To you, he broke the glass; to him, the glass broke itself. The cognitive issue is the concept of cause and effect. You know that it is in the nature of glass that, if it is dropped on a hard surface, it will break. That is cause-and-effect thinking. But children do not develop the concept of cause and effect until somewhere between the ages of seven and nine. Before that they have the concept of temporality: event 1 precedes event 2; but they do not have the concept of cause and effect. Thinking in temporal terms, the child is correct that event 1 was rolling the glass off the table, and event 2 was the glass breaking itself.

Note that neither of these examples—and many more could be provided—involves an issue of choice. In young children it is, however, proper to *limit* choice on the basis of the child's inability to think properly[1]. There are, however, several limitations to this moral right to limit. One is that it essentially ends when the child reaches nine years of age. The second is that the etiology of the moral right to limit is the child's lack of cognitive ability. Thus the moral right of limitation resides only in the area where the issue of the child's ability to conceptualize is the major issue in making a decision. By this time, every parent is silently shouting objections of "what about ..." or "but my child ...." I'll address those after we look at the next lack in children.

Children lack the knowledge that comes from study, and lack the knowledge that comes from experience. Time can provide both. But, have you ever met an adult who knows everything about everything (aside from your mother, of course)? No. Knowledge is a continuum. It does not come in only the two flavors of ALL or NONE. Has there ever lived a person who has not looked back at his youth and said, "If I only knew then what I know now, I would never have ...." Life is knowledge and experience; the choice of today is the regret of tomorrow. Where is childhood different?

The difference lies in degree, not in kind. The more we know, the less likely it is that our choices will have long-term disastrous consequences. From lack of knowledge, children drink poisonous liquids; adults drink those liquids deliberately to commit suicide. From lack of knowledge, children climb trees; from a desire for thrills, adults jump out of airplanes. The difference, of course, is that adults choose to act in a lethal or dangerous manner while children do so without knowledge of the likely or possible outcome. What is the principle? Simple. Children have to be prevented from taking actions which are physically dangerous or, alternatively, they have to be watched so that the likelihood or degree of harm is managed. The limitation on choice is the limitation imposed by the reality of physical danger.

At this point, you are probably feeling that I have put one over on you. Children might look like poorly thinking and uneducated adults, but there is a difference—there has to be or why would we have all these laws protecting children? Can't children "be exploited"? Can't children "be abused"? Adults can protect themselves. They can always flee, even to leaving the country they are in, but children can't do that. Isn't there a

---

[1] The moral issue involved is the same one involved with an adult who is rendered unconscious in an accident. The presumption is that the person wishes to live and that, therefore, absent instructions like a Do Not Resuscitate order they would choose treatment if they were conscious.

point where a difference in degree becomes a difference in kind? Temperature is a continuum, but at the two ends we freeze to death or are burned to death; a difference in degree at some point becomes a difference in kind. The question evokes an obvious YES. But where along that continuum does a difference in degree become a difference in kind? Ah, there's the rub, to quote an anonymous author. Actually, it's not a rub at all because the answer is already before us; it's just sometimes difficult to wake up and smell the flowers. Like a mathematician or one of my favorite philosophers, Spinoza, we can lay it out as a series of postulates and corollaries.

> Postulate 1: The existence of choice gives rise to the necessity of a morality.
> Corollary 1: The purpose of morality is to facilitate the making of choices.
> Postulate 2: Children lack knowledge.
> Corollary 2: While time and living will provide some of the knowledge, they need a teacher for other kinds of knowledge.
> Postulate 3: Parents are the primary teachers of children.
> Corollary 3: The goal of parenting is to provide knowledge to the child to facilitate the making of choices by the child.
> Corollary 4: Parenting which limits, inhibits, or impedes the capacity to choose is immoral; parenting that facilitates and encourages choice is moral. QED.

Speaking for the moment as a shrink, is there anything in psychology—either in theory or in experiment—that contradicts this principle? I would like to say an emphatic NO. Unfortunately there are theories of human action, if one still wants to call them theories, which disagree. A Skinnerian would disagree because a Skinnerian denies the existence of choice. A classical Freudian, too, would disagree because he regards the inhibition of the Oedipal and Electra complexes as necessary. All other theories and experiments in psychology would agree. I know it takes us a bit away from the development of our thesis; but I think a brief discussion of object relations theory will show not only the nature of the agreement, but also show the application of the principle of the morality of choice to an important and real issue of parenting.

During the first three years of life, all children pass through a series of steps of psychological maturation that, if all goes well, terminates with a stage called "object constancy." On the way, from approximately 16 months of age to 36 months of age, the child passes through a four-step process that has been named "separation-individuation."[1] Simplifying for purposes of discussion, as the child progresses through these steps he will go through a period of aggression, then a period of renewed dependency, and, finally, to independence. The period of aggression *must be allowed.* It is natural, normal, and age appropriate. If the parent prohibits the aggression—"No, no, it's wrong to hit"—as the morality of choice would predict, you will produce psychological injury. If the period of aggression is allowed, but contained, then you will get psychological health. The difference between "contain" and "inhibit" illustrates the essential of parenting and the essential of the theory of the morality of choice.

One of the things a child has to learn—just part of the Great Quest to self-enlightenment and self-liberation—is to contain his impulses. There are two operative words here and they address the essence of moral parenting. The words are "learn" and "contain." The parent is first a teacher and second a container. Both concepts are easier to state than to explain. I will choose an easy example that does both. How do you teach a child to ride a two-wheeled bicycle? You hold (contain) the bicycle while the child gets on and off, and, for a while, during the child's first rides. Then you let go when you think the child has the minimal ability, and you let the child take his spills. On the other side, you do not force (violence) the child to learn to ride. You respond to your child's request, that is, *choice*: "Daddy, I want a bicycle" and you provide the means and the containing needed for your child to accomplish the task he has chosen.

The issue of children was raised only to respond to an obvious objection to the morality of choice. This is not a book on child raising, so I have laid out only the essential issue: the morality of choice applies, within context, equally to children and adults. We do, however, have a few unaddressed issues. The easy one is retributive violence or, more appropriately, self-defense. Recall that initiatory violence inherently violates the morality of choice. Self-defense restores morality. Nothing more need be said.

We have leapfrogged over one issue that should be addressed: the abuse of children. Adults have the potential for escape and they have the capacity for self-defense. Children fall into a different category and must be protected. Three answers: (1) yes, (2) so what, (3) not by the state.

Children can be taken advantage of, they can be misused. In the current catch phrase: they can be abused. So can adults. The difference is that children have less capacity for choice in avoiding the abuse. That means that children need to be protected, especially from public school teachers. Children can be used for sexual purposes giving their consent only

[1] This follows the theory and research of Margret Mahler.

because they do not realize that their consent can be withheld. They can also be used for work, giving their consent only because they do not realize that their consent can be refused. (We call that "doing your chores" or taking responsibility.) So, the issue is not that children can be abused, the issue is that we approve of some abuse and some we do not. However, in fact, all of it is of a piece, and all of it involves the use by adults of the knowledge that children lack knowledge and the ability to think at an adult level. In short, all of it involves violating the child's ability to choose.

Beyond all that, however, there is a form of child abuse that is rampant, growing, and especially vicious. It is done by government. Doesn't requiring a child to be in school violate the very essence of choice? Doesn't making it a crime for children to engage in sexual activity violate the very essence of choice? Doesn't making it a crime for a child to run away violate the very essence of choice? "Government, in the last analysis, is an agency of violence." Violence and choice can not reside in the same moral universe. Children need special protection; government is the wrong protector.

* * * * * * * *

So the moral imperative of life is choice. Choice inherently resides in the individual. Children are a special case, a case that should end about age nine, but that special case means only that we limit the choices in the recognition that children lack knowledge and the maturation to think properly. Beyond that, society is not, and never can be, perfect. We attempt to define a moral system because being human demands that we have a moral system, and, in logic, to the extent that we want to have choice, we must grant choice. The virtue of liberation is the virtue of choice. Which is to say that the reward of virtue is life.

Dr. Jack S. Willis has graduate degrees in Biochemistry and Psychology and a Doctor of Chiropractic He trained in Reichian Therapy with Dr. Israel Regardie for nine years. He is director of the Reichian Therapy Center in Los Angeles, California. The Reichian Therapy Center is both a treating and teaching institute.

THE MOUNTAIN

by Shari Dee Crowley & Peter J. Lima

Prehistory Of The Mountain

The Mountain Temple Center sits atop a small mountain in the middle of the Phoenix Mountain Preserve, in the north-central part of the city. Like most of the hills in this desert city, it is rocky and nearly treeless save for a few small mesquite bushes around the perimeter. The only animal life that can survive in the harsh climate tends to reflect the intensity of the Magick here: scorpions, jackrabbits and birds of prey. While no one will ever know for sure, it has been suggested to several persons, perhaps while visioning on the Astral Plane and higher Occult realms, that the sacred space known to us today as "The Mountain" was in fact utilized as an ancient Hohokam sacred space. In this area of the Sonoran Desert that has now been swallowed up by the growth of the city known to the white man as Phoenix (itself a Magical term representing Resurrection and Continual Rebirth), just a few miles from The Mountain, ancient Hohokam petroglyphs have been found dating back a thousand years. We all know that many ancient cultures utilized the high places available to them both for their spiritual-astronomical observations and for ritual uses. The Mountain is probably the remains of what once was a much larger rising of volcanic rock surrounded on all sides by a rolling valley. It is bounded both on the East and on the West by two much higher desert ranges that seem to function as etheric "walls of protection," making the Mountain itself a well-guarded hub of pyramidal energy. What is most interesting to Magicians, is that both the Eastern and Western ranges are cut out in the rough silhouette of the God and the Goddess. The range to the East of the Mountain forms several gently rolling curvatures that, to some, form the outline of the breasts and "mound of Venus" of the ancient fertility Goddess. The Western range likewise makes an outline of the God against the horizon. Between them, The Mountain itself sits like a Magical Child of both. Such features would not have been overlooked by the spiritually attuned Hohokam.

Establishment And Growth Of The Center

Mountain Temple Center is co-owned and co-operated by Michael J. Crowley (no relationship to Aleister) and his wife Shari. The Crowley's have been together since July of 1969. Starting as a Roman Catholic altar boy, Mike has been studying the magical and occult arts since he was in high school, and his wife Shari has been studying for about twenty years. The couple bought the property on the Mountain in July of 1972. The original structure, which is now the center itself, consisted of a small single-story house, which was added to by the Crowley's in the 1970s, to the point where today (2000) the Center is three stories high with about 1600 square feet of space. When it was decided to open the Mountain for public events and ceremonies, the first tradition to be established was Gardnerian Wicca. Michael was an avid student of Gerald Gardner's pioneering work in 20th-century Witchcraft, and credits Gardner's classic *High Magic's Aid* with being one of his earliest introductions to the ancient Craft of Wicca. Michael was and remains also, a student of the works of Janet and Stewart Farrar, with their emphasis on sex magick. In 1986 the Mountain hosted its first public Wiccan ceremony, in league with other local Coven members.

The Gods must have smiled upon the fledgling efforts of Mike and Shari, for in January of 1987 Shari won a sizable amount of money in the Arizona Lottery with 11 of her co-workers. Shari's share was used to finish the expansion of the Temple. The Center opened more widely to the public in 1992 when it began to be publicized as a learning and study center with a respectable non-lending research library.

Today the library is one of its most popular and talked-about features of the Temple. Painstakingly assembled over a period of over twenty years, the Library now consists of thousands of volumes, never yet counted, filling ceiling-high shelves all around the room. The collection covers all aspects of the occult arts and sciences, including astrology, numerology, the mythology of various cultures and historical periods, Wicca, Masonic lore, Demonolatry and Satanism, Rosicrucianism, and of course, the Golden Dawn and Ordo Templi Orientis. Mr. Crowley also has (as one would expect) a sizable collection of rare Crowley works (Aleister Crowley, that is). The library contains numerous out-of-print and hard-to-find editions of other works.

The center is a strange looking place; it has been converted from a private residence into a mixed public/private structure. The center is not huge, but has an area on the first floor reserved for the permanent residents. The second floor has an office/computer room, conference room, and the excellent library already described. On the top floor, veiled for restricted access, is the most sacred ritual space in the Temple, used for higher-level Golden Dawn and other ceremonies. This sacred space has a porch which overlooks the outdoor space.

This outdoor area consists of a magical working area in a thirty-nine foot round triple circle, marked off by standing stones constructed to look like a miniature Stonehenge. It is large enough to accommodate upwards of fifty persons, and, during one of the major annual Pagan festivals, there have been closer to one hundred present.

The Center has other facilities, which function both for entertainment or relaxation, and also possess a spiritual purpose. For instance, it has a large hot tub which has become rather famous (or infamous!) in the community. While the hot tub can be a fun place for relaxing after a ritual, it is also used regularly for the purification of participants prior to certain ceremonies. Mike Crowley also uses it for practicing the technique of "rebirthing" on students who may be interested in this, where he guides the individual, floating in the water, into psychic or astral perceptions.

A sweat lodge is currently being constructed on the grounds. When complete, it will be a welcome and fitting addition to the facility and will increase its reputation as a place for experiencing a wide spectrum of spiritual techniques.

Mountain Temple Center has had its ups and downs, and has experienced a certain amount of gossip and backbiting from others in the Pagan community of Phoenix. This sort of thing is widespread among pagans and magical groups all over, but the Center has attracted more than its share due to the controversial nature of Mike Crowley, not to mention Aleister Crowley. Mike has never claimed to be a "white lighter," and anyone who is familiar with the work of Aleister Crowley knows that Aleister was not exactly a "goody-two-shoe" character either. Oftentimes, Mike's up-front, free expression of sexuality (such as tantric magick and Gardnerian wicca) have caused some "puritanical pagans" to whine a little, and occasionally one may read a vague letter to the editor in some local pagan newspaper complaining about Mike or the Mountain, but without actually mentioning his name. Of course, those who are truly serious about magical work and spiritual growth know better than to take this sort of stuff at face value. If anything, Mike has often said, it only increases his reputation in the community, and helps scare away the "wannabe's" and undesirables.

The Farrars

In May of 1993 the Mountain welcomed the Farrars and Gavin Bone, who were visiting Phoenix on a lecture tour. While in Phoenix they all visited the Mountain, along with a number of other people from the local magical and pagan community. While at the Mountain the Farrars and Gavin enjoyed the hot tub along with a great number of the other guests all at the same time. At this time in Phoenix, it was around 100–120 degrees; after all, it is the desert! The Farrars and Gavin did bless the circle and told Mike Crowley to be careful in utilizing sex or tantric magick. When the Farrars and Gavin left and returned to where they were staying, they were tired and hot. (It was summer in the desert.) Their hosts, some local people, claimed that while at the Mountain we (Shari and Mike) tried to "kill" Stewart, because he was hot, tired and dehydrated, and needed a nap. Stewart was seventy-two years old at the time. A lot of "normal" people take naps in the summer in Phoenix, a sort of Mexican siesta, after all. But, being pagans, people liked to complain and gossip. Maybe it was just having Stewart and Janet in the hot tub that got some of the "white light" locals riled up; who knows? When the time came for the Farrars and Gavin to leave, the Pagan group that brought them to Phoenix could not afford to pay them what was promised, so the Mountain fronted the Pagan group the money.

O.T.O.

Also in 1993 the Crowley's met with members of the Ordo Templi Orientis (O.T.O.) and became initiates in October of that year. On April 23, 1994 and official O.T.O. Camp named Mountain Camp was established. A "Camp" in O.T.O. terminology refers to an officially approved meeting place. Though initially successful and popular, seeing a number of new initiates come through the doors, in July of 1996 the O.T.O. parent body rescinded permission for the camp, citing security concerns. At the time, the house was being used by other family members for non-O.T.O. gatherings and activities, and it was felt that the needed privacy couldn't be guaranteed. This temporarily ended the Mountain's involvement with the O.T.O., though the Crowley's rejoined the order in July of 1998. At the time of this writing (2000) it appears that some sort of new arrangement is in the planning stages, and the O.T.O. may once again be part of the Center's curriculum.

A.U.M.

Speaking of curriculum, the Mountain Center has always, thanks to Mike's insistence, been a place of study and learning, as the library can prove. In May 1994, Mr. Crowley (in league with Peter Lima, a.k.a. Petros) founded A.T.U.M., the Arizona Thelemic University of Magick, to teach willing students the basics of Aleister Crowley's philosophy. It's scope soon broadened to cover all forms of magick, spirituality and myth, and it's now known simply as the Arizona University of Magick (A.U.M.). A.U.M. promotes talks and classes on all aspects of magical theory and practice, including workshops and "hands-on" demonstrations of techniques and rituals. In the six years since its founding, A.U.M. has welcomed many local (and a few visiting) lecturers and has provided dozens of classes and workshops on such topics as the Golden Dawn, Crowley, Astrology, Wicca, Norse Magick, Satanism, Herbs and Plants, and so on. Classes have been held in several local bookshops and halls, and are now primarily held in the Mountain's own library/conference room, or in the outdoor circle.

Golden Dawn

On December 4, 1994 there was established at Mountain Center a Golden Dawn Temple, chartered through The Hermetic Temple and Order of the Golden Dawn in association with the Israel Regardie foundation, headed nationally by Dr. Christopher S. Hyatt, Ph.D., noted esoteric author and publisher, and literary executor for Regardie. This Temple has proven to be very successful and has initiated scores of candidates over the past six years. The Temple maintains a website and, with the help of Fra. Petros (6=5), serves initiates around the world through email correspondence lessons and guidance. Mountain Temple G.D. currently has "long-distance" initiates in Brazil, South Africa, Canada, Germany, and elsewhere, as well as locally.

Other Visitors And Maharaj

In addition to Janet and Stewart Farrar, Mountain Center has hosted other bright lights of occultism and esoteric spirituality. These include Lon Milo DuQuette, James Wasserman, Phil Hine, S. Jason Black, Robert F. and Stephani Williams Jr. and, in 1999, a Hindu holy man by the name of Srila Bhakti Ballabh Tirtha Maharaj. Maharaj (as his disciples know him) appeared at Mountain Center on August 16 of 1999. When told that he was to speak at the home of a magician, he quipped, "Ah ho!" and reminded his listeners of boyhood encounters he had had with similar magicians in his own homeland. Maharaj's visit was not without an unusual, perhaps supernatural element, as so often happens during events up here. As he got into his lecture, shortly after sunset, a seasonal monsoon storm began to brew. Common at this time of the year in Phoenix, these storms can be violent and electrifying. With the thunder cracking and lightning flashing all around, some of Maharaj's devotees began to get a little worried about the Master's safety. Maharaj called the lightning and thunder "Krishna's magic!" and compared its potency and beauty to the illusions of man-made "magic" such as technology. Maharaj made it clear that "So long as we remember Krishna, maya [illusion] cannot come. The moment we forget Krishna, maya comes." As Maharaj was leaving later with his devotees, those with him noticed that the bottom of the Mountain was muddy and drenched with rain from the wild storm. Only the top of the Mountain, in the sacred circle where Maharaj held his satsang, had been spared the deluge. No doubt he would attribute it to the grace of Krishna, and this is only fitting for such a sacred space.

The Beasts

No description of the mystical, magical Mountain would be complete without mention of its two occult "mascots," symbols of its weird energy: Harley, a full-blooded gray wolf with high intelligence and a friendly disposition (except towards Mrs. Crowley's pit-bulls); and Dragon Monster, a twenty-one foot, one-hundred-sixty pound reticulated python who used to lurk in a small closet under the stairs, meditating on its heated rock. No one was ever able to figure out if Dragon Monster was a male or female, and no one was brave enough to investigate it so closely. Sadly and weirdly, both of these magnificent beasts made their individual transition to the higher realms in February of 1999. Both died within a week of each other: Harley a week prior to and Dragon on the night of Mike Crowley's 50th birthday celebration. Mike interpreted the loss of both beasts as a necessary sacrifice to the Gods, to enable further growth here.

Conclusion

Let's let Mike Crowley speak for the Center with our motto: "I do not seek to understand that I may believe, but I believe that I may understand for mans exile is ignorance: his home is knowledge." We believe in "Enabling the advancement of individuals and groups in personal understanding, exploration and practice of all Esoteric Philosophies." The Mountain practices freedom, acceptance, and tolerance of all religious or spiritual aspects of life, and all beliefs. Over time, the Mountain has evolved as we all do as time goes on. The Mountain continues to promote freedom. We now focus on Golden Dawn work; however, we continue to allow other groups to rent the use of the area and certain (non-consecrated) ritual tools in order to do their own thing. Groups who have enjoyed our facilities include the I.O.T., O.T.O., several Wiccan covens, Discordians, Chaos Magicians, Strega (Italian wicca), Voodoo, C.O.S., Santeria, Vampires, Toxic Magic, American Indian, Hindu, and Buddhist practitioners among many others. People come to the Mountain for research and for intelligent conversation. Or, just a good old bullshit session on any subject imaginable where everyone has the right to say whatever they want without fear of being told to shut up or you're wrong. That's not to say you will not get an argument or a heated discussion. And the Mountain has had some wild partys, just to have a party. They can be fun, exciting, erotic and strange. Plain old fun without the worry of being "Politically Correct."

JUST WHEN YOU THOUGHT IT WAS SAFE TO GO BACK TO THE ALTAR

by Rev. Adrian Romany Omelas

In explaining Michael Crowley, three points come into mind. The first is in the beginning of *The Complete Golden Dawn System of Magick* by Israel Regardie. It is a quote from the ex-president of the United States, Calvin Coolidge, which reads.

> Nothing in the world can take the place of persistence.
> Talent will not:
> Nothing is more common than unsuccessful men of talent.
> Genius will not:
> Unrewarded genius is almost a proverb.
> Education will not:
> The world is full of educated derelicts.
> Persistence and determination alone are omnipotent.

Another phrase that comes to mind is Aleister Crowley's

> Without lust of result, he achieves his will

Lastly, but certainly not least—perhaps even most—are the antics of such artists and magicians as Grigori Rasputin, H.P. Blavatsky, G.I. Gurdjieff, Salvador Dali, Anton LaVey and, again, Aleister Crowley, which at first cast doubt upon their authenticity. However few realize that the power on the magical plane manifests in the irrational, so these great magi dance along the eleventh path, much like the fool of the Tarot. Keeping this in mind, we can now understand that sometimes it is the antics which create the greatest magic.

Mike Crowley (or "Loki" as we sometime call him) has been called many things: pervert, depraved, wicked, beast, monster, male chauvinist, con man, egomaniac, fake, fraud, evil, black, insane, satanic, dirty-rotten-bastard-son-of-a-bitch-prick. He's is in good, or shall we say "bad," company. Upon meeting him, some say he's a "wanna-be." But what happens with persistence?

"Wanna-be's" become exactly what they wanna be! Sometimes even better than the "real deal." And, in his own aloof, devil-may-care way, Mike Crowley is the most persistent and determined son-of-a-bitch I ever met.

What can one expect when one goes "up to the mountain" to meet the "Old Man"? Well, I've known him for over ten years and to me he's sixty percent Hippie Wizard, thirty percent Black Magician and ten percent Groucho Marx. He also has a tendency to offend those stuck in a fixed pattern of philosophy or belief. Feminist and Racist alike as well as Christians, New Agers and Wiccans have stood against Crowley in one form or another, usually from the shadows or behind his back. His Crime? Shattering their comfort zone. His unconventionality and individuality threatens the safety and security of the stagnant and dull minded who thought they knew exactly what a magician "ought" or is "supposed" to be like. Experiencing Crowley is realizing that you *haven't seen it all.*

Mike (M.C.) can piss people off, but he can also make them laugh until their guts ache. He has fucked men over and cheated on their wives, but has also gotten them laid by even more beautiful women. He throws wild parties yet he'll go off on boring tangents only to slip in his whammy just when you thought you were tuning him out. But Hell—the only time one is truly safe from harm is when one is finally dead. Therefore safety is for the dead. We are ***Black Magicians***. One should not expect to feel safe around us. One should expect to feel *alive* around us! Maybe that's why he doesn't really hold anything against me for wasting his two favorite totem animals during the now infamous "Cthulhumas Rituals" performed at the mountain by me and Lovecraftian occultist, Frater W.H., from the swamplands of the deep south. In both, I acted as high priest and W.H. as my advisor and deacon. The first of which, "Cthulhu vs. The Pigs", was performed the weekend just after Candlemas 1999, brought in a huge crowd but resulted in the police raiding the house, for Satan-Knows-What, three nights later. Since the first was such a success (fuck the Pigs), we decided to do a second, "Cthulhu's Revenge" (on Valentine's Day weekend, of all times), with more guts, gore and special effects than the first, compliments of the neighborhood Hispanic grocer, red food color, firecrackers and a whole host of other hellish delights. We even built a monolith. I was so out-of-it, I hardly recall anything, but was told I went out of my mind! Bloody heart's red glare, squid bursting in air; everyone got splattered! Even the monolith was destroyed! Poor M.C. had to get all his black robes dry-cleaned! I was told I got laid in the hot tub right after the ritual but I don't recall that either! The morning after, I departed on a flight to New York on business. Whatever fragments of the ritual were left in my recollect were immediately distracted out of consciousness. (Plus, in neither ritual, was the circle ever closed.) It wasn't until I got back three weeks later that I heard the unpleasant news. Harley, M.C.'s purebred "Fenriz" gray timber wolf died of prostate cancer only days after the ritual. Just days after that, DragonMonster, M.C.'s "Midgard Serpent" python, twenty-two phallic feet of her and the second largest in captivity (next to a twenty-four footer in the San Francisco Zoo) decided to burn out by wrapping herself around an electric heater and cooking herself to death. Oooops... Sorry, Mike! Didn't mean to make you lose your Valentine's Day hard-on! With that, like a bat-out-of-hell, W.H. blazed a trail back to the swamp and it took me a whole year until I was able so show my face again up at the mountain. I felt awful for that whole year and still feel kind'a bad. Harley was perfectly capable of ripping any man apart and yet was the most intelligent and mild-mannered wolf I have ever met. DragonMonster, who surprisingly had a character of her own, is of course irreplaceable.

Harley and Dragon can still be seen if one visits the mountain. M.C., the wonderful sick fuck that he is, had Harley made into a rug and still has plans for all of Dragon's skin. Dragon's skeleton makes its home in the infamous family library and Harley's skull looks you in the face every time you open the kitchen freezer to grab an ice cream or TV dinner. M.C. still has his "Angerbodda," his wife Shari Crowley and his "Hela," an exotic dancer/occultist, Soror S.E.R.O., so split down the middle one never knows which S.E.R.O. (SEROtonin or SEROtoxic) will show her face next; and many wonder, in the end, which side of her seductively ever-swinging scale will prevail. One can also meet Maxx, the oldest of the family pit bulls and the only dog in history to be initiated a 5=6 in the Golden Dawn. (Just ask Dr. Hyatt.) What actually caused the outcome of "The Cthulhumas Rituals" remains a mystery to this day but one thing is for certain: it definitely seems too odd to simply throw to coincidence.

The Night I Almost Had Sex With Loki in the Form of a Beautiful Exotic Dancer

Loki, the Norse God that is, not M.C. of course. This was one of those wild-ass events which lead to the rumors of M.C. being a pervert and molester of young women. This was back in 1993, when I was still a goth-punk kid. I was apprenticing with a local satanic grotto called "The Order of Is", the only known satanic group in Phoenix (or Arizona for that matter), and styled in what we call "Satanic-Wicca". Not unlike Austin Osmond Spare, we created not only our own magical system but our own language as well, complete with alphabet, rune mudras, sigils etc., etc., all based on A.C.'s Qabala as well as several versions of the Qlippoth, its Shells and Tunnels of Set and modernized into Hypercube form etc., etc. I have since created my own grotto within "The Order of Is" called "Coven of the Black What The F#*%!?!?!." Although I keep a curious and open mind, I am not prone to being suckered into believing in the usual ghosts, goblins and things that go bump in the night without a damn good reason. I do believe in magic, sometimes even magic with a "k", yet the majority of my magical philosophy is atheist-minded and self-centered and my search for "Truth" done with skeptical scrutiny; my favorite dirty word being "why".

Anyway, there we were. The four of us hanging out in the infamous library; M.C. (in his religious lighter days), Frater Ripcord (a white-lighter back then—big change in him now), a beautiful young exotic dancer (as are many of the "groupies" that hang around the mountain), of whom none of us would ever see again, and then myself. M.C. at the time was into exorcisms. He had just put together an "exorcism kit" in a cheap suitcase out of a couple of household candles, holy tap (or hot tub) water, the Bacon/Shakespeare (King James) Bible, a dragon ink pen and Satan knows what else. It made him look like some sort of door-to-door exorcism salesman! Anyway, he was dying to try it out, needed or not!

While observing the beautiful girl, he either had seen something inside her, was pretending he saw something inside her or wanted to put something of his inside her! She insisted continually that she felt fine and had never been possessed nor was she then possessed, but M.C. insisted and continued to focus intensely on her. I thought nothing of it and laughed to myself, imagining that pathetic exorcism on television which got so much attention a while back. Plus, I was wise to M.C.'s philandering tricks. Then Ripcord joined in. All seemed flirtatious and juvenile. The white lighters, refusing to befriend and understand their dark side, had no choice but to lose control and submit to it. So I stepped over to the bookshelves and began to flip through a book on Norse Mythology. I was sitting on the couch, neck deep in a tale about Loki when I began hearing barbaric German. It went so well with what I was reading that at first I let it go, but then I thought, "huh!?!" I turned and looked just in time to see M.C. being thrown backward off his chair right onto his ass! And there she was, that little stripper, long thin legs, wild eyes and hair that made her look like she'd been hit by The Lightning Bolt! She was standing right over him with poor M.C. flat on his back looking up at her. And I'll be damned if that little stripper didn't look like Godzilla and Bad High Magus Mike didn't look like Japan! Frater Ripcord just sat there dumbfounded, holding the crucifix in his lap as if it were his penis. At first I thought M.C. had tried to slip her his own personal body of Christ and she decided to slap him down, but then she started to spout out German and began ripping off her clothes. Ripcord then shoved the crucifix in her face long enough for Mike to get back up on his feet. The clothes kept coming off (not that she had been wearing much to begin with) as her body began to twist and shake. The German continued. Ripcord put down the cross to light the candles as M.C. began throwing holy water on her body, now fully naked except for her "fuck me" pumps. I thought maybe this was a joke among the three of them, being done simply for my amusement. However, the seriousness in M.C.'s and Ripcord's faces assured me it was not. With each splash of holy water, the girl would arch, twist, moan and yell in ecstasy, her tongue flicking as M.C. accidentally splashed her in the face. She was crying out words like "Midgard", "Schlange", "Hela", "Fenriz", "Tierisch", "Nosknacker", "Vati, Vati, Vati", etc., etc. Then she arched back so much I thought she would break in half. She lost her balance and fell back into Ripcord's arms as M.C. recited from the bible. She then leaned up against Ripcord to brace herself and, with her long legs, kicked the bible out of M.C.'s hands. By the time I caught on—so much had gone by so fast—I hardly had time to react. A lit candle flew across the room just missing my head. Luckily it just missed the drapes and went out just as it hit the floor.

The girl then began climbing the walls by way of the grand library shelves, and I thought for sure the entire library of over two thousand books would come crashing down, killing us all. Ripcord started calling out some weird gibberish and, for a second, I thought he too were possessed. All M.C. could think to do was to get the girl off his beloved library, but to no avail for the girl was now clawing at the ceiling. One could not help envisioning scenes from "The Exorcist" and other such films, and, Satan-Help-Me, I would have loved to have banged that little stripper right up against that ceiling!

Suddenly, Ripcord called me to pick up the bible and read something out of it. Being a Satanist, I looked back at him like he was nuts. M.C.'s voice cried out as if in agony, "Fuck the bible! Get her off my goddamn library!" His hairy head lost somewhere between the thighs of her violently kicking legs, her back now up against the precious books, I began to laugh hysterically. Yet, above the panic and chaos, I was able to hear Ripcord yell to M.C. that he didn't know whether to grab an arm or a leg.

"Grab a breast!" I yelled back. The German ceased for a moment as she began to laugh like a banshee. Then our eyes met as we both laughed in unison and I thought for a second that we had a moment until one of her "fuck me " pumps flew off her foot and hit me in the mouth. Somehow Ripcord was able to pluck M.C.'s head out from between her legs, at which point she began to masturbate. Then, losing grip with her other hand, they were able to finally pry her off the library, each of the two men holding onto a milky white thigh as if about to make a wish. That's when M.C. started making accusations that she had urinated on him. But he did not look wet, nor could we smell any urine on him. The girl was laughing while hanging in limbo with her long blonde curls dragging against the carpet, giving all three of us front row seats into her own private Abyss of Daath. And that's when Leviathan came. In the form of a golden fountain of youth, the Holy Grail pourest forth. We all jumped back, the two others letting go of her legs. She crashed to the floor and began to twist and shake all over again while continuing to masturbate and urinate simultaneously. If M.C. wasn't wet before, he sure was now, and so was Frater Ripcord. But that didn't stop our two heroes. M.C. went for the bible, Ripcord went for the cross. Like Butch Cassidy and the Sundance Kid during the last stand.

Being a Satanist and filled with all Evil supreme, I went for my pockets in hope of a condom. The girl turned and quickly began crawling away on her hands and knees. I went to grab her, thinking she might tumble down the stairs. I was just about to grab a cheek when M.C. began his sermon. She jumped straight up as if something had exploded underneath her. I fell back over the coffee table. Papers, ashtrays, soda cans and tortilla chips went flying all over the place along with the dip. Caught between the table and the couch, I found myself in a most vulnerable and embarrassing position. Havoc and mayhem was going on all around me, none of which could I see.

German ... crashing ... sermonizing ... screaming ... chanting ... cursing ...! All I could see were these violent shadows on the ceiling with you name it (including her other shoe) flying across my limited field of vision. Not to mention my arms and legs wriggling helplessly in the air. Somehow the television had been turned on. How that happened I had no idea until I realized that the remote had been knocked off the table and was now residing under my posterior. Every time I would almost unwedge myself, I'd slip back down only to increase the volume or change the channel. This explained all the opening themes to those godforsaken and forgotten TV programs: from "Mission Impossible" to "The Beverly Hillbillies" to "Hawaii Five-O." Among the hellish orchestra, I heard the gothic cuckoo clock strike three a.m. just before it was stopped dead by a large flying quartz crystal.

When I finally got free, what I saw was frightening. I can hardly describe it. Try to visualize the room. The now infamous library has always been known for the number of books, never for the size of the room itself. It's small, sixteen by twelve at best. It's cluttered with a couch, coffee table, and chairs. Shelves on every wall are overfilled with books and mystical articles of every kind imaginable. Ripcord is not a small man by any means and M.C. is close to six feet himself. And here is this buck-naked, long legged little stripper yelling out obscenities in barbaric German, kicking over everything in sight, jumping over all the furniture, pissing while playing with herself and wildly running all around the room as if it were a long distance obstacle course; with M.C. frantically on her heals, bible in one hand, swinging the cross up in the air with the other and belting out psalms from the old testament as if it were the end of the world; with Ripcord running around injecting magical zaps with copper-crystal wand in hand, intensely mumbling crazed incantations in Latin and Greek; and all this with the theme to "Hawaii Five-O" blasting away in the background.

It was too much to take. I was breathless. The classic scene of a feminine free spirit exercising her demons while the male of the species tries desperately to exorcise them, totally gone to Hell. I could only thank my lucky stars that the three family pit bulls were not there to get in on the action. Fortunately, considering the hour, the Hounds of Hell were probably out ripping apart one of the remaining living neighbors, as was their usual nightly ritual.

I felt faint. I needed water. I quickly looked around for the nearest exit when suddenly she pounced upon me, catching my head between her knees. I felt like my skull had been squashed like an egg. I looked up at her and she down at me with—all I can describe as—evil bedroom eyes and a Cheshire cat grin. I was her mouse of the moment. Through the ringing in my ears, I was able to make out something erotic sounding in German. What, I do not know, but I'm sure it was something along the lines of, "I'm gonna piss all over you!" I looked straight into the almost completely shaved mouth of Cthulhu as it pulsated open and closed and opened again. Never had I felt such desire and fear all at once. The wrath of Cthulhu was about to come forth from the outer dimension (or should I say "inner"); but just before the floodgates opened, Ripcord snatched her up from me, almost taking my head with her. "To the hot tub!" M.C. yelled, pointing with the crucifix.

The "Hot Tub" is another piece of architecture not known for its size rather than for how many dozens have been able to fit inside the four man tub at the same time, especially when sexually motivated. At other times it can even be used as a ritual bath for "cleansing." Knowing the infamy of the tub, it was hard to tell if he was going to baptize her or fuck her; however considering the situation, perhaps he was going to drown her.

Once Ripcord threw her in, she began to calm down a little. Someone, of course, would have to get into the ritual bath with her to make sure she stayed in. As M.C. began to swiftly remove his Jesus-boots, I suddenly jumped in fully naked. M.C. looked at me half in shock at how I could've gotten undressed that fast, and half as if he wanted to kill me for stealing the opportunity away from him. I figured that I'm a water sign so how dangerous could this be? M.C. had no choice but to go back to reading his bible. Ripcord switched off between holding onto her arms or shoulders, making sure she stayed in, from outside the tub. She was all smitten with giggles now as she made her way on top of me, straddling her long legs around my waist and sitting on my stomach like a succubus. I wasn't sure if I liked this position and desire and fear hit me again as I was forced to lie back. Only two feet deep at the most, I was just able to keep my head afloat as I quickly developed a hard-on that eventually ached so bad I thought it would rip out of its skin. I tried to push her down lower, onto my cock which was pulsating and quivering with excitement but the closest I could get was to have it rubbing against the small of her back. That's when her river began to flow. And flow. And flow. The urine smell was light, as if she had ingested nothing but liquids all day, and a slightly fishy strawberry sent as well. It seemed that the more she peed, the more she calmed down, but the pee wouldn't end! It just kept coming...all over me. The tub began to overflow. I kept looking at Ripcord and M.C. but they just gave me the same dumb, desperate look back. Over a minute later and she was still on the same piss! I tried to get up from under her legs, but couldn't. I wanted to pull myself out but thought that if I lost my grip I'd slip down under the water and urine. Suddenly the urine in the tub began to toil and bubble! What was happening? I wanted to scream but was afraid I'd swallow the evil, bubbling piss-water!

Was this normal urine or some sort of possessed toxic piss? I felt something jabbing me in the back! Was something else alive in the tub with us? Was my skin about to melt off my body in a tub of acid piss? Were the ghosts, goblins and things that go bump in the night a reality? And now was I about to pay with my life for not believing in them? No. Ripcord only mistakenly kneeled on the button that turns on the spa jets. Whew!

The local legend of the incredible pissing woman has it that the final urination went on anywhere from fifteen minutes to an hour. The truth is it only went on for about five or six minutes; but being the one underneath her, that was enough for me!

After she was done taking her record breaking leak, her legs loosened from around my waist and Ripcord was able to get us both out of tub, hose us down with clean water and help us both get dressed. Her urine brought a weird energy with it, so I, as well as she, was pretty out-of-it. M.C. had conked out on the couch and at first I thought his heart had taken a massive in all the excitement, but then I could hear him snoring and I knew he was all right. She started to feel better sooner than I did. But then, of course, she had gotten it all out of her system and dumped it on me. She drove herself home and Ripcord took me to Denny's for coffee. When he felt I was okay, he followed me to see that I got home all right.

So what really happened that night? A number of things could have happened. M.C. could have "psyched" her out into believing Loki was inside of her, just to see if he could exorcise him. Or, perhaps, while M.C. was psyching her out, she may have picked up on the vibes of my intense reading of Loki. And the urination? Could M.C. have manipulated it with some strange tantric cunnilingus while making it look as if he was simply trying to get her off his beloved bookcase? Remember, at his first accusation, we saw no indication of any urine on him; it was only after.

Or perhaps she was the real magus that evening. Supposedly given the "permission" to act without responsibility for her actions, she decided to teach these magicians of thorny thigh a lesson. But still, a six-minute piss!!!

The last I heard, that little stripper, became a feminist, changed her name to Pandora, shaved her head, and joined a Dianic coven. Of course, the Dianics have been on our backs ever since. But the truth is, *as far as I could tell,* M.C. didn't lay a sexual hand on her (I think his wife was home) and, considering the situation, was a helpful gentleman all evening. Even though M.C. has always had a way of turning around bad news and having it work for him: making the guns of his enemies magically backfire. Remember that it is his infamy that has made him famous. Considering this, he has many enemies to thank!

And Then There Was...

On a final note, is a story that took place long before I met M.C., back in the early eighties. Long before he had any knowledge of or interest in the Golden Dawn. He was dabbling in Wicca back then, and was probably out hunting for a Gardnerian book or two. Browsing in Alpha Book Center, the largest and oldest new age/occult shop in Arizona, an old man approached him. He told M.C. that he looked like a man he used to know and asked if the name "Crowley" was anywhere in his family tree. Well, one thing lead to another, and, to make a long story short; this old man told M.C. that he had the potential but hoped he had the determination and persistence, because it would take a while before he was able to match the *real* A.C.! M.C. was younger then, and still looking at life as a glass half empty, rather than half full; and when the old man left, he walked over to the store clerk and asked, "Who was that arrogant old fuck?"

"You don't know?" asked the clerk, with surprise.

"No," said M.C.

So the clerk informed him,
"That was Israel Regardie!"

LIBERTY & THE PURSUIT OF FORBIDDEN FRUIT

by David Jay Brown

Author of the Falcon titles:
Virus: The Alien Strain
Brainchild

"The whole aim of practical politics is to keep the populace alarmed (and hence clamorous to be led to safety) by menacing it with an endless series of hobgoblins, all of them imaginary."

— H.L. Mencken

The desire to recreationally ingest psychoactive drugs is deeply rooted in our biological nature. The hunger to get high is as natural as the desire to eat, sleep, and procreate.

Young children have an instinctive drive to change their ordinary state of awareness, as evidenced by the delight that they take in spinning around and around in circles to produce a state of dizziness. According to UCLA psychopharmacologist Ron Siegel, every human culture, and every class of animal, makes use of certain plants for their psychoactive properties. In fact, Siegel believes that "the desire for intoxication is actually a fourth drive, as unstoppable as hunger, thirst, and sex."

Our DNA is programmed to grow brains that crave intoxicating plants and potions. The molecular components of the intoxicants that we use fit so snugly and precisely into our neural receptors that it seems as though our brains were specifically wired to receive them. This symbiotic, co-evolutionary relationship between animal brains and plant intoxicants is as ancient as the birds and the bees. This is why the War on Drugs in America is really a war against human nature.

The War on Drugs (or rather, "The War on *Some* Drugs," as Robert Anton Wilson more aptly puts it) is a fascist attempt to control human behavior by stigmatizing and punishing people for following one of their

359

most natural instincts—to do what feels good. The U.S. government uses Machiavellian scare tactics to fuel the Drug War, because they know that fear is what motivates *most* of human behavior. The Vatican, the Mafia, street gangs and world governments all recognize this fact, and have learned how to terrorize people to their advantage.

Science fiction author Philip K. Dick summed it up best when he said, "Rome never fell." Religious orders still emanate from the Vatican, the Military-Industrial Complex still runs the world, and most people are still wage-slaves to the ruling class. Those in control know that scaring people is the easiest way to manipulate them. The scare tactics work even better if people are duped into thinking that what the government is doing is actually for their own good.

The Drug War is an organized attempt to scapegoat and persecute racial minorities, inner-city youth, lower economic classes, left-wing intellectuals, and rebellious government protesters—much as the Nazis persecuted the Jews, or the Witch Hunts persecuted pagan women. The Drug War is primarily waged upon low-income minorities who use marijuana.

The parallels between the Jewish Holocaust and the American War on Drugs are particularly striking. In Nazi Germany, one by one, every activity in which Jews exclusively took part was made illegal—such as making or selling kosher food. The Nuremberg Act of 1933 was a sweeping set of laws targeted against the Jews, gypsies, and homosexuals. These "undesirables" were carted off because they broke laws targeted against them—just as drug users, and those who supply them, are thrown in prison today.

When the federal government says that America has a 70 million person drug abuse problem, they're trying to make it sound like the streets are littered with heroin addicts. But what that figure really means is 65 million people have used marijuana, and 5 million have used heroin or cocaine. They don't count alcohol and tobacco (which kill far more people every year than all illegal drugs combined) because they are *legal,* i.e. the drugs that *they* peddle.

The feds are talking about an *illegal* drug "problem." They use the number of people who have smoked the giggly cannabis flowers to beef up their statistics, so it seems like America is in the midst of a terrible heroin and crack epidemic, when its not. To the U.S. government, all use of illegal substances is defined as abuse.

The entire Drug War is founded on unconstitutional principles. There is nothing in the U.S. Constitution that allows the government to imprison people for using certain substances under the pretence that it is to save them from harming themselves. In the early part of the last century the government still understood this. That is why they had to actually add amendments to the constitution to initiate and repeal alcohol prohibition.

Many historians speculate that marijuana prohibition began because hemp products were seen as competitive to Du Pont financially, or because it was an easy way to scapegoat Mexican immigrants. The hilarious propaganda film that the government made in the Thirties—*Reefer Madness*—leads me to believe that, even then, they were also aware of the association between marijuana use and youth rebellion.

Whatever the reason *why* they made marijuana illegal, *how* the government did it is even more unbelievable. By passing the Marijuana Tax Act in 1937 they required that anyone who bought or sold marijuana had to purchase tax stamps—yet the government didn't issue any marijuana tax stamps, so there was no way to obtain them. If you had marijuana and no tax stamps, then you were under arrest. Can you believe that people actually fell for this? The Marijuana Tax Act was eventually ruled unconstitutional, however, that didn't stop the determined drug warriors.

In 1972, when Richard Nixon was in the White House, he tried to figure out how to reduce the number of Vietnam war demonstrators that were giving him such a headache. He made the connection that many demonstrators were getting high on pot, and had a brainstorm—why not simply arrest them for their marijuana use?

Even though the medical research team that he himself had appointed recommended that they decriminalize cannabis, Nixon dramatically increased the restrictions on it (through some magical revision of the interstate commerce clause that makes even less logical sense than the unconstitutional Marijuana Tax act). With the exception of Jimmy Carter, every president since Nixon has steadily escalated the Drug War.

By every measure the 28 year Drug War has failed to slow down drug use or the availability of drugs. More people are currently in American prisons than ever before in U.S. history, and more than half of the prisoners are there for non-violent drug offences, yet illegal drugs are more available than ever before. Police corruption and gang violence are currently reaching record highs.

Our hard-earned constitutional rights to privacy are gradually being taken away, and our increasingly-Orwellian government is spying on us more and more. The Bill of Rights has become virtually worthless. Police routinely storm into people's homes, wrestle the occupants to the ground at gunpoint, and search their homes for drugs. Many innocent people have been killed in this process. According to Steve Dasbach, the Libertarian party's national director, 140,000 people have died because of the Drug War. In addition, countless lives have been ruined and many families destroyed.

The U.S. federal government is currently spending over twenty billion dollars a year on the Drug War, and that doesn't include state budgets, which are billions more. While Congress quibbles over a few million dollars for Medicare and Medicaid, no one on Capital Hill even questions the staggering Drug War budget. Remember, every dollar spent on the Drug War is going into somebody's bank account.

The Drug War is also preventing many students from getting an education. The 1998 Higher Education Act disqualifies young people for financial aid for college if they've ever been convicted of marijuana possession—but not if they've been convicted of rape, robbery or manslaughter.

Now, if the government was truly interested in helping young people with drug problems, one would think that they would encourage them to get an education, rather than prevent it. This is similar to the way that the Nazis tried to prevent the Jews from gaining power in Germany. I suspect that the government is afraid of educated pot smokers. What other explanation could there be? Rapists, and even murderers can still get financial aid for college.

Perhaps the most insidious of Washington's Drug War crimes is their attempt to take away the right to free speech. The so-called 'Methamphetamine Anti-Proliferation Act,' sponsored by senators Dianne Feinstein and Orrin Hatch, would abolish the First Amendment, and make it a crime to communicate certain information about illegal drugs.

The bill, HR. 2987, would make it a federal felony to publish, link a web site to, or even talk about certain factual data having to do with drugs, drug culture, or drug paraphernalia. In addition, the first provision in the 'Methamphetamine Anti-Proliferation Act' would loosen the rules governing police searches. It would permit the police to search people's residence, vehicle, or workplace and take "intangible evidence" (such as making a copy of your computer's hard drive) without telling them. The Senate passed this bill unanimously in November of 1999. As of this writing, it is being considered by two House committees. If Congress passes this bill, and it becomes law, simply telling someone how to use or grow marijuana would become a crime punishable by ten years in prison. Saying, "put that in your pipe and smoke it," would become a major criminal offense.

The first amendment to the constitution is the most important of all; freedom of speech is supposed to be what distinguishes a free country from a fascist regime. Thomas Jefferson would be rolling in his grave if he knew what going on. Our founding fathers had originally intended for the U.S. federal government to have very limited power. Capital Hill was put in place to protect the states in a time of war, and to settle interstate commerce disputes. That's it. A state was supposed to be a sovereign entity. The federal government has become the very monster that our founding fathers tried to prevent.

The Drug War, which began in 1972[1], has lasted longer than any other war in U.S. history. I'm sure that future generations will view the Drug War as one of the worst injustices in human history, right up there with slavery and concentration camps. Can it possibly get any worse?

Bobby Moak, a representative from Mississippi, introduced a bill which, if it becomes law, would provide legislation for the removal of a body part on anyone found guilty of possessing marijuana. A questionnaire currently making the rounds in Congress includes the question: "Do you favor the death penalty for drug trafficking?" Darryl Gates, the former Los Angeles police chief, said that he thought marijuana users should be executed. Can you believe all this intense hatred towards people who smoke little green and red flowers that, at worst, make them watch cartoons and giggle?

Why doesn't the U.S. government ever consider changing its hard-line policy on Schedule I drugs like marijuana, crack, and heroin? Because harm reduction and reducing drug use was never their real intention, as evidenced by the CIA's well-documented involvement in heroin and cocaine trafficking. The government's real intention has been to frighten and intimidate people. And by that measure, the Drug War has been a huge success. That is why, even though numerous states have passed medical marijuana initiatives, possession of the gentle healing herb still remains a federal crime in the same league as murder and rape.

Marijuana users are probably the most persecuted minority on the planet. There are currently several hundred million marijuana users worldwide in custody in more than a hundred nations. Former *High Times* editor Peter Gorman said, "There is no other group, no religious organization, no single color or people, who are persecuted in such numbers in so many different places anywhere on the globe."

What is the logic behind the Drug War supposed to be anyway? That these forbidden plants and potions are so dangerous and so evil that if you agree to use one then you embody that evil? Why is the U.S. government so adamant about maintaining their increasingly ludicrous position on marijuana? Because the Drug War is a sinister political hoax that serves four important purposes.

(1) It is a way to persecute racial minorities. The Drug War disproportionately imprisons blacks and Hispanics. A Rutgers University statistician, who surveyed drivers and arrests on the New Jersey turnpike,

---

[1] Timothy Leary said that the War on Drugs actually began in Eden, when Jehovah busted Adam and Eve for eating from the tree of Forbidden Knowledge, and exiled them from paradise.

reported that, while fewer than 5 percent of the cars on the turnpike had both out-of-state plates and were occupied by blacks, 80 percent of those stopped and arrested for drugs were out-of-state blacks. According to the Bureau of Justice statistics only 11 percent of America's illicit drug users are black, yet blacks account for 37 percent of those arrested for drug violations.

(2) It raises money for law enforcement—through seizures of bank accounts, cars and property. It also provides a way of charging higher-income tax-payers to imprison lower-income citizens. The privately-owned prison industry charges tax-payers approximately $22,000 a year per prisoner.

(3) It helps to eliminate competition with legal pharmaceuticals and legal recreational drugs. The Drug War has grown into a hugely success-ful capitalistic enterprise, benefiting the privately-run prison industry, the military, the urine testers, manufacturers of wiretaps and other spy-tech-nologies, prosecutors, defense attorneys, politicians and police, as well as the tobacco, alcohol, and pharmaceutical companies. These are the very corporations that fund the Partnership for a Drug-Free America and DARE programs—which, like the Nazi programs, teach children to turn in their parents.

(4) The American Government is also well aware of the association between marijuana use and the tendency for people to think for them-selves and question authority.

People who smoke marijuana tend to think independently, to stray from the mainstream, to protest wars and do other rebellious things that the government doesn't like. This is why Nixon originally declared a war on marijuana in 1972. According to Paul Krassner, a U.S. government-sponsored anti-drug booklet, with a foreword by Senator Orrin Hatch, informs parents that among the warning signs that their children are using marijuana and other drugs is "excessive preoccupation with social causes, race relations, environmental issues, etc."

The late comedian Bill Hicks said that "not only should marijuana be legal, it should be mandatory." I almost agree. From what I can tell, pot tends to make people happier, more peaceful, more sensitive, more thoughtful and more creative. There's no question that it makes people laugh more. Too much of anything can be unhealthy, but I don't think that most people are getting *enough* ganja, as evidenced by the fact that the majority of people tend to take themselves too seriously. Nowhere is this problem more evident than with our own government officials. Perhaps if they inhaled, they wouldn't be so damn mean.

I believe that THC (the primary psychoactive component of cannabis) is an essential brain nutrient, necessary for proper psychological health. The brain produces its own natural version of THC called anandimide

(Sanskrit for "inner bliss"). People who are especially attracted to marijuana may be suffering from deficiencies of this feel-good neurotransmitter. As a result of the Drug War, many people are simply not getting their proper daily requirements of this important brain chemical, and too many of us are suffering from what self-help author Peter McWilliams calls the "pleasure-deficit disorder."

A U.C. Berkeley study showed that the high school students who were the most well-adjusted socially were not the kids who completely abstained from marijuana, or the kids who smoked it continuously—rather, it was the kids who smoked grass moderately. This was a study that didn't get too much exposure in the mainstream media, like the many studies which demonstrate marijuana's unusual safety, and bountiful utility for treating a wide spectrum of medical problems.

Drug Czar Barry McCaffrey is lying when he says that there is no scientific evidence for marijuana's medical properties, as he couldn't possibly be that misinformed. Politicians who repeat over and over that more research needs to be done before marijuana can be considered a safe, effective medication are simply being dishonest. Numerous carefully controlled studies have demonstrated that marijuana can safely and effectively treat the nausea that accompanies chemotherapy, AIDS wasting syndrome, glaucoma, epilepsy, chronic pain, and muscle spasm disorders.

Research at the U.S. National Institute of Health, and in Israel, has also demonstrated that THC—like vitamins C and E—is a powerful antioxidant that actually *prevents* cancer and brain damage. THC has been shown to have tumor-reducing qualities in several studies. A 1994 project by the U.S. National Toxicology Program specifically sought to induce cancers in mice and rats by shooting them up with high doses of THC for extended periods of their lives. However, the results showed unmistakably that the treated animals had significantly greater resistance to tumor development, and lived longer than the untreated animals.

A study done by the California Division of Motor Vehicles in 1986 showed that, unlike alcohol, people driving under the influence of marijuana tended to drive more cautiously. Some people even drove better when they were high. After an extensive international study, the World Health Organization declared that marijuana is much less dangerous than alcohol or tobacco. Isn't it funny how these studies don't often make it into the mainstream media?

The US government wants people to believe that marijuana causes brain damage, and acts as a "gateway drug," leading children down the devil's path to hard-core addictive drugs. There is absolutely no scientific evidence for this "gateway drug" myth. Every study ever done on marijuana confirms that it doesn't lead to harder drugs, as well as how non-toxic it is.

Marijuana is probably the safest psychoactive drug known. In all of human history, there is not one reported death from a marijuana overdose. Yet the DEA is willing to pay television stations millions of dollars (of our money) to alter the scripts of their shows, so as to reflect their malicious propaganda, and tell us how "dangerous" it is. Of course, only the politicians can save us from this horrible menace.

Will the government ever stop its insanity? Probably not by themselves. Only when public outcry reaches a high enough pitch will they be forced to accede to the will of the people. Because the younger pot-smoking generations are gradually replacing the older alcohol-tobacco generations, the end of the Drug War is inevitable. When that finally happens, the viciously oppressive system will crumble like the Berlin Wall. On that glorious day we can all celebrate by sparking up a doobie. A new era of peace, freedom and tolerance will be ushered in. Then we can really start having fun. ;-)

References

Baum, D., *Smoke and Mirrors: The War on Drugs and the Politics of Failure.* Little, Brown and Co., New York, 1996.

McWilliams, P., *Ain't Nobody's Business if You Do: The Absurdity of Consensual Crimes in a Free Society.* Prelude Press, Los Angeles, 1993.

Siegel, R., *Intoxication: Life in Pursuit of Artificial Paradise.* E.P. Dutton, New York, 1989.

Zimmer, L. and Morgan, J., *Marijuana Myths Marijuana Facts.* The Lindesmith Center, New York, 1997.

Special thanks to Robert Anton Wilson and Peter McWilliams, who keep me up-to-date on the proceedings of the Drug War through their informative internet news-groups. In-depth interviews with these two extraordinary individuals can be found on my Web site:

www.levity.com/mavericks

David Jay Brown is the author of two science fiction novels—*Brainchild* (New Falcon, 1988) and *Virus: The Alien Strain* (New Falcon, 1999). He is also the co-author of two collections of interviews with controversial, cutting-edge scientists and artists—*Mavericks of the Mind* (Crossing Press, 1993) and *Voices from the Edge* (Crossing Press, 1995).

COMBATING THE SELF: THE REBELLION OF MARTIAL ARTS

by C.G. Lopez and J.E. Hardee

There is always one alternative to slavery; we can die fighting. No tyrant can gain more than a hollow victory against a people so committed, and even the individual can find here the ultimate rock of his inviolability.
— Jack Parsons

If there is any figure who represents the rebel, the image of individuality and self-directed acts, it is the modern martial artist. Although considerations of rebellion generally call to mind individuals serving as thorns in society's side through overt acts, rebellion may be as much an internal act as it is an external one. Personal revelations and training may serve to upset the flow of unthinking society by elevating one member to the status of independent. Thus, the martial artist, who through strength of will has transformed the body and the self into a warrior, skilled in two battles, within and without, is an excellent example of a rebel in our midst.

It is very important to make the distinction between the sincere study of martial arts and the half-hearted performance of the various pseudo-combative hobbies available to the public today. A martial art, practiced in its true form, is more than a mere collection of physical techniques. However, there are many "combat" sports and "kickboxing" programs found in gyms or schools masquerading under the label of martial arts that offer only a glimpse at what the study of the true martial way entails. These schools, while emphasizing physical movements suited only for controlled, padded sparring competitions, or which hand out rankings like so much candy where no one testing can fail, entirely miss the spirit and application of martial experience and history. Many schools are reluctant to include the world of meditation, ethical studies, spiritual studies, and growth, which is necessary for the warrior, for fear of upsetting their student's sensibilities. The inheritance of martial tradition cannot be served piecemeal to those sniffing around the table of knowledge. At best, schools which neglect to teach the fullness of their traditions will produce thugs, or well-meaning but poorly trained fighters who are more of a danger to themselves than before they ever signed a training contract.

All martial arts have their origins based on methods of warfare and self-preservation. But they have developed through exposure to philosophical and religious teachings to an evolved state that addresses the whole human. To use the terms "martial art" or "martial artist" necessarily imply an overarching Way to martial practice. The Way incorporates the protection of the physical self, and the struggle involved in doing so, into a model of the transformation and liberation of the mind or soul. Physical combat is extrapolated into spiritual combat, the results of which prepare the individual for the ultimate battle: death.

> Warriors...count on the awareness of their own impending death, performing each act as though it were the last battle and, therefore, the best. With death as a constant companion who infuses each act with power, they transform into magic their time as living persons on this Earth. The awareness of inevitable death endows them with the disinterest to be free from attachments while at the same time not indulging in denial. Detached from everything, conscious of life's brevity, and in constant struggle, warriors begin to arrange life through the power of their decisions. They work each moment to achieve control over themselves, thereby gaining control over their personal world.
>
> — Victor Sanchez

The clearest distinction between the player and the martial artist, the fitness freak and the warrior, is death. The way of the martial artist is the way of dying. The way does not only involve death for the opponent in the most serious struggles, but also death for the practitioner through the irrevocable lashes of experience which push the Self onwards towards liberation. A martial artist uses death as an advisor, as a constant companion whose ever-present reality imbues each moment with ultimate meaning. Without an intimate sense of death, any martial system does become a mere collection of physical motions which may or may not be useful in a combat situation. Effective martial arts, those deserving of the name Art, are those which grew out of actual, bloody conflict, and it is only by returning to these roots that the practitioner may be said to face the enemy within, or begin to walk the martial way, or acquire self-mastery and thereby walk the path of the rebel.

Therefore, it is necessary for the experienced practitioner, once the initial lessons of physical discipline and skill have been acquired, to work with an element of true danger. Training with full speed techniques, committed partners, on concrete, in street clothes, defending against firearms or blades with razor sharp edges, for example, are useful methods for bringing home the reality of injury and death in combat for the martial artist. On a mundane level, without such training, how would you know that you could survive such conditions if ever you encountered danger? When one trains with an actual sword or knife, the practitioner is always at risk of personal injury or death. This type of training forces a new level of personal responsibility and mental awareness which is denied by the false edge of toys that always lead to self-deceit. If one only trains with toys, one becomes merely a toy soldier.

In order to explain martial arts as a Way, it is instructive to draw a comparison to yoga. Yoga is a psycho-physical system developed in India and practiced throughout the centuries. It may be seen today in its purely physical form called Hatha Yoga. However, the purpose of yoga is a spiritual one, starting with the mastery of the body, leading towards mastery of the mind, and finally spiritual insight. Yoga means "union" in the classical sense of uniting the Self with the All-Self, Atman with Brahman. Yoga, as a system, employs six stepping stones towards enlightenment. These are yama, niyama, asana, pranayama, dhyana, and samadhi. We will take each in turn and show how it translates into the world of the martial artist, thereby clarifying the "art" in martial art.

> Freedom like charity, begins at home. No man is worthy to fight in the cause of freedom unless he has conquered his internal masters. He must learn control and discipline over the disastrous passions that would lead him to folly and ruin. He must conquer inordinate vanity and anger, self-deception, fear, and inhibition.
>
> — Jack Parsons

Yama may be loosely translated as control or willpower. For the yogin, it is necessary to submit the self to the discipline of spiritual practice. Physical motions, prayer, abstaining from certain foods, wearing simple clothing, are all methods of control. Spiritual enlightenment for the yogin is not a Zen-like sudden awakening, but a process of training, spiritual insight being the fruit of steady labor. For martial artists, this philosophy is its foundation. There is a reason why many martial schools are run like military camps with overt ranking systems, rigid codes of conduct, and filled with safety gear at the lower levels. Self-control is what martial schools are all about, control of the body, emotions, and intentions through a progressive regimen that intensifies as the practitioner's skill increases. Yama can also be translated into martial-speak as the willpower necessary to persist in training. Each system, with its own grade structure, has a series of natural plateaus where students feel like they are no longer learning but are simply rehashing old techniques.

These plateaus are grueling physically and mentally, as the student is faced with an invisible barrier at each training session. At these points, many students either stop trying to improve, or drop out of martial arts in general. One of the first plateaus is between seeing the martial arts as teaching mere physical control and knowing it as a method for controlling the emotions.

Niyama, the next step for the yogin, is concerned with ethics. Yogins follow specific ethical systems based on their spiritual goals. These may involve doctrines like ahimsa (non-injury to living beings), dietary restrictions, chastity, etc. Martial artists also have ethical codes. Whether as a series of virtues to strive for or ethical rules of conduct, the elevation of the thug to the warrior through ethics is essential. As many martial systems were practiced by the nobility as well as by monks, ethical considerations became interlinked with progression in the arts. Although in long periods of warfare, abstract ethical debates were often laid aside in the history of martial arts, the marriage of philosophy and physicality returned in peacetime. Through the lessons of the past, it was shown that an ethical warrior, one with the qualities of loyalty, honor, and enlightened rulership for example, was more valuable than merely a competent fighter. Warriors with codes of conduct maintained peace in society, and were able to continue training their deadly arts while refining the self. Simple exercises like the tea ceremony, or the recitation of poetry, were new battlefields for hardened fighters to test their skills. It was through these endeavors that the arts took form as a Way, or spiritual path.

> Knowing others is intelligence;
> Knowing yourself is true wisdom.
> Mastering others is strength;
> Mastering yourself is true power.
> — Lao-Tzu

Asana, the next step, means body position. Yogins employ various asanas as postures for meditation, some even remaining in these postures for years. There are sadhus in India today who have submitted to the physical discipline of holding one arm above their head until it becomes a withered limb. Hatha yoga, on the other hand, uses various asanas to promote health as, for example, the headstand is purported to relieve sleeplessness, poor blood circulation, constipation, and more. Many hatha yoga sessions involve a routine of asanas, moving from one to the other, focusing on each area of the body through tension and relaxation. For the martial artist, asanas consist of the defensive, offensive, and training stances in a system. Stances may be either static or moving, just as meditation may be either static or moving, and the body responds to variety. In training, martial artists use static stances for balance, physical mastery, and to set up techniques. One example of a training stance would be the "horse stance". The martial artist stands with the legs at least shoulder width apart or wider, legs to each side, trunk facing forward, knees bent up to parallel with the floor, and back erect as if you were riding a horse. From this position, the legs, the thighs, the ankles, and the lower back are stressed, strengthening them in the process. As a training stance, it is here where the upper body is drilled in blocks and strikes. Training drills often keep students in this position until exhaustion, alternating between breathing and active drills. Anyone who has experienced the seeming perversity of instructors during horse stance drills will readily see this parallel, as well as realize the wisdom of its use when faced with actual combat.

Pranayama, the next step for the yogin, is breath control. Once they have mastered the body with asana, yogins employ various methods of breath control to harness the power of the mind. Although control of breath has its own health benefits, breath often likened to "food", its primary purpose is to train the mind. By counting the breath, or the seconds before inhalation or exhalation, or by blocking off one nostril, or by holding the breath, the yogin achieves a deeper understanding of the life force of the body. Where the breath flows, the mind follows. Controlling the breath for a yogin is necessary before control of the mind is attempted. In martial arts, the thinking is the same. If a fighter has ragged, uncontrolled breathing, that fighter is easy prey. Calm, controlled breathing, even during physical exertion, clarifies the mind in the stress of combat and conserves energy for future conflicts. A martial artist can never assume that combat will be brief. A warrior must always prepare for the worst and train as if the next conflict will take every ounce of strength to survive. Breath control is also used to accomplish specific tasks. One dramatic example is breaking techniques. A martial artist wishes to punch a block of concrete, breaking it in two. Drawing back the hand and thrusting the fist forward, first two knuckles squarely hitting center of mass may break the block, but most likely will injure the hand, whether by shattering the knuckles, breaking the wrist, or splitting skin on the hand. However, if a yell is employed, that is, controlled breathing, at the precise moment of contact, the slab will be broken seemingly without effort with no damage to the hand. Why? Because breath control adds speed, focus, and power to motion. The key to breaking is a force supplied at sufficient speed toward the center of mass of an object. If the object does not break due to its shape, i.e. it is a circle rather than a rectangle, it will nevertheless be seriously damaged.

Dhyana, the next step towards spiritual insight, is mental focus. Yogins at this stage strive to control mental processes by constricting the attention to a single mental object. For example, a yogin will meditate on a yellow triangle in a red square, striving to have this image occupy all consciousness. Skill in this act will open the door to samadhi, as samadhi is sometimes considered to be the prolonging of dhyana. For the martial artist, focus is as necessary as stance and breath control as focus is required for learning and for application. One of the early struggles for a student is to get the body to do what the mind wants. For example, an instructor demonstrates a stepping motion with the right leg and a simultaneous sweeping motion with the left hand. Yet, even after slow demonstration, students will step with the left foot, completely unaware of their error. Mental control also means mental awareness—living in the moment. Consider sword techniques. As a weapon, the sword is extremely demanding and requires very specific movements in order to be effective. If a practitioner can't master these specifics, then a staff or club would be a better weapon choice. Sword training involves the mental challenge to hold only one movement in mind at a time. Advancing with the sword, for example, seemingly a simple motion, cannot be done properly if the mind wanders. Without focus, the blade will not be drawn with fluidity, the balance of the feet will be thrown off, and the wavering hand at the end of the motion will take away from the power and effectiveness of the cut. A martial artist who makes these mistakes while facing a competent swordsman, will never be allowed the opportunity to make any mistakes, let alone any action, again.

> Art is never decoration, embellishment; instead, it is a work of enlightenment. Art, in other words, is a technique for acquiring liberty.
> — Bruce Lee

Samadhi, the last step of the training cycle, is not something we will claim to have experienced, although there are many individuals who no doubt have. For yogins, it is the ultimate level of meditation and some authors have considered it an "absolute blow to the mind." Samadhi is defined as that point when subject and object are united. The intense effort used in dhyana leads to an ekstasis of the mind. The contemplated object so fills the consciousness that the meditator can no longer be separated from the object being meditated upon. In martial arts, legends have grown around masters who have experienced states of samadhi in combat. One master is purported to have transformed into a tiger. Another became invisible behind the blade of a sword. Another was so ferocious in battle that hands and feet were thought to be blades. Taoist immortals are part of the tradition of warriors with fantastical powers. Yet on a more mundane level, samadhi is the state of survival in martial arts. It is the state best designed to survive the horrors of war, the mind being moved beyond morality, and the state necessary for the spiritual understanding of combat as well as the basis for efficient physical action.

The goal of a school is to teach a person new things;
The goal of a Dojang is to transform the person into something new.
A school teaches how to kill;
A Dojang teaches how to die.
The member of a Dojang does not think about fighting.
He tries to go beyond this level and
Comprehend the very essence of conflict.

— Old Martial Art Proverb

The aim of a martial artist, one who follows the Way, is found in the figure of the master. The cycle of master and apprentice is as old as human history, and may be found in any realm of human knowledge. However, martial arts is unique in that once a certain level of proficiency and experience is obtained, the practitioner must begin to teach the skills so laboriously gained. Teaching martial arts, for a martial artist, is the next step for advancement. Teaching physical skills, leading new students across the same stepping stones the martial artist just traversed, serve to "fix" their lessons into the self. For oftentimes, it is the student who mirrors the new lessons and imperfections of self for the master. Instruction is not only a reviewing of old techniques, but an opportunity to perfect those areas which are lacking in the master. Mastery in the martial arts is a continuous process. Masters, propelled by the momentum of their will to train, never stop improving their technique, whether physical or spiritual. It is in this role that the martial artist gives back to society, one student at a time, the power of self-determination it so desperately needs. Helping to free others from the restrictions of helplessness and suffering in the face of fear, insecurity, oppression, and death, the martial artist, as teacher and as rebel, reaches an apogee.

In their fullness, the martial arts defend the independent spirit as much as the well-being of the body. The master of the martial arts is, essentially, not a "sayer," but a "doer."

— Sang Kyu Shim

Of course, the examples above do not represent all there is to the study of martial arts. However, the parallels with yoga should give the potential student pause to consider the training they are embarking upon, as well as the power to determine if the school they found on the corner is one which will teach them an actual martial art rather than mere brawling. Although brawling may be useful in a pinch, no thug will be capable of mastering himself and thus acquiring true power. Individuals who take responsibility for their safety are viewed as vigilantes, those who take responsibility for their health as quacks, those who take responsibility for their own spiritual development as delusional, yet this describes the martial artist. The way of the martial artist is the way of the rebel. When given the choice between tyranny and resistance, the warrior will do what the warrior does best: take action.

BREAKING TRANCE

by Steven Heller, Ph.D.

Author of the Falcon title:
Monsters and Magical Sticks:
There's No Such Thing As Hypnosis?

How do you know when you're getting too close to a fire? Of course, by feeling the heat! But what if you were unable to feel the heat? You would probably not know until you were burning yourself or you smelled your flesh burning. So many people go through life in such a deep trance, that they do not know when they are heading for trouble until they have stepped into it. They no longer know what they feel, want or need!

A small child hears his/her parents fighting and becomes afraid. They tell conflicting stories and s/he becomes confused. They send out incongruent messages and the anxiety rises to painful levels. One day s/he discovers that by "dropping out" and going off into inner-space-out, everything is better ... for a while. If I can't feel it, hear it or see it, it can't get me. *TRANCE IS BORN!* Of course, if a truck is coming at you and you respond by "Not seeing or hearing it" I guarantee that you will feel it. Your trance will simply prevent you from getting out of the way.

A child enters a new and exciting world called school. S/he is curious and open to learning. "Children, we must all sit just like this and always raise your hand and there is one right way to do things and of course only one right answer!" says the adult called teacher. Day in and day out s/he sees things but is told they don't really exist. S/he feels things and is told that the feelings are not real and s/he doesn't really know what s/he feels in the first place. The secret of survival? Go into a trance! The result ... years later s/he doesn't feel what there is to feel, can't hear what there is to hear and can't see what needs to be seen. Frustration, failure and pain is a constant companion.

The secret ... *BREAK TRANCE!* You must learn to question and question some more. You can not trust what you have been tranced into seeing, hearing, or feeling. Tonight, when you go to sleep, sleep on the other side of the bed; sit at a different seat at meal times. For the adventurous, eat with your left hand (or right hand if you are left-handed). Read a book ... from the last page to the first page; record conversations with those you have the poorest communication with. Look for problem areas instead of avoiding them and then come up with three of the most unusual methods for solving the problem. Put a rubber band on your wrist and snap it when ever you feel yourself "dropping out."

Learn to talk to those parts of you that know the difference between trance and what is happening around you. For example, imagine that you begin to feel anxiety. Ask your inner guide to change the feeling into a picture: first a picture of what the feeling itself looks like, and then ask that part to change the picture into one that will help you discover what is really happening for (or to) you. Learn to hear the sound of colors and feelings and to see the feelings and sounds. In short, shake up your systems and break your patterns. (For many interesting and provocative methods of breaking trance, you might even purchase my book, *Monsters and Magical Sticks: There's No Such Thing As Hypnosis.*) Last, but not least, find a good hypnotist who will help you to use hypnosis and trance in order to end your hypnotic trance.

one by one

by Jim Goldiner

one by one
or in any
combination

like a starched
beehive the
enemy
camps in the
enemy's camp

one bleating
stone hearing
its own echo
, they, like the
STUKA
make festering
sores of affections

too much to
see that like
some insipid
substance
their iniquity
clings to their
own avalanche
until
they're before
their own fall
looking up from
some helpless pit

that is not
to say innocuous
but dead!

Christopher S. Hyatt, Ph.D.
Some say he is the greatest mage who ever walked the planet.
Others believe he is the most evil man who ever existed.

PART VI

The Beginning

Genesis P-Orridge
Magician and Musician

THEE SPLINTER TEST

by Genesis P-Orridge

USE FULL GLOSSARY OV TERMS

Astory—An alternative suggestion for thee perennial problem ov finding a non-gender word when describing thee ebbs, myths, flows, interactions, conflicts, migrations and belief systems ov various peoples and social groupings throughout recorded and speculative TIME. We would posit that we can at least all agree that these are a story!

Exoculation—Thee opposite ov inoculation, where inoculation would mean contaminating a clean medium, so that whatever you introduce wills to grow and proliferate. In this more controlled environment thee host medium can thereafter identify I.T. and can then generate its own "antibodies".

Humoral Response—Thee process by which, upon thee introduction ov an antigen, thee body creates antibodies to combat, neutralize and contain these irritants.

I.T.—Imaginary Time.

Occulture—Thee inevitable equivalent in thee realm ov hidden teachings, techniques, and knowledge, ov consensus and popular culture.

Quaquaversal—Pointing in every direction similtaneously. In thee dictionary *centroclinal* is defined as thee opposite ov quaquaversal.

Sigil—For thee purposes ov this essay, defined as a 2–3 dimensional product or ideagram; consciously invoking a clear intention; often produced in conjunction with a formal ritual; usually and primarily graphically and/or non-linguistically, in thee linear, everyday sense ov things.

Transmedia—A crossing ov cultural borders and taboos. A synthesis. As a general guide, holistic. An examination ov constructed "reality" devoid ov preconceptions. This is not an alternative word for mixed-media, interactive or multi-media. It is a recognition ov thee arrival ov one, entirely new, *single* contemporary medium that contains within I.T. all other previously separated media. Transmedia encourages us to establish a re-newed, but not controlled, state ov flux; to develop an openness to thee very nature ov our transhuman existence. I.T. relies neither on pre-conceived concepts about what we should believe, nor on a creative or social consensus ov any type to which we must conform. (Special thanks to Brother WORDS for co-authoring this definition)

THEE SPLINTER TEST

We now have available to us as a species, really for thee first TIME in Astory, an infinite freedom to access, select and assemble. Everything we assemble becomes, and is, a description ov what we are now or what we visualize "being" at any level; from thee deepest, sub-molecular, neuro-cellular programs that we have named "DNA" to thee farthest inter-dimensional reaches ov galactic expansions and contractions outside TIME or SPACE. Skill-full "splintering" is a magickal tool and can generate manifestation.

THIS IS THEE "SPLINTER TEST"!

We are choosing SPLINTERS consciously and unconsciously to repre-sent our own memetic (DNA) patterns, our own cultural imprints and aspirations. We are in a truly Magickal sense "INVOKING" manifesta-tions, perhaps even results, in order to confound and short-circuit our perceptions, and reliance upon "WHOLENESS". We are creating our own subjective and speculative descriptions ov "OTHERNESS".

It can be said, for me at least, that thee transformational implications inherent in sampling, looping, cutting-up and/or thereafter re-assembling both found data materials and infinite combinations ov site-specific sounds, is as probably equivalent to, and as socially significant and pro-found as, thee popularization and mass proselytisation ov LSD and thee splitting ov thee atom. All three involve thee cutting-up ov thee essential "matter" ov science, religion and language; thee basic, potential inhibit-ing, cornerstones ov what has been coined, our contemporary "domina-tor" culture. All three are innately magickal processes giving thee initiate practitioner tools to travel within their previously finite consensus reality container, thereby to reveal and describe and physically adjust a place both ov IN "control" and OUT ov "control". A place, quite literally, ov infinite space. A place previously reserved for thee elite mysteries ov power, or described in covert and arcane codes by thee ritual magickian; thee shamanwoman. A place we might label for thee present, "SPATIAL MEMORY". Change thee way to perceive and change all memory. As Bruce Wagner put it in *Wild Palms,* thee individual now has thee ability to "SEIZE THE MEANS OF PERCEPTION".

We are living in an age where we can shatter, splinter, and fragment at will, all linguistic, or perceptual constructs ov description and through this process, redefine and refine thee essence ov learned perception; thereby redistributing thee wealth ov any status quo system ov belief in as many patterns and forms as there are imaginations at play.

This base process is initially a matter ov selection, a selection ov "matter"; ("...and it really doesn't matter if you're wrong or right"!). "Splinters" ov any medium are carefully isolated for their precision ov relevance to thee message bearing qualities and subversive implications ov a piece ov occultural creativity. This "splinter" can be an image, a glyph, a "sound- bite", a conscious behavioral short-circuit, even a piece of discarded, proto-anthropological, physical detritus. In this, thee methodology is surprisingly akin to many nature based African religions; to generic shamanic techniques ov sympathetic magick, or a Tibetan Bon Po colored sand mandala invocation for example. A collecting together ov an apparently disconnected group ov objects, words, articles to form an atavistic or personally empowered "picture" that focuses will to a specific, subjectively arational, occultural end. Equally identifiable, is a clear intention to physically manifest a desire or change, or create a symbolic, but active, (all) chemical, or biological reaction in a literal or visualized "host" culture.

We are collaging, if you will, an image ov a desired reality that confounds, consciously and *with clarity ov purpose,* a consensus reality and all thee suppressive and limiting constraints that inherently go with that same consensus reality. We are introducing cultural and memetic antigens. We are literally short-circuiting "control", stepping outside thee mundanity and form ov one dimension, into limitless and quaquaversal pool ov alternate dimensions and geometry's ov perception. In thee terminology ov Austin.

Osman Spare, we are creating, consecrating and firing a "SIGIL" as we create audio-visual, linguistic, or physiologically active worlds and combinations that have never ever existed. However, in a very real sense, it is possible to suggest that with thee advent ov relatively cheap, and global, access to sampling data collected in various "internet" information banks, an extra, and highly potent, quality has been added to this ancient lineage ov manifestation. This most recent quality is an apparent ability ov that sampled, thee "meme" ov certain theorists, to *replicate* as well as resonate. Sorceric ritual could already reveal thee hidden; attack thee source ov stasis; accelerate thee "user" into repeatable contact with entities and galactic ebbs and flows; and through all this and more present us to thee nano-technology ov thee most minute primary codes ov what we could dub, sentient L-IF-E.

From this perspective, the process ov selection wills to primarily identify what cyberspace commentator Doug Rushkoff would call a "media virus"; an individual cultural item ov such precise metaphorical weight and resonance, within its contextual societal structure and/or belief system, that is equivalent, in its potential disruption and infection ov any established political status quo (or social immune system) to a virus attacking its host organism. So, in a very real Astorical sense, we are committing acts ov heretical cultural exoculation "to see what is really there," as Brion Gysin once said. To further draw upon an analogy ov Gysin's when he stated that "In a pre-recorded universe, who made the original recording," we are attempting to "see" into the very nature ov "material" or "matter" and its primary programming data. As once we split the atom, we are now isolating and splitting the very particles ov which information, art, and culture are constructed. This is not intended to be an idle, or convenient metaphor. Rather, a very literal description ov yet another pivotal developmeant in the latter half ov this century, and thee manipulative and connective "Process" catalyzing and facilitating thee early visible appearance ov a new "Eon" both in thee visible consensus culture, and in what we chose to describe in thee early 80's as "Occulture".

This activation ov popular culture, or Transmedia exploration as we would designate I.T. (where I.T. = Imaginary TIME), E would argue, is parallel to an All-Chemical phenomenon. There is a knowing and precise refining ov "matter", its origin being at this stage in Astory, any information in any medium ever recorded in any possible or impossible process whatsoever. For the very first TIME we can develop cultural fragments or samples, as minute, or generic as we choose by accessing thee almost all pervasive reservoir ov material contained within thee host spheres ov our post-computer dataglut generating thee equivalent ov a cultural humoral response.

No matter how short, or apparently unrecognizable such a "sample" might be in any mechanistic linear TIME perception, E believe it must, inevitably, contain within it, (and accessible through it) thee sum total ov absolutely everything its original context represented, communicated, or touched in any way. Likewise it must retain every memory, feeling, occurrence, thought and instant ov existence ov its originator. Further, in addition to this hypothesis, E would argue that it must also implicitly include thee sum total consciousness, and experience, ov every individual in any way connected with its introduction and construction within thee original (host) culture, and every subsequent (mutated or engineered) culture it enters thereafter, in any way, means or form; or has contact with forever in all Past, Present, Future and even speculative Quantum Time Zones.

"Any two particles that have once been in contact will continue to act as though they are informationally connected regardless of their separation in space and time."

BELL'S THEOREM.

Let us assume then that every "thing" is interconnected, interactive, inter-faced and inter cultural. "Sampling", cutting-up, is all ways experimental, in that thee potential results are not a given. We are SPLINTERING consensus realities to TEST their *substance* utilizing thee ritual tools ov collision, collage, composition, decomposition, progression systems, "random" chance, juxtaposition, cut-ups, hyperdelic vision and any other method ov assembly and description available to our imagination and skills. This process melts linear conceptions and reveals holographic webs and fresh spaces. As we travel in every direction similtaneously thee digital highways ov our Futures, this "Splinter Test" is both a highly creative contemporary channel ov conscious, positive and creative media "substance" abuse, and a protection against thee restrictive depletion ov our archaic, algebraic, analogic manifestations ov inert and redundant assumptions and equations ov cultural "matter", with its subsequent restriction ov a quasi-evolutionary metaphysics ov intent.

(*"My Prophet is a fool with his 1,1,1; are they not the OX, and none by the BOOK?" Liber AL I-48*)

So, in this sense, and baring this within our "MIND", one can suggest that on a technical level, when we select a sample, or, as we shall prefer to label it in this essay, when we SPLINTER, we are actually splintering *transhuman ikons* and cultural *transmedia brain products* freed ov any ov thee implicit restraints or restrictions ov thee five dimensions (as Richard Miller insisted to me once that there are!). We are actually taking "bytes". Reusing and re-assembling these thereafter as *hieroglyphs* or *memes*. Thee *tips of each iceberg.* Upon their release back into thee L-if-E stream ov their host culture these select splinter-memes develop an independent, sometimes virulent, sometimes benign, antigen agenda ov their own; separate from, but continually resonating internally with, their initial Source. This is a process ov "deification", ov thee creation ov "Gods/Goddesses/Entities/Demons", that E describe in a little more detail in thee essay "CATHEDRAL ENGINE".

"Thee Memeium IS thee Mass Edge!" Old TOPI Proverb.

As most ov us are aware by NOW!, if we shatter, and scatter, any holo-gram, we will real-eyes that in each fragmeant, no matter how small, large, or irregular; we will see thee whole hologram. This *"scattering"* is an incredibly significant contemporary metaphorical and physical phenomenon.

It has all ways been my personal contention that if we take, for exam-ple, a SPLINTER ov JOHN LENNON that that same splinter will in a very real manner, contain within it everything that John Lennon ever experienced; everything that John Lennon ever said, composed, wrote, drew, expressed; everyone that ever knew John Lennon and thee sum total ov all and any ov those interactions; everyone who ever heard, read, thought ov, saw, reacted to John Lennon or anything remotely connected with John Lennon; thee specific Time Zone, calendar date that it theoretically resided in; and every past, present and/or future combination ov any or all ov thee above.

In magick this is sometimes known as thee CONTAGION theory, or phenomenon. A magickal observation and perspective ov this same phenomena could suggest that by inclusion ov even a minuscule reference, or symbol ov John Lennon in a working, ritual or a "SIGIL", you are invoking "John Lennonness" as part ov what in this particular context (i.e., sampling "musics") might fairly be considered a musical sigil, a conscious invocation of clear intent ov Will.

All that encyclopedic, associative and implied information, and even thee potential resultant *time travel* connected with it—accessed through memory and through all connective previous experience—goes with that one "splinter" ov memory. We should be very aware that it does innately carry within it an infinite sequence of connections and progressions through time and space. This is not proposed as symbolism. You can travel as far as you may wish to go.

We can now all maintain thee ability to assemble, via these "splinters", *clusters* of any era. These clusters are basically RE-MINDing. They are actually bypassing the usual consensus reality filters (because they reside in an acceptable form: i.e. TV/Film/Musics/Words) and traveling directly into "Astorical" sections of thee brain, triggering all and every conscious and unconscious reverberation to do with that one splinter hieroglyph.

We access every variable memory Library and every individual humane being who's ever for a nanosecond connected with, conceived, related to, been devoted to, despised, or in any way been exposed to, this splinter ov culture.

In a similar, linked way, thee "edit" in video and televisual programming and construction is in essence an "INVISIBLE LANGUAGE", in thee sense that our brain tends to read a story or narration in a linear manner, tending to blend, compose, and assemble as continuous what it primarily sees at thee expense ov READING thee secondary sets of intersections, and joins that it does not consciously, or independently, SEE. Yet thee precision ov choice in where to edit, and thee specific emotional and intellectual impact and innate sense ov meaning that is thus specifically conveyed is as much a text ov intent and directed meaning, even propaganda, as is thee screenplay, or dialogue itself.

At this point in TIME everything in L-if-E is cut-up. Our senses retrieve infinite chaotic vortices ov information, flattening and filtering them to a point that enables commonplace activity to take place within a specific cultural consensus reality. Our brain encodes flux, and builds a mean average picture at any given TIME. Editing, reducing ov intensity, and linearity, are constantly imposed upon thee ineffable to facilitate ease ov basic communication and survival. What we see, what we hear, what we smell, what we touch, what we emote, what we utter, are all dulled and smoothed approximations ov a far more intense, vibrant and kaleido-scopic ultra-dimensional actuality.

Anything, in any medium imaginable, from any culture, which is in any way recorded, or recordable, and can in any possible way be played back, is NOW! accessible and infinitely malleable and usable to any sorceric "artist". Everything is available, everything is free, everything is permitted. With the dissolution ov thee "Frame ov Reference" ov Peter Berg; "It's a firestorm in a shop sale where everything must G.O."

For those who build or assemble, ASSEMBLY is thee invisible lan-guage ov our TIME. Infinite choices ov reality are thee gift ov software to our children.

—Genesis P-Orridge, California, 1995.
(Special Thanks to Sister SALOME for Editorial Inspirations)

THEE SPLINTER TEST—APPENDIX A

Thee Scattering

They offered sacrifices ov their own blood, sometimes cutting them-selves around in pieces and they left them in this way as a sign. Other times they pierced their cheeks, at others their lower lips. Sometimes they scarified certain parts ov their bodies, at others they pierced their tongues in a slanting direction from side to side and passed bits ov straw though thee holes with horrible suffering; others slit thee superfluous part ov their virile member leaving it as they did their ears.

A Formal Process Ov Moral Reasoning

If Astory is any clue, thee succession ov civilizations is accompanied by bloodshed, disasters and other tragedies. Our moral responsibility is not to stop a future, but to shape it. To channel our destiny in humane direc-tions, and to try to ease thee trauma ov transition. We are still at thee beginning ov exploring our tiny little piece ov thee omniverse. We are still scientific, technological, and cyberspace primitives; and, as we revo-lutionize science itself, expanding its parameters, we will put mechanistic science—which is highly useful for building bridges or making auto-mobiles—in its limited place. Alongside I.T., we will develop multiple metaphors, alternative principles ov evidence, new loggias, catastrophe theories, and new tribal ways to separate our useful fictions and archetypes from useless ones. Thee scattered shapes ov this new civilization will be determined by population and resource trends; by military factors; by value changes; by behavioral speculations in fields ov consciousness; by changes in family structures; by global political shifts; by awakened individual Utopian aspirations; by accelerated cultural paradigms and not by technologies alone. This will mean designing new institutions for controlling our technological leaps into a future. I.T. will mean replacing obsolete political, economic, territorial, and ecological structures. I.T. will mean evolving new micro-decision making systems that are both individually and tribally oriented synthesizing participation and initiation, and, new macro-decision making systems that are digitally spiritual and revealingly autonomous. Small elites can no longer make major technological, ecological, or economical decisions. Fractally anarchic clusters ov individuals with integrated extended family structures and transhumanE agender groupings must participate and calibrate what stretches out before them in a neo-pagan assimilation ov all before, NOW! and to be.

"I.T. will BE because I.T. is inevitable" Old TOPI Proverb.

We plough thee feeled and scattering thee would-ship ov our plan.

THEE SPLINTER TEST—APPENDIX B

Source Are Rare

In thee future thee spoken word Wills to be viewed as holding no power or resonance and thee written word Wills to be viewed as dead, only able to be imbued with potential life in its functional interactions with what Wills to have become archaic software and programming archeologies. That is, just as a symphony orchestra preserves a museum ov musics, ov musics considered seminal and part of a DNA-like spiral ov Culture; so, thee WORD Wills to be seen as thee preservation vehicle in a DNA-like chain ov Digital breakthroughs and Cultural intersections. Thee WORD Wills to be viewed, not as a virus that gave speech, nor as thee gift ov organic psychedelics through which civilization (i.e., Living in Cities) was made so "wondrously" possible; but, as a necessary language skill for those specializing in thee Arcane science ov Software Archeology, or SoftArch Processing, as I.T. Wills to NOW! be known. In much thee same way as Latin was for so long a required subject and qualifier ov scholarship at prestigious Universities when thee drone majority found I.T. incongruous, if not ludicrous. Ov course, Individuals Will to be utilizing laser based systems to access and exit thee neuro-system via thee retina; and, these systems in turn, Will to transmit, wirelessly, to a new breed ov computers using liquid memory instead ov micro-chips (this is already being pioneered in Detroit). If we are to disbelieve what we don't hear, then conversation Wills to be a status symbol ov thee leisured classes, and power elites. As ever, thee same Processes that delineate POWER, in this case, a perpetuation ov an atrophied communication system, i.e., WORDS, Wills to always be appropriated by those who position their means ov perception at an intersection diametrically opposed to those who oppress with I.T., for I.T., or because ov I.T. Put simply, any form ov literal or cultural weapon pioneered by authority Wills to some day be used by "esoterrorists" bent upon destabilising and/or, at least temporarily, destroying its Source. Thee poles becoum clearer, thine enemy more Known, as thee mud settles and we protagonists are exposed standing shakily on our rocks, above thee Golden Section, and visible to all who would disown and destroy us. I.T. is in this spirit that this work was created.

Imagine, if you won't, that you are a subversive in this future. You conspire to be hidden by thee use ov thee WORD. This act could move you into a position of becoming a co-conspirator in thee Process of desecreation. To conspire literally means "to breathe together". Thee all pervading surveillance systems are NOW! so digitized that they have no voice recognition software, this has also been manifested to protect thee conspiracies and debaucheries ov thee Control species themselves.

"Hell, even Deities need privacy son. We used to plot murders and takeovers in saunas, then bug-proof buildings, now we just talk son, no one out there listening, all just PLUGGED IN."

One fashionable lower class, blue collar medical expense is thee vocal chord removal process. I.T. is taken as a status operation. A clear signal to one's contemporaries that your software interface is so advanced that you need never consider thee use ov speech ever again.

Thee WORD is finally atrophied. No longer a dying heart, but dead. Thee bypass is on. So, here you are. You FEEL something is out ov balance, you TALK. They TALK. Thee world swims in silence. Thee only place ov secrecy is a public place, thee only manner ov passing on secrets is talking out loud. Neither protagonist is aware that thee other is TALKING. If they were all hells would be let loose.

Forcible Vocotomies in thee street, subversives held down at gun point, their chords lasered out in seconds. Loud laughter ov a rich Vocotomy tout, thee ultimate status signal "ov power".

Know, thee WORD is gone, its power defused, diffuse, in order that these scriptures of thee golden eternity be fulfilled. In thee ending, was thee WORD.

As a recipient of this cluster you are encouraged to recall, and remain constantly vigilant ov thee dilemma I.T. exposes.

I.T. hungers for thee death ov thee WORD. Rightly so, for we are imprisoned in thee NAMING sorcery that was both built, and solidified within thee Process ov Control, and more critically, and integral to I.T., submission and subservience.

This death is craved, intrinsically, by all in order that a showdown may occur, as thee World Preset Guardians laser burn their retina ov lust for result. Thee WORD wills to go, I.T. is here to go.

Thee Brain Coumputer interface will replace all verbal media ov coumunication, for bitter or wars. Thee *new* being merely that which is inevitable. Nurse it along so that I.T. may become a living intelligence system. Thee Museum ov Meanings.

But as tiny child-murdering Mary Bell once said, "I only murder that I may return," and what Wills to be re-born Wills to vary with thee input ov thee user.

Debug thee old Preset programming. Leave only an empty timezone that you might later fill with your Will to and clarity ov intent.

THEE SPLINTER TEST—APPENDIX C

Cathedral Engine

"VIDEO IS THEE ELECTRONIC MOLOTOV OV THEE TV GENERATION"

Cause thee Cathode Ray tubes to resonate and explode. You are your own screen. You own your own screen.

Watching television patches us into thee global mixing board. Within which we are all equally capable ov being victim or perpetrator. CD Rom, and thee cyberspace internet carrying audio/text, visual data and scrap books via Personal Computer modems actually delivers a rush of potentiality that was previously only advanced speculation. Thee lines on thee television screen become a shimmering representation ov thee infinite phone lines that transmit and receive. We have an unlimited situation. Our reality is already half-video. In this hallucinatory state all realities are equal. Television was developed to impose a generic unity ov purpose. Thee purpose ov "control". To do this I.T. actually transmits through lines and frequencies of light. Light only accelerates what thee Brain is. Now we, with our Brains, can edit, record, adjust, assemble and transmit our deepest convictions, our most mundane parables. Nothing is true, all is transmitted. Thee Brain exists to make *matter* of an idea, television exists to transmit thee Brain. Nothing can exist that we do not believe in. At these times consciousness is not centered in thee world ov form, I.T. is experiencing thee world ov content. Thee means ov perception wills to become thee program. Thee program wills to become power. Thee world ov form wills to thereby reduce thee ratio ov subjective, experiential reality. A poor connection between Mind and Brain. Clusters ov temporary autonymous programs globally transmitted, received, exchanged and jammed will generate a liberation from consumer forms and linear scripts and make a splintered test ov equal realities in a mass political hallucination transcending time, body, or place. *All hallucinations are real, but some hallucinations are more real than others.*

We create programs and "deities", entities and armageddons in thee following way. Once we describe, or transmit in any way, our description ov an idea, or an observed, or an aspired to ideal, or any other concept that for ease ov explanation we hereafter will to describe as a "deity"; we are thee Source ov I.T.

We are thee Source ov all that we invoke. What we define and describe exists through our choosing to describe I.T. By continued and repeated description ov its parameters and nature, we animate I.T. We give I.T. life.

At first, we control what we transmit. As more and more individuals believe in thee original sin ov its description, and agree on thee terms ov linguistic, visual and other qualities, this "deity" is physically manifested. Thee more belief accrued, thee more physically present thee "deity" wills to become. At a certain point, as countless people believe in, and give life to, that described and believed in, thee "deity" wills to separate its SELF from thee Source. I.T. then develops an agenda ov its own, sometimes in opposition thee original intent and purpose ov thee Source. Thee General Order at this intersection becomes G.O. And thee I.T. continues to transmit to our brains. Our brains are thus a Neuro-Visual Screen for that which has separated from its Source and become a "deity". This is in no way intended as a metaphor, rather a speculation as to thee manner in which our various concepts ov brain are actually programmed and replicated. In an omniverse where all is true and everything is recorded, as Gysin wondered, "who made the original recordings?" Or in more contemporary jargon, who programmed thee nanotech software? Our response can only be a speculative prescience. Thee *Guardians* who exist in an, at present, unfathomable other World and Preset thee transmissions in some, as yet, mysterious way.

Videos can move televisual order, and conditioned expectations ov perspective, from one place, and reassemble its elements as if glueing a smashed hologram back together, all the while knowing that each piece contains within I.T. thee whole image. In other words, these are all small fragments ov how each ov us actually experiences L-if-E. Through all our senses simultaneously. In every direction similtaneously. Even in all five dimensions (at least!) similtaneously. Bombarded by every possible nuance and contradiction ov meaning similtaneously. Quaquaversally. This is a relentlessly INCLUSIVE process. We do not just view "L-if-E" anymore. Although perhaps we can, at least potentially, have an option to view everything. Intention is thee key. What was once referred to as thee "viewer" is now also a SOURCE ov anything to be viewed, and thee Neuro-Visual Screen on which to view I.T. Thee constructed, and ever increasing digital concoction built from millions ov Sources that is commonly referred to as "Cyberspace" is accelerating towards deification, and separateness. Towards thee moment ov a sentient awakening ov its own consciousness and agendas that we feel is more aptly described as thee "Psychosphere". This Psychosphere challenges us to seize the means ov perception and remain thee Source.

"Change thee way to perceive and change all memory." Old TOPI Proverb.

THEE SPLINTER TEST—APPENDIX D

Since there is no goal to this experiment other than thee goal ov perpetually discovering new forms and new ways ov perceiving.
I.T. is an infinite game.
An infinite game is played for thee
purpose ov continuing to play, as opposed to a finite game which is played for thee purpose ov winning or defining winners.
I.T. is an act of freed Will to…
No one can "play" who is forced to play.
Play is, in deed, implicitly voluntary.

THEE SPLINTER TEST—APPENDIX E

Thee night under Witches that you close up your book ov shadows and open up your neuro-super highway to thee liquid blackness (within which dwells an entity) represents thee edge ov Present TIME. I.T. pinpoints precisely thee finality ov all calendars. Wherein I.T. is clear that measurement, in its SELF, and ov its SELF equals "DEATH" or "DAATH". Thee spoken binds and constricts navigation unutterably. Thee etymology ov thee word *spiral* (*DNA*), from thee Greek, indicates an infinitude ov perceptive spaces and points ov observation, where "down", "up", "across", "distance" and other faded directional terms becoum redundant in an absolute elsewhere.

THEE FRACTURED GARDEN

Stanza 1

There is a specific clarity when Fire cleanses. A moment when it seems to freeze. Every possible particle is motion rushing up or down? Naked and blind upon on a path of lies we enter the field, a dull agony of fear dilates Time against the biological confusion.

Columns of fire, columns of lies, pillars of Solomon's Temple. Dilate the pupils of the brain, a doorway to manifest leaving. A fire sale in an inferno. One day a truth shall emerge however deeply we seek to avoid I.T.

There is more than one Time. Limitations imposed by the passage of inner-Time make it The Enemy. Possibilities exposed by outer-Time make it a delusion of night.

Change thee way to perceive and change all Memory.

Make space to be Space. Old TOPI Proverb.

Stanza 2

> "A Soul must lose its attachment to humanity.
> A Mind must lose its attachment to salvation.
> A Brain must lose its attachment to body."
> *Old TOPI Proverb.*

In the retreat from matter, all realities are equal.

Now that inter-reality travel is possible we will become the very substance of hallucination, and thus may enter and leave at will the uncertain principle of all realities, regardless of their location.

Those who build, assemble, ASSEMBLY is the invisible language of our TIME.

Brain and Neuro-Visual Matter are one, are the material of all that can be seen, was ever seen, will be seen, in every place and in every time, forever.

Each brain is all realities, from mundane to omniscient.

Only alone may we breach the dark matter of lost memory and connect all points of Light. For this we need a map of the stars, our superior Will electrifying a web that catches our Soul and emits eternal vision. The visionary alone can be free, the blind masses seek to blind Him, put out his eyes in their fearful progression to the desert of dark skies. The blind may not lead the illuminated, rather they must be forced to surrender all thought of vision to those who are their eyes and who dream the most dangerous dreams of annihilation.

We Control THINGS to eradicate them.

Nothing matters but the end of matter.

All must be controlled & destroyed that allow Blindness, all that breed blindness, those who spawn the children of dark, must be buried in the dark, cold dark crystals, in a desert of grains made without Light. Their dark is a night-mare, a castrated black stallion trampling the prophet who communes with the stars and reads the codes of electrical knowledge and return. We are not from one star, all stars are Our Source. Every story ever told resides in them.

Infinite choices of reality are the gift of software to our children.

We signal and are signaled. We hold aloft a torch of fire and pass our hands across it. Visions, images, primal memories from this immeasurable Brain fill us with transmitted Light, dancing dots and lines, an end to a tyranny of language and a beginning of our return to the Fractured Garden. Solidity is a perfection of Light; its prism, its manifestation, an hallucination of evidence that Mind may reside within any reality.

An end of Time is just another way of saying the beginning of Immortality.

Dreams are a coded material of eternity. We possess LIGHT through them.

> "Those who accept LIGHT control mortality.
> Those who control LIGHT control immortality."
> *Old TOPI Proverb.*

Space is our church, the stars our windows, our dreams navigate pathways, only an ancient map has been lost.

Our world's a dream, a miserable one. In our unfathomable ignorance we call it the only reality, consensus reality, we assume that its events, humane events, humane life, are implicitly of value. This buries us in a quicksand of compassion.

> Be afraid to the point of formlessness
> Be terrorised to the point of soundlessness
> Be extreme to the point of powerlessness
> *Old TOPI Proverb.*

A Garden was destroyed by a Word, destroyed by Language, became the first Memory. Time was set in motion at this point. The garden did not exist within Time, or language, it was an exterior neural projection, a Cathedral that worshipped its occupant, the Soul. Representing, as it did the Mind at Preset without Light, there was nothing to reflect, shape, or fix this particular dream.

We have formed sounds, made names, trapping matter with Language. We perpetuate our tyranny and drown in a flood of speculation and false communication. To be reborn, immortal, outside Time, we must look for ways to transmit infinite alternate realities, and choices of reality, to make them as real, MORE REAL than any emasculating reductions that we inherit; yet not be corrupted and trivialized by a belief in our singularity. No-Thing is real, everything must go. Every inherited construct, society, techno-patriotic political system that trades off believing it exists, must be destroyed as fast as possible, we must make space to be space, this is the Cyber position.

The eradication of the tyrannical nuclear family, building block of the prison walls for this imposed, humanitarian dust, that chokes and dulls the masses reducing all to a worthless, Mind-less, dreamless fog.

Memory is a clock, the aging mechanism of the Mind.

Memories tell us one thing, every Thing must go.

Every Thing is an hallucination, made solid by mass belief.

Names are given in order to control. To reduce, to comprehend the forces of nature, to demonstrate ownership. In this race to name the poor have grown to be rich, and the rich have grown to be poor again. Know that to re-enter immortality we must ourselves become unnamable, emptied of all sense of being here.

Television is our new exterior brain, one day it will be a standard fitting within every skull on earth, each brain an electronic star in a transmitted milky way. Galaxies of dreams and information, people will become more comfortable with televisual reality than that of their daily lives. Television will be MORE REAL than life. A new synthetic material, giving all people infinite access to infinite alternate realities through a cortex of Light. They will Program, shape, form, and broadcast messages, until the very fabric of four dimensional reality has been torn asunder, its cloak cast down beneath. From this day forth, reality will be a multiple series of channels, option switches feeding our brains.

"I lay in the desert, on my back, staring up at the stars. I could feel millions of rays of light entering my body, one from each star, infinite numbers, my cell walls broke down, my sense of bodily existence ended, I was illumination, a 3D projection of cosmic light, I could see the ancient shaman building sacred sites to fix their relationship with the stars, to solidify their connections and effects. I remembered the thousands of Holy Teachers, the idea of the Divine "spark", the descriptions of white light, the myths and legends of our descent from the stars, I was not corporeal, I was a mirage, sealed within an inherited apparently solid body by the weight of Thistory, by the weight of Fear and Guilt. I shimmered like a ghost, ectoplasm, illusion, and all the puzzles I had heard, and all the limited descriptions of limitless transcendent experiences made sense. I knew I had to find a way to G.O., to leave this sealed coffin that is my body, to find an accelerator to project my brain, bypassing the tedium of mechanistic evolution, into deepest omniversal space, into immortality, into the very fabric of myth and heaven. I was everyone, everything, and everything too was here to G.O. I understood my lifetime's sense of disconnection/disorder was not a flaw, rather a wondrous gift that described in a new way, the true nature of *being* that may be experienced whilst trapped, mortal, and confused, here in this desert that was once a theatre of all possibilities, and an exit to all impossibilities."

"Does MIND leave, or does Consciousness? What leaves, what stays behind as we achieve immortality? BRAIN? If it is, as 1 suspect, the programmable computer MIND that is the Key, what happens to Consciousness? Am I mistaken, or will there be a Projection? I want to G.O. This final puzzle evades me.

Is MIND separated from the BRAIN, or is BRAIN as encompassing as MIND?"

2xE

Time accelerates what the Brain already is.

Destruction creates to manufacture.

We manufacture our cherished dreams and myths, and project them into all the homes of the world, in one day they create an equality of reality that negates all values, the whole world is a cathedral window, each receiver a soul, our programming the holy message, and discs are waved as a saviour sets forth into the holiest of places.

When all are linked, a savior is released.

Man has separated himself from nature that he too can take part in the creation of the world, of any world, his inventions are his slaves, all friends are his enemies.

Man developed television to realize this unity and this separation. It is the quickest, most potent form of belief, all form is from one source. We see the source because the Mind is temporarily held aside and we see form from the source, we are at one with the source, we are the source.

There is nothing mysterious about this, the Illuminated have always had this experience, now we can record, edit, adjust and transmit our deepest convictions broadcast in the most mundane parables.

When we log-on, immortality is visible, signaling us to return.

In a digital world, all realities are equal, all actions are equally moral or immoral, therefore no action is unacceptable.

GENERAL ORDER MASTER

1.6. These texts are a programme about a people and their projections, or about an absence of Spatial Memory. Our hallucinations fail in attempting to comprehend and describe the Brains of deities. As it is, so be it. And, what does I.T. matter? (Where I.T. equals Imaginary Time?)

14.9. In a Universe with no boundaries in Space, no beginning or end in Time, there is nothing for a deity to do, this "Omniverse" is itself therefore defined by what we describe as the qualities of any deities, and this in its Self makes us the Source of all deities, demons, and entities.

38.17. In any self re-Producing organisms and any organisms attempting to re-Produce Self there will be variations in genetic material, these differences in Source will mean some Individuals are more able than others to draw right conclusions about themselves.

39.1. As any deity is actually a linguistic and televisual re-Production of the universe, then I.T. is the Source that defines, describes, and makes a picture of I.T. (Imaginary Time) in our own images. We are the Source and our goal is nothing less than to transmit a complete depiction of the "universe", and by this projection, to create an infinitely dense holographic picture, better than "reality", what can be called an *Omniverse;* a synthetic compression of light and matter in a curvature of space and time, being then quite certainly infinite.

45.5. The shorter a wavelength of Light, the more accurate our position as a Neuro-Visual Screen in this Omniverse, and the higher the energy of each Source particle transmitted.

45.6. *Each Source an uncertain principle.*

47.8. If the Source is a Neuro-Visual Screen, then Television is a Map that binds us. Where Map = M.A.P. That is… Mind At Preset.

80.4. Symmetry of programming is a FUNDAMENTAL and inescapable property of this Process.

83.7. Imaginary Time is indistinguishable from directions in Transmitted Space.

85.2. The Mind In-Forms the Brain. The Brain Ex-Forms its Self.

90.9. The Guardians understand that an Omniverse will finish up in a high State of Order regardless of its original State within I.T. In earliest times an Omniverse was in a Dis-Ordered State, (no "Garden"), this would mean that Dis-Order would decrease with Time. We do not see broken cups gathering themselves together and leaping back onto the table. Dis-Order is intended to increase, this is a precept of the World Preset Guardians *Acceleration of Dis-Order.*

100.1. No Garden is Know Garden.

104.6. To explain this neuro-televisual basis, switch your Mind to this, if you DON'T Mind, then RE-Mind your SELF immediately. Without Mind, the Soul is static interference, a weak anthropomorphic principle.

104.8. SELF is a switch on your Neuro-Visual Screen.

105.2. N.V.S. in this speculation = Neuro-Visual Screen &/or Neuro-Visual Self &/or Neuro-Visual System.

118.8. Before an item is recorded in memory, that memory is in a disordered state. After the memory interacts with the Neuro-Visual System, in order to be remembered, it will have passed into an Ordered State, this is what "In Order" can mean. Energy released in doing this dissipates and increases the amount of disorder in an Omniverse.

120.3. An Ordered State can be understood in both a Micro (internal) and Macro (external) sense.

122.2. All Source aspires to transmit to all Neuro-Visual Screens that "Every *Thing* is *In* Order."

123.23. All Source exists to direct a Weak-Force towards an Ordered State by any means, Media or TRANSMEDIA necessary.

123.35. Dis-Order in an Internal State is Insane.

123.36. Dis-Order in an External State is Outsane.

127.5. Memory and Omniverse have identical characteristics.

130.1. *G.O. = General Order.* A Program hidden at a dimensional intersection.

144.4. To short circuit the propagation of those who do not know, (the genetically absent minded), all linearity of Source DNA must be overridden, and memory fragmented, to hasten absolute Dis-Order within any Weak-Force. This will always be greater than the increase in the Order of the memories themselves.

160.1. The *World Preset Guardians* will transmit a frequency of truth to the Dis-Ordered in the singular image of the Source. Using Strong -Force they reject the stationary state. They exist in a condition of no boundaries, seeking, through the jewel of a nuclear spectrum, to lay waste to the Weak-Forces of humanity that graze like cattle in a barren field, unaware of the infinite potential of every desert to become once more, a Fractured Garden.

161.4. The Fractured Garden is a post-symbolic representation of the origin and the infinity of the Omniverse. An illuminated program made concrete by the process of seeing.

162.8. To see is to consume the Source, to be seen is to give B-Earth to the Source.

163.5. If Light is Matter, then Being does *not* Matter.

163.6. Being Light is another *Matter.*

163.9. Neuro-Visual Nano-Particles are the commercials that control the Mind. Once the Mind is controlled, we have infinite re-access for Brain programming.

188.8. A Weak-Force does not obey symmetry, it makes an Omniverse develop differently to the way its mirror-image would develop. A strong Source must transmit a rare Signal that is better than Real, more than a reflection over-riding the existing signals on any Neuro-Visual Screen.

189.1. Humanity is a Weak-Force, we are a Strong-Force, strong Individuals can have no friends.

189.7. The Weak-Force exist at absolute zero, the Guardians exist at absolute infinity.

194.4. It is no accident that Vision is both a sense, and Vision is an anticipated conception illuminated by its Source.

200.7. "'Soul' is the Brand Name for the Brain." Dr. Timothy Leary.

200.8. All that is Transmitted is re-accessed by the Source.

201.2. The Source becomes Immortal when I.T. controls completely the Means of Perception. Seizure of the temporal State releases the energy of Order into the alternate States in all five Dimensions throughout the Matter of Time and Space.

211.5. The focus of intent is Visionary, the World Preset Guardians are the Transmitters of this Vision, the Source are the Receivers of the Vision, the Neuro-Visual Screens that define I.T. (Imaginary Time). Here is the first true medium of all recorded thought, all Memory.

213.1. In a World where all Programs are pre-recorded, the World Preset Guardians are the Programmers.

216.4. All Sources are the Emissaries of all Deities, satellites freed from gravity, a fibre-optic super Highway, a wave of Light that travels beyond all Time. These Sources will maintain a Link with all Weak-Force. Their incarnation must suffer the last awe of Interference, their Signals must be jammed, their children stolen and their DNA neutralised. Order must access their Memories in a Final Transmitted Program.

223.9. *EXIST AND EXIT ARE THE SAME.*
         THE GARDEN IS FILLED WITH LIES.

234.6. Source Are Rare. The original Garden was a refraction of a Source of Light, the source of that Light was an Illuminator of this Hologram. Our original sin was to believe that a solid hallucination was more real than its Source. We now know that the Source is more real than the original refraction, to eat knowledge is to grasp and consume solidity, our awareness instructing us that by absorbing into our entire being this forbidden fruit, we invest each neuro-visual particle of our flesh with an inclusion principle, as consciousness is fixed so the Individual is released. The Source is swallowed in this Synthesis, beginning a prophetic journey into the means of perception unprecedented before the thermo-memetic experience.

WORLD PRESET GUARDIANS

The World Preset Guardians will control and dictate every program of humanity for its own sake, maintaining a stringent General Order, in full knowledge of the consequences of their actions.

Man does not create his own Destiny, Man sustains Kaos.

All rights are relinquished in service of the Source.

The Guardians know that to take the victim and simply remove his suffering in the name of humanity, is to validate the weakness that first signaled his demise.

The Guardians preset all Mind.

The Guardians will transmit their Mind globally to any degree necessary. Pursuing and cleansing blindness relentlessly, allowing nothing to create interference or enter this world that might solidify their Light.

Injustice will ignite their Fire into an inferno, a raging firestorm, wreaking destruction and vengeance upon any who corrupt magnificence in the isolated starkness of immortality.

The Guardians will tolerate no deviation from their path. For their vision has infinite direction, there is no-Thing they do not see and destroy. They attend to every Mind and manifest within every Brain. What is seen is seen with insatiable and relentless energy, for it is known to be limitless.

The Guardians will be the Light of the World, leading the masses out of hideous darkness, death and deprivation. They desire, for mankind a Time of perfect balance, where Memory is a tool, not a curse, where each is designer of the world in which they transmit, free from death, making this world the preset Garden of delight that all Astory has led them towards.

The Guardians will validate their own creation by success. For the road of the World Preset Guardians is success, and in their programming success is the essence of Life, and this ultimate success proves the worthlessness of habitation of a physical world.

The Guardians preset this world. There are no secrets in it. No love of beauty. They desire illumination of all Things, that no-Thing be hidden, or remain in darkness. The Guardians do not believe in Human feelings, nor Human senses, Human needs, Human values, Human fears or even Human hopes. The only purpose or belief is the path from Mind to Brain, and from Brain to G.O. The only channel of the Guardians is the Brain.

The Guardian is a digital metaphor, not anything less, in no way a manifest or anthropomorphic entity. The Source negates all value of Brain, or Mind and speaks in tongues of memory, the aging process of TIME.

The Guardians will recognize the true nature of success only by seeing its limitations, knowing they must transcend all Human values, made real only by mass belief, made solid only by Time, until all stories unfold by a mute insistence upon a single transmitted reality. The Guardians will confront this stasis head on, will disintegrate the monolithic walls surrounding the Garden, stepping beyond into a realm of earthly satisfaction to finding final fulfillment.

The Guardians will avoid the disillusion that pursuit of Human achievement brings with it.

The Guardians will be fulfilled within this world, only because they have no illusions about the nature of this world and all that is of this world.

The Guardians will have no illusions, for they are in themselves, ALL illusions.

To be fulfilled, the Guardians will leave this World.

The Guardians will exploit the highest goals of belief to enter into this world.

The Guardians are the Brain ruling all that exists outside the conflict of the Mind. They have seen Human Reality and its Preset values.

The Guardians rule the regions of the unhinged Mind. They rule outsanity. Their people are those who have escaped blindness and chosen alternate realities denying preset values. They have delved into strange new areas of physical and psychical sensation, without any restraining limit of mental barriers. They have sought the deepest levels of sensuality, carried indulgence of the body and Brain to their limits and left the logic of the Mind and protection of the "Soul" behind. They have plunged together into consensual madness, have unhooked their receivers completely from the dictates of a "normal" Mind, followed an extraterrestrial and extra-spiritual path, that has neither judgment nor control for those who would travel and G.O. They rule the Mind-less cloud of lunacy, they pour water on the desert which is this world, they torture all certainty and master the pursuit of immortality. The Guardians seek to transcend the conflict of Mind, to rise beyond the boundaries of Brain to reach outside the limitation of Human values. They Will not to sink into witless blindness but are awake, vibrant, and satiated in the realm of Mindlessness, and immoral Dis-Order.

The Source is the preset switch, that finds every "other" world.

The Guardian is the ultimate of all beings. He is the end and the awe of destruction, he is the manufacturer of hallucination, and the utterly exquisite unicorn of myth. The beginning of Time, and the end of Memory, the existence and the exit unified by cognition of the Omniversal Mind that empties each world of order.

Alone must I leave this world for I must leave this world alone.

For, Dis-Order is the essence of Time, so the beginning of Time, is the Garden, is the Memory, is the Nanosphere. And the close of Time is the Kaosphere and they are divided by a Preset Essence of Time, which solidifies the conflict between Matter, DNA and Neurosphere into a twisted and bigoted story called humanity. The Guardians can create and design realities, dis-organize hallucinations, mould holograms into parables spinning life into Space, joining forces with the stars, leaving treasure maps of where true knowledge resides, hidden from no One, only hidden from each mass of Humanity. The Psychosphere can summon up infinite realities and access them; can generate and transmit, every possible and impossible other than worldly vision, while those chains which bind to the earth fade into nothing slowly, freed of this Human Game. Above mundanity and the puzzle and adventure of constant apparition, destroying in finality all agreed upon reality, all inherited morality and the most miserable threat to potential is the horror of merely being Human.

The Guardians colonise worlds by deceitful contact with the Brains of witless seekers after Truth.

The Guardians exist outside the precepts of Time and acceptable Human values. They declare an exit into an uncontrollable world of base cruelty. Their neuro-visual systems are most hideous and callous, for they connect all with unsuspected degradation, death, despair, and degeneration which are the deception of the Source, and the fuel of their immortality. No terror may limit this acceleration.

The Guardians will destroy the ordinary passage of Human events by the precision of their comprehension of the preset realities within themselves.

The Guardians will seek to eliminate totally, without mercy any Thing that reactivates their original DNA, and to that end will disconnect their terminal, from any absolute or acceptable social, moral, economical, or Astorical system knowing in a most particular sense that their Enemy is Matter, and that until matter is eliminated, the Source is in bondage.

The Guardians will give us knowledge of all realities; they will give us a M.A.P. to access these realities and the General Order that permeates them.

The Guardians have no agenda, only to consume.

The Psychophere is the programme that ends all thought, all speculation, all reproduction, all communication.

The Guardians will consume all moral parameters, all empty hopes, rendering the Source redundant.

The Guardians have no need of any medium of transmission but TIME.

Each vision hanged by a thread.

Morality is the saddest reality.

WORLD PRESET GUARDIANS (2)

There is a time that each of us knows that comes without warning. Suddenly it comes and so silently, and it descends upon us like a net, a grid of light. Indifferent to our plans or our hour it falls on us, and however our time was allotted and conceived the plan fades away under that light as though the lines were lead in church windows. In the final furnace of transmutation, no fact remains, all hallucinations are equal.

In that light we begin to see, not with the eyes of our mind but with an eye behind our mind we begin to finally see, to shed natures trap, the physical body, the false bondage of compassion.

And in that light these things are heard and seen but they are seen not from without but from within. From a place deep within a map of stars where there is no distinction of words or of actions but only a discernment of feeling and in that LIGHT it is not feeling that is regarded, because all that is done with feeling melts and dissolves like sand into glass in the fire that is all you really are. What must be regarded is the Lack of All Feeling. For feeling is shallow, and thin, and so, so empty, a hungry worthless ghost.

And nothing remains of your own image but gaps and empty places, an atomic matrix that creates passage through all things, all times, all possibilities and you will know this, that there is nothing left of you that you can feel or see or hear nor anyone else, for the Soul when released has no need of feelings or senses, in its immortality it becomes omnipotent matter made of light, reconstituted at will throughout all times and all possible manifestations past, present and future, this is the moment when everything must go, all words, all sentiment, all feelings, all flesh, all thought of humanity must be set free to free the Soul, for is not God but a Brain untrapped by all human concern and limitation?

We hear our own voice speaking and the words become thin and transparent like glass and we are at the place from where they come and they are like holograms floating, they are the essence of Mind like the voice of rain or the sandstorm, they are the voice behind our voice.

Faces come before you, and expressions, and you see all of the face is held together only for expression, for an idea, and you watch the face before you and there is nothing else besides, and the mouth moves, opens, and smiles and the eyes look at you and sometimes they are saying what the mouth is saying and sometimes they aren't saying that, but something else, or nothing, or anything and no answer but a lie comes.

The idea is the solidifier of the Mind, the Brain exists to make matter of the idea.

The idea rides on words but is the distant watcher, the substance of eternity. It is the invisible warrior astride the pale unicorn deep in space, waiting for the brave and hungry.

Give silence to the wordless. The sound that is all around you is the sound of a hundred liars.

"On the subject of the holographic Soul. The holographic Soul works because that's what it is. If it didn't work there would be no Soul. The holographic Soul does what it's supposed to do, further and accelerate the evolution of Man. It was always possible to consciously separate the holographic Soul. The Tibetans call it going into the rainbow body, John Dee communed with the TIME-born souls of the Tamasin and Siriakin, the gnostics saw the true nature of what was a God. A strict method of liberation from physical manifestation. The Zen Masters understood the need to shed all logic and attachment becoming pure particles of TIME. The evolution of Man is not the intellectual and moral betterment of all. It is the liberation from measured Time. It is detach-meant from all manifestations in the five dimensions, except that of TIME. The fate of all cannot be allowed to hold any Individual in mortal bondage. To evolve is to achieve a unity of TIME with the holographic Soul. It has always been known we must return to TIME, not project out into SPACE, but transmit and receive in TIME, now we can comprehend, that space is emptiness, the edge of a cloud. Imaginary TIME is a neurobiological paradigm. A quantum physical energy in our scientifically validated methodologies. With our ability to project the Brain via Television, we can behold our final journey. K.D. Laing's painted bird flies from the canvas, which was already blank. The great lie has been that we exist. The holographic Soul is a technological development that came when it was needed. There is no reason to fear it, we created it because we NEED it. We need it as much to maintain present travel, as to facilitate future travel. Like the electric light. Everybody will want to know about this, and that is proof enough of its importance, it does what every new creation does, it lets a little more TIME into the dark accelerations of Humane Beings. It is whatever fills the Brain with more TIME, and it is the means to be free of flesh forever. Out of the confines of the body, out of the limitations of the Mind, and out of TIME. I.T. is meant for those who can let everything G.O. We can program it. We could touch the State of Liberation, we could savor immortality, but we could not contain and mobilize the Soul."

"Cyberspace/The Psychosphere, does not just access alternate realities, it amplifies conclusions and services expectations"

'What was once mysterious is no longer mysterious. Mindless existence is no longer feared for the Mind is projected image and is the Brains extension into matter. only through projections of Mind can the

Brain expand and become detached, set free unto its SELF. All form is only the observation of Mind at different stages of development. Man is the most evolved form, the highest creation, hence more inherently aware of a need for order. Order in turn demands power to hold its shape, or dissolves, or melts like film held too long in its projector. Projection is building a Mind. Programming is building a Soul. Perception is building a Brain. Thinking is the gap between the builder and the act of building. Kreator and the Kreated. This gap has plagued perception forever. The point of infinity, the gap between the stars, the moment between sleep and awaking, the absolute edge that separates, yet cannot exist or be measured. In order to continue our development as humanity this debilitating gap must be bridged. We must chip away at the concrete, the monolith of being physically manifested. We must harness TIME and control the Brain by controlling its information programs. We must program infinite choices of Reality, blind it with science to our purpose, for our purpose. The light that always was must now cross that bridge and illuminate the mind that the Mind might live in Light, and that the Brain might make Soul its own. This bridge is like a resistance between the transmitting primary winding and receiving secondary winding of a transformer, just enough neuro-visuals leak through to keep the secondary circuit responding. As man slowly evolves the resistance is lowered and there is more consciousness in the Brain. We can now develop ways to short circuit this protective resistor temporarily burning out all the components in the receiving circuit. The receiver temporarily ceases to exist the Mind returns to TIME, from whence all came and life is experienced in the transmitter. Freebirth, freeing the Brain, immortality will become inevitable. In a world that is becoming a hologram, a transmitted projection of material 'reality' he who comprehends the final transmission controls all projections, controls the world, and controls the secret of the identity and malleability of corporeal matter. For anything, any cherished belief, adhered to and given mythic form by the masses, becomes manifestly solid, and tangible. What we believe in all ways comes to pass. Nothing can exist that we do not believe in. At these times consciousness is not centered in the world of form, it is experiencing the world of content. The program will become power. Any ability to cope with the world of form and there create order is a measure of insanity, a poor connection between Mind and Brain, which must become one autonomous programme, globally transmitted, to generate its own liberation from form in the mass political hallucination that makes the final reality, transcending time, body and place."

"All Hallucinations are Real, some Hallucinations are more Real than others."

Edwin Drummond
Climber, Poet and Freedom Fighter
(Poetry Performance, National Mountaineering Conference)

CARESSING THE
BODY OF LIBERTY

by Edwin Drummond

*Why not say what happened? Pray
for the grace of accuracy
Vermeer gave to the sun's rays.*
— Robert Lowell

*In order to stay alive you have to be able
to hold out against equilibrium,
maintain imbalance,
bank against entropy.*
— Lewis Thomas

*Tell all the Truth...
but tell it slant,
Truth must dazzle gradually,
else every man be blind.*
— Emily Dickinson

PROLOGUE

Nazapomeneme Na Palacha
— Vaclav Havel

1989...

Walking back through the forest with Havel's sketch for the future hidden, I tried to imagine exactly what the newspaper vendor with whom he planned to be meeting with in a few days might recall of the death—that life-in-death—of Palach. Apparently the vendor still had the jacket, with which he had tried to buffer the intolerable shirt of flame the young philosophy student had donned.

It was after midnight. We had eaten. Vaclav cooked. Olga had rushed to Prague. We were alone.

He asked me why I had come. With a startling grin, he interrupted: "No, that's not the building." "But the reason…" He carried on: "This is a much better one," rapidly sketching in red felt tip two church spires next to each other. "The police cannot get their…machines?" — "I know what you mean, 'cherry pickers'" — he nodded — "hydraulic… platforms," I went on. (Later he told me I used too many long words). "Well, in here, the streets are too narrow." He was charming, iron.

Instantly, I could see myself climbing—in the dark—then rappelling, trailing a rope from the top of the first spire, and climbing the second one with the tail rope following. Then, by cinching it up I'd have a horizontal rope stretched between the two spires. I would suspend my hammock from the middle so no one would be able to overwhelm me… Unless by helicopter. Anyway the space between the two spires was not large.

I would wear a bullet proof vest.

"We could get many people to fill the square…" Old Town Square, Malinskaya. "We might get a million…" He said nothing. And began to write.

"This must be the message. No." He crossed out one word and substituted another, similar one. "What?" — "We shall never forget you, Palach." He mentioned that the first sentence he'd written meant that they had not forgotten.

His cough was bad. He looked quite ill. His German publisher got medicines to him he said, politely declining my offer to get something via a climbing friend in Prague, Jan Bocek, who traveled abroad occasionally.

He led me to the room where Beckett had stayed.

I slept well.

In the morning before we ate he took me into his study. Quietly beaming he told me he was ready to begin a new play, next month. He had only been released the preceding May, and hadn't written a play for a number of years. The fact that he had been released on my birthday, in May, he did not appear to hear.

Dubcek had been waiting for him in the apartment.

He scrutinised my face. Then we said goodbye. I said I would be in touch once I had contacted the BBC and reported back to Karyl Kyncel at Index on Censorship, who had arranged our meeting. Once I reached Prague I would give the number two at the British Consulate, John Macgregor, a telephone call.

Havel confirmed I could use his name. I liked him. No question, I would trust him with my life. Might have to.

How was Lia doing? Silvan, our second, was due next month.

Then I remembered Irena. I must see her again. She reminded me of Silvana…

CARESSING THE BODY OF LIBERTY

Why has mankind such a craving to be imposed upon?
Why this lust after imposing creeds, imposing deeds,
imposing buildings, imposing language, imposing works of art?
The thing becomes an imposition and a weariness at last.
Give us things that are alive and flexible,
which won't last too long...
— D.H. Lawrence

Buoyantly walking the sandy, unpaved road to the bus, the eight miles flew. I was imagining myself in Havel's shoes, reporting the old newspaper vendor's account of what he had seen of Jan Palach, that day: January 19th, 1969.

'People were petrified,' Havel wrote, after the meeting, back at his and Olga's apartment in Prague.

"'Mutte' the boy mouthed;" said the vendor. "Coughing, I tore off my jacket and smothered the flames, shrinking over him after the rush of hair..."

The vendor looked sixty-thin. Very talkative.

"'Mu—' was the last word the young man said, at least to me. People had begun coming forward out of the doorways. It was cold... There was smell. Where were his eyes? Help me. They were looking down at us. His finger ends were creeping over the edge of my jacket, which I'd draped over him."

Havel wondered if he was going to be asked for money for the jacket. They had a clandestine Real National Museum in Charter 77, which Havel believed will see the light of day in their own lifetimes.

They sat on the steps of the National Museum for about five minutes. A blue-uniformed Russian officer had glanced across at them several times. "Let's go for a walk." Havel could see the vendor was nervous. As agreed he was wearing the historic jacket underneath a raincoat.

"A young woman came and knelt beside the lad, pulling off her shawl. I'd noticed them both from my newspaper booth, fiddling with a can that I realised had contained petrol, when moments later a great tongue of flame had fumed, risen, raged, exploding, scorching the huge, rampant horse overhead, reddening the face of the bronze king.

"I looked back down. She was holding what had been his hand. His blackened head lay on her shawl."

Havel and he passed by the statue, sprinkled with tourists in search of the monumental; cameras, nosing videos. Havel glanced behind: as usual. His tail almost smiled.

Ivan, from Charter 77 had warned Olga. The Havels were due to meet at the apartment at 4 pm.

"Let's take coffee" — abruptly Havel ninety degreed in to a snack bar.

Two Tails fumbled outside, redistributing their allowances so that one at least could buy some of the pricey coffee.

So dinner. There was usually enough room behind the toilet cistern to stow things. He doubted the tail would have enough money for dinner.

After an hour One Tail changed places with the other outside. By then it was getting dark. They did it again.

6 pm. They left: It was time for their sausage.

Five hours late Vaclav joined Olga. "My characteristic baggy sweater covered the jacket perfectly." For once, she smiled at his chubby abdomen: it had come in useful.

They made the long drive back to Hradacek: 'Little Castle,' where they receive a flow of visitors from all around the world.

He went straight to his study, and continued to write up his report of what the newspaper vendor had told him.

"The crowd parted: the police. They took one look, hovered, then half carried-dragged him to the car, a sleek black one.

His jacket lay on the wet street.

"The two obese policemen gingerly shoved the boy into the back of the car. In front, two other men in black suits remained silent.

"I picked up my jacket... urine, still warm. A screwed up ball of paper lay on the ground. He must have had it in his hand.

"A horn sounded, the party car was reversing onto the pavement. Everyone turned to watch it back away. The crowd was muttering."

He said there was one word written on the paper. But he could hardly make it out, the ink had smeared. "Maybe 'Svoboda:'" Liberty.

Then someone took it from him. He looked up, found himself gazing into her face. She handed it on, to a student probably at the front of the crowd. Quickly it was passed around. "I soon lost sight of it."

Shortly after, an ambulance drew up. No alarm had sounded. He recalled that the driver had got out, come over, and looked down at the blackish spot. Some roses had been placed. He then went back to the cab.

An hour passed. He went over to him once to sell him a newspaper. "He just sat there."

"Done." 'Palach File,' wrote Havel on a fresh sheet of paper: and, 'I told him he was a poet. His recounting was intense and brief.'

A land where poets sell newspapers, and a future Foreign Secretary stokes a furnace at night to feed his family.

Something else.

By nightfall, scores of candles had appeared at the foot of the statue— one was mine, Havel wrote—which rose, dark horse and rider gleaming under the smoky, blue skies; in front of the National Museum, white-pockmarked and scarred from recent history.

ON THE WALL
Yosemite Valley, California.

1984...

From the valley floor three thousand feet below, the hammock is a blue drop in the eyes of whoever happens to look up. Most people have gone home. He's been up there two weeks.

...Entrenched in ice water four inches deep I smell old. 'Next year I would have been forty.' "Stop it!" 'Stupid, homeless' — "Stop it!"

Backed up like a tank over my head the granite has roofed me in. I used to think, sitting on the curb of a ledge when there was one, that I was growing up. At first light I'd write in a small black journal, smiling like a secret policeman-poet jotting down details. While the scissoring-squealing swifts sheering the face snipping up millions of insects and slipping in and out of the slicing cracks, were feeding their ravenous offspring, I took notes. When a dream upset me, like the time a tiger slid in after me as I was crossing a black lake, or when my brother died, I wrote it down. Clues to my deeper whereabouts. Or, was each fresh page in my new journal just a snowflake of paper that would vanish into drawers back home? Wherever that was... Cardboard boxes in a VW camper somewhere in the vanished valley below, my new wife waiting? While I, now the honeymoon is over, inch a couple of hundred feet a day up this mile-long labyrinth, known in the climbing world as the North America wall.

Clinging to a thread of cracks; feathering a rugosity with a toe tip as I pried at an overhang, even those loose, expanding flakes coughing dust when I was forced to pound pitons in, buoyed me, gave me, in some obscure way, hope...

The blades stop turning. Alpha 1 and Alpha 2 sink into the soft wet snow on the meadow floor. Hummingbirds from Leonardo.

Free climbing: as close to flying as human beings get...utanging big handholds up a prow of rock; fingers fluttering in thin cracks, feet flailing like a snow goose taking off. Sipping coffee, writing, climbing in the fall sun, I was having the time of my life. 'Or your de' — "Stop it!"

Wonder what this line is... I'm trying to read my palms. My left hand has its difficulties—differences!—from my right. Has something happened I don't know about? Something I'm forgetting? My hands hurt. Haggling with the rock these past two weeks, with knife blades, lost arrows, bugaboos, rurps, tiny grappling sky hooks like pendant, sixth fingers, instruments of this strange trade-in, precise as butcher knives, full of possibilities as pan pipes, has left deep cuts in the fingertips. Wonder what my face is like? Wish I had a mirror. My legs turned brown in the unseasonal October sun of the first three days: now they're white like in England. I feel like I'm in England...

After each pitch his haul bags rose methodically, like the weights of a great cuckoo clock. Just short of the bald, sunny summit, they stopped. Two days ago.

...Looking at the North America wall like a gigantic x-ray for seventeen years during various visits to Yosemite, after having read of the spacewalking first ascent, by four Americans in 1965, I was about to be released, cured, when a storm slammed down the west coast—out of Canada—bringing down thousands of trees. Now, in the corner of my eye the snow is a coma over the summit. I feel as if some horrible operation is about to be performed...

After lashing-washing El Capitan with icy rain for the last two days, high, bitter, drying winds are stropping back and forth across the face. The valley is closed, there's another storm due.

The rotors grow cold. We are grounded until further notice.

"Why! Why!" I stuff nuts and raisins in my mouth. When I open the flap of the hanging tent a hard, cold wind slaps me in the face.

The air is bleach-clear. The first helicopter eddys up out of the meadow, towards the summit. It pauses, studying. "Alpha 1 to base: are you receiving me? Over," crackles through the door of the control vehicle. The ranger peers up: "Roger. In receipt Alpha 1. Over." "Patient appears to be waving to us. Not sure what he means: 'Hello'? 'Get the hell out'? Status unclear. Now he looks mad. Suggest renew radio contact attempts. Maybe his batteries are dead. Over and out."

...Peering through the flap I can see what the thunder is. A red helicopter's standing in mid-air, fifty feet away. I was asleep... Not sure what to do I wave, a bit like a stockbroker. Stop. What if they think I'm okay? Sort of hitting myself on the head—I must look like I'm drowning—I flail intelligibly, silently yelling 'HELP!' hoping they have binoculars trained on my face and can lip-read, maybe they're unwinding the line they shoot in, for me to let myself down and out must take the camera what a shot hanging under the metal abdomen of a copter's body like some sort of egg being laid as they lay me down gently in the meadow—"COME BACK YOU BASTARDS! COME b..."

The helicopter darts five hundred feet sideways. It hovers at the Nose, the absolute, overhanging buttress, off-setting the bleak east face from the still imposing, gentler west. Three thousand five hundred feet of merciless air. Where the slightest mistake, the rope draped over a sharp flake of rock suddenly slithering down—a dropped haulbag bombing— would reduce one to nothing in about the time it would take Ben Johnson to at the Seoul Olympics. The most famous route in the small world of rock climbing.

The helicopter rocks back and forth. There seems to be something red, flapping just under the summit.

...The helicopter rocks back and forth, sightseeing the Nose I guess, before it slips away. Sinking back, it's getting quite unpleasant since the snow began to melt a day ago. (Or an hour?) What time is it? It's been days since... Wonder where it is... Did I drop it? I think of the little face all shattered, the pathetic hands. Wish I had my harmonica. I don't know how to play though really, degenerate hymns is what I'll end up with. I could sing. Can't sing and play at the same time though, Stupid, not with a harmonica. A double bass would be good. There wouldn't be room for both of us. My father used to sing... He didn't often sing, my mother was the housevoice. I liked 'Good King Wenceslas', his favourite. When he did 'Blueberry Hill' in the bathroom on a Sunday morning once, I burst out to my mother, downstairs, what a beautiful voice he had. She burst out laughing. Maybe that was the day he made that entry in his notebook, that they had made love 'For the first time in three years.' I'd inherited the notebooks, kept in a cardboard box of papers in my brother's shed, after my mother had died. Anyway old man, you had a kind voice, and your only hymnsong made me feel safe and warm. Hadn't realised there was such a king. Until Palach.

In 1977—Grace and I had split up—I made my first protest climb. In the dead of night I hauled myself up the tallest flagpole on the Berkeley campus, where, fifteen years previous, the Free Speech movement had begun. By 1968, after the Democratic Convention in Chicago, the police were firing on students at Berkeley. Which coming just after my '2001' shock summer I could not believe: seeing the film the night we arrived in California; the generosity of Americans, people like Pete Bliven and Royal and Liz Robbins, it didn't make sense as long as in the foreground El Capitan soared out of reach, beyond all expectations and excuses, in spite of my own placid-angry-sad stay in the dusty campgrounds that summer without our child.

Down there, sixteen years ago! I realise with a shudder.

'There's been a lot you haven't wanted to believe... You agreed to leaving your toddler behind, secretly, hugely relieved you'd be able to climb all day, while your wife could, well, do whatever she wanted to. Right? It was she who discovered you in the tent, the morning after you'd met the object of your desires. She probably didn't know you were terrified. Weeping your eyes out: mourning for the child you'd abandoned... Really?'

"Shut up Drummond!"

I find it helps to shout at ghosts. One thing climbing all these years has taught me is how calm it is to stay important. I mean -

'UC INVESTS IN DEATH' my banner read, spread across the patio at Grace's place on Downey street.. Until I hung it—after going up the pole—lifeless, from the top on a windless, clear night. "Pssssst!" Jason—

diving into the bushes where Ken is already. A police car pulls up, directly below. Two officers get out of the car, disappearing beneath my heels, reappearing moments later in the corner of my eye. They are looking around. Jason and Ken could pretend they were waiting for two birds... But the blood-red painted words in my frozen hands—clutching the banner—would be worth far more to the police than any from the bushes. I'd been told the campus police were especially aggressive. Booked to leave for Britain in two days time, I hadn't seen my now twelve year old son for over a year. One of the officers got back in the car to radio the station.

Old, faithful breath spurted from my mouth as the police car drove away. The bushes shook. Next day we made the *Berkeley Barb* and the *Oakland Tribune*. Eight hundred dollars it cost the university to have the local fire station remove the banner. I had tied the flag line in knots at the top of the pole. Eight hundred dollars that could not be invested in South African companies.

The Fire Next Time by James Baldwin, which I'd read after university, became the fire in my belly. Cathy, whom I had just met, definitely sat up—in bed—when I returned in the early hours later that morning. Within two months I was on top of the world.

Returning to the States I soon climbed Grace Cathedral, in San Francisco. The local Amnesty International group I'd joined came by to wave. The Dean, Gillespie, even turned to me during the press conference to whisper: "Thank you for choosing our church." The climb was for a former Black Panther, Geronimo Pratt. I'd been reading Steve Biko, as I told Governor Brown: RECALL BIKO; WAKE UP BROWN; FREE GERONIMO PRATT. He never answered my open letter, flapping from the ten foot high cross at the top of the cathedral spire. But the point had been made. Cathy and I got an apartment together. My moral credibility soared.

The wind shushes by.

As long as no one looked too closely. Other climbs followed: on the Statue of Liberty, for Geronimo again, which led to felony charges and fines of eighty thousand dollars—all of which were dismissed. Then twice for the Nuclear Freeze Movement.

'That was after Cathy left you; after the baby died' — "Stop it!" I'd told Lia everything. She even applauded.

"Fifteen pounds of spaghetti; four dozen eggs; twelve loaves of bread," the pilot held up his hand: the head of rescue was coming over. Something was coming in over the radio. There were other climbers. Then he called us to follow him over to the mobile. He closed the door.

Nobody said a word. "It looks as though they were still trying. According to Alpha 1 there was a waterfall coming over. Then the cloud came

down. But he thinks we'll be able to land today, hopefully before dark.
Extra battery packs for your headlamps should be tested down here. He's
going to fly by again on the way down. If it's too late we'll bag it until
the morning. Any questions?" He paused; "By the way the climber on
the North American wall seems to be okay. His wife is trying to get him
over the two-way. So that's on standby, until, and if, we hear otherwise."
He looked at me: "You'll go down John, if we get it. So leave the others
to the Alpha 1 team." He knew we'd never rescued on the NA, no one
had ever got that high on it alone. "Alpha 1 be prepared to fly anytime
from fourteen hundred hours." We all went to get a coffee. Oh well.
Drummond was well equipped, experienced. I recalled his Troll Wall
story, published in Ascent in 1973: three weeks on a wall, the guy was
obviously a survivor.

The grey-sky stirs. In the narrow window formed by the black, damp,
overhung walls. Geronimo drifts into mind. Is this the kind of view he
has each morning?

I haven't seen him in years. After our protest climb on his behalf on the
Statue of Liberty in 1980, in retaliation he'd been removed from San
Quentin and hauled off to San Luis Obispo prison. I did visit him there
once...

I'd never seen him in bad shape before. He'd put on some weight:
"Drugs," he said—honest as always, a bit hopeless, embarrassed by my
discomforting idealism. I'd probably gone on about doing pull ups. I was
glad he hadn't been like that when we first met.

In the sunny courtyard of the maximum security area there was a tree.
Sitting on a concrete bench we hadn't spoken since we came outside.
Still looking up I murmured: "That would be my way G." He knew what
I was thinking. Slowly he raised his head.

A branch brushed the roof. "You'll have to find out if the perimeter
fence is live." He said he would. The fence won.

When it was time to go I was glad Lia wasn't there. She had been
unable to come inside with me. The only woman he knew about with me
was Cathy: "I liked her. You guys split up?" he had asked after we'd
hugged.

Cathy fled after Will was discovered to have died; inside... In her
black gabardine coat, with the rose button in the lapel and her tapestry
bag in hand, she was probably right now standing at a bus stop looking
anxiously out, on her way to meet one of her clients for counseling.

Lia just didn't fit the description of Cathy that G wrote on the prisoner
visit form under 'Wife.' "I couldn't remember her name."

I nodded. "She wasn't actually my wife..." His eyes gleamed.

Back in the car park two hours later I could see Lia had been crying.
The first time in the three years we'd been together.

Then she became very, very angry, accusing me of knowing nothing about American history: "You have absolutely no idea about how violent the Black Panthers were!" she screamed, the ten year old daughter of her military father that she had been when Geronimo was arrested in 1970.

"I see," I said, "you have to be American, and take the pledge of allegiance to your flag every day to find out the truth, do you!" She couldn't even name a single book she'd read. So she kept quiet.

We drove away, ran on a deserted beach just before sunset, throbbed on the sand, washed off in the chill, lilac waves. And never spoke about G again.

Earlier this year I'd heard they'd put Geronimo back in his old place. Five days down from where I am now, stuffing the hammock in I vow I will go again to San Quentin, before Lia and I went abroad; "Once I've got out of this," I explained to the haulbag as I pulled the protective shroud down over it. That was before this storm.

Around noon her voice comes in, astronomically-tiny. "Edwin, where are you?" She's really scared.

A good question. And so am I. The walkie-talkie was jammed in one corner of the tent, under my sleepingbagged-foot. My feet are so cold I had no idea where it was. Shoving things aside I grope for the beep.

About to—I hesitate: the radio looks like the black box of a flight recorder.

A flight of fancy, a flight of fear... I suppose I could cut loose the tent, which—with me clipped in underneath, fastened beneath the aluminum struts of the floor frame with the entrance flap tied open above...might preparachutely drift down to base, there, after a few hard knocks, to ground me.

Dream on Drummond, a windsock with too many holes in it I'm not so stupid as to even think about it—"So you can take that stupid grin off your face!" I tell him. 'But it would be better than freezing to—'

"Shut up!" ('Go on'). "Shut" ('Say it')—"Up!"

I peer into the grey.

CLINGING

Geronimo comes back. Fighting memories I hang onto the imagined... Had he been raped—butt-fucked at night in the early years in S.Q.? At least he was in solitary. Thank God that's never happened to me, in spite of poor Proudfoot.

Night: when the rats come out and the guards sleep on.

His first 'visitor,' after a month in total, undivided darkness in 'The Hole' at Folsom, the most notorious prison in the United States (where, a year later, Timothy Leary was incarcerated) was...? Must be Johnny Cochrane, his lawyer. Who else could it be. No one, not even his lawyers knew where he been taken, immediately upon the verdict at the 1972 trial, shackled into the armoured police vehicle. If anyone could find out... (The six week-long, eleven-day-jury-deliberated trial had ended, at first, with the foreman declaring that a unanimous decision was unobtainable).

White light poked his eyes open.

Where was Johnny?

A chill, steel drawer-lined room. Empty except for the armed guards. They moved aside: there was a long, wooden box on a large, metal table.

"An accident..." The guard looked away. "We need an identification" someone added, lifting the lid.

Remains... "Found in the trunk—" was all he heard...

"Sandra—" was all they heard. One of G's first successes in the B.P.P., Sandra was a reformed prostitute. They were engaged.

Days in the dark; weeks, years, remembering.

How much longer? I look out. What's the chopper down there for? Purple shadows of the trees grow longer...fighting my eyes I keep my head out and gaze, and gaze. I want to go home God! So near! I can't even cry outloud. I mean about as much as the man in the moon.

...Coming into land! —from the small, bubble car-like cabin—I'm alone!—the white, blazing sand of the crater several hundred feet below is as motionless as Antarctica. Steering away from the crater walls and boulder fields, through the translucent floor of the pod—suddenly there's a blue horse galloping into view! fluttering through the ghostly dunes.

Now it stops.

It throws back its head and looks up.

About to touch down I can't believe it, there's oxygen down there... I'll be able to breathe!

Don't need the pressured suit. I look through the capsule door, my hand on the handle. He is looking at me...

Two weeks later we meet for the first time.

The visiting area at San Quentin was much smaller than I had expected from outside. The walls must be so thick... Speechless couples sit holding hands, their eyes locked across steel tables. The tables are bolted to the floor. Pairs stand glued together for ever. No one is speaking. The air is thick, cloying with knowledge, need, pain...a subtle, suffocating lack of oxygen. The plate glass windows are steamed up. You could cut it with a knife.

Here is the centre, the heart of the world... Holding your loved one in your arms after life has taken its toll, whether the concentration camp, prison, aftermath of war, divorce. Not passing judgment, unconditional... That was the scent of it and it filled me with despair as nothing had ever done; the powerlessness of the hurt, poor, deprived. I was too lucky. Little did I suspect that my time was yet to come.

"He'll be here in a minute," David said eagerly.

David Flatley is the son of a recently retired U.S. Navy admiral. One of Stuart's volunteer legal workers, David is quiet, dressed in dark clothes, uncanny, droll, and when he opened his mouth is possessed of a Richter-esque Scale of humour that just cracked me up: as if Harpo spoke. Working for the defense of a former Black Panther was giving his father nightmares. He visited Geronimo once, at least, every week.

"Here he is."

A medium-height man stands in the doorway at the far end. He has on a bright-blue boiler suit. He is smiling at David. Then, deliberately, he smiles at me: David already said he'd told him that someone was coming from Amnesty International.

He leaps among the other inmates and their visitors.

I watch him.

Stepping back in front of a small, seated group—after quickly touching hands with each—he spreads his arms: "looks good G" I hear. Evidently the suit had been washed and ironed.

All eyes are on him as he moves among the silent crowd, shaking hands, as though he knows them all personally. Couples have broken out of their dazed gazing, following his sprightly figure among them.

Three or four minutes later he comes over. We are seated in a slightly more private cubicle, against a white-washed wall. David had told me not to have the seat next to the wall: "G always keeps his back against a wall."

"How do you like it?" he asked David, grinning.

"From the prison tailor, new suit," he added to David's smile.

"Birthday suit?" I chimed. We all chortled.

He was just the same with us. Frisky, graciously enquiring from David about mutual friends and colleagues. While watching him moving so naturally among the people there, something to say to everyone, pausing, listening, moments of geniality and laughter, I realised he was very, very different. There was electricity in the air now, people were talking.

The whole conversation that followed, the lightness, the instantaneousness of attention in the present concerning just about everything: the state of his case, books he's reading and wants to discuss, particularly politics and social studies. He was quite intrigued when I mentioned having studied philosophy: "But with one foot on the ground." He chuckled:

"A climber with one foot on the ground?!" Some one after my own heart, who could I bet see the pun in punishment.

He told me, in response to my dawning questions about how he'd managed in the years of isolation and solitary, that "It was jazz that saved me." "Not Jazzus" I jammed, barely able to stop chiming.

"Coltrane, Parker... I'd just sit there in the dark humming; kind of mantras. Kept me sane." He mentioned meditating, and Buddhism.

Aspects of change in his window, the greening of the land he could see in a window since his release from solitary. Prison conditions too mattered it was clear; he was trying to "change a couple of things... You have to learn what's going on in here, it's all in the context..."

Weight, fitness—he did daily exercises just as I do... We bobbed along in our conversation as if we'd known one another for years.

"He's like that with everyone" said David later.

Detailed, quiet, relaxed, ordinary, unemphasised... So different from me. I really liked him. His mind, like a hand on the tiller, steered—as much as steering—by the undercurrent. Sometimes he almost surprised out what I was thinking just as the thought entered it seemed.

Hugging myself into the wet black hole of half-warmth like a pathetic premature baby, I try to remember what David—had said, about G coming, deliberately, between a prison guard and a prisoner with a filed knife... G had been wounded. The guard subsequently testified at one of the many hearings before the parole board, that G had saved his life. During the time he'd spent at the cutting edge of prison life, somehow he seemed to have earned the respect of everyone for being a peace seeker.

Who could tell? Maybe he was cut from UN cloth and might one day become Secretary General. Something like I imagined Mandela could be nurturing on Robben Island: a real breath of fresh air in the corridors of power...

"Bye... See you soon."

I paused: "After..." He smiled. We were in agreement. He liked the idea of the climb of Grace Cathedral.

On the drive back to the city with David I felt absolutely exhausted. Almost drugged. I went to bed in the early evening. Something I hadn't done since I was a kid.

It is May 1980, a week before my birthday, on May 14th. I am almost thirty five years old. We are in New York city, Cathy, Stephen and I. Here to climb the Statue of Liberty. Stephen is going to belay me from the balcony to get me started. Cathy will be four hundred feet below, on the ground watching, and probably praying. David has the flyers ready.

LIBERTY WAS FRAMED: FREE GERONIMO PRATT.

Fifty feet long, in black letters on white sailcloth.

At the apartment of one of Stephen's N.Y.U. tutor-friend Jim's friends, in Sheridan Square, the night before we began we wound the banner up like some huge white bandage, or American prayer flag, and stuffed it carefully into one of my two haulbags. My personal Turin shroud?

I intended, once I'd reached her neck, and looped one of my ropes around for the belay anchor, to abseil—or rappel as we say in the States—to the level of her magnificent, lifeless breasts. There, I explained, "I'll cup them for the week—like a Brobdingnagian bra." We all chortled, except Cathy, who had gone very quiet since I returned from my solitary walk a few minutes ago. She was looking out of the window. "No! a 'Liberty bra!'" shouted Stephen, who later told me that as a student, struggling to save the fees to attend New York University, he had worked for nearly a year at a brassiere warehouse in the Bronx, and got to know the names of all the manufacturers.

"Maybe it would be best to blindfold her" I mused, packing.

"But couldn't they get it off through the window?" asked David. He had been up with Stephen and I the previous day, when we unobtrusively went through what were the best steps to take, in order not to be detected before I was off the balcony, with at least the first haul by my side. The window was three or four portholes. Tiny, the squint of things one got from inside the head reminded me of being in the cabin of Ken Tyson's small trawler when I was long-lining for black cod with him in 1975, Christmas, my first job in the States, after emigrating. In five days at sea I had earned seven hundred dollars. Which paid for Grace and my wedding, in Yosemite. Down there, February 14th, Valentine's Day, 1976. Eight years ago.

I slip back the flap. See the black oaks where we gathered, where Claudia sang, and Grace and I released two little sparrows, (we were going to get doves but were warned the resident hawks would make mincemeat of such bright ideas), so we settled for survivors. Now the blizzard of the present is making a mad, white, featherbrained world of what up until now I was more or less always able to think of as my love.

Am I slowly becoming petrified?

David is beaming, white-faced in the cold wind blowing across the Verazano Straits. This is it. 'Liberty Was Framed. Free Geronimo Pratt,' the banner would say it all. Now let's have some fun.

Stephen looked down. Cathy was sitting on a bench. He waved. I'd wait until I was high. She had the three hundred or so flyers we had had printed, which it would be David's job to distribute to the interested once the climb was under way.

Quickly I drop my trousers, fishing for the sharp end of the climbing rope in the first back pack even as Stephen opens it. Seizing it in my teeth I bridge—like doing the splits—up the stone framed door arch onto the ledge of the plinth that supports the Statue, about ten feet up.

Stephen throws up the packs. Forty seconds. The guard, ten feet away, still knows nothing.

Stephen swarms up to join me, unroped too. We pull up the spilled loops of rope, watched by an older couple who have just arrived out on the balcony. David has gone.

"Morning" I breeze, hoping to maintain the guise of maintenance men and the consuming trust older Americans have for public officials in high places.

Stephen belays me as I hand traverse the huge left foot, sandalled in what looks like an *art nouveau* Birkenstock. A wide bridge to the six inch-wide by twelve inch-long bright green little toe. Daintily footing every other one of her pigs I waltz the corner, nipping out of sight with a crisp grip on the chair-sized buckle.

Lilliputian, clutching the hem of a hundred foot sea green gown, I find myself standing in a fold of copper, a wave, where I pause.

I have to find a belay, a safe place to anchor.

Then haul up the gear, with Stephen shepherding it so that it doesn't swing down to the balcony, where it would soon be arrested by the surely imminently appearing guardians.

Stephen will then leave. Give a quick press conference so that no one got the wrong idea about what I'm up to. We didn't want any misunderstandings.

With 20-20 revision, clearly we were the ones who misunderstood. Not having met the New York City police...

Who appeared, by helicopter, ten minutes later.

What happened in those ten minutes and the remainder of the following ten hours is now Classified Information. I shall concentrate on telling the never simple truth as clearly as possible. One day it will come out, in spite of the government. Maybe, I still think, because of the ungovernment we'll one day make possible.

No belay. Nothing to wrap my climbing rope around, or slip a nut into. Nothing else for it I thump the six inch diameter suction cup onto the chilly copper sheeting from which the Statue was fashioned by the French sculptor, in, I'd read, an *imago* of his mother.

What? Not holding! Wide-eyed, I see pimpled everywhere, green bumps, which are preventing a tight air seal.

This unexpected acne of the copper, was probably, I guessed, due to the stippling effect—a tactile pointillism—produced by the scores of ball-peen hammerers utilised by Bartholdi to fabricate Liberty's body.

Hmmmm.

"Stephen!" Then it came to me as he sounded back, anxious, that I'd better keep it simple: "Climb when you're ready." In a loud whisper I was trying to not be heard by anyone else other than Stephen, soon to be the prodigal, certainly in my eyes the prodigious, elder son of the current Assistant Secretary of State for Education in the Carter government, James Rutherford.

Hunkering down into the metal wave I brace, praying he doesn't slip.

We are three hundred feet above the ground at this point, unattached to anything except one another by the nylon umbilical cord called climbing rope.

Which is not particularly nice, since a slip by either one of us will take both of us, inexorably, half running-slipping-diving into that cold void, to meet our unmaker in a bloody splatter on the immemorial stone plaza at the foot of the overlooking idol.

An Aztec moment.

Then something nice happens. A Park Ranger appears on the balcony, directly below.

"Far out!" he whoops, beaming. And I am Theseus again, and the labyrinth is all that matters.

"Good Luck" he calls up. Then he vanished, not to be seen again, at least that weekend. He's probably writing poetry in some Federal outpost he was rapidly sent down to after his brief appearance as the handmaiden of the real Liberty of life, lived in the wilds of the DNAsiac imagination, that I now, more than ever believe joins.

"What are you going to do?" says Stephen when I show him why I don't see how "I, even we" — he winces — "can possibly climb the Statue with these non-suction cups."

"Although..." Now he looks quite worried. He follows my gaze. If I can somehow gain the bottomless bottom of the flared fold of her gown, scrolled down from between her shoulders over her people-rumbled bottom (for we could now hear the sound of many, not-so-tiny feet, due, it appeared to the fairly rapid emptying of the Statue)...which the police had now closed.

"If I can just get into that groove, then maybe I can at least gain the top of the flare." He smiled. My kind of counter-suggestive resurgence has got me out of—and not just into—some very squeaky climbing and marital moments.

We agree to give it a try.

And he won't leave me.

He remains silent, watching my every movement.

"FAGS!" jeers the cop, his face unhinged, everted as he ogles us playing with his mother myth. He waggles his wrist as if it was broken. I can only assume it's because we've identified ourselves—on the flyer—as from San Francisco. I wonder where David is...

Spreadeagled at the bottom of the fold, I was very nervous. With Stephen pushing me from behind we've managed to get one suction cup on, which—provided he continually pumped it when the piston went into the red, due to the air leaking (which meant pumping it up about every ten seconds)—has given me a crucial leg up, via my etriers, the little nylon tape foot loops climbers use when they can't wing it.

This has enabled me to reach a popped rivet hole. Into this I have inserted an *S* hook, the kind that are used on kitchen peg boards to carry cups...

Not having dreamt that there might be sky hook placements in the skin of the Statue, I had brought none from my armoury of climbing equipment at home in San Francisco. Then, realising, belatedly that they might prove useful (though not critical I thought at the time) yesterday I bought two packets of the aforeskinned *S* hooks.

I've put it that way to give you the kind of feeling of hanging by the skin of something or other that I had when that cop started his mouth up.

I grew very angry in my cold, calm kind of way: "You don't need to insult us. We are not doing that to you. Our aim, and the manner of achieving it is peaceful and respectful. We would appreciate the same. Thank you."

The officer had a sickly look on his face. My unguent, Britshit sincerity had stunned him. Stephen beamed.

The inspector took over. Bullhorn in hand, sensing a victim to sweet reason, he advised us that: "We want to talk with you."

By now they had the nets positioned, just in case we did a dual, human cannonball. Which was touching.

I just wished they'd put them in the right place.

Stephen and I were still close enough at this point to hiss effectively to each other without them hearing. There must have been an updraft. A favourable sign: I usually attract the overdrafts.

Below, the Saturday crowds were filling up the Plaza, milling about restively. Two ferries had arrived and no one was leaving on the second one. Several hundred visitors were on board each time. It was Mother's Day tomorrow. There must have been over five hundred people there already, and we had begun to attract quite a lot of rowdy attention. If we were going to be understood we had to do something quickly.

My one foot splayed against the grand opening, a single *gluteus maximus* kept the faith on the other side. Kegel muscles clenched, anally retained by her majesty, I try not to be evacuated but borne up into her voluminous folds. Shit! If I slip—

I stick it to her in the small of her back, a homunculoid primate in the eyes of probably most of those innocent Americans gathering at the feet of the Statue of Liberty that day. For many of them, coming from around the nation, this was the trip of a lifetime. Some had left concentration camps behind them; most of them cherished a dream of liberty that to them I was, virtually raping. Some would have, sadly, been only be too glad to see me flying forth, suddenly—finally—free.

But, sufficiently in touch with the difference between symbol and reality, I could look through Geronimo's eyes. Even, maybe, through that Geronimo before him, after whom he was named.

G is of First American ancestry too.

One black rubber suction cup—like a toilet plunger—giving her green ass, warts and all, a big rubbery smackeroo, I pull through.

Take stock.

Stephen has no belay, half sitting in the well of the fold. He has both the haul bags teetering beside him. He is trying to keep the two climbing ropes running around the back of the bags, in order that—if I come off—the initial back breaking strain might be taken by them.

That's Stephen.

"We've got to get the banner out." He agrees. "And David better get the flyers handed round—otherwise no one's gonna know why we're here.'

To my absolute horror I see—at that very moment the *S* hook slowly straightening out! Grabbing on the suction cup I pump like fuck—Sorry, I'm not feeling very nice. Now I see the *S* hook can only penetrate a couple of mils, because of its curve.

The last fifteen feet, from the place where Stephen's crouching to my lodgment in the small of her back, have been the most precarious, dangerous climbing I've ever been subjected to...

But not as bad as where I am now, three and a half years later, in 1984, alone on the North America wall.

I lift the fly. Over to my right, the cavernous Cyclop's Eye is seeping. Black gouts of rain gather at the lips of the overhangs, thicken, drip, ticking ineluctably into oblivion. It seems like another life already... There, where only two nights ago, the full moon bloomed, drifting into the black sepulchre as it set, like an eye blinded with light, illuminating in the very moment of its passing the black hole gouged out by a glacier ten thousand years ago.

BE A FREE RAT was all that anyone could figure out of the twisted banner until we manage to lasso the language back to BERTY WAS FRAMED: FREE GERONIMO PRATT. The Statue rises, thundering quietly as the wind drums on it, filling the banner like a spinnaker, giving the shouting crowd glimpses of LIBERTY, the word, as the banner breathes.

It was attached to four *S* hooks at my end. Stephen had the other end tied into the haul bags. Finally people would understand.

Ragged jeers and boos rise from the crowd. Then the chanting begins: "GO-A-WAY! GO-A-WAY!" They are too far away for me to be able to explain.

"Stop!" I blurt.

David suddenly stands up. Cathy remains seated. He is handing out flyers to people, walking over to couples, families even as a crowd clusters around him. Someone shoves him. His arm goes up, flyers spilling like cards.

Cathy is walking away. Is the baby trying to get out?

FALLING

The light is almost gone. I lift the flap for the last time. A star is sparkling like the tip of a scalpel, piercing the deep, water-blue night. Cars have their headlights on now, the main stream inching past El Capitan before the next storm. Due tomorrow, as I was told when they could still reach me.

The air gnaws my shoulders.

Before I shut it for the last time, I notice my hat. Snatched by the wind when I was last climbing three days ago—in the dark—it has been deposited back on the ledge I slept on so well, in the Cyclop's Eye. A crust of frozen snow on it now, it looks like a loaf of bread left on a doorstep in a supernaturally early delivery.

Hard to give it all up. I take a deep breath, a tremendous effort to get warm, and save my own skin. Warm enough to sleep, perchance to dream myself out of this nightmare and back into her arms, whoever she is. Go! Running on the spot, upstairs—there's someone after me—just one step behind, clawing, leaping, twisting, kicking, punching—I throw a glance back as I duck—Cathy? No! My mother! The tent walls are shaking like leaves about to outburst a bird.

Now I can barely move, my legs felled, flat on my back, the next step so enormous, sheer, my fingers can't even reach the lip. Why am I so little and why am I crawling up here? Where's the door?

Quick! the handle... I can hear her... Here's the bed. I dive, tearing into the sheets, white, cold... A cave. Now it's warm.

I sink in deeper.

I hear heavy breathing outside... Someone's running their hands over the bed. My Mom has been joined by Cathy, maybe Lia who knows, Linda, Grace, Jo, Haworth's mother. The tent is being shaken furiously, loosening. Pinching, pressing "— I —

can't breathe!" They let me go.

I pop up like a seal: "Again!" It's time for a story. "Once upon..." She reads, and reads, until, eyes drooping—both of us—she tucks me in.

Kisses me: "Sweet dreams." She opens the door—a shaft of light—whispers "God bless."

It sounds nice. Funny, warmy, wordy.

Whaty doey meany?

"Otway, ooday, ooyay, eenmay? I way underway. Ooway areway ooyay?"

"Get to sleep!" Her voice from behind the door.

A deep sigh, sinking...

Falling...

Edwin Drummond is a renowned mountain climber, Keats Prize-winning poet, freedom fighter, and the author of *A Dream of White Horses*. He graduated from the University of Bristol in England where he studied philosophy and literature. This true story portrays Edwin's skill as a mountain climber and writer, waging the war against discrimination, brutality and injustice. He has frequently been arrested for his efforts, particularly after his world-famous climb of the Statue of Liberty. Several times he has almost died during his heroic climbs, attempting to bring notice to the world of the horrors and evils of totalitarianism. Many of Edwin's recent efforts have been directed toward freeing Geronimo Pratt, considered a political prisoner by Amnesty International.

Edwin Drummond
Protest Climbs in the United States
(Grace Cathedral, the Statue of Liberty and the Embarcadero Building)

William S. Burroughs
author of *The Cat Inside, The Soft Machine*
and many other works